Shojo Beat

Godchild™

Earl Cain Series 5

Vol. 6

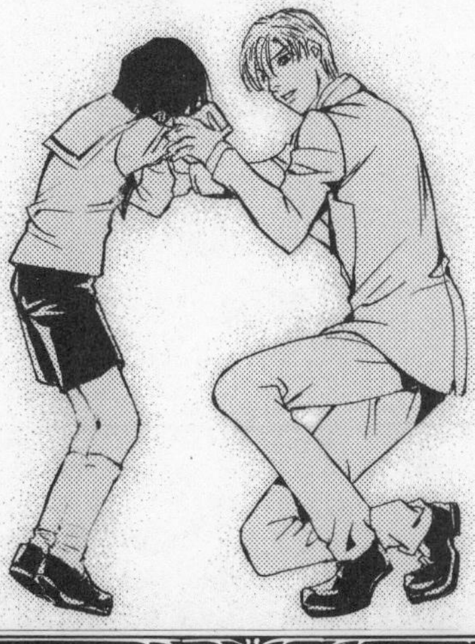

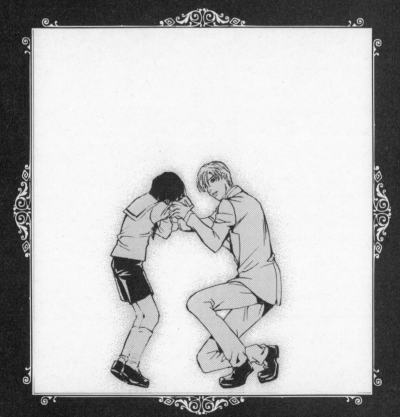

Story & Art by Kaori Yuki

Contents

IN THE LATTER PART OF THE NINETEENTH CENTURY, VICTORIAN ERA ENGLAND WAS SECURELY CENTERED ON LONDON SOCIETY. IN THIS CITY OF FOG, A YOUTHFUL EARL NAMED CAIN HAS A HOBBY COLLECTING POISONS, AND A GROWING OBSESSION WITH DESTROYING A SECRET ORGANIZATION CALLED DELILAH THAT MAY BE RUN BY HIS FATHER, ALEXIS, PREVIOUSLY THOUGHT TO BE DECEASED. PREVIOUSLY, CAIN LEARNED THAT A NOBLEMAN, LORD GLADSTONE, PURCHASED AN AREA KNOWN AS THE PRECIOUS GARDEN, LOCATED DIRECTLY IN THE MIDDLE OF THE PROPERTY OWNED AND OPERATED BY DELILAH. INCOGNITO, CAIN INFILTRATED THE GLADSTONE MANSION AND DISCOVERED THE LORD WAS ACTUALLY CASSANDRA, A HIGH PRIEST OF DELILAH. CAIN REVEALED THE TRUE NATURE OF THE HIGH PRIEST TO HIGH SOCIETY IN FRONT OF A FULL HOUSE AT THE OPERA, CAUSING DELILAH TO TURN ON CASSANDRA. DR. DISRAELI THEN CONDUCTED AN EVIL EXPERIMENT, AND TRANSPLANTED A DYING CASSIAN'S BRAIN INTO THE RUINED CASSANDRA'S BODY. WITH ITS HIGH PRIEST OUT OF COMMISSION, DELILAH HAS EVEN MORE REASON TO HUNT DOWN CAIN - IF HE DOESN'T FIND THEM FIRST. CATCH UP ON THE STORY SO FAR BY READING THE ENTIRE *EARL CAIN SERIES*, INCLUDING *THE CAIN SAGA* 1: *FORGOTTEN JULIET*, 2: *THE SOUND OF A BOY HATCHING*, 3: *KAFKA* AND 4: *THE SEAL OF THE RED RAM*, AND THE EARLIER FIVE VOLUMES OF *GODCHILD*.

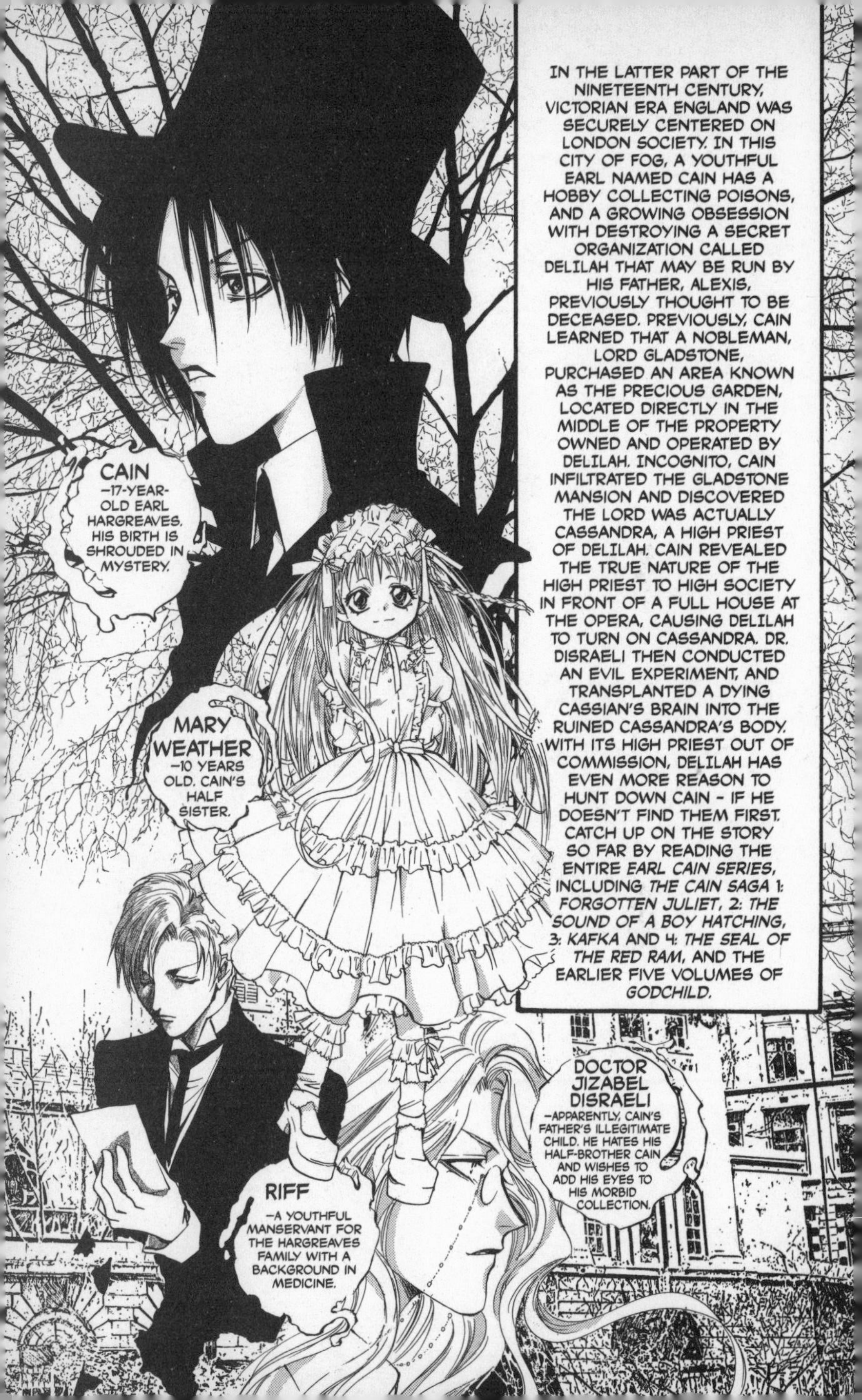
CAIN
–17-YEAR-OLD EARL HARGREAVES. HIS BIRTH IS SHROUDED IN MYSTERY.
MARY WEATHER
–10 YEARS OLD. CAIN'S HALF SISTER.
DOCTOR JIZABEL DISRAELI
–APPARENTLY, CAIN'S FATHER'S ILLEGITIMATE CHILD. HE HATES HIS HALF-BROTHER CAIN AND WISHES TO ADD HIS EYES TO HIS MORBID COLLECTION.
RIFF
–A YOUTHFUL MANSERVANT FOR THE HARGREAVES FAMILY WITH A BACKGROUND IN MEDICINE.

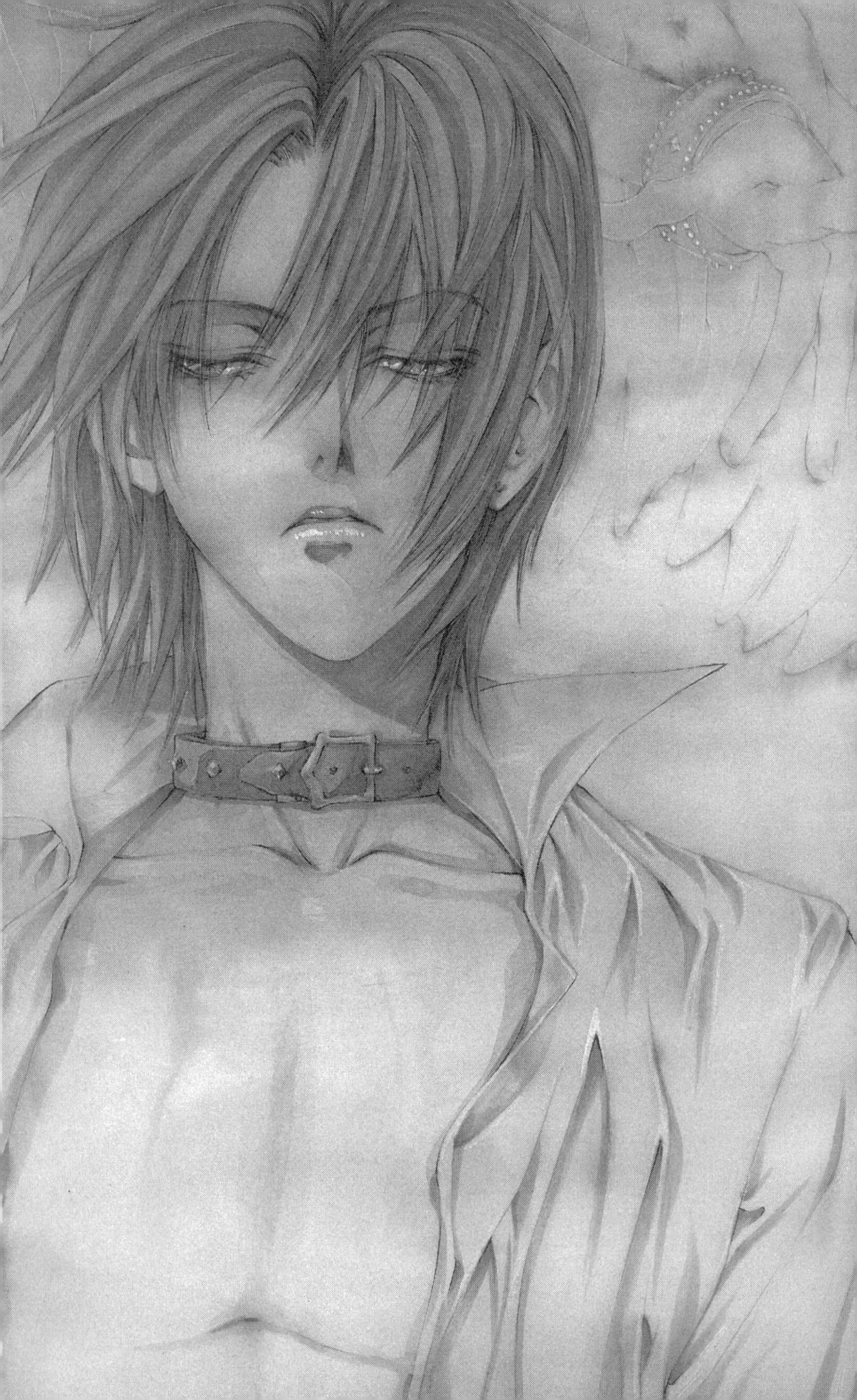

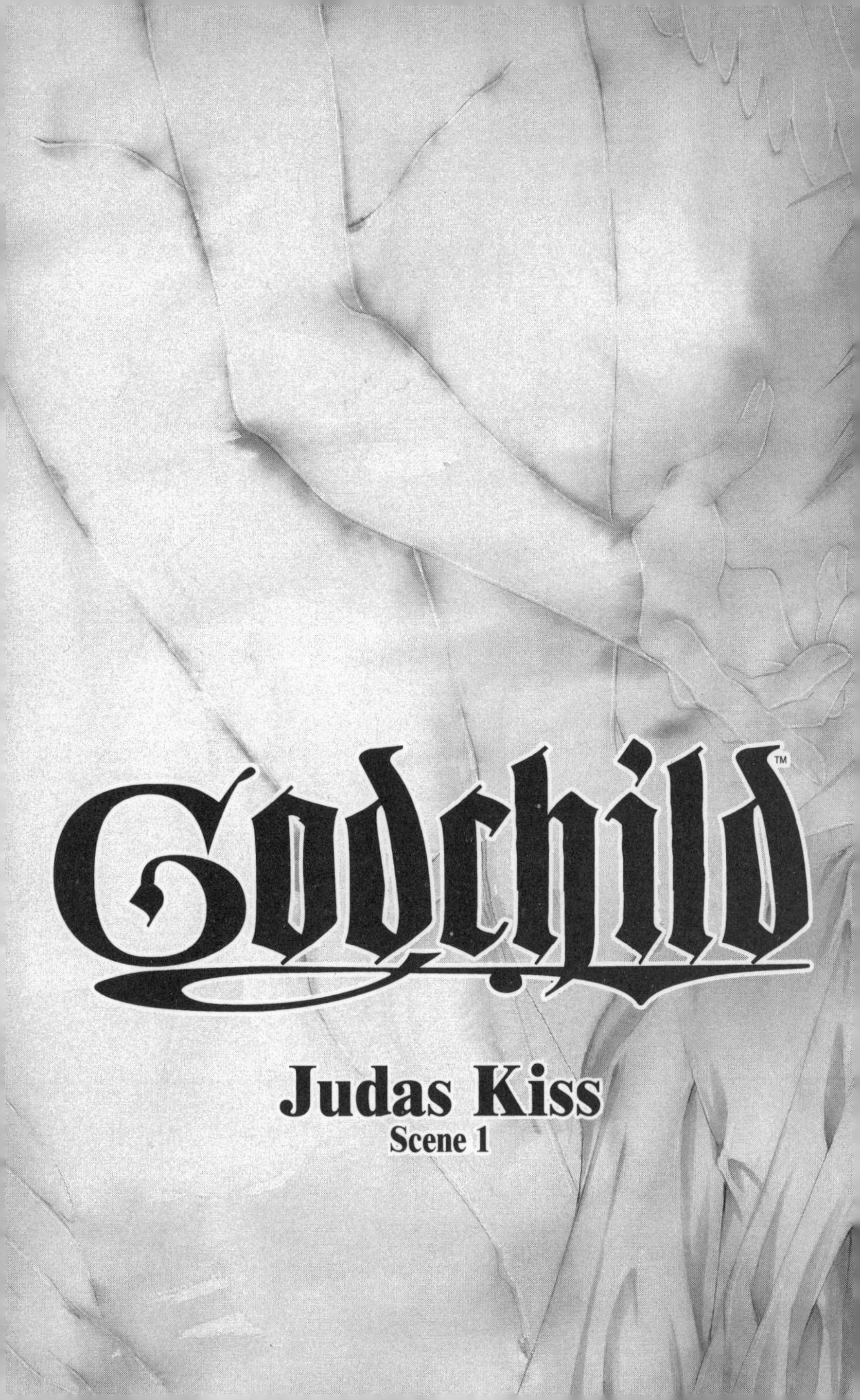
Godchild™
Judas Kiss
Scene 1

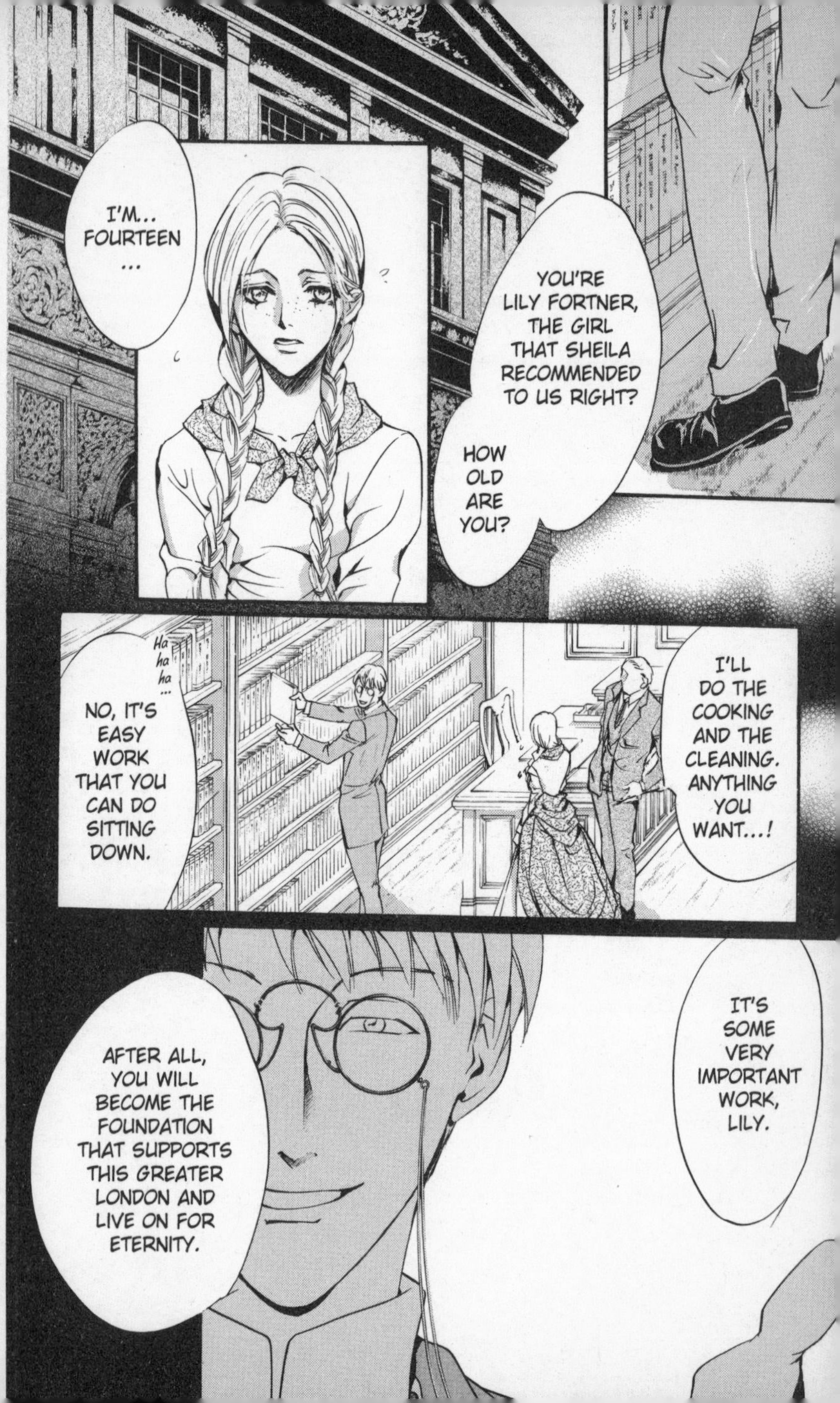
YOU'RE LILY FORTNER, THE GIRL THAT SHEILA RECOMMENDED TO US RIGHT?
HOW OLD ARE YOU?
I'M... FOURTEEN ...
I'LL DO THE COOKING AND THE CLEANING. ANYTHING YOU WANT...!
Ha ha ha...
NO, IT'S EASY WORK THAT YOU CAN DO SITTING DOWN.
IT'S SOME VERY IMPORTANT WORK, LILY.
AFTER ALL, YOU WILL BECOME THE FOUNDATION THAT SUPPORTS THIS GREATER LONDON AND LIVE ON FOR ETERNITY.

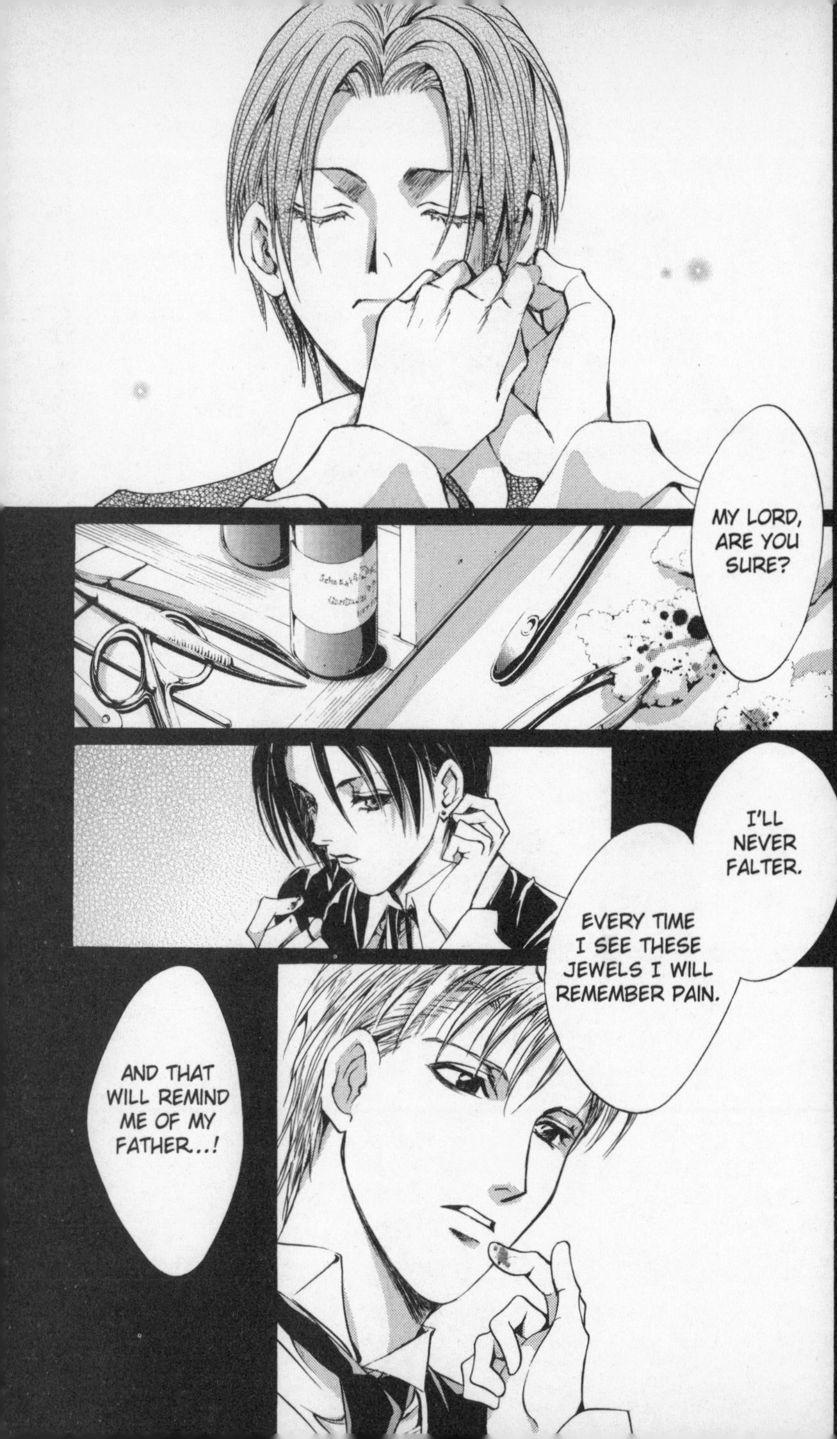
MY LORD, ARE YOU SURE?
I'LL NEVER FALTER.
EVERY TIME I SEE THESE JEWELS I WILL REMEMBER PAIN.
AND THAT WILL REMIND ME OF MY FATHER...!

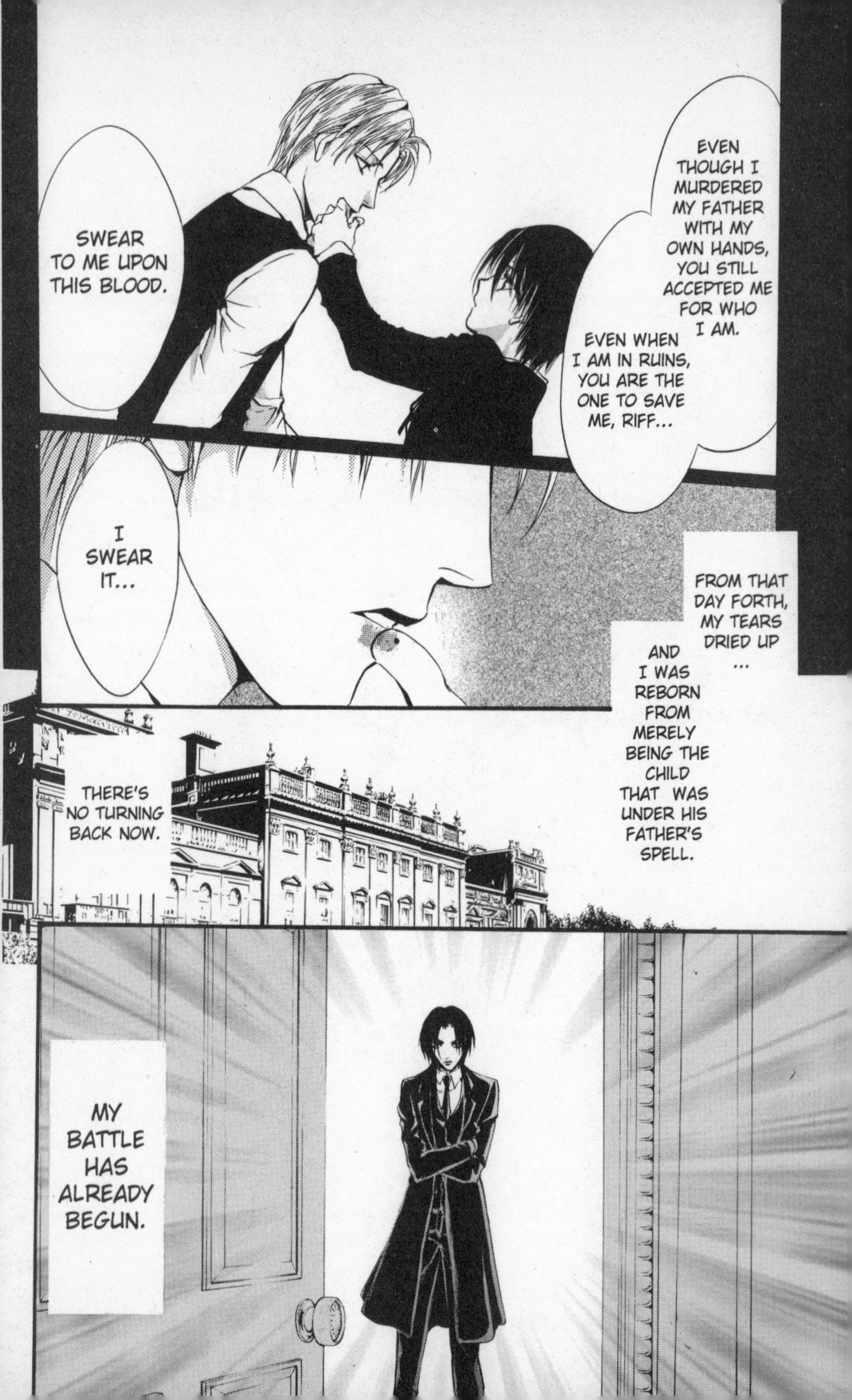
EVEN THOUGH I MURDERED MY FATHER WITH MY OWN HANDS, YOU STILL ACCEPTED ME FOR WHO I AM.
EVEN WHEN I AM IN RUINS, YOU ARE THE ONE TO SAVE ME, RIFF...
SWEAR TO ME UPON THIS BLOOD.
I SWEAR IT...
FROM THAT DAY FORTH, MY TEARS DRIED UP ...
AND I WAS REBORN FROM MERELY BEING THE CHILD THAT WAS UNDER HIS FATHER'S SPELL.
THERE'S NO TURNING BACK NOW.
MY BATTLE HAS ALREADY BEGUN.

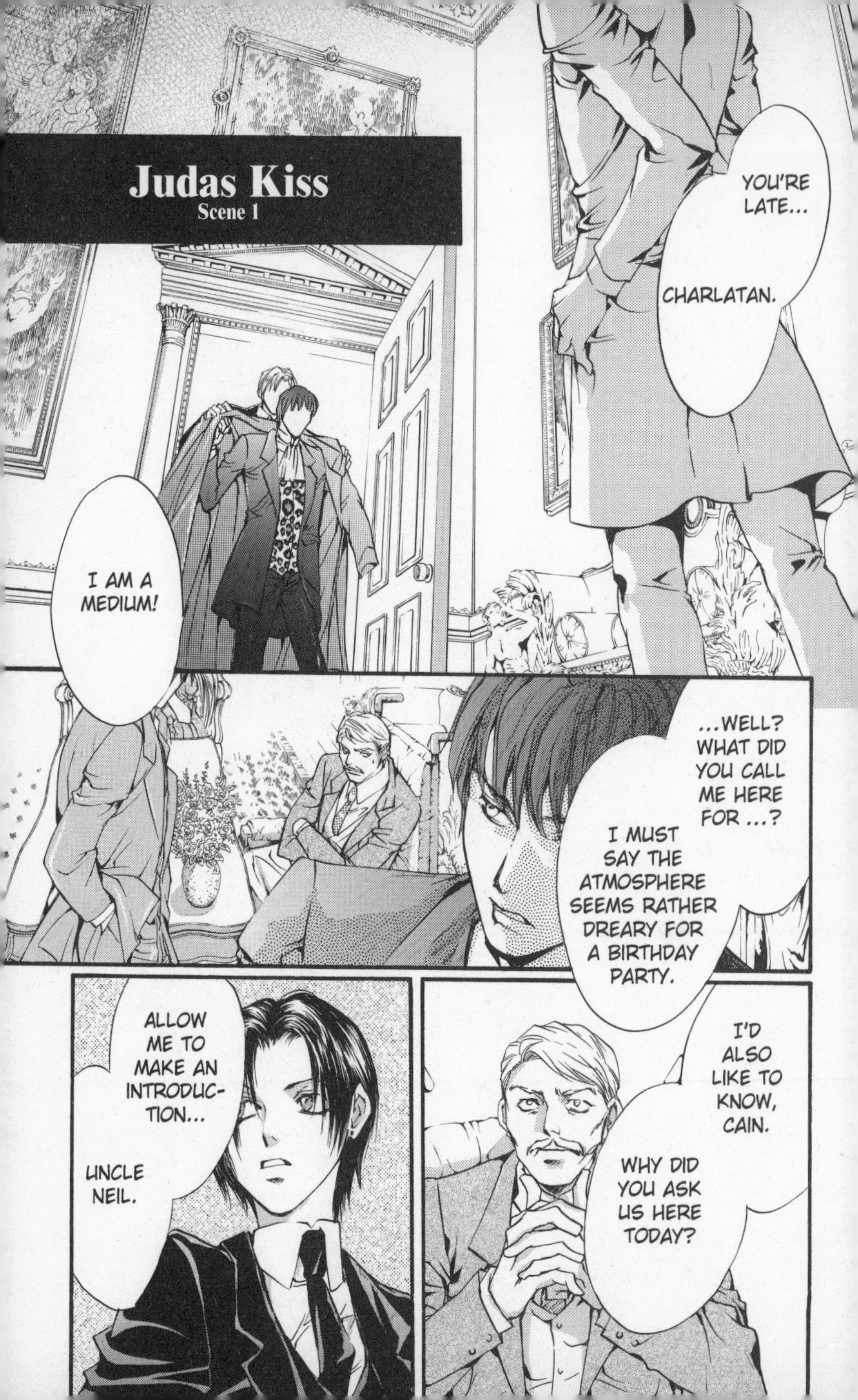
Judas Kiss
Scene 1
YOU'RE LATE...
CHARLATAN.
I AM A MEDIUM!
...WELL? WHAT DID YOU CALL ME HERE FOR ...?
I MUST SAY THE ATMOSPHERE SEEMS RATHER DREARY FOR A BIRTHDAY PARTY.
I'D ALSO LIKE TO KNOW, CAIN.
WHY DID YOU ASK US HERE TODAY?
ALLOW ME TO MAKE AN INTRODUC-TION...
UNCLE NEIL.

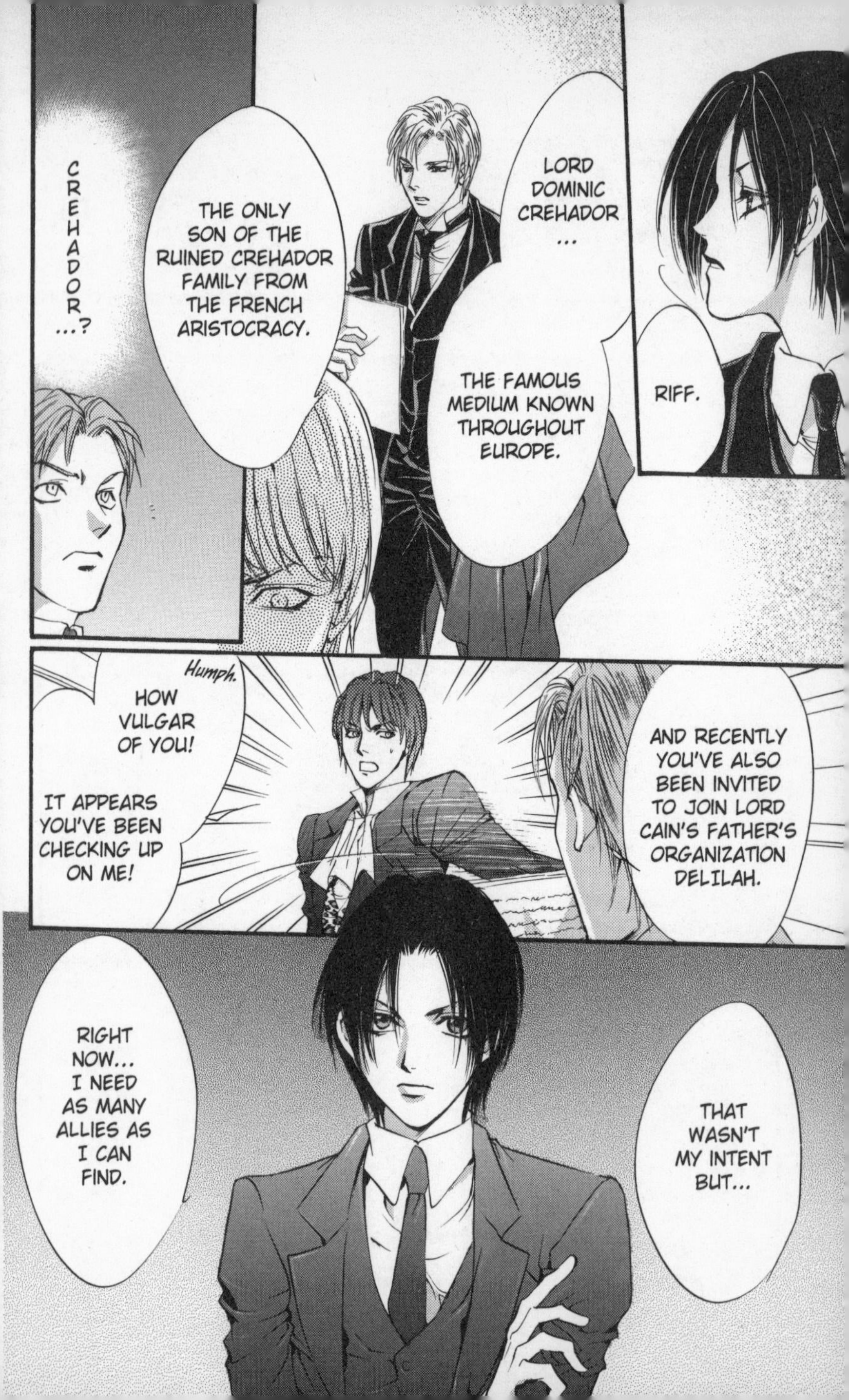
RIFF.
LORD DOMINIC CREHADOR...
THE FAMOUS MEDIUM KNOWN THROUGHOUT EUROPE.
THE ONLY SON OF THE RUINED CREHADOR FAMILY FROM THE FRENCH ARISTOCRACY.
CREHADOR...?
AND RECENTLY YOU'VE ALSO BEEN INVITED TO JOIN LORD CAIN'S FATHER'S ORGANIZATION DELILAH.
Humph.
HOW VULGAR OF YOU!
IT APPEARS YOU'VE BEEN CHECKING UP ON ME!
THAT WASN'T MY INTENT BUT...
RIGHT NOW... I NEED AS MANY ALLIES AS I CAN FIND.

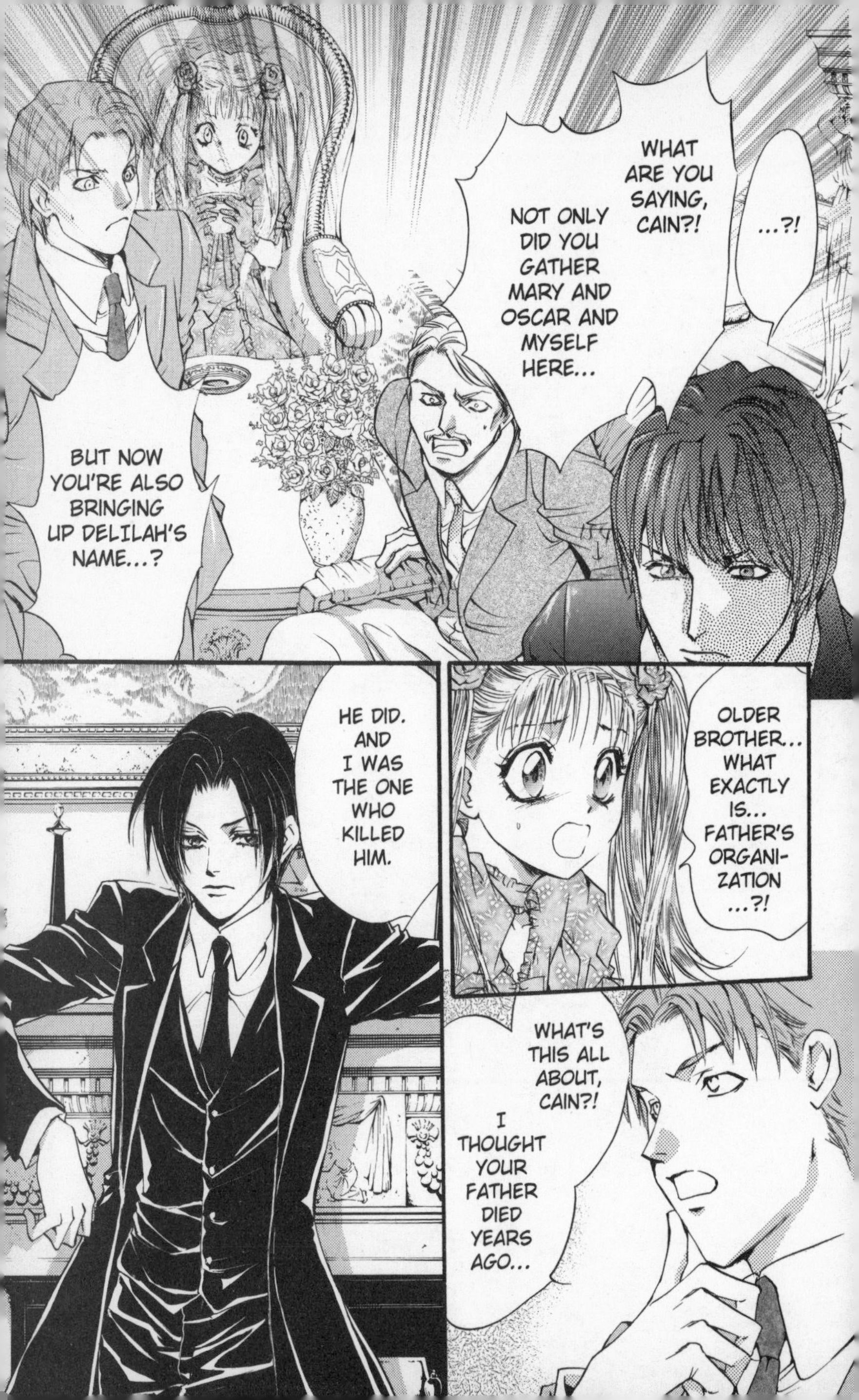
...?!
WHAT ARE YOU SAYING, CAIN?!
NOT ONLY DID YOU GATHER MARY AND OSCAR AND MYSELF HERE...
BUT NOW YOU'RE ALSO BRINGING UP DELILAH'S NAME...?
OLDER BROTHER... WHAT EXACTLY IS... FATHER'S ORGANI-ZATION ...?!
WHAT'S THIS ALL ABOUT, CAIN?!
I THOUGHT YOUR FATHER DIED YEARS AGO...
HE DID. AND I WAS THE ONE WHO KILLED HIM.

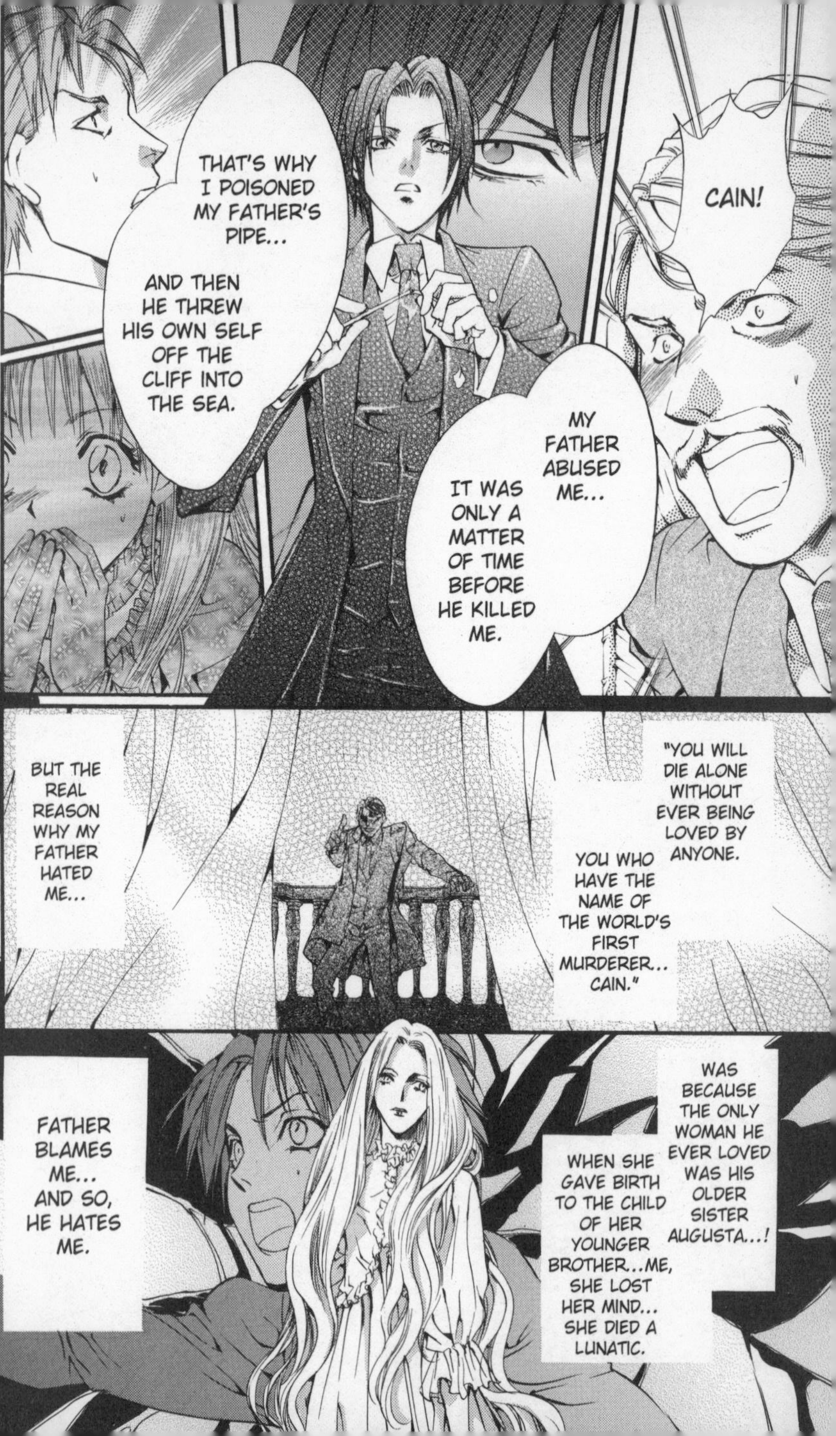
CAIN!
MY FATHER ABUSED ME...
IT WAS ONLY A MATTER OF TIME BEFORE HE KILLED ME.
THAT'S WHY I POISONED MY FATHER'S PIPE...
AND THEN HE THREW HIS OWN SELF OFF THE CLIFF INTO THE SEA.
"YOU WILL DIE ALONE WITHOUT EVER BEING LOVED BY ANYONE.
YOU WHO HAVE THE NAME OF THE WORLD'S FIRST MURDERER... CAIN."
BUT THE REAL REASON WHY MY FATHER HATED ME...
WAS BECAUSE THE ONLY WOMAN HE EVER LOVED WAS HIS OLDER SISTER AUGUSTA...!
WHEN SHE GAVE BIRTH TO THE CHILD OF HER YOUNGER BROTHER...ME, SHE LOST HER MIND... SHE DIED A LUNATIC.
FATHER BLAMES ME... AND SO, HE HATES ME.

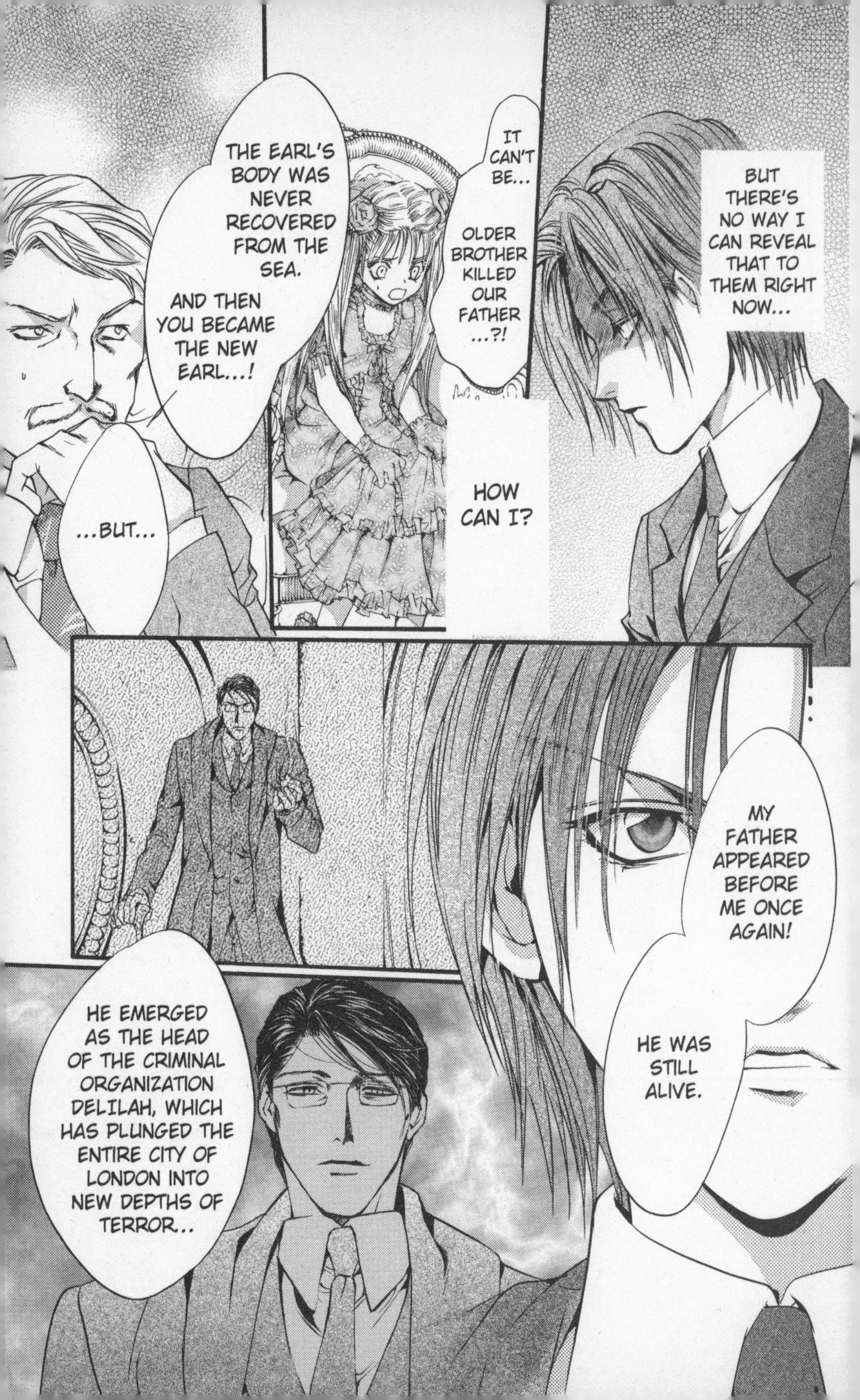
BUT THERE'S NO WAY I CAN REVEAL THAT TO THEM RIGHT NOW...
HOW CAN I?
IT CAN'T BE...
OLDER BROTHER KILLED OUR FATHER...?!
THE EARL'S BODY WAS NEVER RECOVERED FROM THE SEA.
AND THEN YOU BECAME THE NEW EARL...!
...BUT...
MY FATHER APPEARED BEFORE ME ONCE AGAIN!
HE WAS STILL ALIVE.
HE EMERGED AS THE HEAD OF THE CRIMINAL ORGANIZATION DELILAH, WHICH HAS PLUNGED THE ENTIRE CITY OF LONDON INTO NEW DEPTHS OF TERROR...

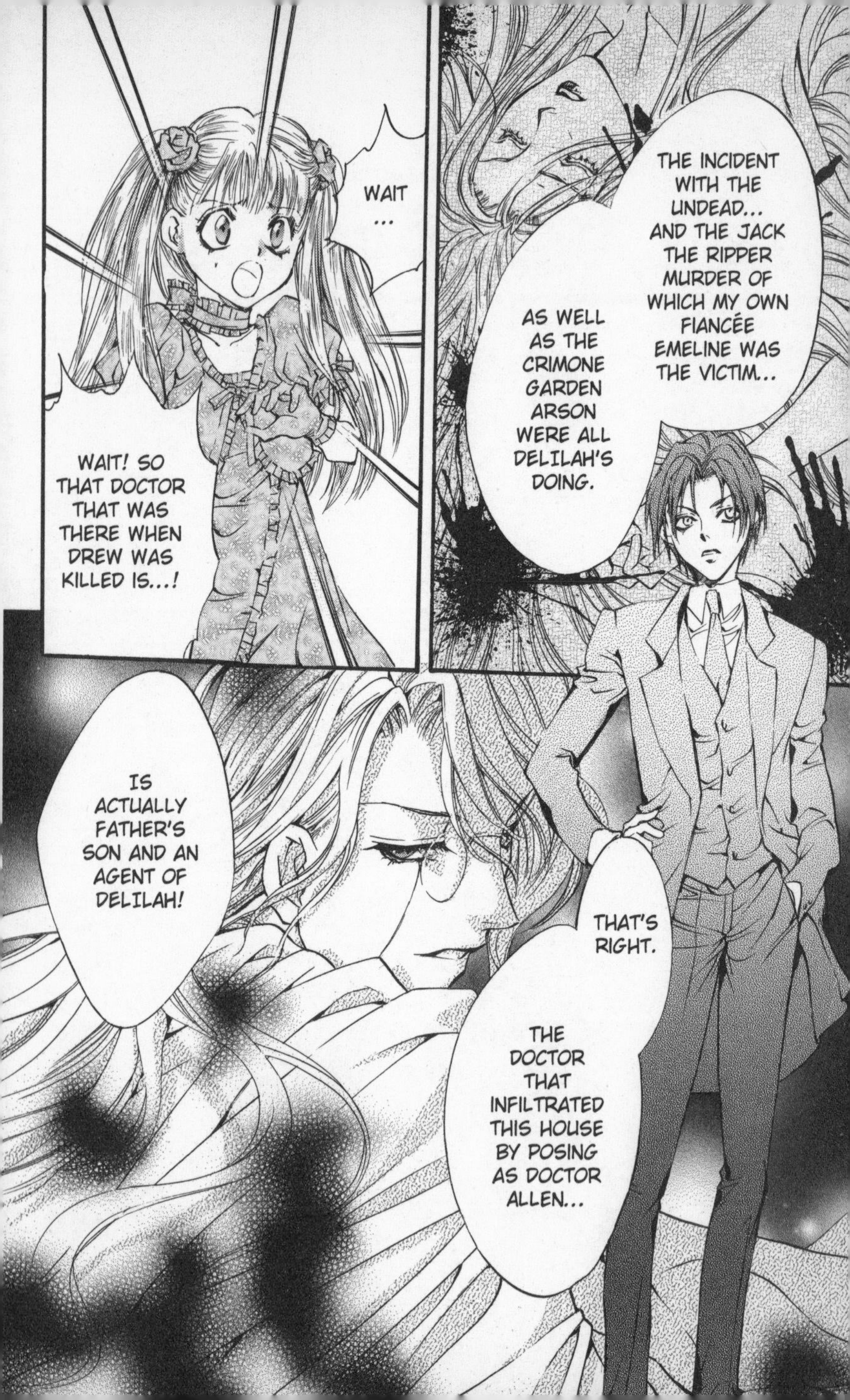
THE INCIDENT WITH THE UNDEAD... AND THE JACK THE RIPPER MURDER OF WHICH MY OWN FIANCÉE EMELINE WAS THE VICTIM...
AS WELL AS THE CRIMONE GARDEN ARSON WERE ALL DELILAH'S DOING.
WAIT ...
WAIT! SO THAT DOCTOR THAT WAS THERE WHEN DREW WAS KILLED IS...!
THAT'S RIGHT.
THE DOCTOR THAT INFILTRATED THIS HOUSE BY POSING AS DOCTOR ALLEN...
IS ACTUALLY FATHER'S SON AND AN AGENT OF DELILAH!

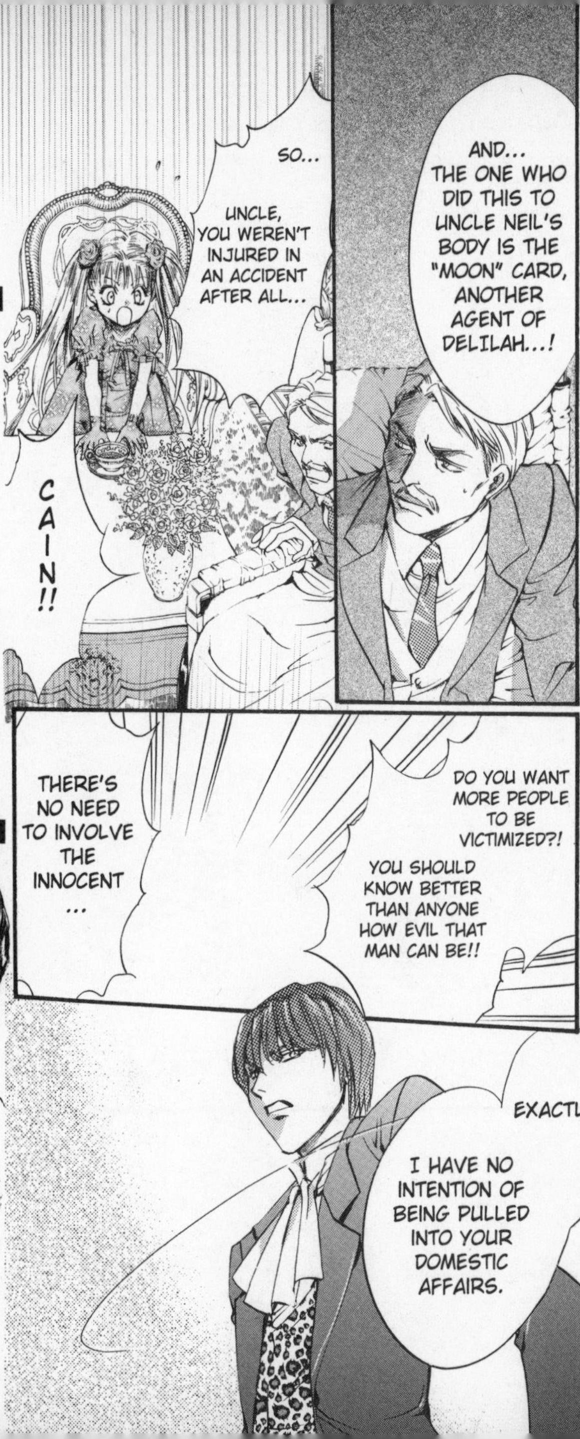
AND... THE ONE WHO DID THIS TO UNCLE NEIL'S BODY IS THE "MOON" CARD, ANOTHER AGENT OF DELILAH...!
SO...
UNCLE, YOU WEREN'T INJURED IN AN ACCIDENT AFTER ALL...
CAIN!!
DO YOU WANT MORE PEOPLE TO BE VICTIMIZED?!
YOU SHOULD KNOW BETTER THAN ANYONE HOW EVIL THAT MAN CAN BE!!
THERE'S NO NEED TO INVOLVE THE INNOCENT ...
EXACTLY!
I HAVE NO INTENTION OF BEING PULLED INTO YOUR DOMESTIC AFFAIRS.

This is the sixth volume. To me it seems like it took a bit too long for it to come out. The character Sheila is the same woman that Crehador had with him at the costume ball... I'll be happy if there were at least a few people out there that figured it out. In this volume there is one episode in which I restarted the series in order to do a story that I really wanted to do. At this point I'm thinking to myself that I've finally come this far...

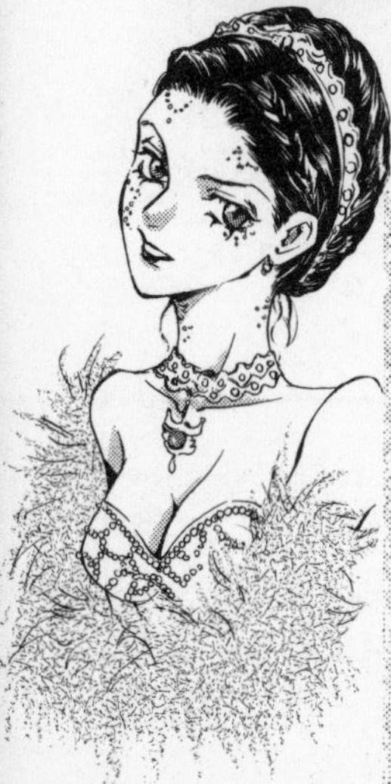

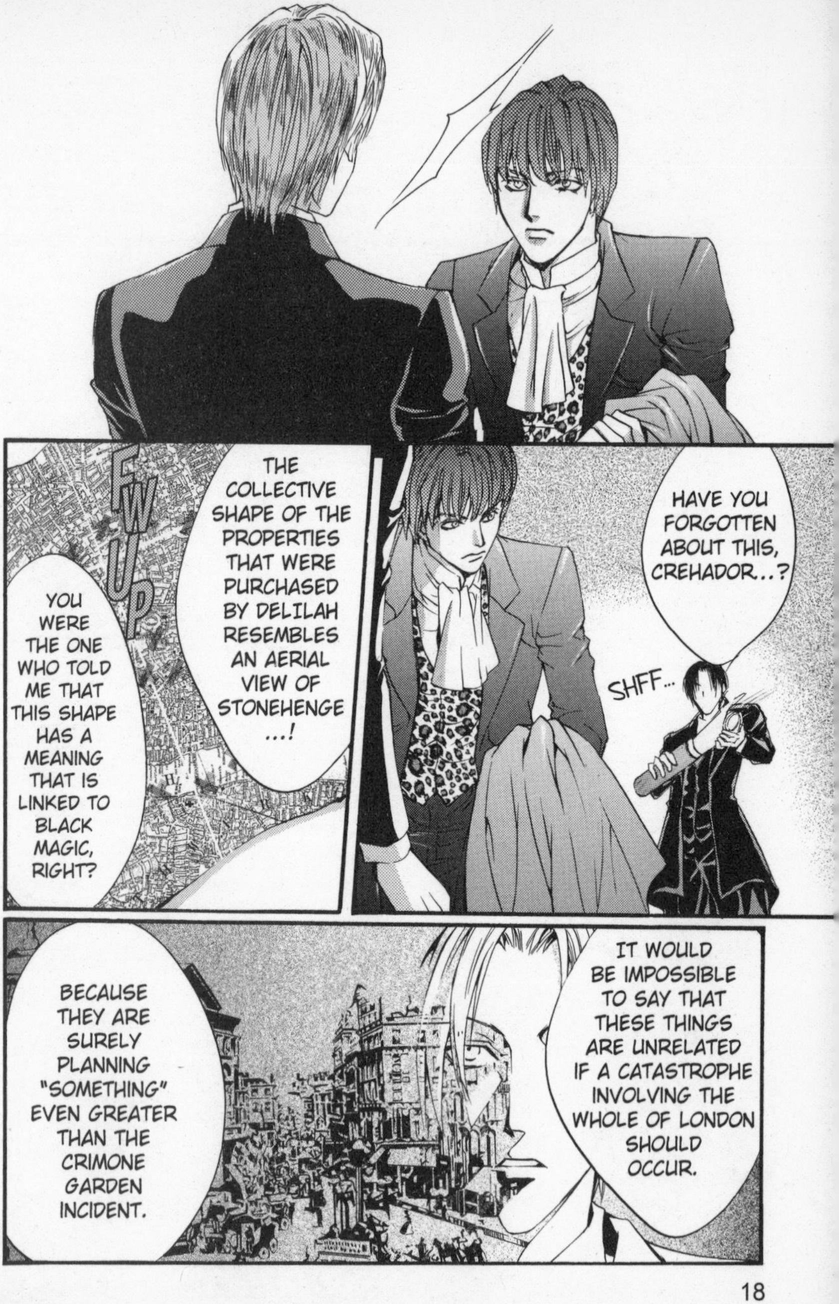
HAVE YOU FORGOTTEN ABOUT THIS, CREHADOR...?
SHFF...
THE COLLECTIVE SHAPE OF THE PROPERTIES THAT WERE PURCHASED BY DELILAH RESEMBLES AN AERIAL VIEW OF STONEHENGE ...!
FWUP
YOU WERE THE ONE WHO TOLD ME THAT THIS SHAPE HAS A MEANING THAT IS LINKED TO BLACK MAGIC, RIGHT?
IT WOULD BE IMPOSSIBLE TO SAY THAT THESE THINGS ARE UNRELATED IF A CATASTROPHE INVOLVING THE WHOLE OF LONDON SHOULD OCCUR.
BECAUSE THEY ARE SURELY PLANNING "SOMETHING" EVEN GREATER THAN THE CRIMONE GARDEN INCIDENT.

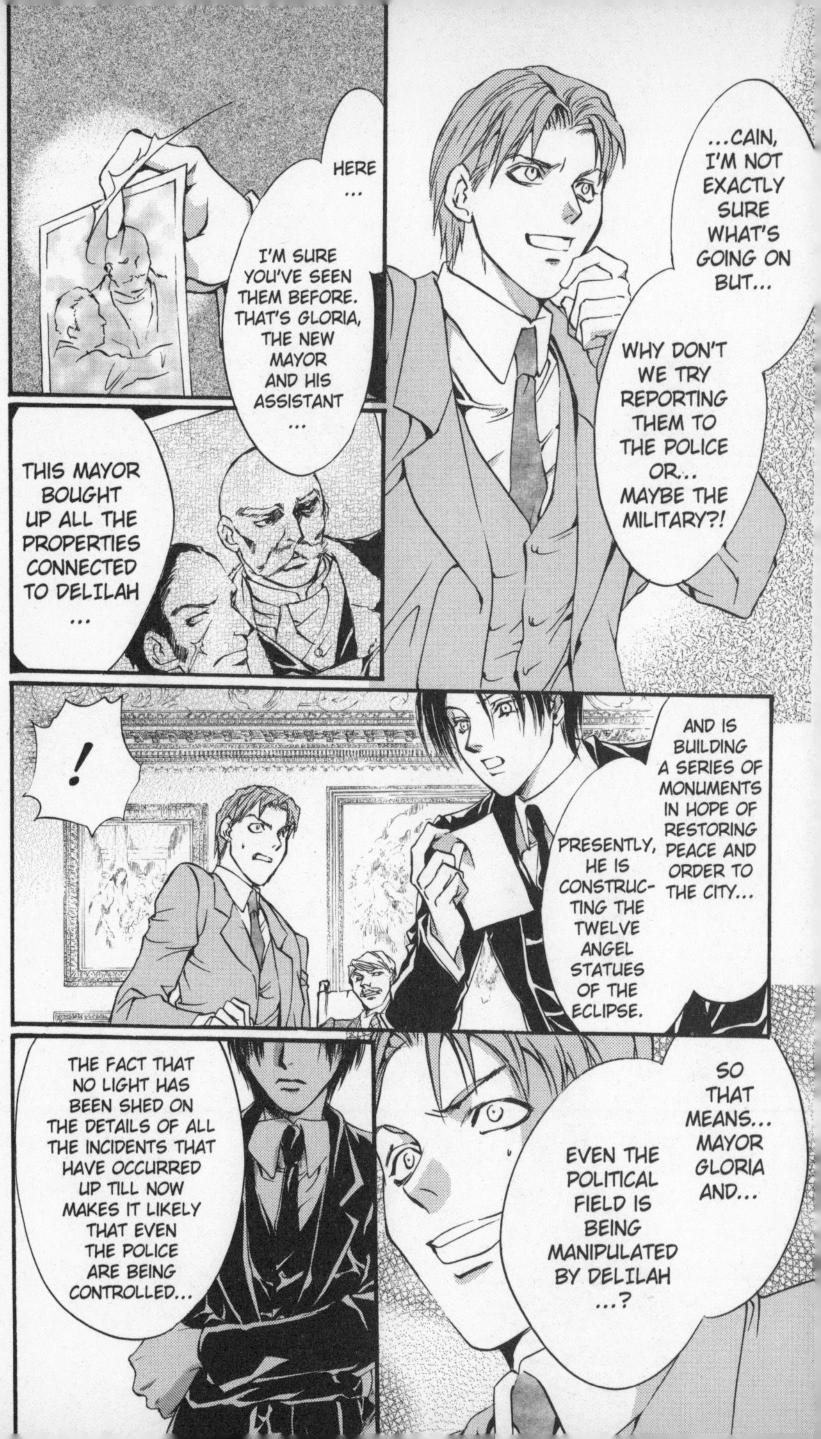
...CAIN, I'M NOT EXACTLY SURE WHAT'S GOING ON BUT...
WHY DON'T WE TRY REPORTING THEM TO THE POLICE OR... MAYBE THE MILITARY?!
HERE...
I'M SURE YOU'VE SEEN THEM BEFORE. THAT'S GLORIA, THE NEW MAYOR AND HIS ASSISTANT...
THIS MAYOR BOUGHT UP ALL THE PROPERTIES CONNECTED TO DELILAH...
AND IS BUILDING A SERIES OF MONUMENTS IN HOPE OF RESTORING PEACE AND ORDER TO THE CITY...
PRESENTLY, HE IS CONSTRUC-TING THE TWELVE ANGEL STATUES OF THE ECLIPSE.
!
SO THAT MEANS... MAYOR GLORIA AND...
EVEN THE POLITICAL FIELD IS BEING MANIPULATED BY DELILAH...?
THE FACT THAT NO LIGHT HAS BEEN SHED ON THE DETAILS OF ALL THE INCIDENTS THAT HAVE OCCURRED UP TILL NOW MAKES IT LIKELY THAT EVEN THE POLICE ARE BEING CONTROLLED...

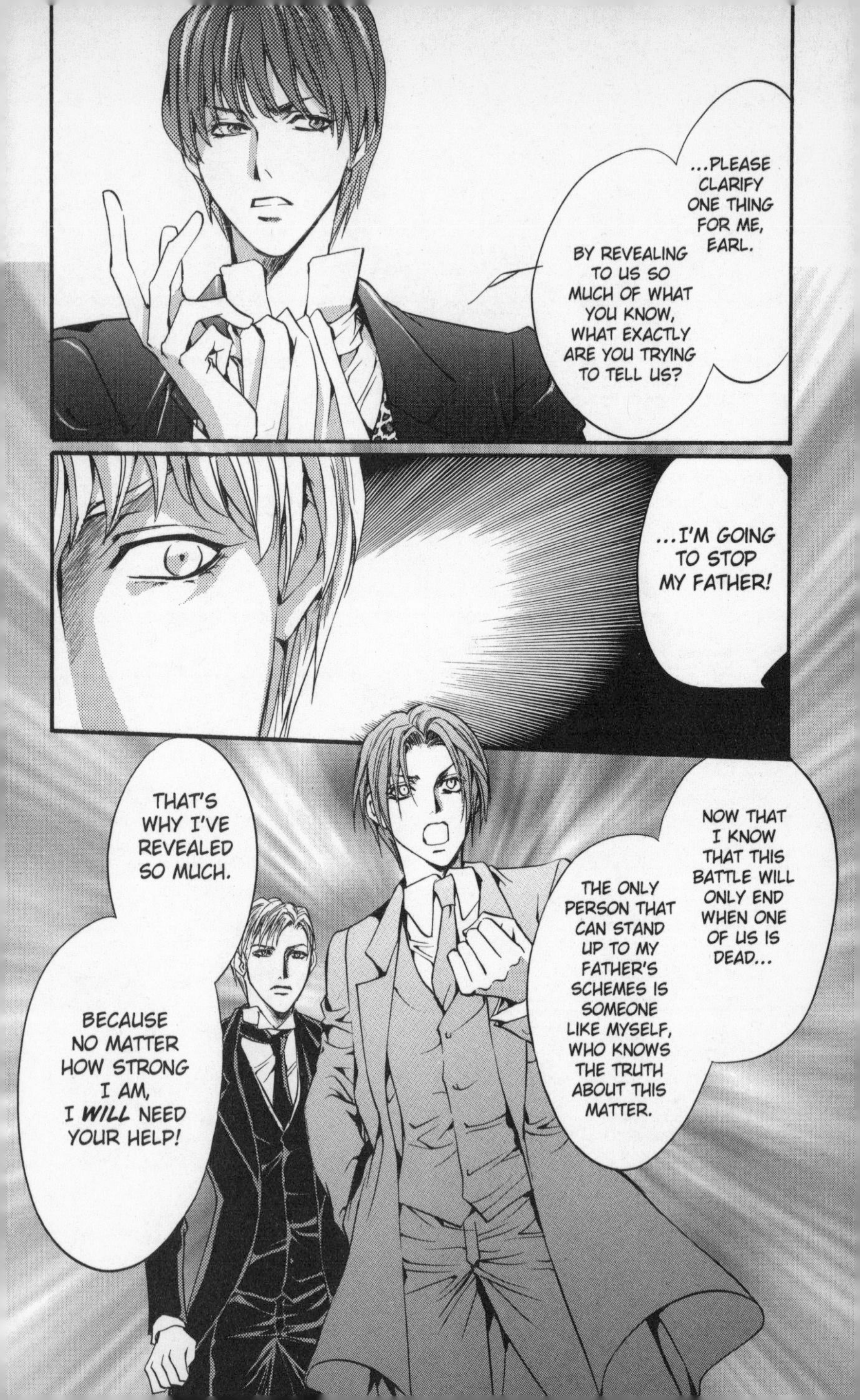
...PLEASE CLARIFY ONE THING FOR ME, EARL.
BY REVEALING TO US SO MUCH OF WHAT YOU KNOW, WHAT EXACTLY ARE YOU TRYING TO TELL US?
...I'M GOING TO STOP MY FATHER!
NOW THAT I KNOW THAT THIS BATTLE WILL ONLY END WHEN ONE OF US IS DEAD...
THE ONLY PERSON THAT CAN STAND UP TO MY FATHER'S SCHEMES IS SOMEONE LIKE MYSELF, WHO KNOWS THE TRUTH ABOUT THIS MATTER.
THAT'S WHY I'VE REVEALED SO MUCH.
BECAUSE NO MATTER HOW STRONG I AM, I *WILL* NEED YOUR HELP!

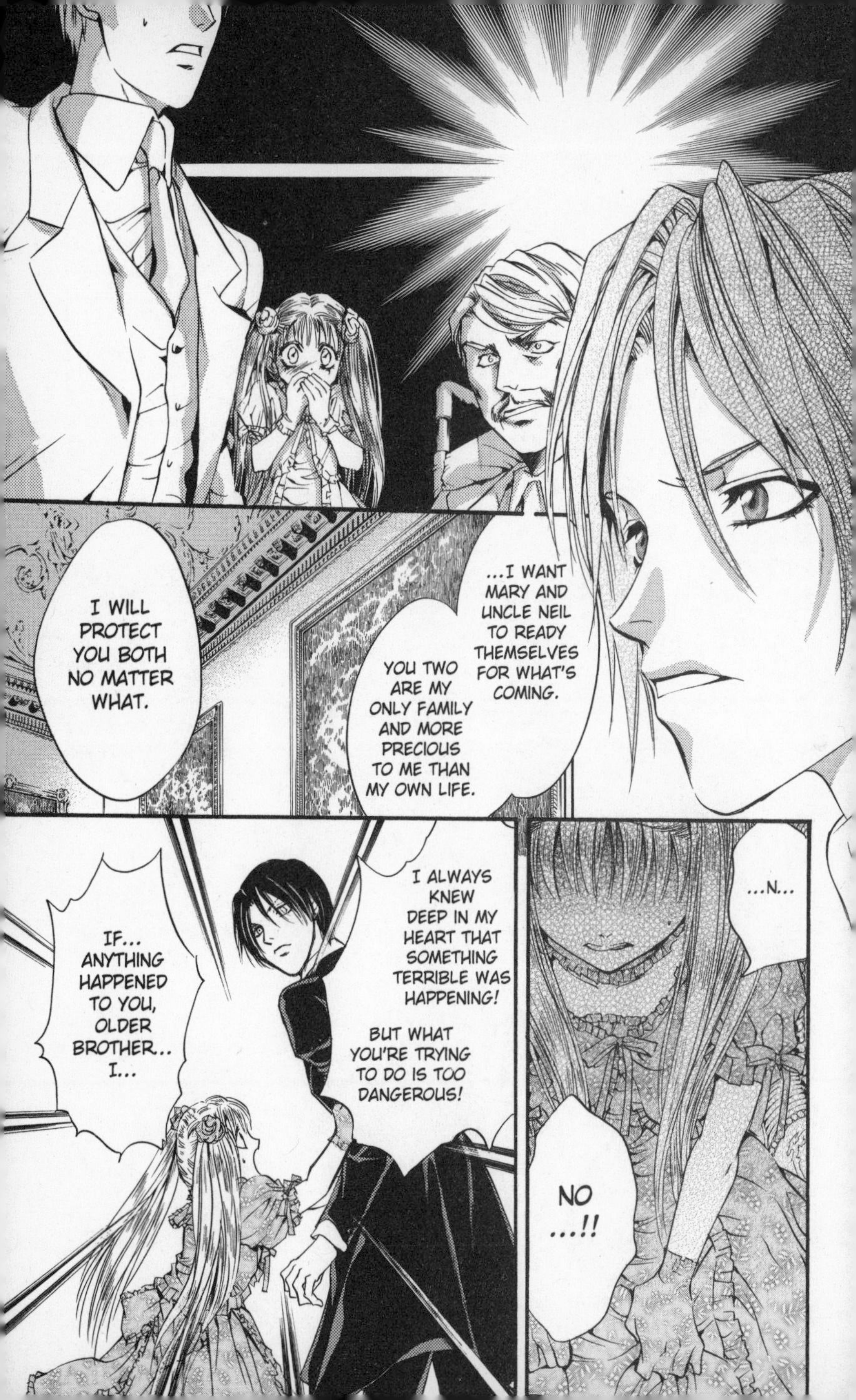
...I WANT MARY AND UNCLE NEIL TO READY THEMSELVES FOR WHAT'S COMING.
YOU TWO ARE MY ONLY FAMILY AND MORE PRECIOUS TO ME THAN MY OWN LIFE.
I WILL PROTECT YOU BOTH NO MATTER WHAT.
...N...
NO ...!!
I ALWAYS KNEW DEEP IN MY HEART THAT SOMETHING TERRIBLE WAS HAPPENING!
BUT WHAT YOU'RE TRYING TO DO IS TOO DANGEROUS!
IF... ANYTHING HAPPENED TO YOU, OLDER BROTHER... I...

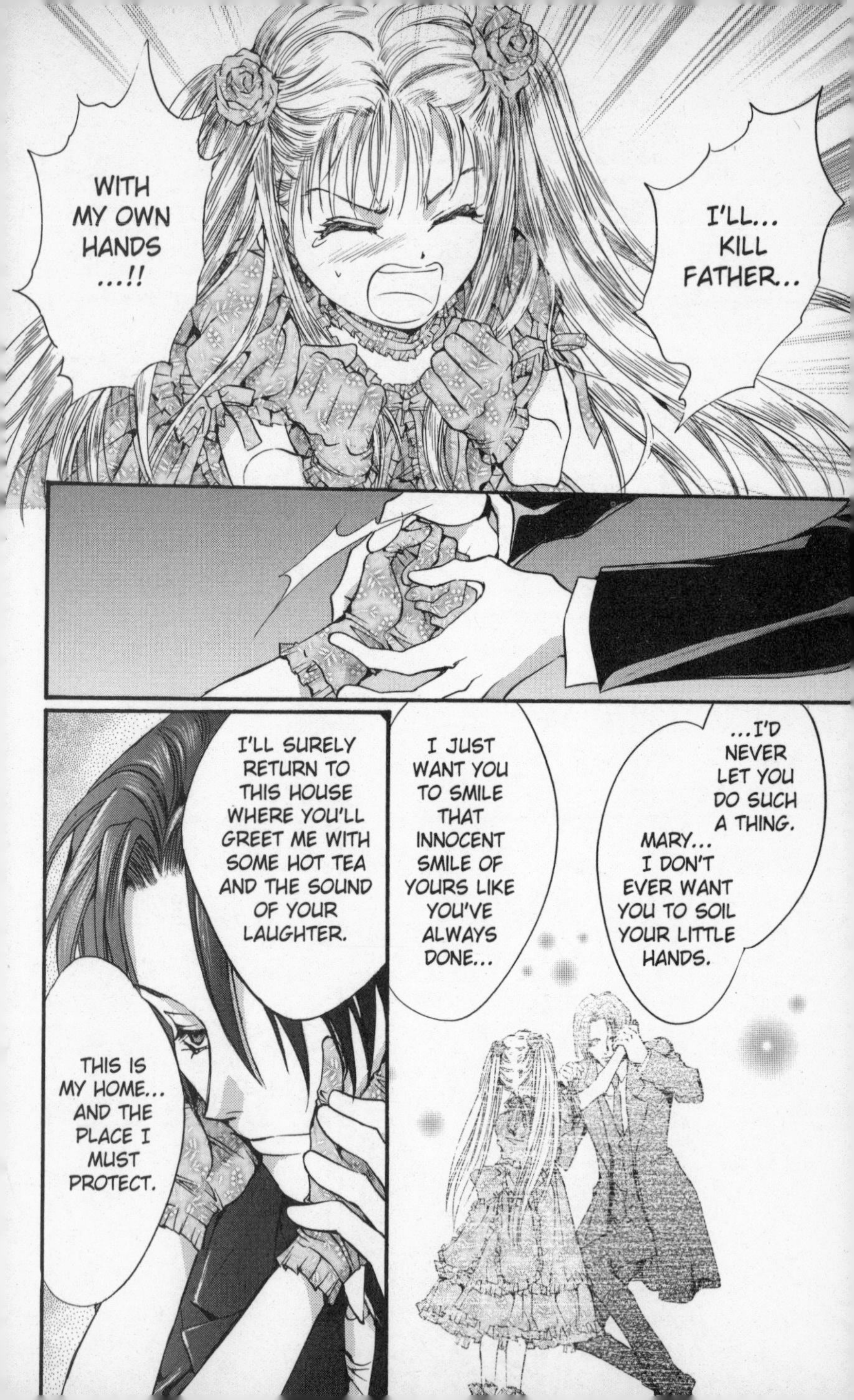
I'LL... KILL FATHER...
WITH MY OWN HANDS ...!!
...I'D NEVER LET YOU DO SUCH A THING. MARY... I DON'T EVER WANT YOU TO SOIL YOUR LITTLE HANDS.
I JUST WANT YOU TO SMILE THAT INNOCENT SMILE OF YOURS LIKE YOU'VE ALWAYS DONE...
I'LL SURELY RETURN TO THIS HOUSE WHERE YOU'LL GREET ME WITH SOME HOT TEA AND THE SOUND OF YOUR LAUGHTER.
THIS IS MY HOME... AND THE PLACE I MUST PROTECT.

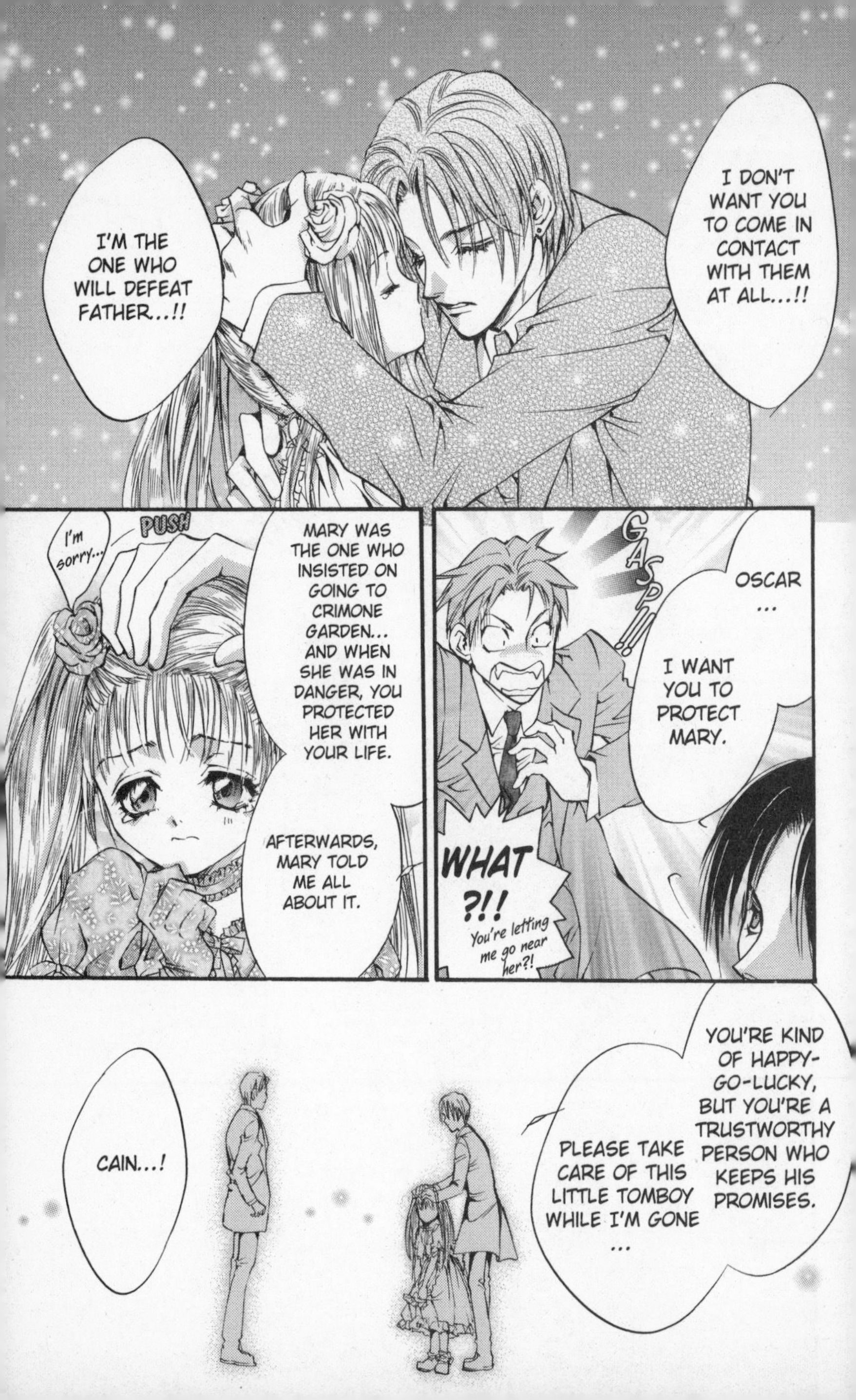
I DON'T WANT YOU TO COME IN CONTACT WITH THEM AT ALL...!!
I'M THE ONE WHO WILL DEFEAT FATHER...!!
GASP!!
OSCAR ...
I WANT YOU TO PROTECT MARY.
WHAT ?!!
You're letting me go near her?!
MARY WAS THE ONE WHO INSISTED ON GOING TO CRIMONE GARDEN... AND WHEN SHE WAS IN DANGER, YOU PROTECTED HER WITH YOUR LIFE.
PUSH
I'm sorry...
AFTERWARDS, MARY TOLD ME ALL ABOUT IT.
YOU'RE KIND OF HAPPY-GO-LUCKY, BUT YOU'RE A TRUSTWORTHY PERSON WHO KEEPS HIS PROMISES.
PLEASE TAKE CARE OF THIS LITTLE TOMBOY WHILE I'M GONE ...
CAIN...!

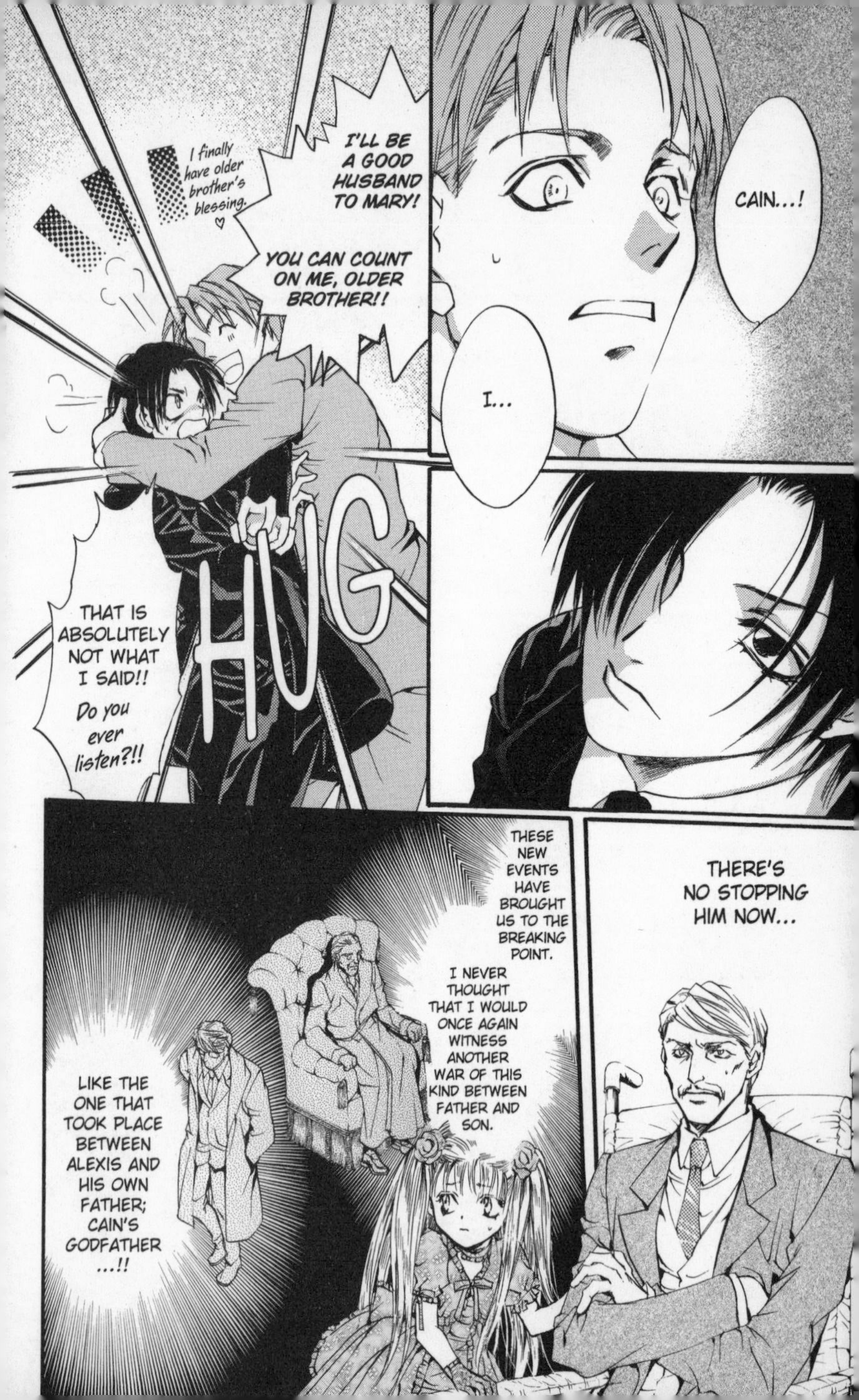

CAIN...!
I...
I'LL BE A GOOD HUSBAND TO MARY!
I finally have older brother's blessing. ♡
YOU CAN COUNT ON ME, OLDER BROTHER!!
HUG
THAT IS ABSOLUTELY NOT WHAT I SAID!!
Do you ever listen?!!
THERE'S NO STOPPING HIM NOW...
THESE NEW EVENTS HAVE BROUGHT US TO THE BREAKING POINT.
I NEVER THOUGHT THAT I WOULD ONCE AGAIN WITNESS ANOTHER WAR OF THIS KIND BETWEEN FATHER AND SON.
LIKE THE ONE THAT TOOK PLACE BETWEEN ALEXIS AND HIS OWN FATHER; CAIN'S GODFATHER ...!!

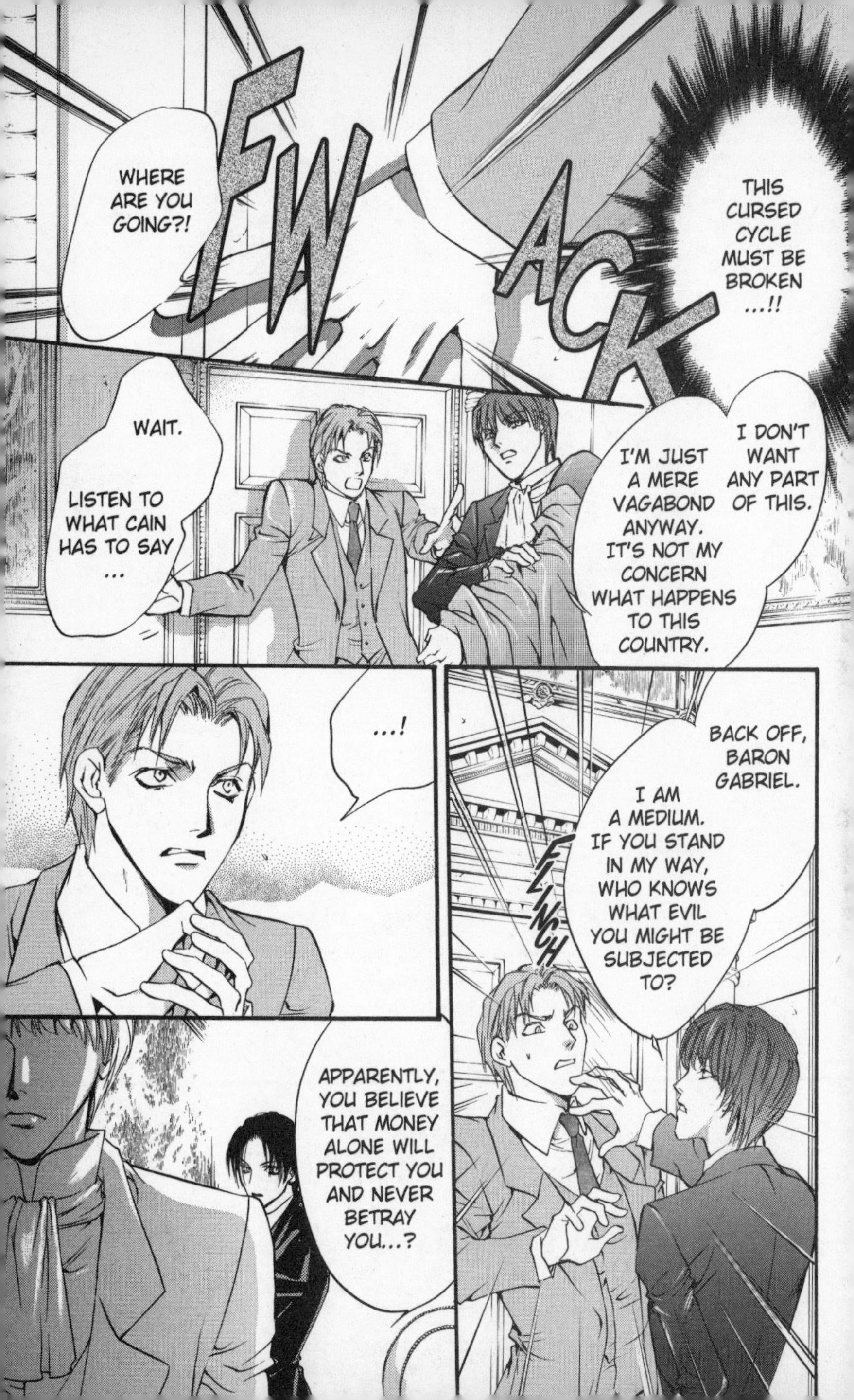
THIS CURSED CYCLE MUST BE BROKEN ...!!
FWACK
WHERE ARE YOU GOING?!
I DON'T WANT ANY PART OF THIS.
I'M JUST A MERE VAGABOND ANYWAY. IT'S NOT MY CONCERN WHAT HAPPENS TO THIS COUNTRY.
WAIT.
LISTEN TO WHAT CAIN HAS TO SAY ...
BACK OFF, BARON GABRIEL.
I AM A MEDIUM. IF YOU STAND IN MY WAY, WHO KNOWS WHAT EVIL YOU MIGHT BE SUBJECTED TO?
FLINCH
...!
APPARENTLY, YOU BELIEVE THAT MONEY ALONE WILL PROTECT YOU AND NEVER BETRAY YOU...?

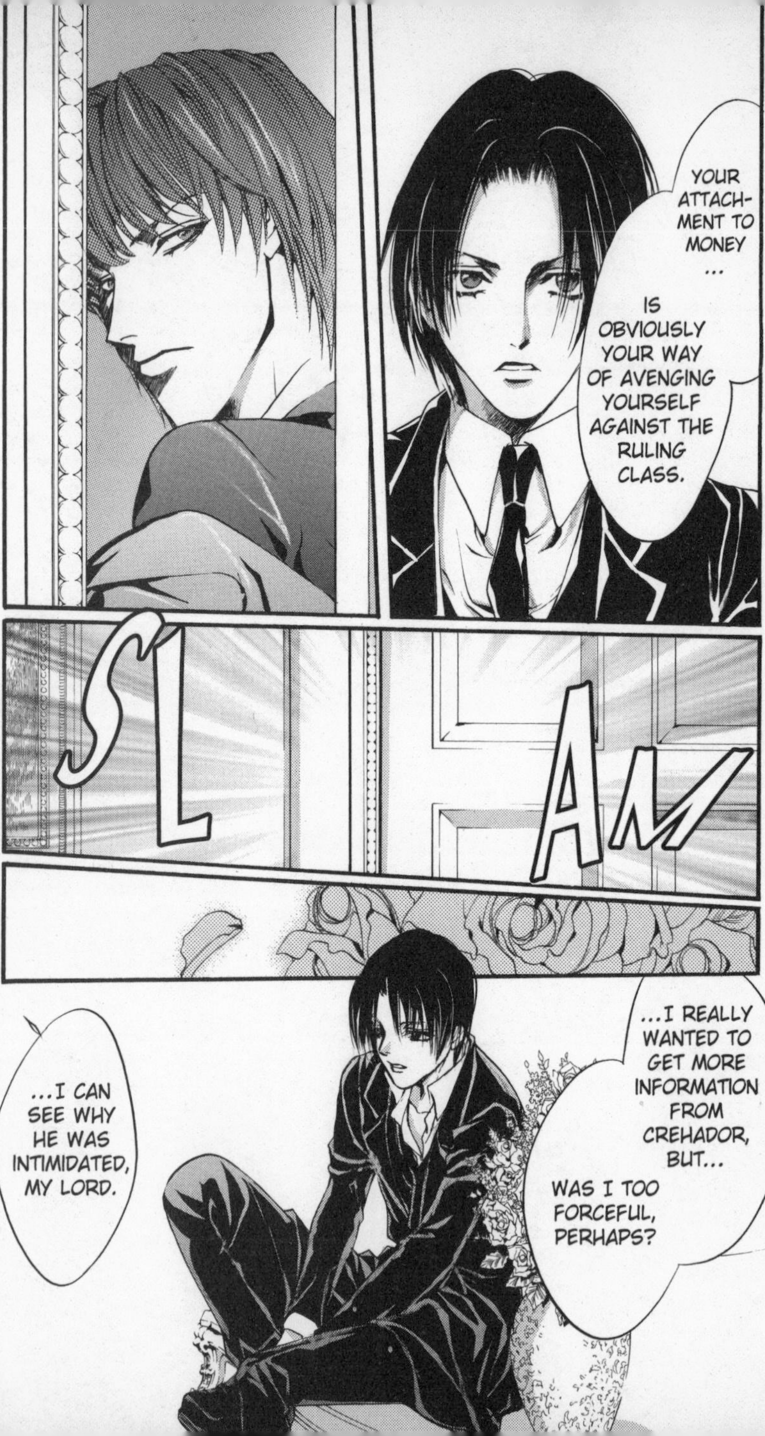
YOUR ATTACHMENT TO MONEY ...
IS OBVIOUSLY YOUR WAY OF AVENGING YOURSELF AGAINST THE RULING CLASS.
SLAM
...I REALLY WANTED TO GET MORE INFORMATION FROM CREHADOR, BUT...
WAS I TOO FORCEFUL, PERHAPS?
...I CAN SEE WHY HE WAS INTIMIDATED, MY LORD.

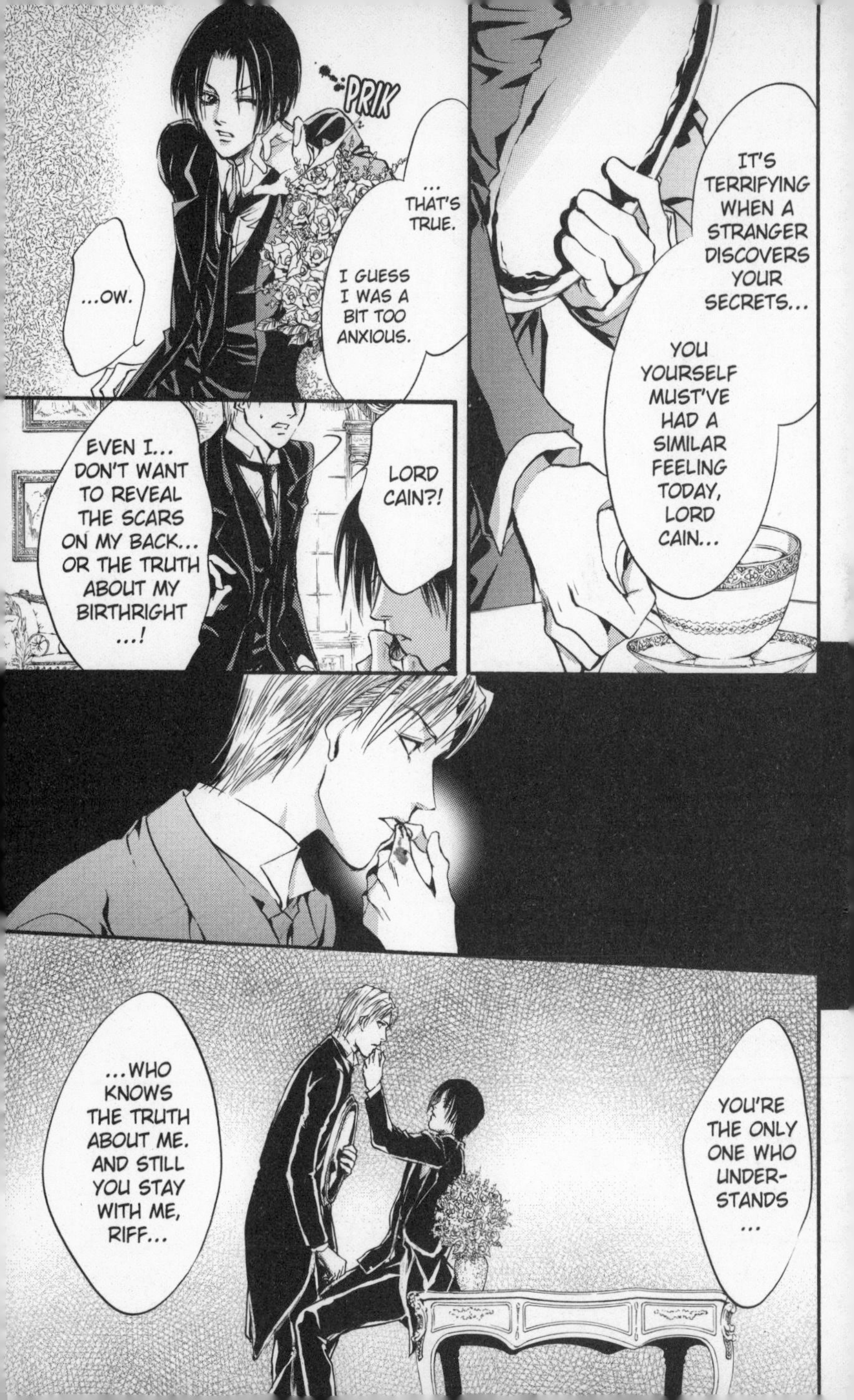

IT'S TERRIFYING WHEN A STRANGER DISCOVERS YOUR SECRETS...
YOU YOURSELF MUST'VE HAD A SIMILAR FEELING TODAY, LORD CAIN...
PRIK
... THAT'S TRUE.
I GUESS I WAS A BIT TOO ANXIOUS.
...OW.
LORD CAIN?!
EVEN I... DON'T WANT TO REVEAL THE SCARS ON MY BACK... OR THE TRUTH ABOUT MY BIRTHRIGHT ...!
YOU'RE THE ONLY ONE WHO UNDER-STANDS ...
...WHO KNOWS THE TRUTH ABOUT ME. AND STILL YOU STAY WITH ME, RIFF...

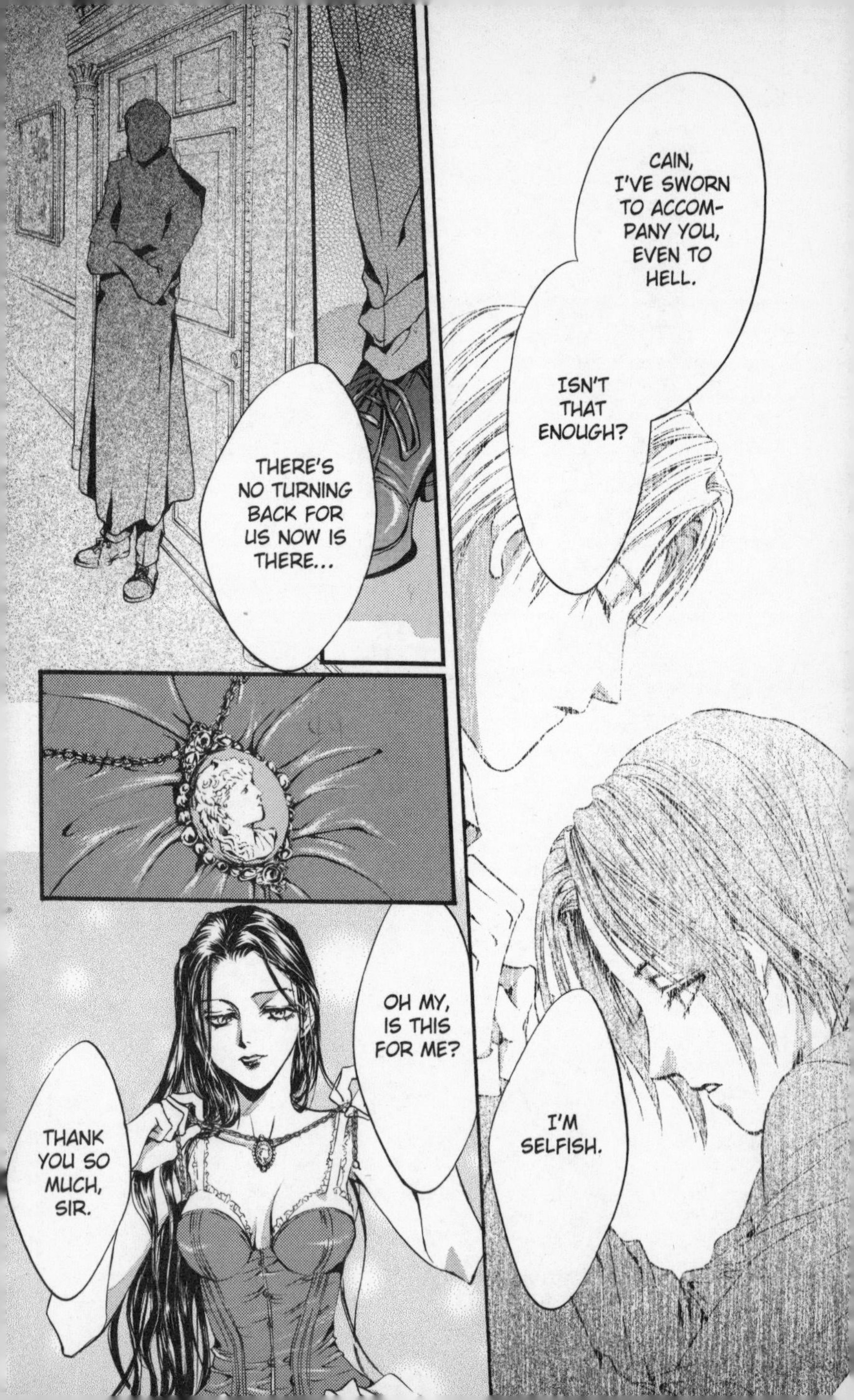
CAIN, I'VE SWORN TO ACCOMPANY YOU, EVEN TO HELL.
ISN'T THAT ENOUGH?
I'M SELFISH.
THERE'S NO TURNING BACK FOR US NOW IS THERE...
OH MY, IS THIS FOR ME?
THANK YOU SO MUCH, SIR.

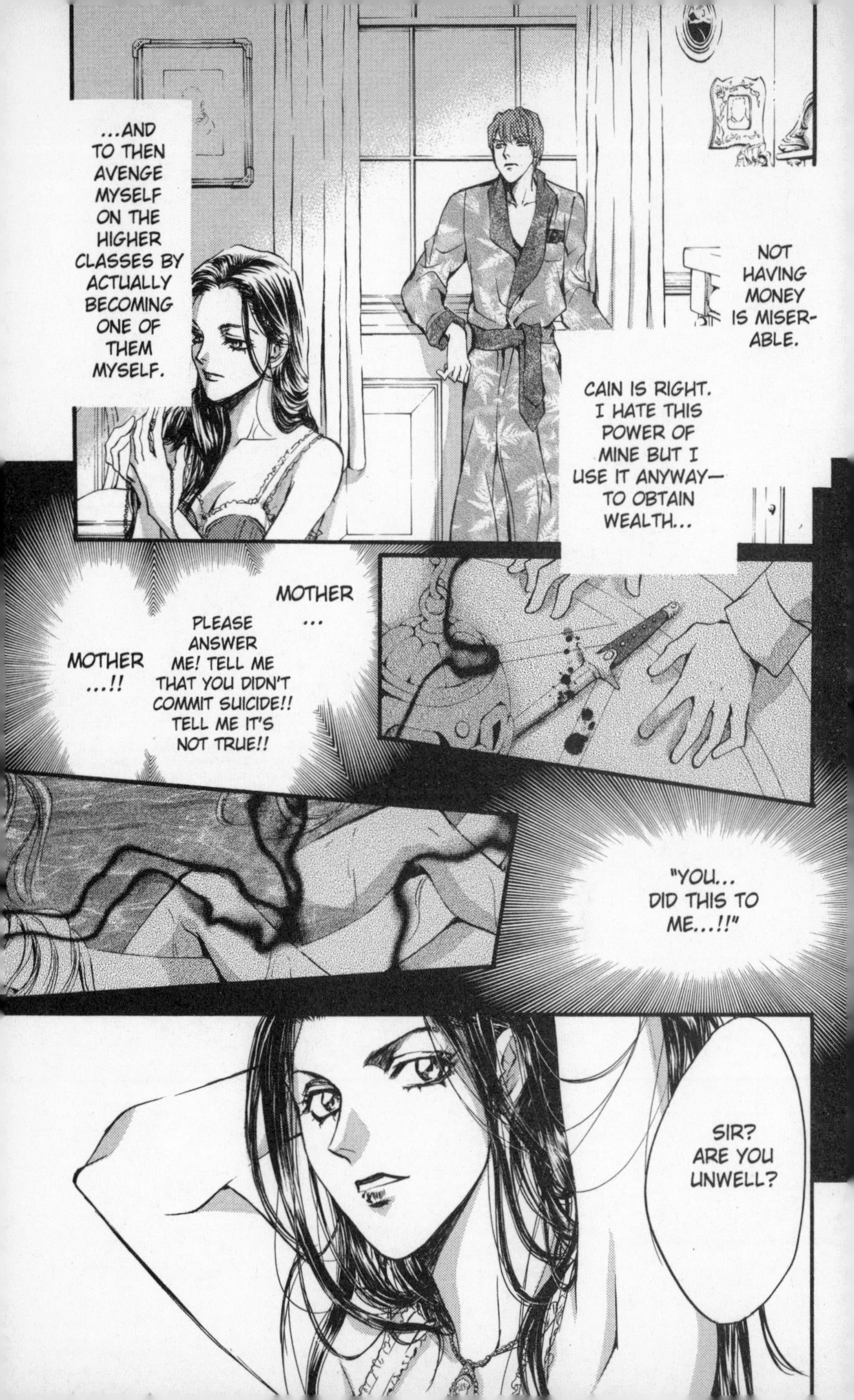
NOT HAVING MONEY IS MISERABLE.
CAIN IS RIGHT. I HATE THIS POWER OF MINE BUT I USE IT ANYWAY—TO OBTAIN WEALTH...
...AND TO THEN AVENGE MYSELF ON THE HIGHER CLASSES BY ACTUALLY BECOMING ONE OF THEM MYSELF.
MOTHER ...
PLEASE ANSWER ME! TELL ME THAT YOU DIDN'T COMMIT SUICIDE!! TELL ME IT'S NOT TRUE!!
MOTHER ...!!
"YOU... DID THIS TO ME...!!"
SIR? ARE YOU UNWELL?

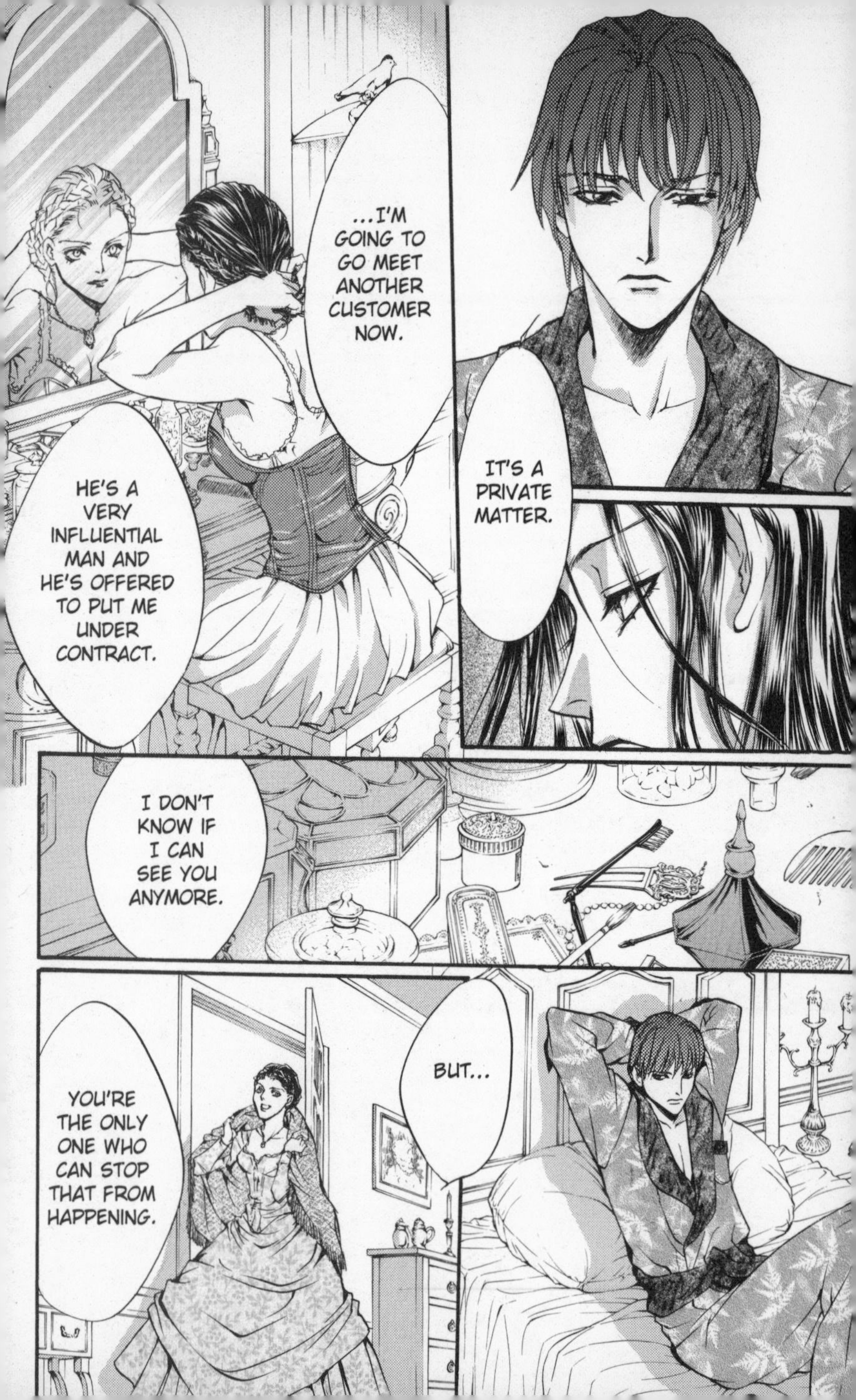
IT'S A PRIVATE MATTER.
...I'M GOING TO GO MEET ANOTHER CUSTOMER NOW.
HE'S A VERY INFLUENTIAL MAN AND HE'S OFFERED TO PUT ME UNDER CONTRACT.
I DON'T KNOW IF I CAN SEE YOU ANYMORE.
BUT...
YOU'RE THE ONLY ONE WHO CAN STOP THAT FROM HAPPENING.

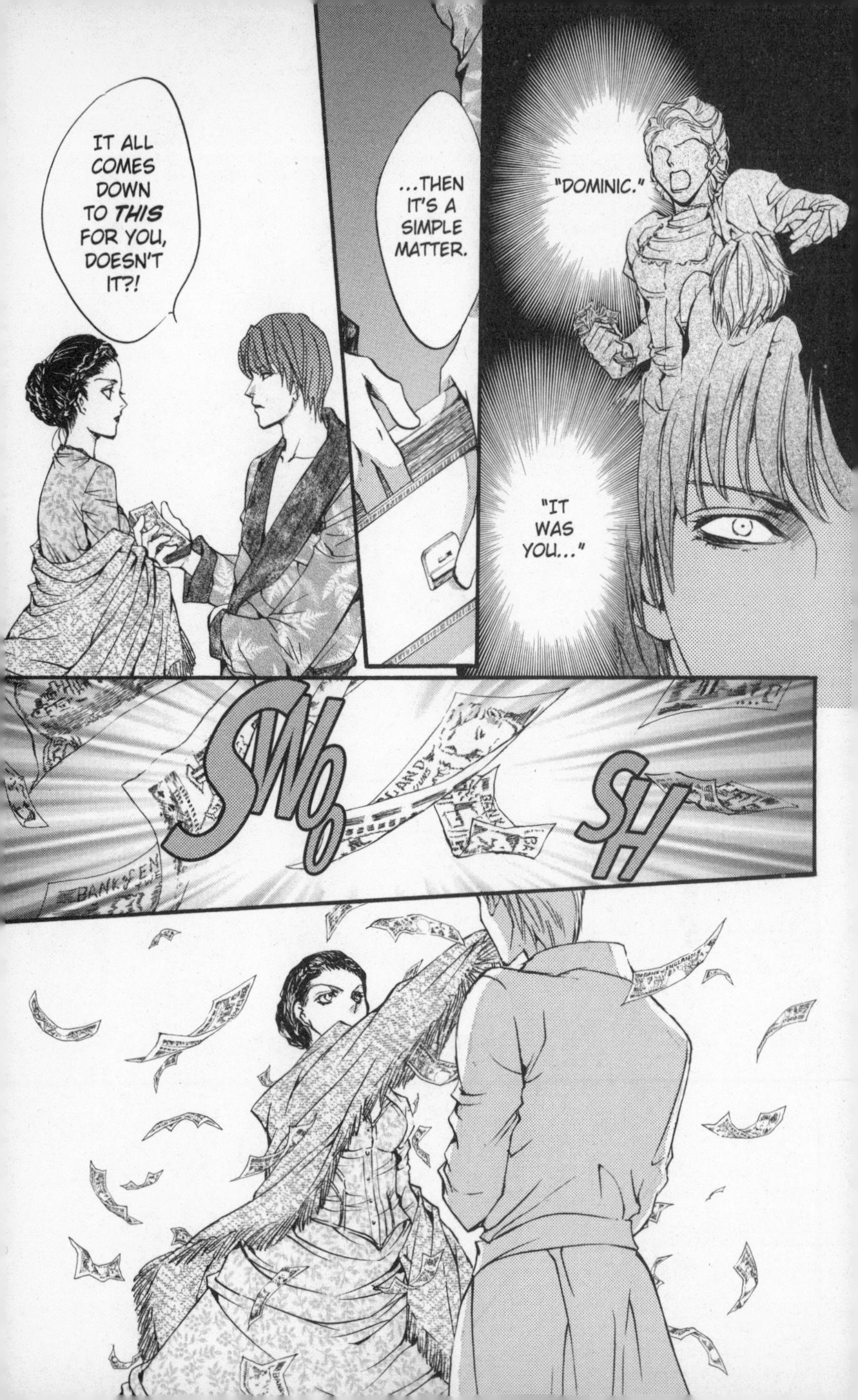
"DOMINIC."
"IT WAS YOU..."
...THEN IT'S A SIMPLE MATTER.
IT ALL COMES DOWN TO ***THIS*** FOR YOU, DOESN'T IT?!
SWOOSH

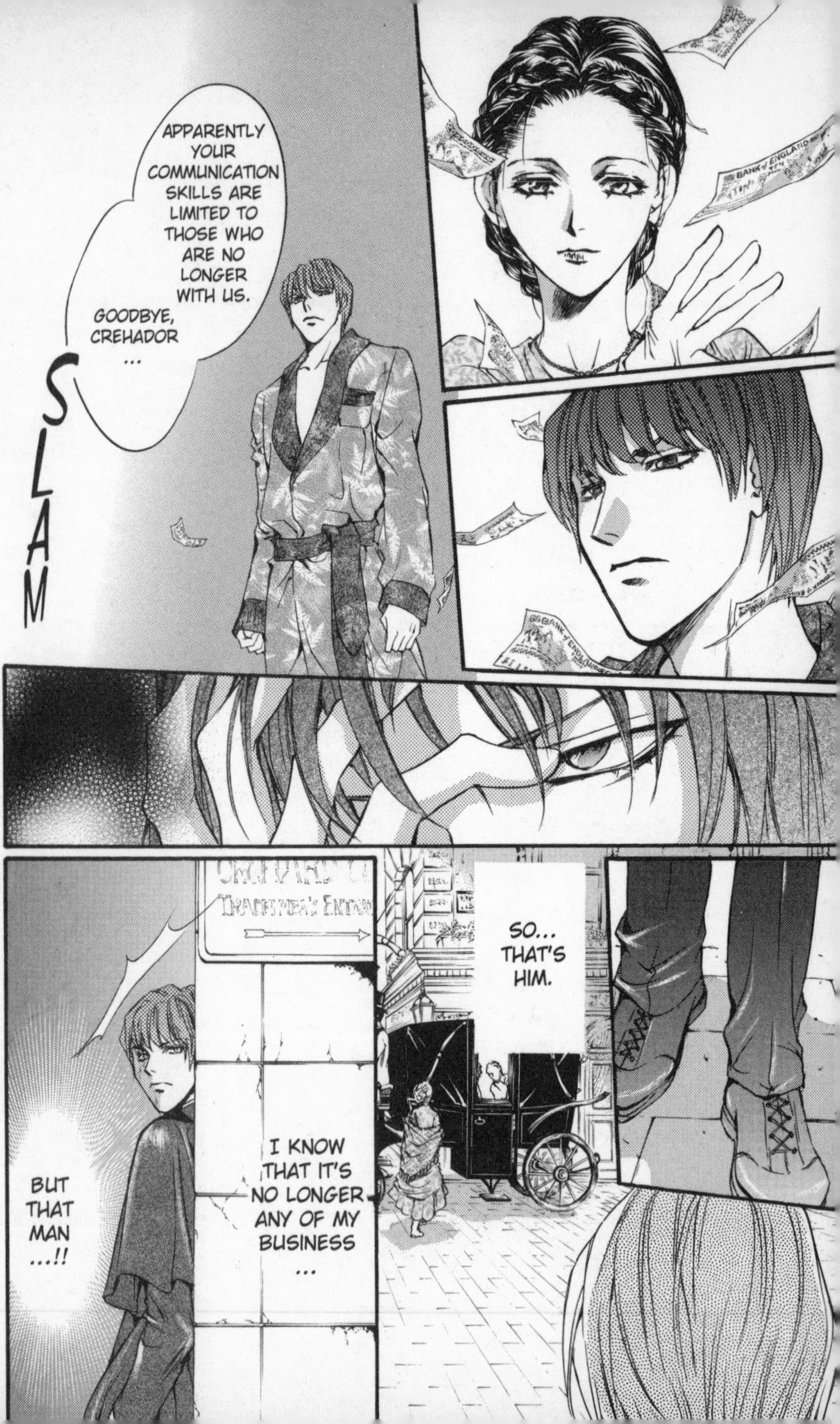
APPARENTLY YOUR COMMUNICATION SKILLS ARE LIMITED TO THOSE WHO ARE NO LONGER WITH US.
GOODBYE, CREHADOR ...
SLAM
SO... THAT'S HIM.
I KNOW THAT IT'S NO LONGER ANY OF MY BUSINESS ...
BUT THAT MAN ...!!

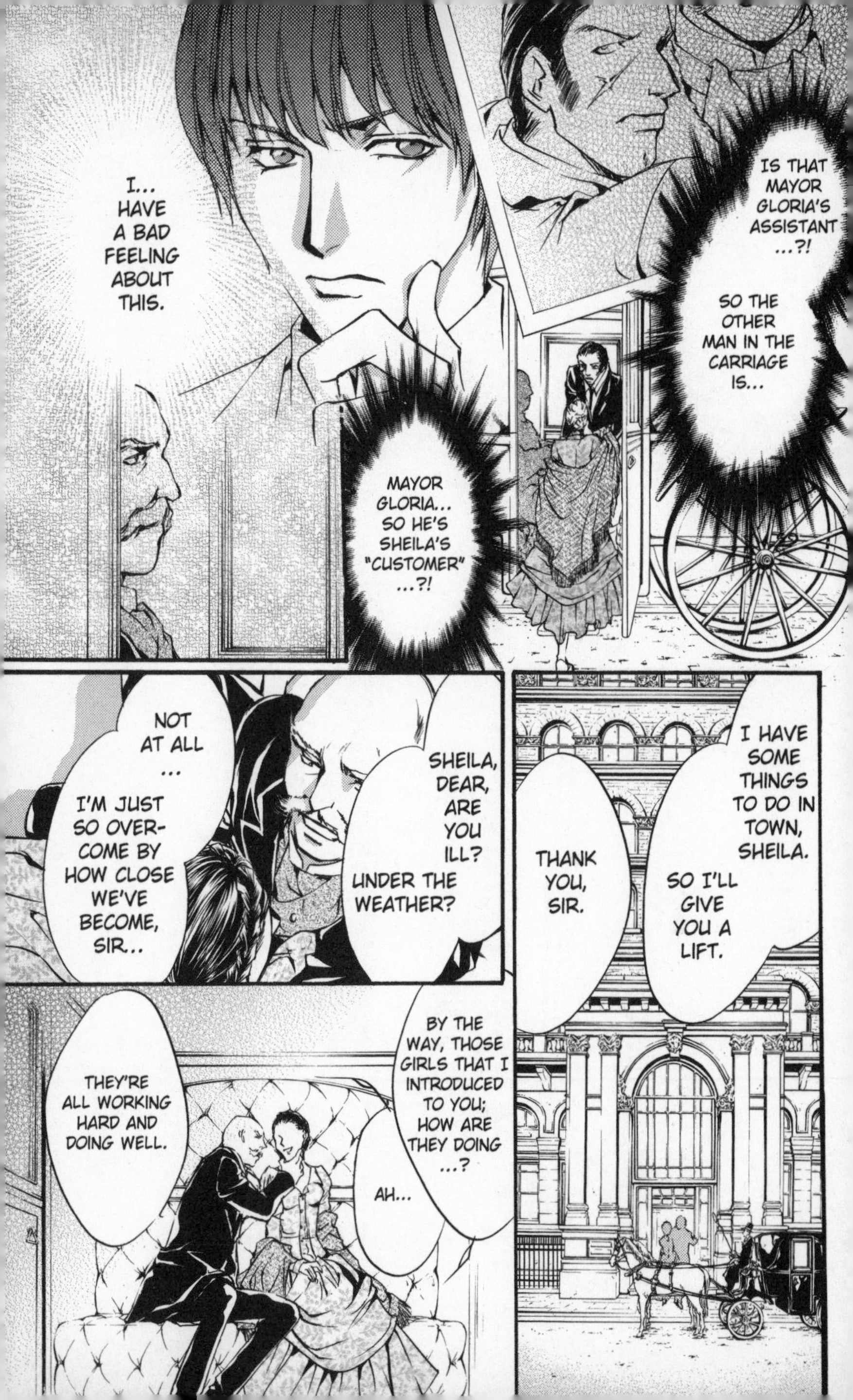

IS THAT MAYOR GLORIA'S ASSISTANT ...?!
SO THE OTHER MAN IN THE CARRIAGE IS...
MAYOR GLORIA... SO HE'S SHEILA'S "CUSTOMER" ...?!
I... HAVE A BAD FEELING ABOUT THIS.
I HAVE SOME THINGS TO DO IN TOWN, SHEILA.
SO I'LL GIVE YOU A LIFT.
THANK YOU, SIR.
SHEILA, DEAR, ARE YOU ILL?
UNDER THE WEATHER?
NOT AT ALL ...
I'M JUST SO OVER-COME BY HOW CLOSE WE'VE BECOME, SIR...
BY THE WAY, THOSE GIRLS THAT I INTRODUCED TO YOU; HOW ARE THEY DOING ...?
AH...
THEY'RE ALL WORKING HARD AND DOING WELL.

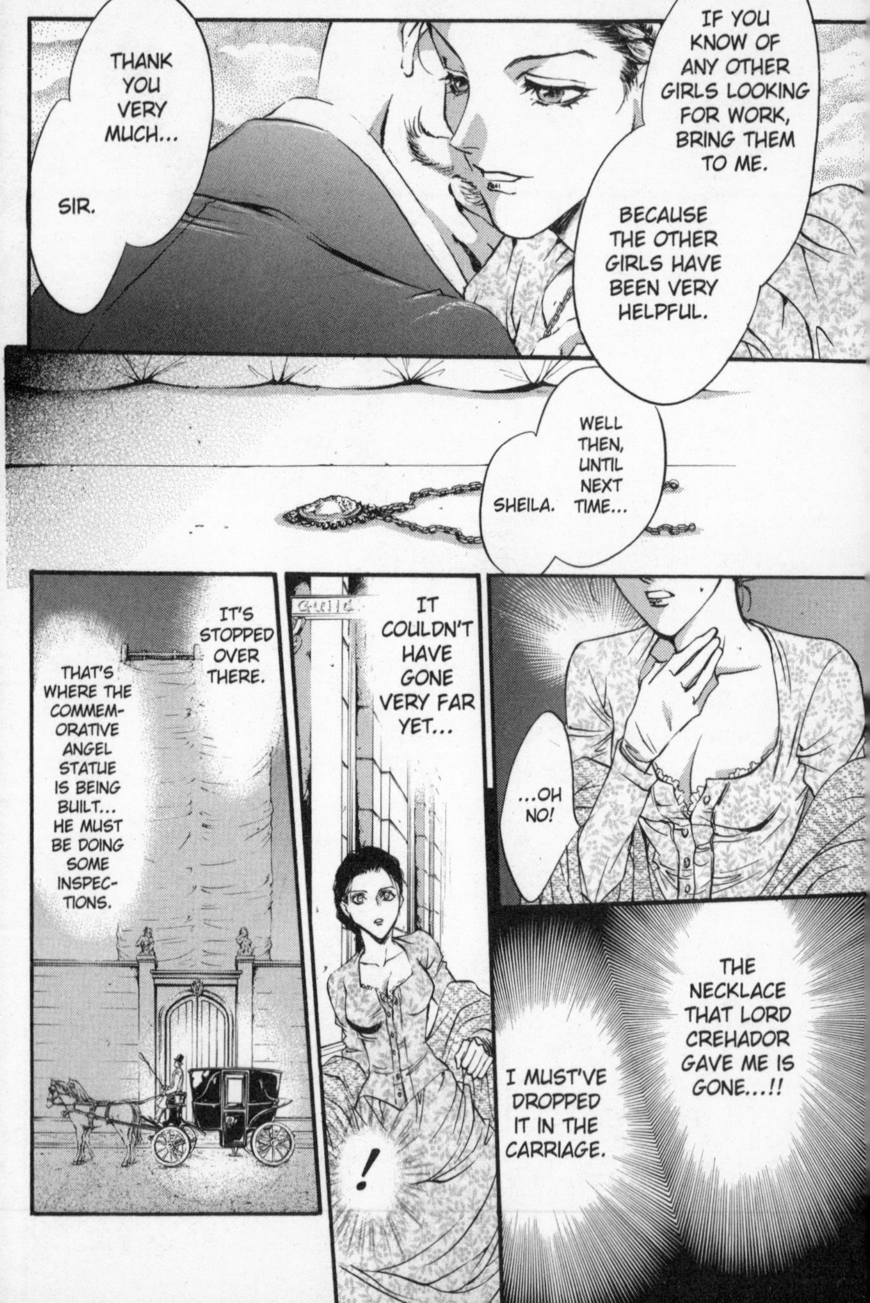
IF YOU KNOW OF ANY OTHER GIRLS LOOKING FOR WORK, BRING THEM TO ME.
BECAUSE THE OTHER GIRLS HAVE BEEN VERY HELPFUL.
THANK YOU VERY MUCH...
SIR.
WELL THEN, UNTIL NEXT TIME...
SHEILA.
...OH NO!
THE NECKLACE THAT LORD CREHADOR GAVE ME IS GONE...!!
I MUST'VE DROPPED IT IN THE CARRIAGE.
IT COULDN'T HAVE GONE VERY FAR YET...
!
IT'S STOPPED OVER THERE.
THAT'S WHERE THE COMMEM-ORATIVE ANGEL STATUE IS BEING BUILT... HE MUST BE DOING SOME INSPEC-TIONS.

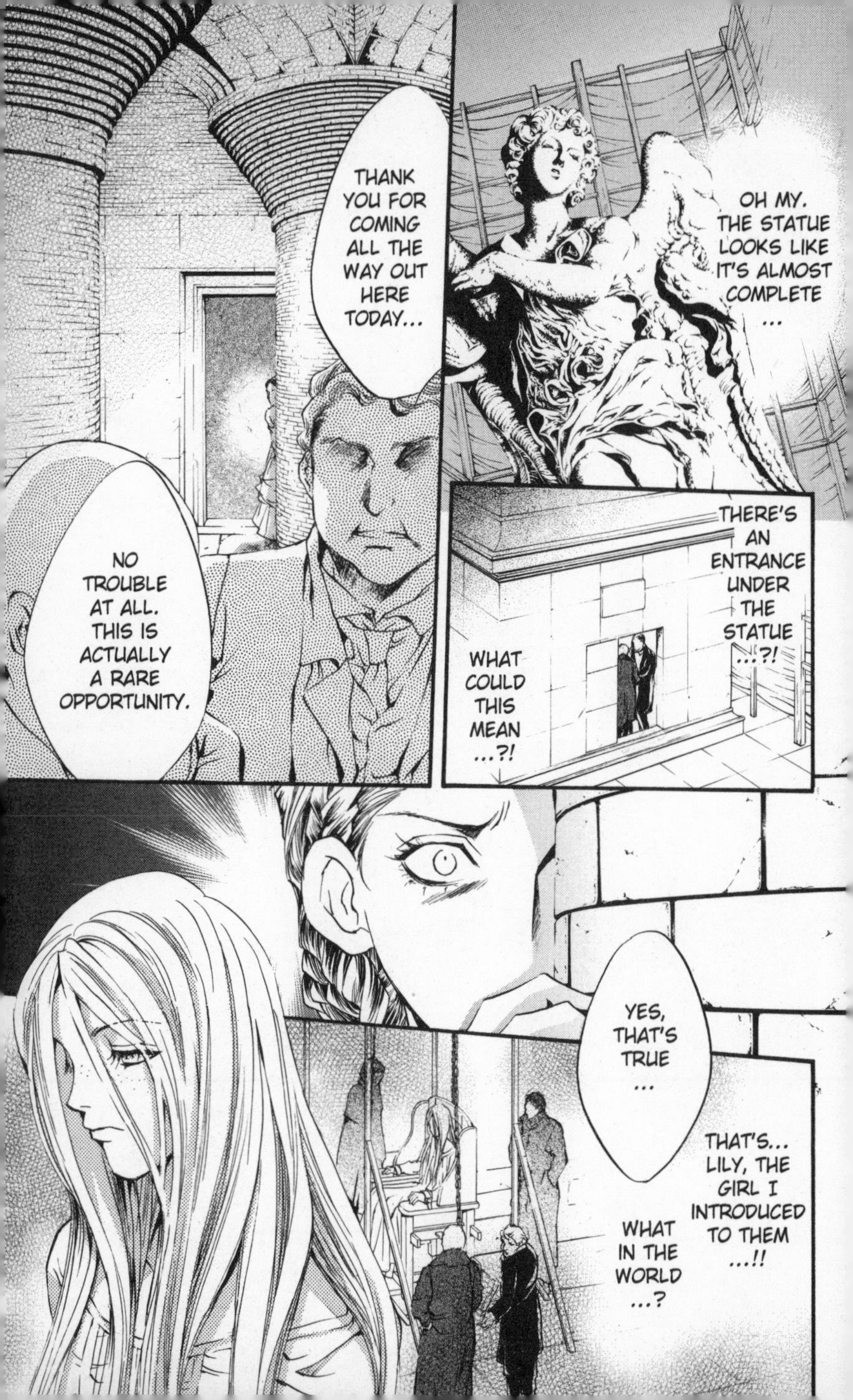
OH MY. THE STATUE LOOKS LIKE IT'S ALMOST COMPLETE...
THERE'S AN ENTRANCE UNDER THE STATUE...?!
WHAT COULD THIS MEAN...?!
THANK YOU FOR COMING ALL THE WAY OUT HERE TODAY...
NO TROUBLE AT ALL. THIS IS ACTUALLY A RARE OPPORTUNITY.
YES, THAT'S TRUE...
THAT'S... LILY, THE GIRL I INTRODUCED TO THEM...!!
WHAT IN THE WORLD...?

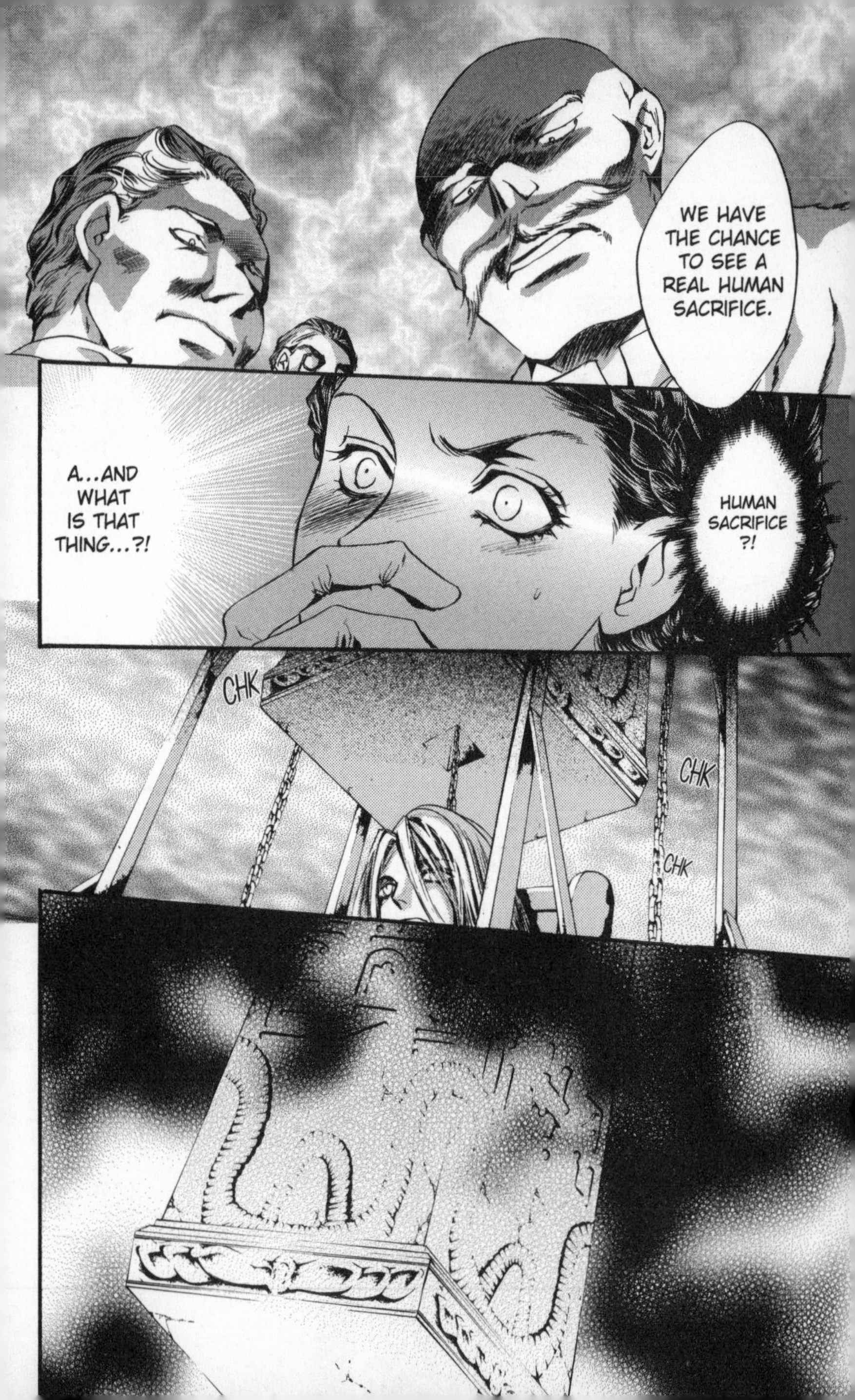
WE HAVE THE CHANCE TO SEE A REAL HUMAN SACRIFICE.
HUMAN SACRIFICE ?!
A...AND WHAT IS THAT THING...?!
CHK
CHK
CHK

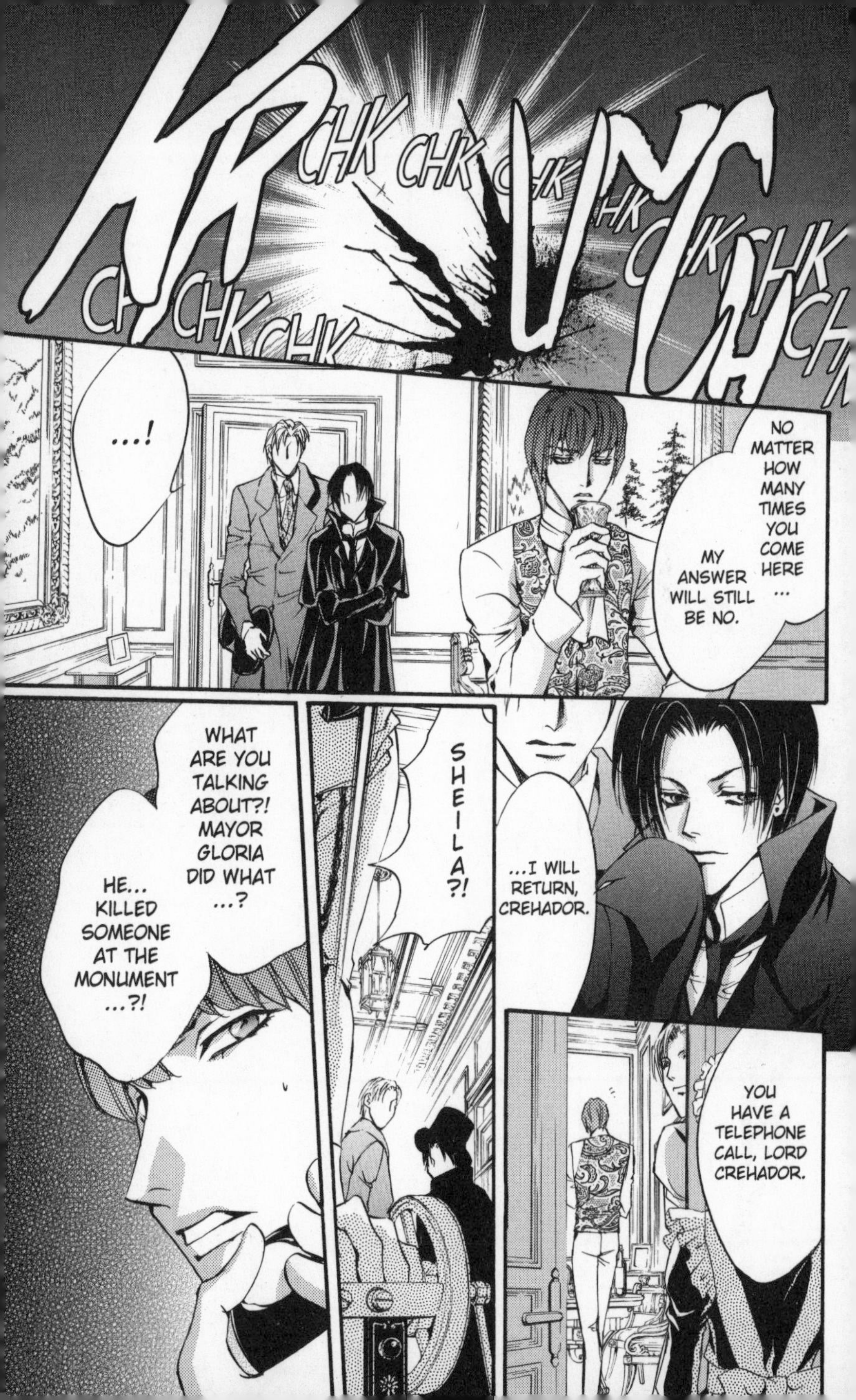
KRUMCH
CHK CHK CHK CHK CHK
CHK CHK CHK CHK
NO MATTER HOW MANY TIMES YOU COME HERE ...
MY ANSWER WILL STILL BE NO.
...!
...I WILL RETURN, CREHADOR.
YOU HAVE A TELEPHONE CALL, LORD CREHADOR.
SHEILA?!
WHAT ARE YOU TALKING ABOUT?! MAYOR GLORIA DID WHAT ...?
HE... KILLED SOMEONE AT THE MONUMENT ...?!

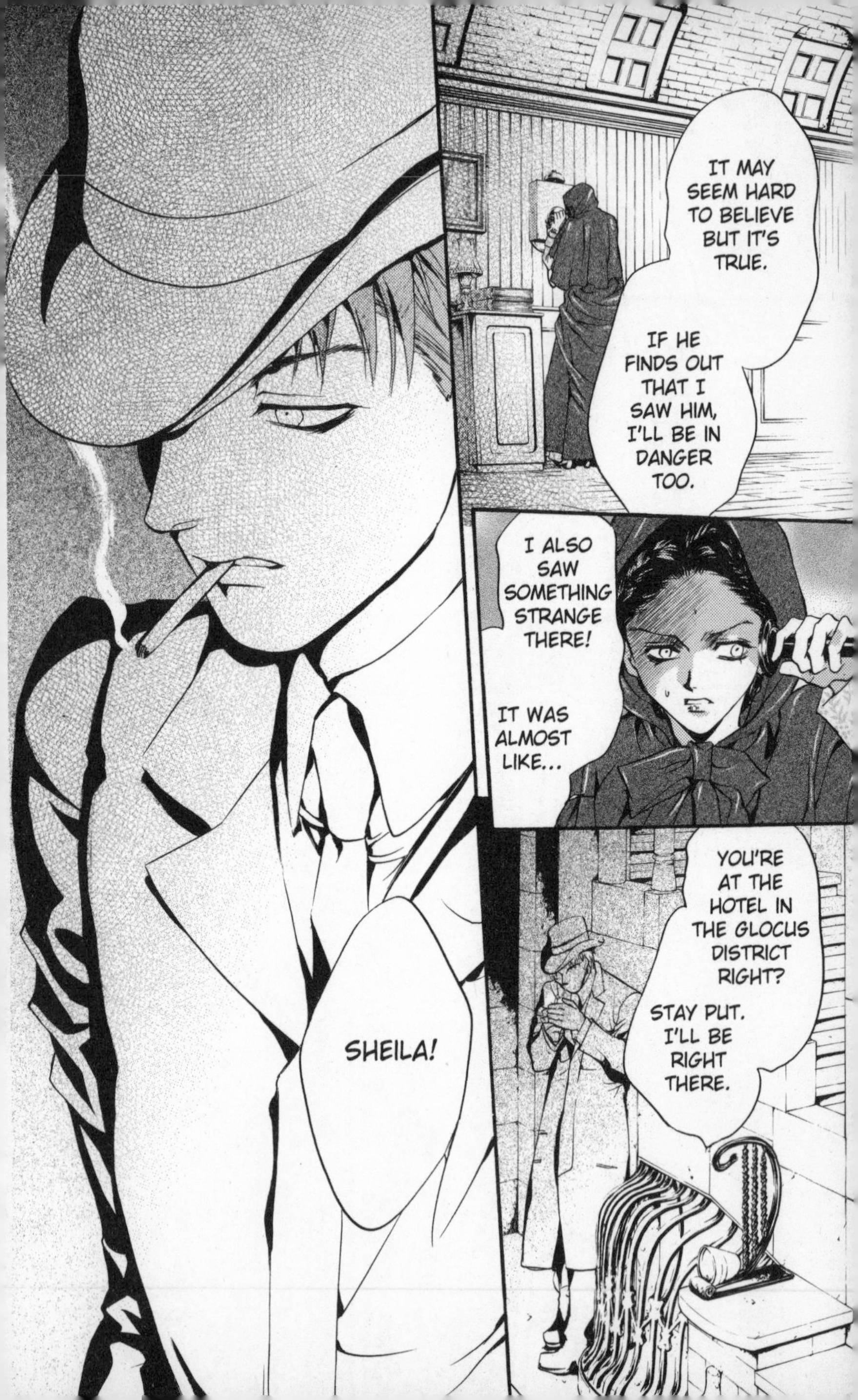
IT MAY SEEM HARD TO BELIEVE BUT IT'S TRUE.
IF HE FINDS OUT THAT I SAW HIM, I'LL BE IN DANGER TOO.
I ALSO SAW SOMETHING STRANGE THERE!
IT WAS ALMOST LIKE...
YOU'RE AT THE HOTEL IN THE GLOCUS DISTRICT RIGHT?
STAY PUT. I'LL BE RIGHT THERE.
SHEILA!

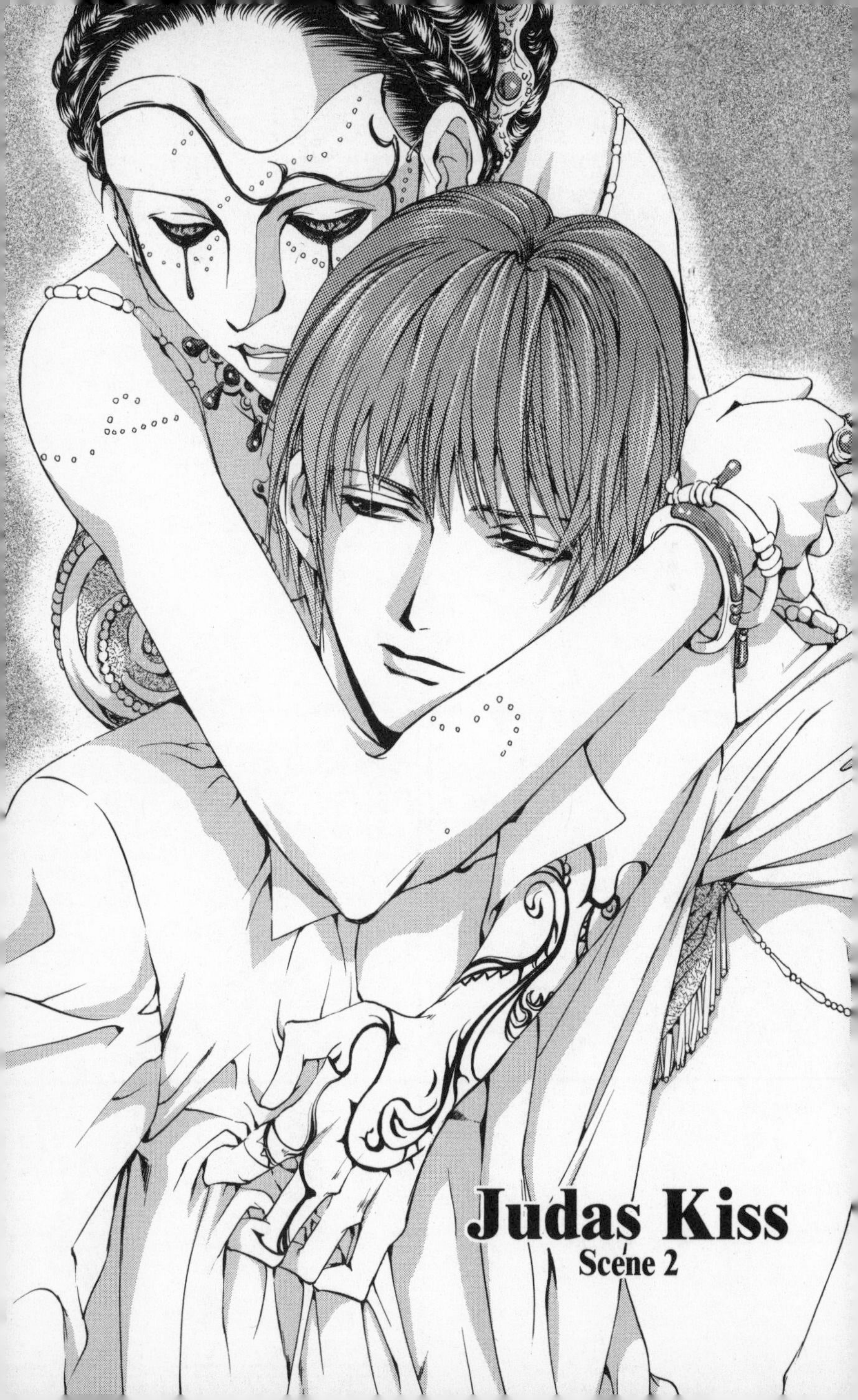

Judas Kiss

Scene 2

Judas Kiss
Scene 2

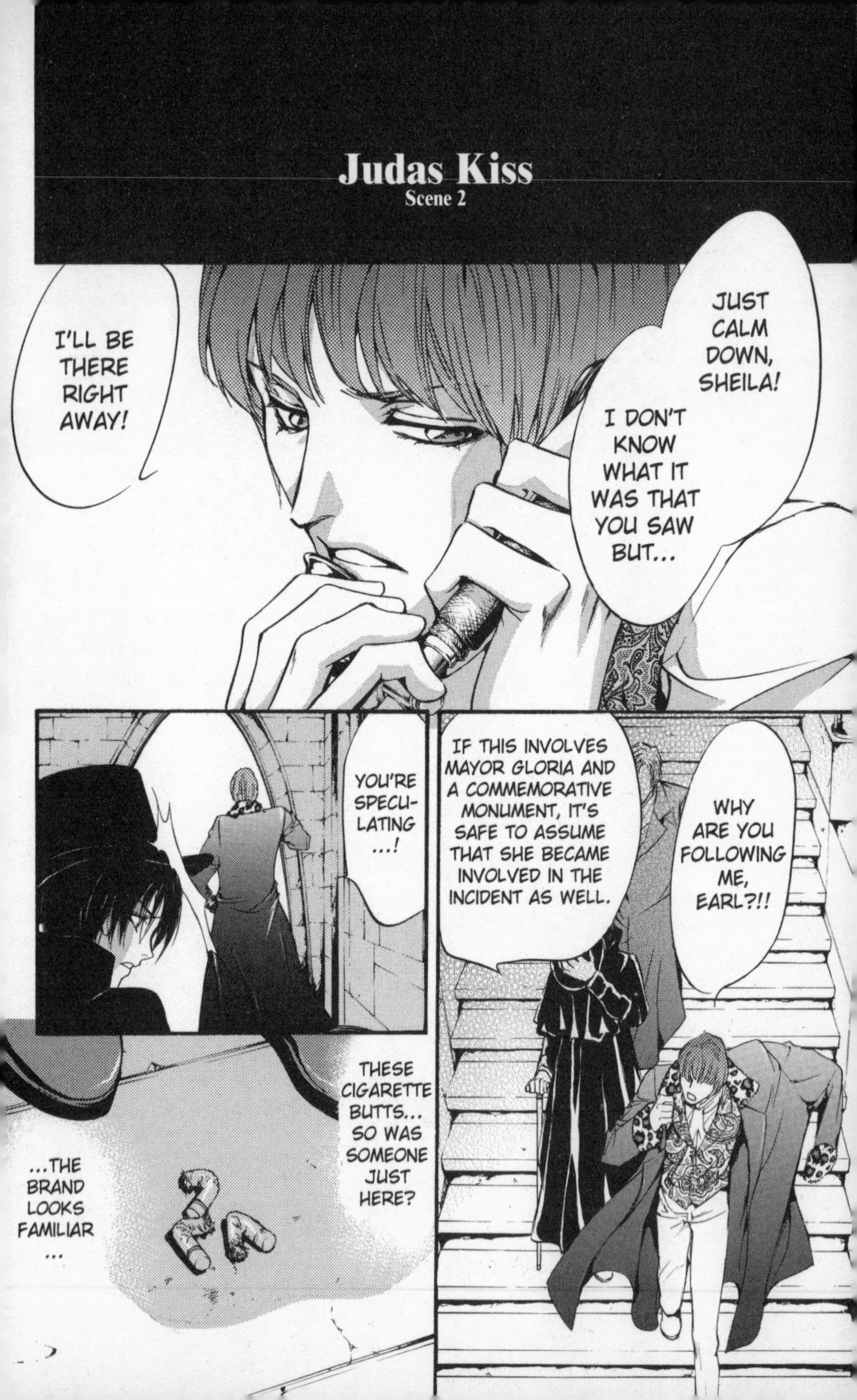
JUST CALM DOWN, SHEILA!
I DON'T KNOW WHAT IT WAS THAT YOU SAW BUT...
I'LL BE THERE RIGHT AWAY!
WHY ARE YOU FOLLOWING ME, EARL?!!
IF THIS INVOLVES MAYOR GLORIA AND A COMMEMORATIVE MONUMENT, IT'S SAFE TO ASSUME THAT SHE BECAME INVOLVED IN THE INCIDENT AS WELL.
YOU'RE SPECU-LATING ...!
THESE CIGARETTE BUTTS... SO WAS SOMEONE JUST HERE?
...THE BRAND LOOKS FAMILIAR ...

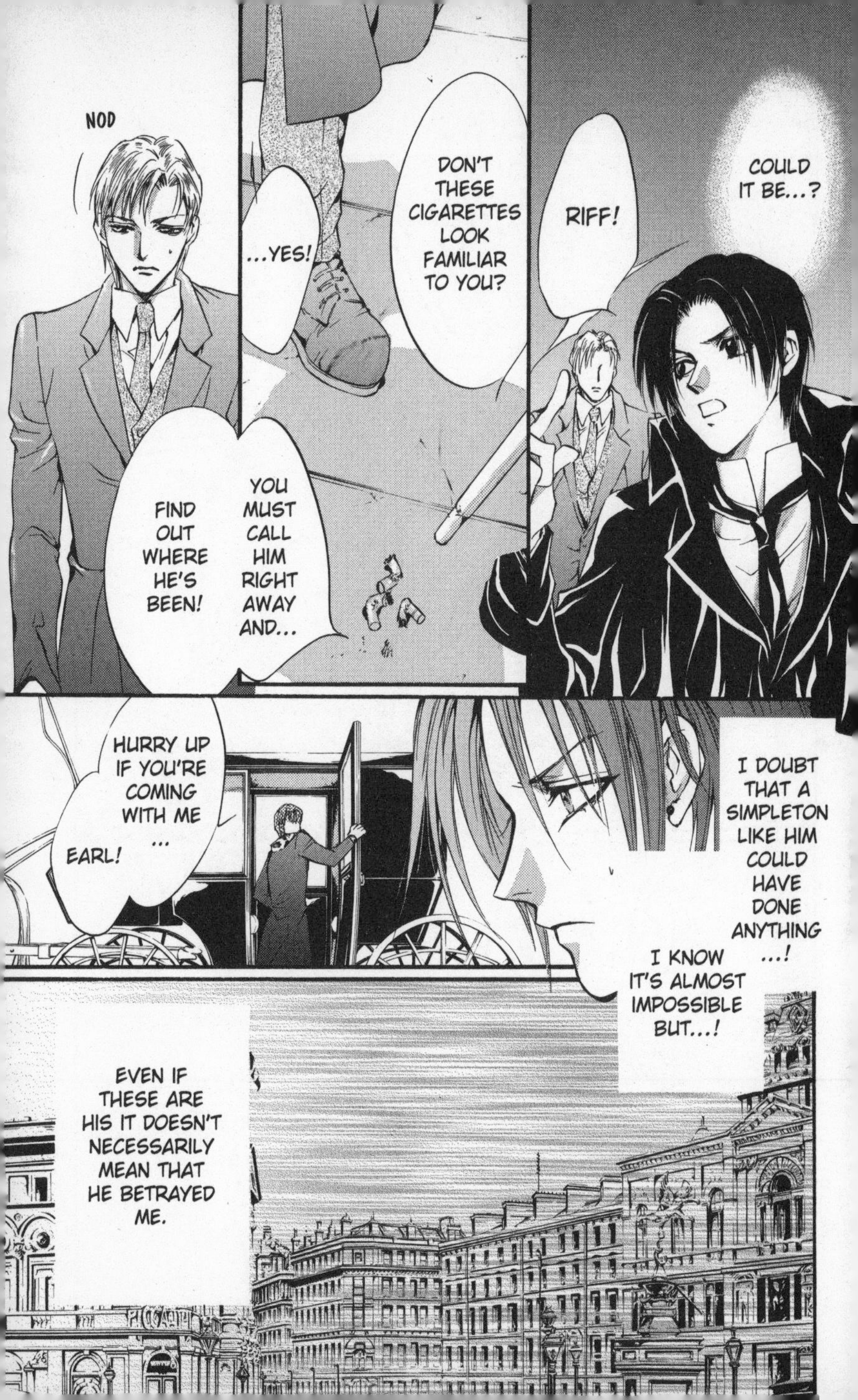
COULD IT BE...?
RIFF!
DON'T THESE CIGARETTES LOOK FAMILIAR TO YOU?
...YES!
YOU MUST CALL HIM RIGHT AWAY AND...
FIND OUT WHERE HE'S BEEN!
NOD
I DOUBT THAT A SIMPLETON LIKE HIM COULD HAVE DONE ANYTHING...!
I KNOW IT'S ALMOST IMPOSSIBLE BUT...!
HURRY UP IF YOU'RE COMING WITH ME... EARL!
EVEN IF THESE ARE HIS IT DOESN'T NECESSARILY MEAN THAT HE BETRAYED ME.

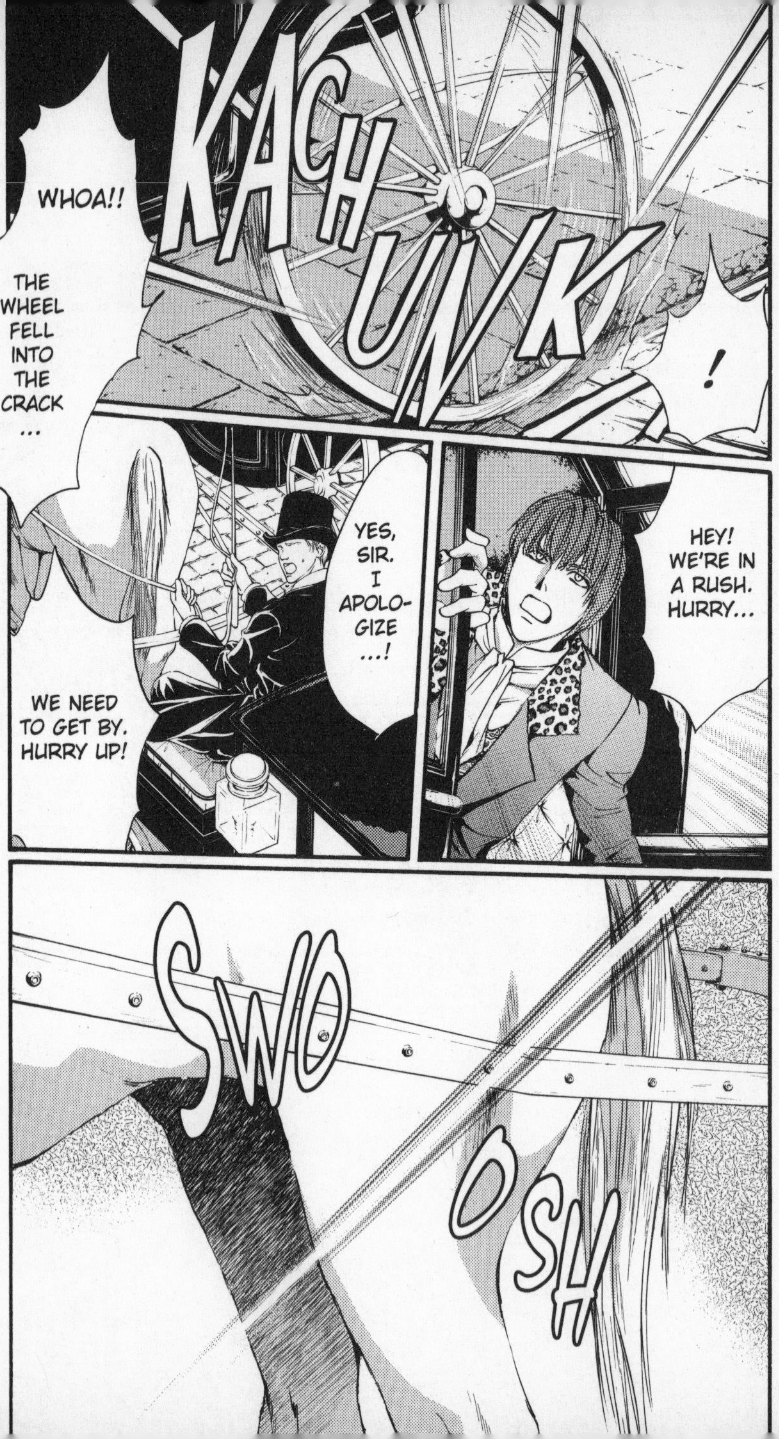
!
KACHUNK
WHOA!!
THE WHEEL FELL INTO THE CRACK...
HEY! WE'RE IN A RUSH. HURRY...
YES, SIR. I APOLOGIZE...!
WE NEED TO GET BY. HURRY UP!
SWOOSH

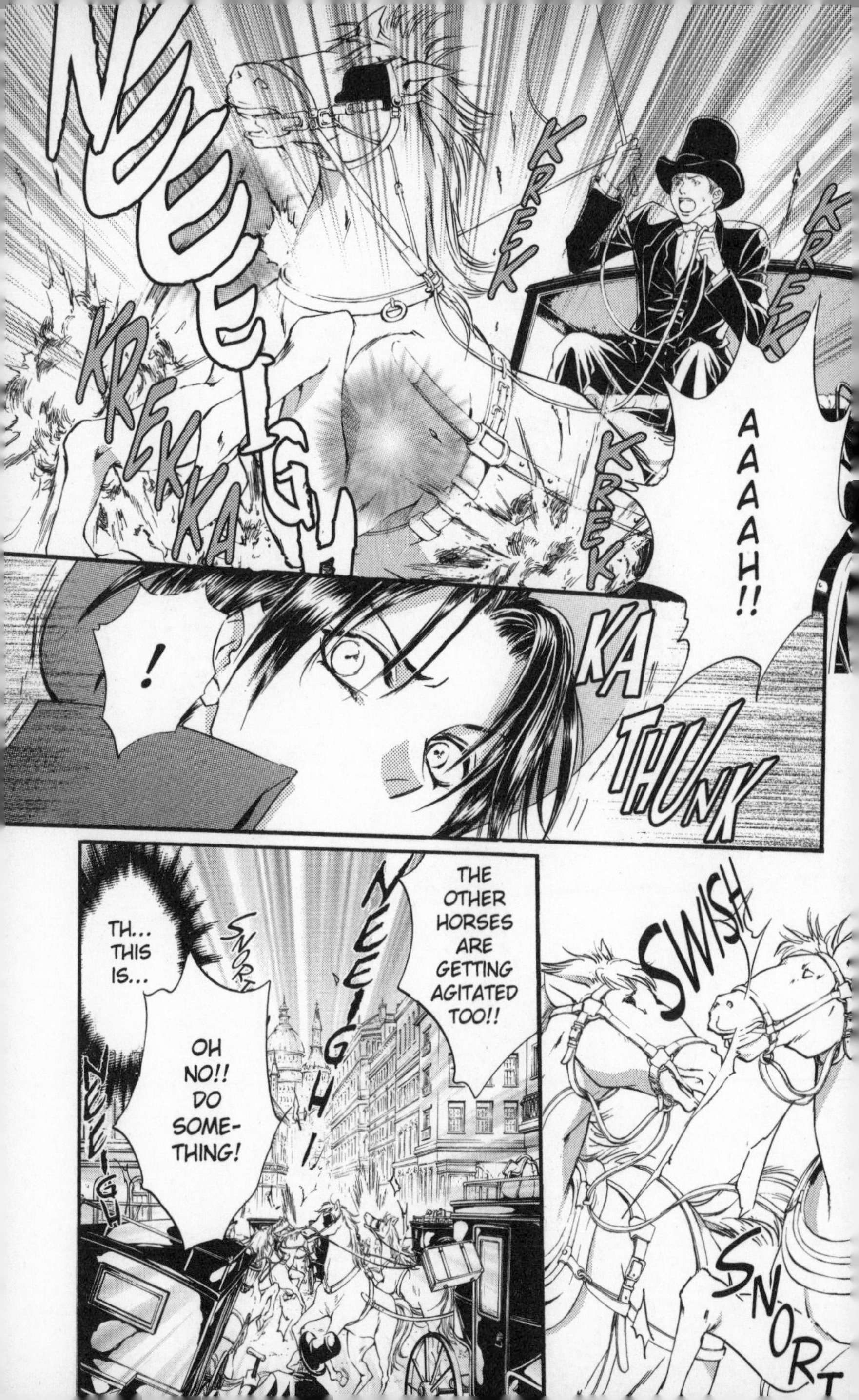
KREK
KREK
AAAAAH!!
KREK
KREK
KREK
KREK
KA
NEEEIGH
KREKKA
KREKKA
!
KA
THUNK
SWISH
SNORT
THE OTHER HORSES ARE GETTING AGITATED TOO!!
NEEEIGH
SNORT
TH... THIS IS...
OH NO!! DO SOME-THING!
NEEIGH

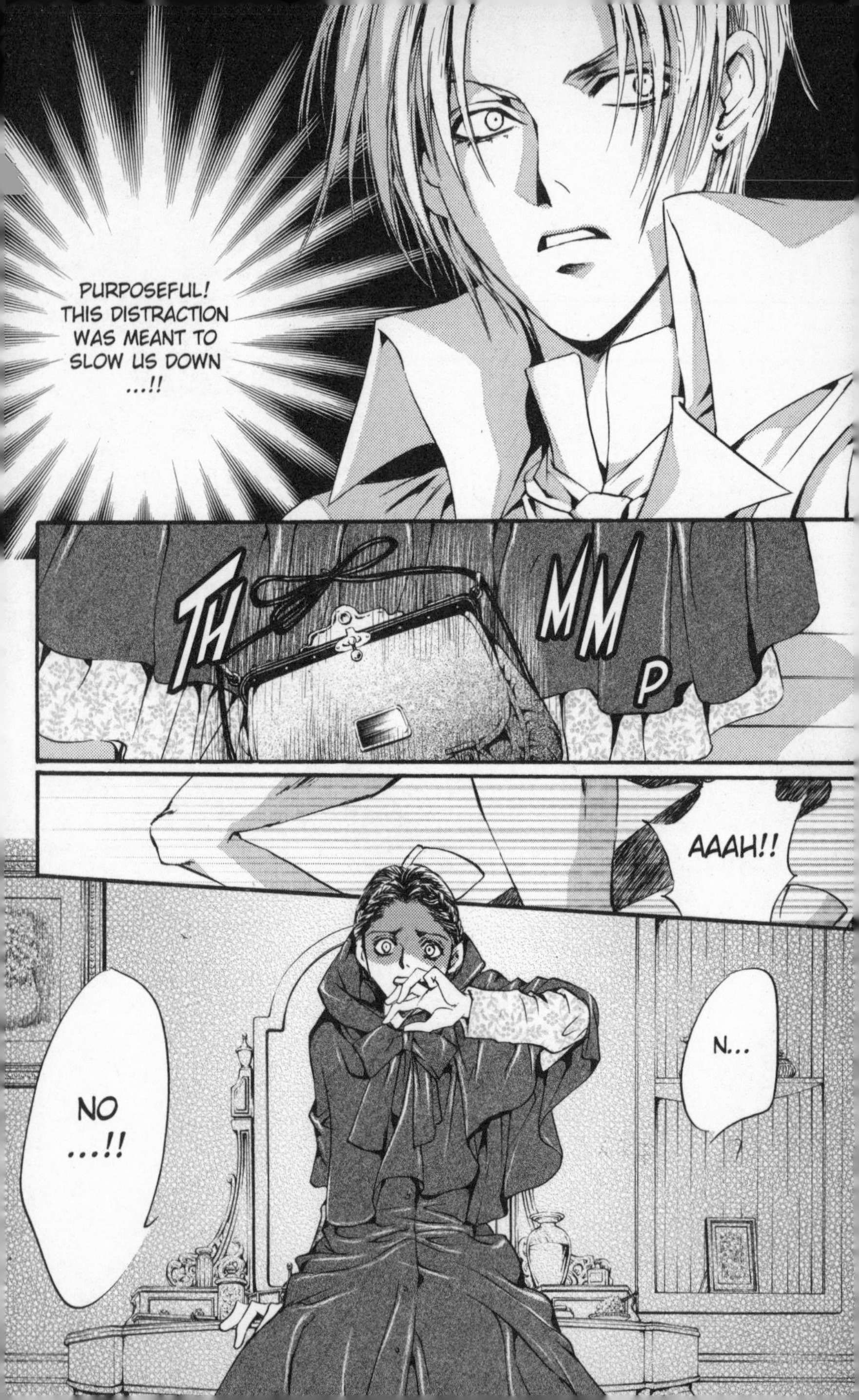
PURPOSEFUL! THIS DISTRACTION WAS MEANT TO SLOW US DOWN ...!!
THMMP
AAAH!!
N...
NO ...!!

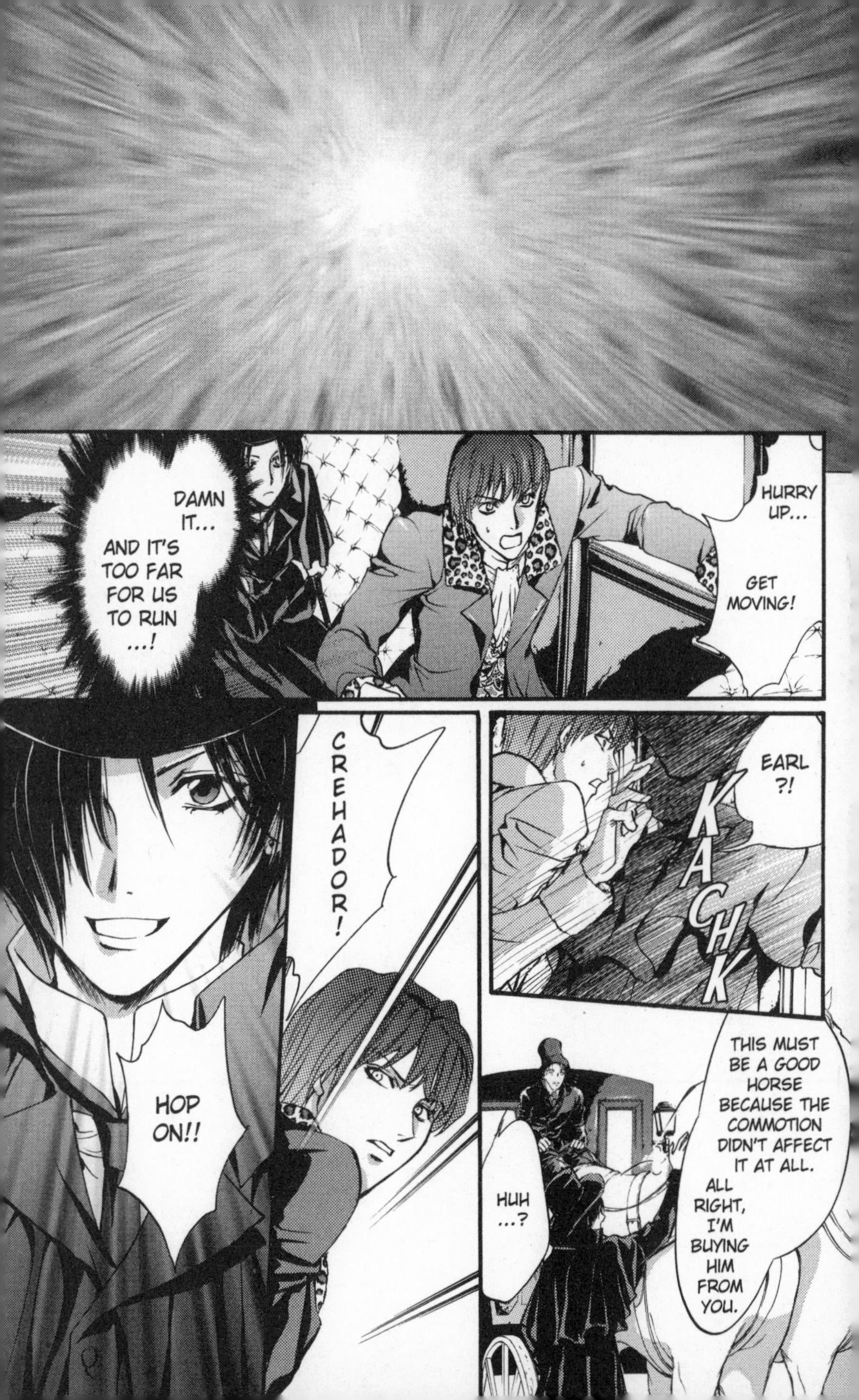
HURRY UP...
GET MOVING!
DAMN IT... AND IT'S TOO FAR FOR US TO RUN ...!
EARL ?!
KACHK
THIS MUST BE A GOOD HORSE BECAUSE THE COMMOTION DIDN'T AFFECT IT AT ALL.
ALL RIGHT, I'M BUYING HIM FROM YOU.
HUH ...?
CREHADOR!
HOP ON!!

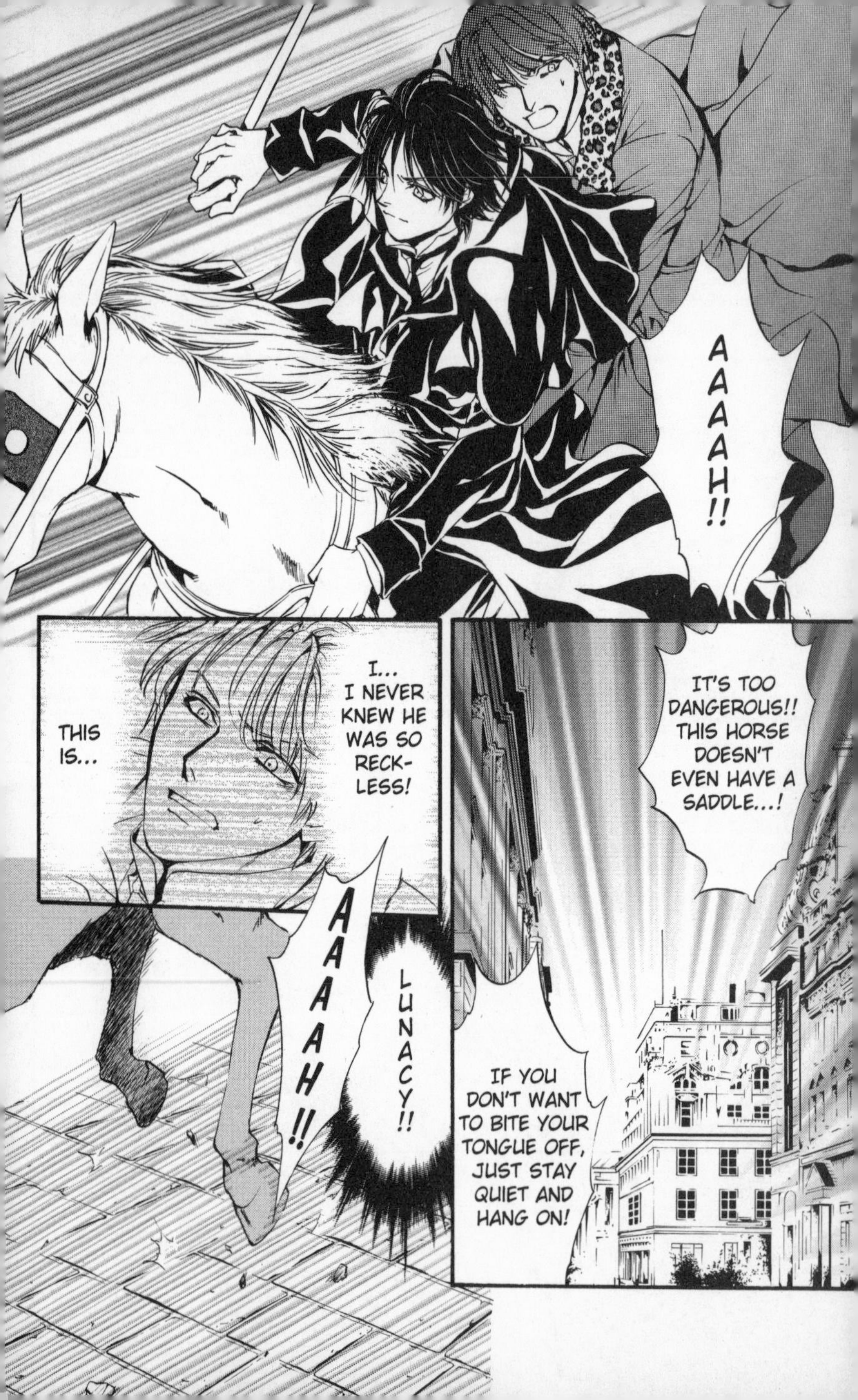
AAAAAH!!
IT'S TOO DANGEROUS!! THIS HORSE DOESN'T EVEN HAVE A SADDLE...!
IF YOU DON'T WANT TO BITE YOUR TONGUE OFF, JUST STAY QUIET AND HANG ON!
I... I NEVER KNEW HE WAS SO RECKLESS!
THIS IS...
LUNACY!!
AAAAAH!!

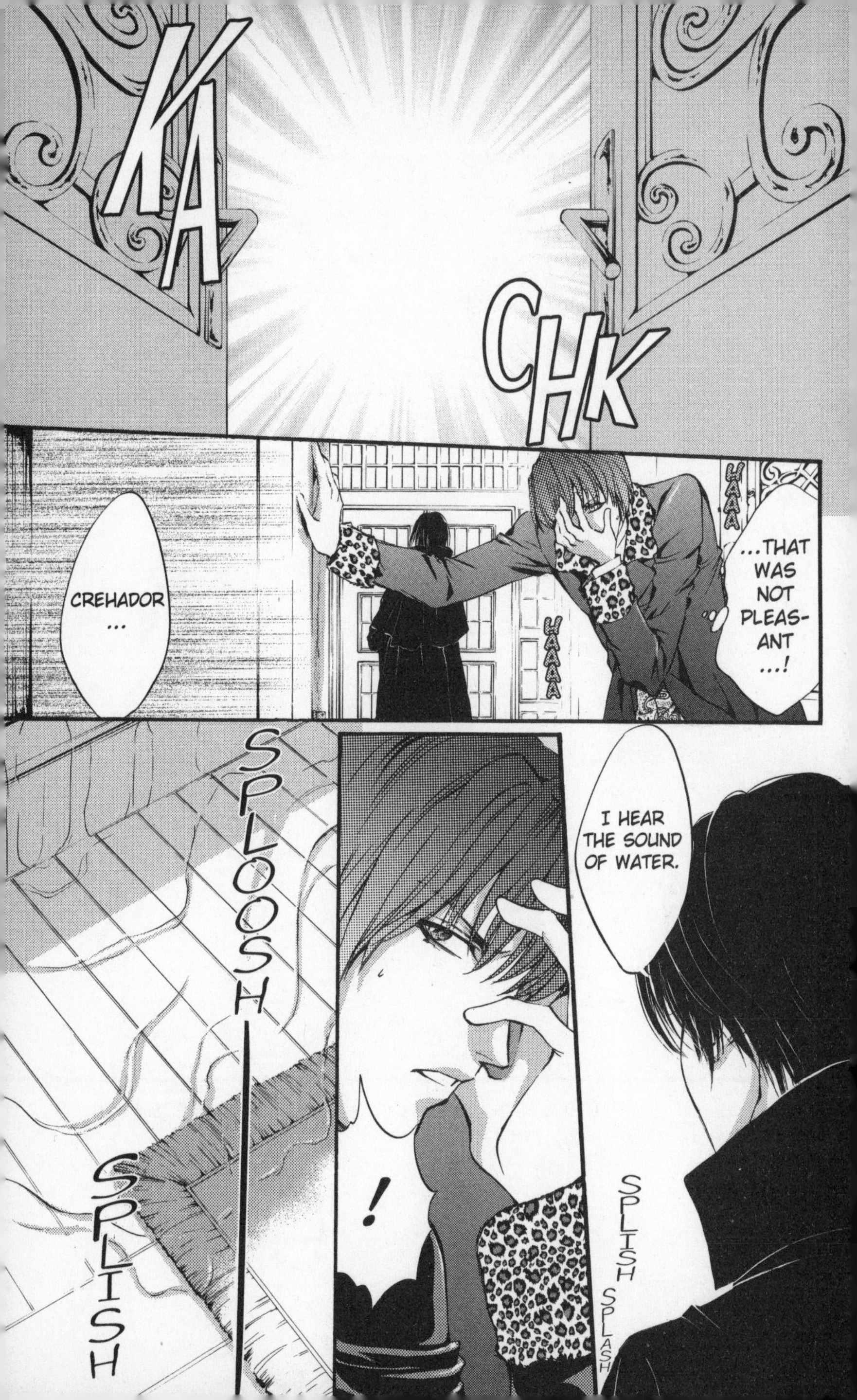
KA
CHK
HAAA
...THAT WAS NOT PLEASANT...!
HAAA
CREHADOR ...
I HEAR THE SOUND OF WATER.
!
SPLISH SPLASH
SPLOOSH
SPLISH

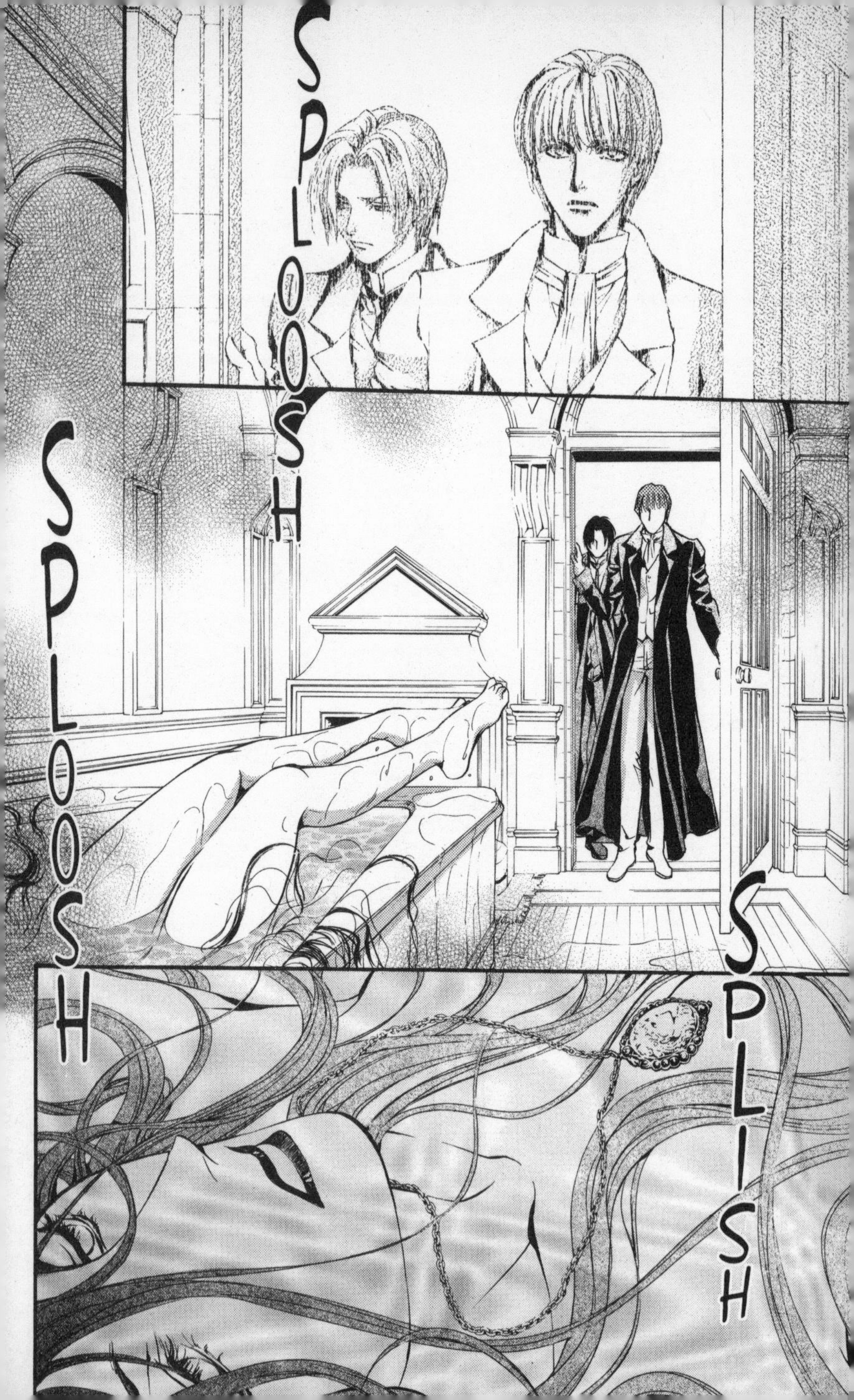
SPLOOSH
SPLOOSH
SPLISH

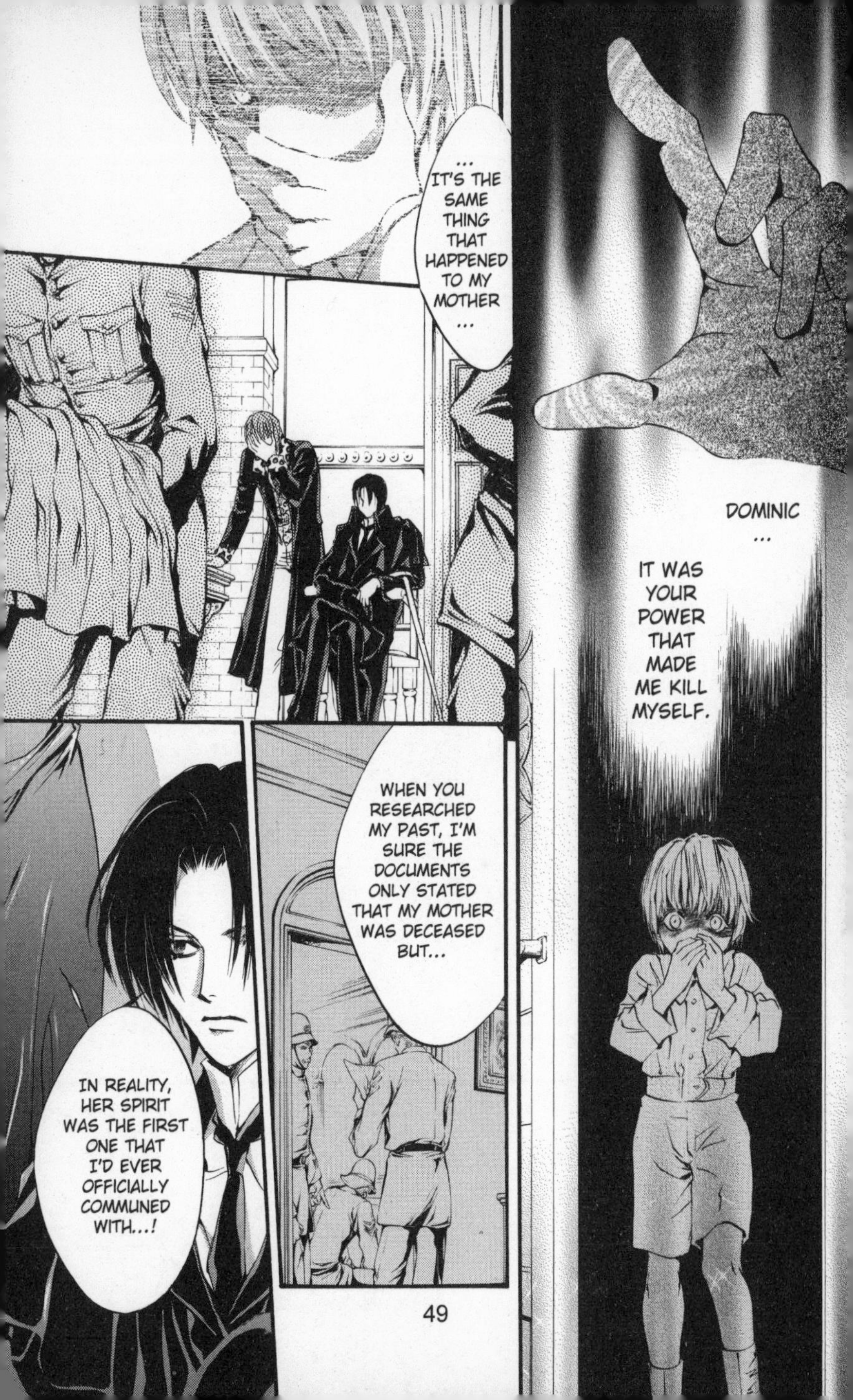
DOMINIC ...
IT WAS YOUR POWER THAT MADE ME KILL MYSELF.
... IT'S THE SAME THING THAT HAPPENED TO MY MOTHER ...
WHEN YOU RESEARCHED MY PAST, I'M SURE THE DOCUMENTS ONLY STATED THAT MY MOTHER WAS DECEASED BUT...
IN REALITY, HER SPIRIT WAS THE FIRST ONE THAT I'D EVER OFFICIALLY COMMUNED WITH...!

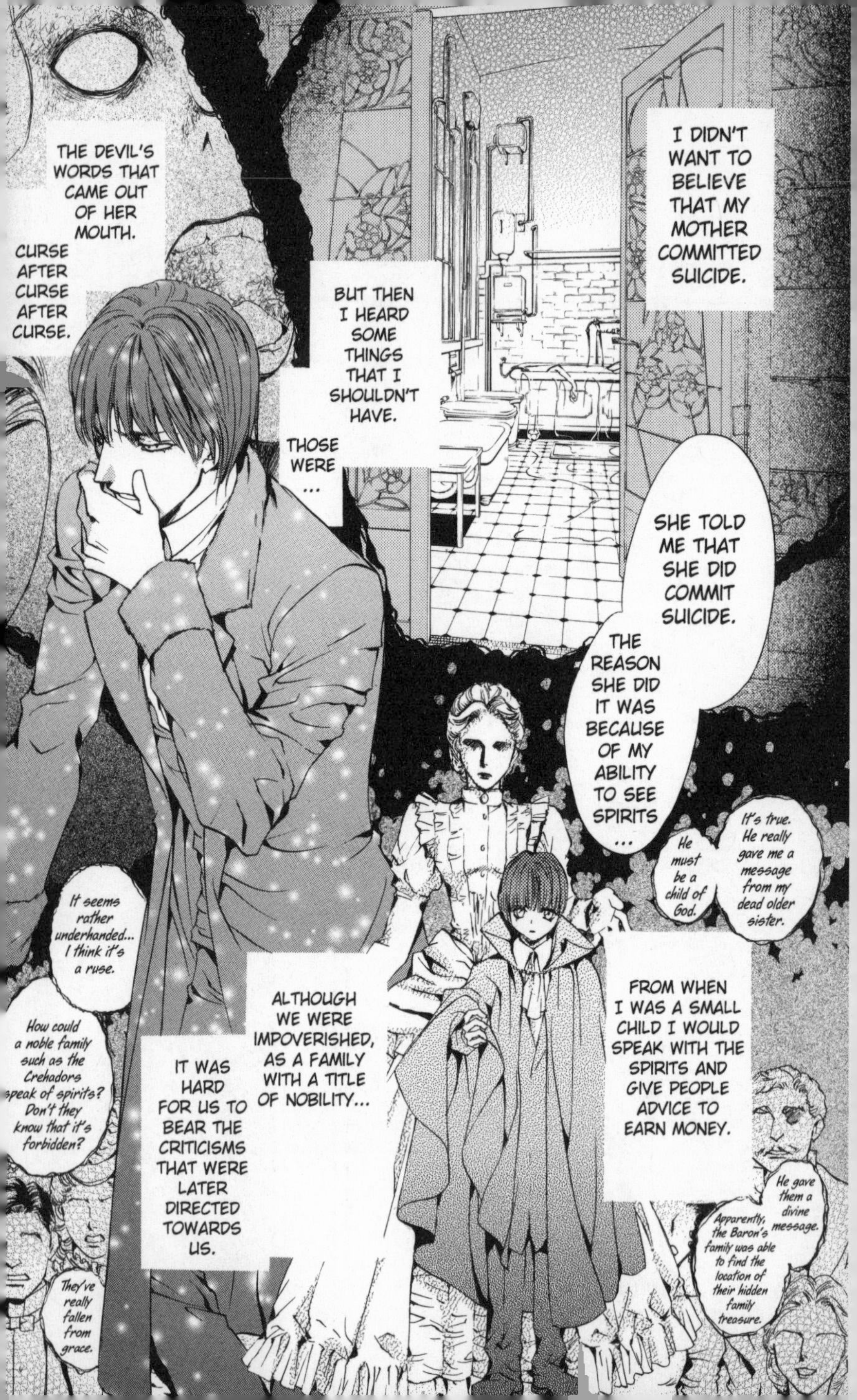
I DIDN'T WANT TO BELIEVE THAT MY MOTHER COMMITTED SUICIDE.
BUT THEN I HEARD SOME THINGS THAT I SHOULDN'T HAVE.
THOSE WERE ...
THE DEVIL'S WORDS THAT CAME OUT OF HER MOUTH.
CURSE AFTER CURSE AFTER CURSE.
SHE TOLD ME THAT SHE DID COMMIT SUICIDE.
THE REASON SHE DID IT WAS BECAUSE OF MY ABILITY TO SEE SPIRITS ...
It's true. He really gave me a message from my dead older sister.
He must be a child of God.
FROM WHEN I WAS A SMALL CHILD I WOULD SPEAK WITH THE SPIRITS AND GIVE PEOPLE ADVICE TO EARN MONEY.
ALTHOUGH WE WERE IMPOVERISHED, AS A FAMILY WITH A TITLE OF NOBILITY...
IT WAS HARD FOR US TO BEAR THE CRITICISMS THAT WERE LATER DIRECTED TOWARDS US.
It seems rather underhanded... I think it's a ruse.
How could a noble family such as the Crehadors speak of spirits? Don't they know that it's forbidden?
He gave them a divine message.
Apparently, the Baron's family was able to find the location of their hidden family treasure.
They've really fallen from grace.

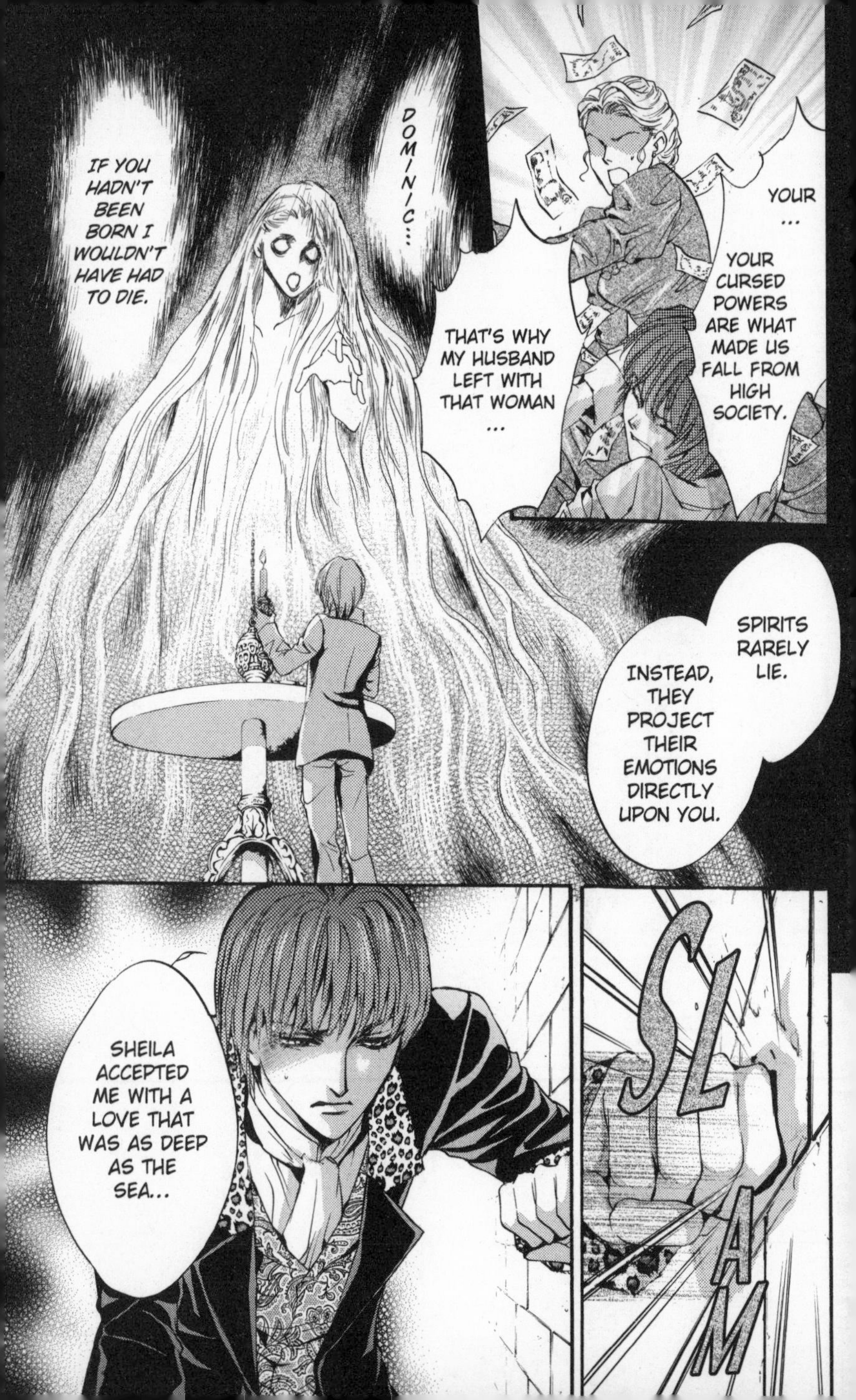
YOUR ...
YOUR CURSED POWERS ARE WHAT MADE US FALL FROM HIGH SOCIETY.
THAT'S WHY MY HUSBAND LEFT WITH THAT WOMAN ...
DOMINIC...
IF YOU HADN'T BEEN BORN I WOULDN'T HAVE HAD TO DIE.
SPIRITS RARELY LIE.
INSTEAD, THEY PROJECT THEIR EMOTIONS DIRECTLY UPON YOU.
SLAM
SHEILA ACCEPTED ME WITH A LOVE THAT WAS AS DEEP AS THE SEA...

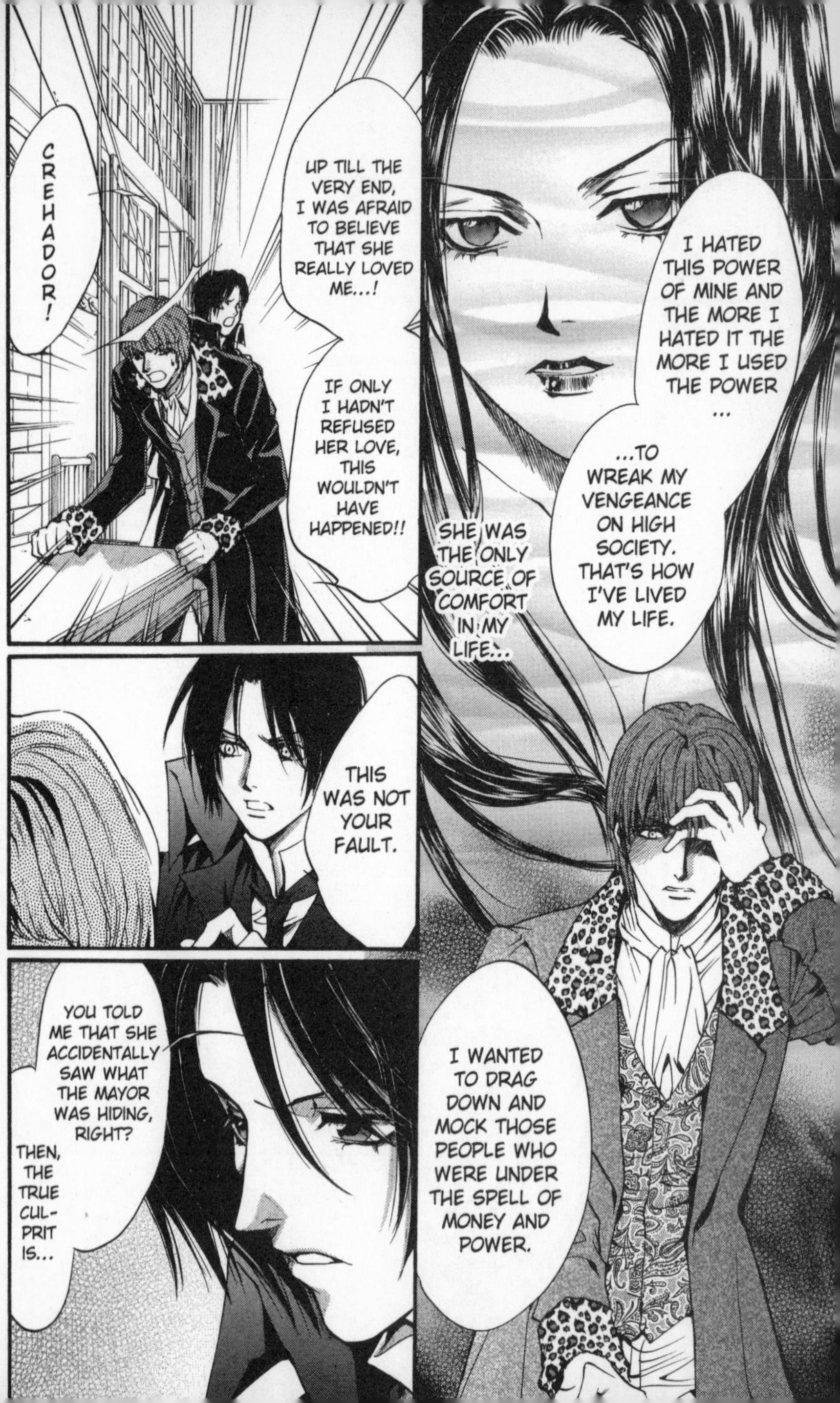
I HATED THIS POWER OF MINE AND THE MORE I HATED IT THE MORE I USED THE POWER ...
...TO WREAK MY VENGEANCE ON HIGH SOCIETY. THAT'S HOW I'VE LIVED MY LIFE.
SHE WAS THE ONLY SOURCE OF COMFORT IN MY LIFE...
I WANTED TO DRAG DOWN AND MOCK THOSE PEOPLE WHO WERE UNDER THE SPELL OF MONEY AND POWER.
UP TILL THE VERY END, I WAS AFRAID TO BELIEVE THAT SHE REALLY LOVED ME...!
IF ONLY I HADN'T REFUSED HER LOVE, THIS WOULDN'T HAVE HAPPENED!!
CREHADOR!
THIS WAS NOT YOUR FAULT.
YOU TOLD ME THAT SHE ACCIDENTALLY SAW WHAT THE MAYOR WAS HIDING, RIGHT?
THEN, THE TRUE CUL-PRIT IS...

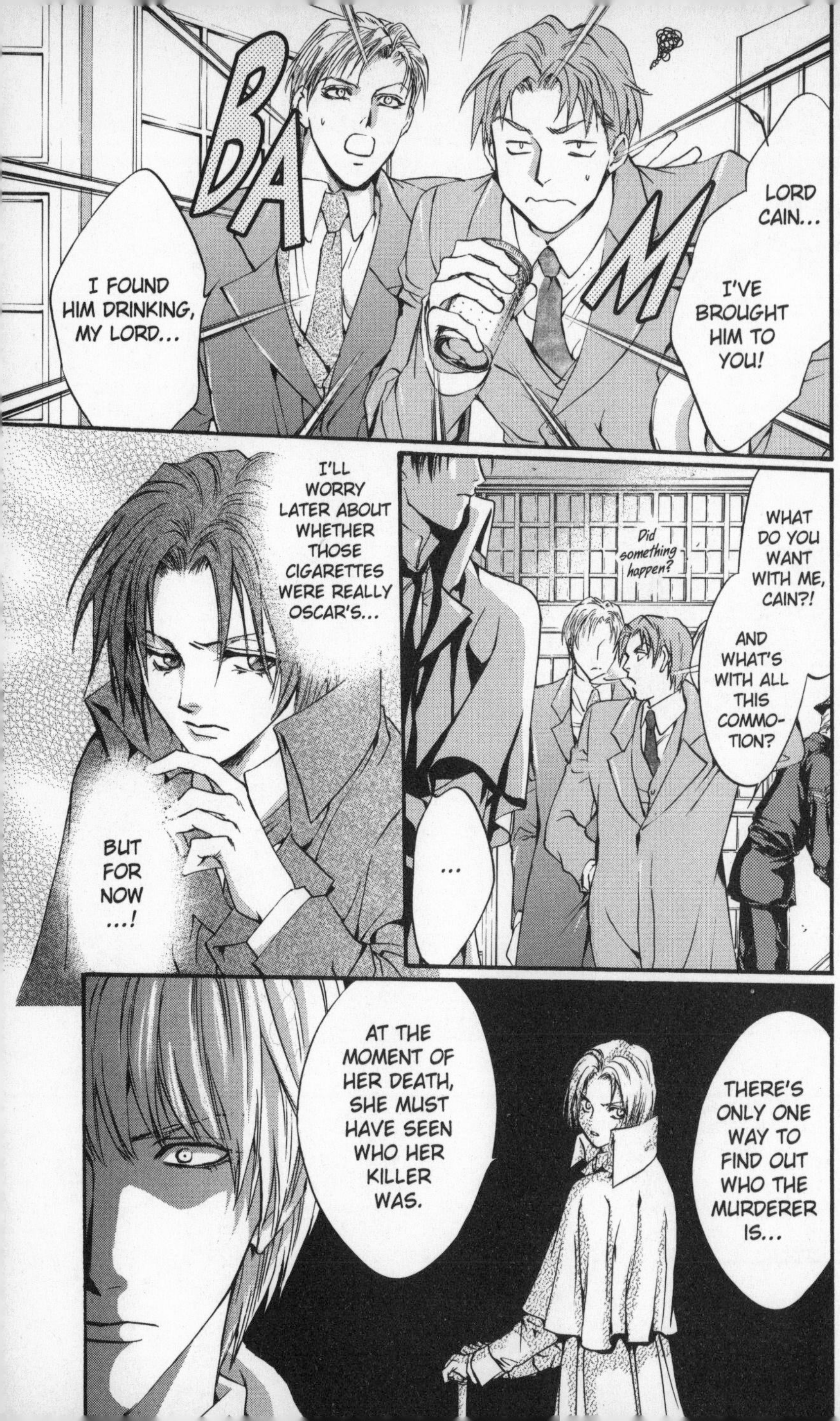
LORD CAIN...
I'VE BROUGHT HIM TO YOU!
BAM
I FOUND HIM DRINKING, MY LORD...
WHAT DO YOU WANT WITH ME, CAIN?!
AND WHAT'S WITH ALL THIS COMMO-TION?
Did something happen?
...
I'LL WORRY LATER ABOUT WHETHER THOSE CIGARETTES WERE REALLY OSCAR'S...
BUT FOR NOW ...!
THERE'S ONLY ONE WAY TO FIND OUT WHO THE MURDERER IS...
AT THE MOMENT OF HER DEATH, SHE MUST HAVE SEEN WHO HER KILLER WAS.

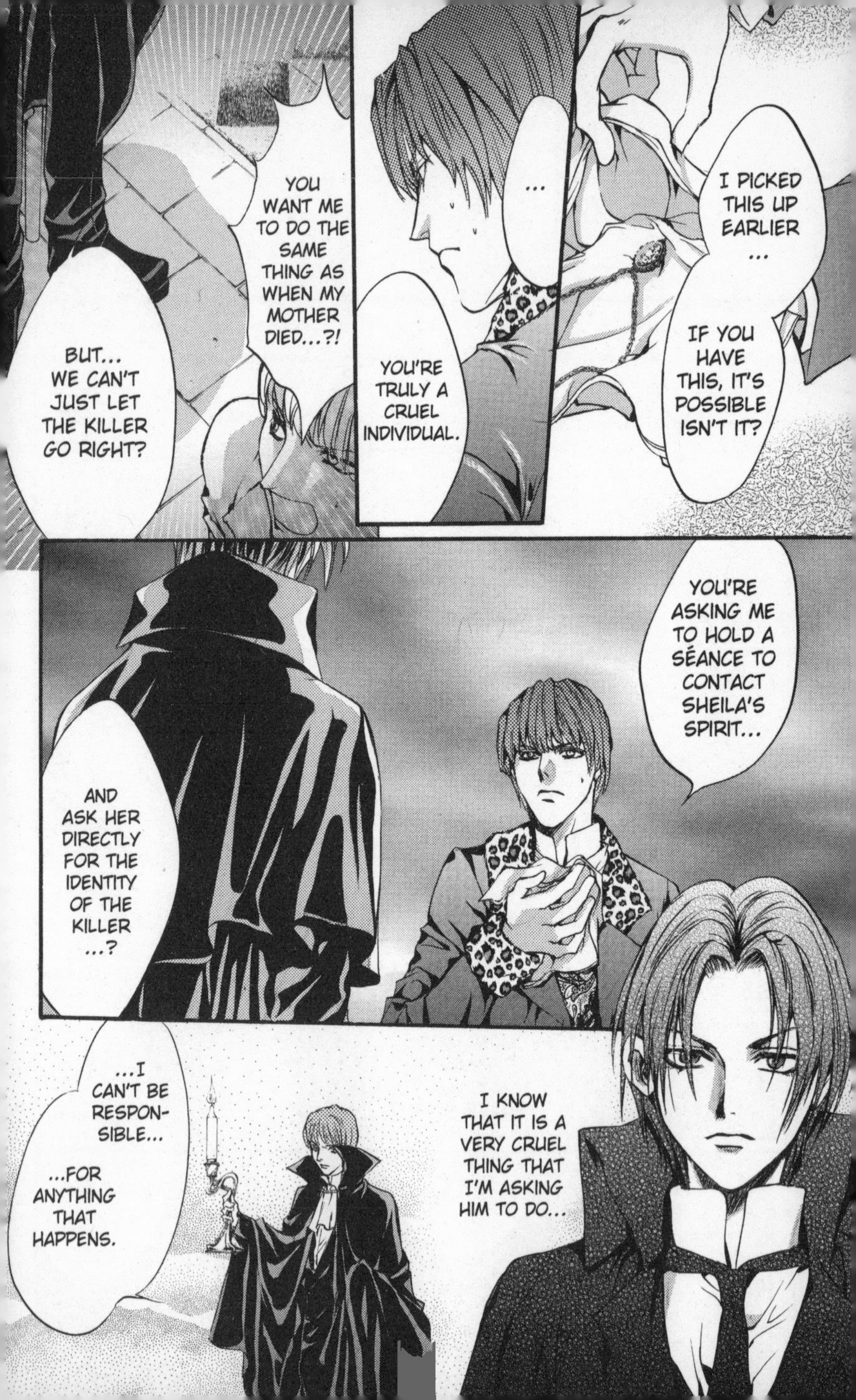
I PICKED THIS UP EARLIER...
IF YOU HAVE THIS, IT'S POSSIBLE ISN'T IT?
...
YOU'RE TRULY A CRUEL INDIVIDUAL.
YOU WANT ME TO DO THE SAME THING AS WHEN MY MOTHER DIED...?!
BUT... WE CAN'T JUST LET THE KILLER GO RIGHT?
YOU'RE ASKING ME TO HOLD A SÉANCE TO CONTACT SHEILA'S SPIRIT...
AND ASK HER DIRECTLY FOR THE IDENTITY OF THE KILLER...?
I KNOW THAT IT IS A VERY CRUEL THING THAT I'M ASKING HIM TO DO...
...I CAN'T BE RESPONSIBLE...
...FOR ANYTHING THAT HAPPENS.

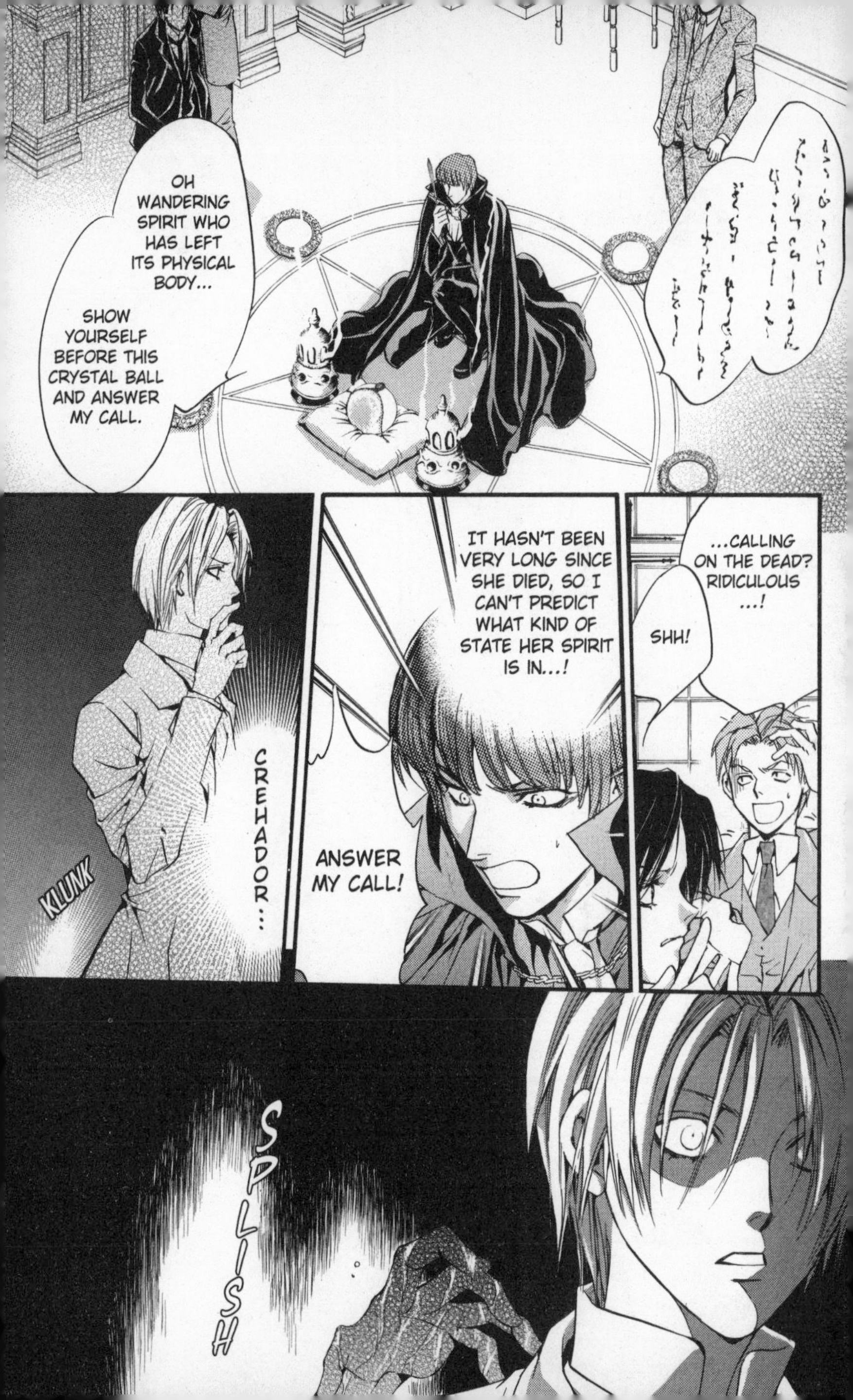
OH WANDERING SPIRIT WHO HAS LEFT ITS PHYSICAL BODY...
SHOW YOURSELF BEFORE THIS CRYSTAL BALL AND ANSWER MY CALL.
...CALLING ON THE DEAD? RIDICULOUS ...!
SHH!
IT HASN'T BEEN VERY LONG SINCE SHE DIED, SO I CAN'T PREDICT WHAT KIND OF STATE HER SPIRIT IS IN...!
ANSWER MY CALL!
CREHADOR...
KLUNK
SPLISH

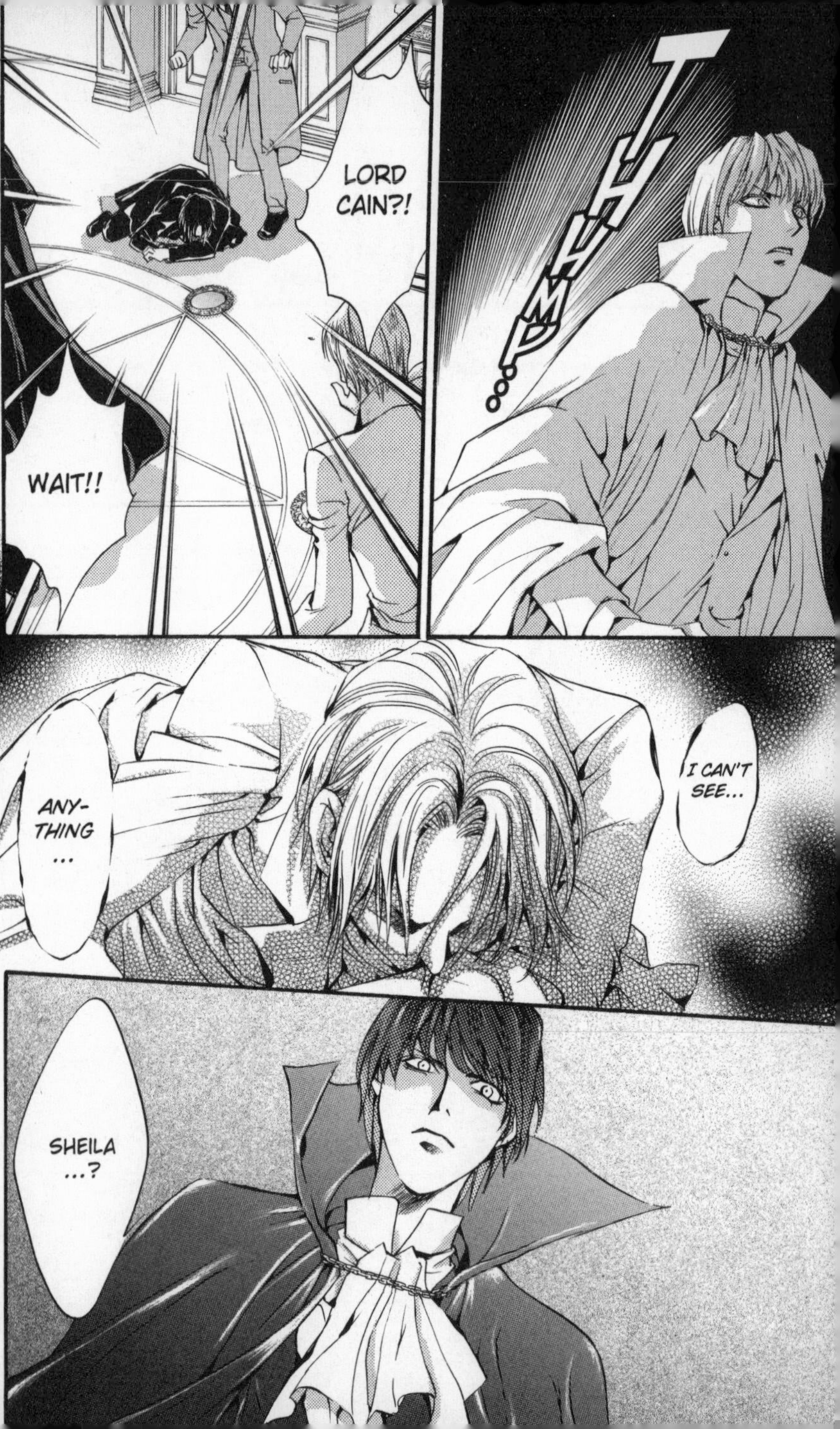
THUMP...
LORD CAIN?!
WAIT!!
I CAN'T SEE...
ANY-THING...
SHEILA...?

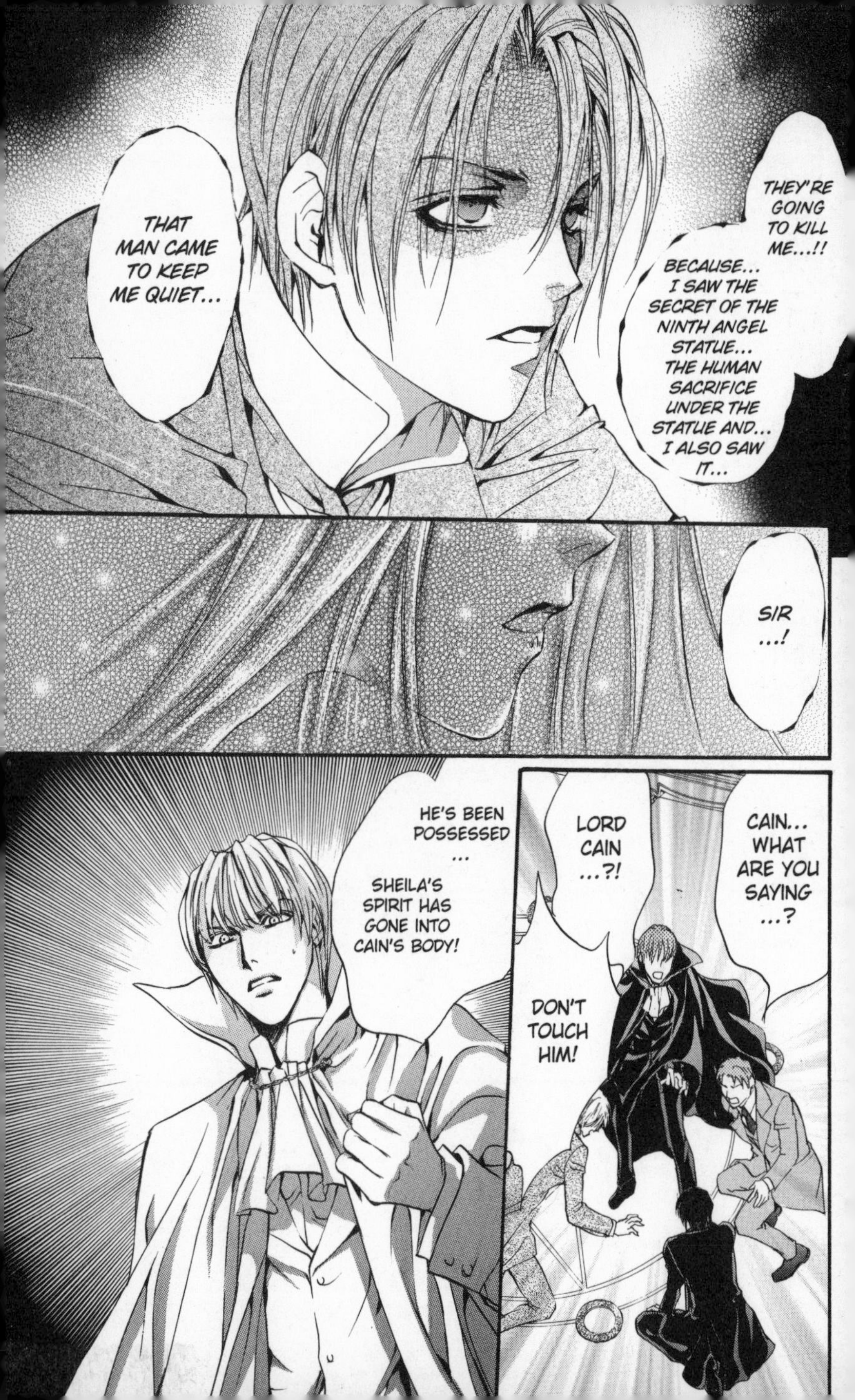
THEY'RE GOING TO KILL ME...!!
BECAUSE... I SAW THE SECRET OF THE NINTH ANGEL STATUE... THE HUMAN SACRIFICE UNDER THE STATUE AND... I ALSO SAW IT...
THAT MAN CAME TO KEEP ME QUIET...
SIR ...!
CAIN... WHAT ARE YOU SAYING ...?
LORD CAIN ...?!
DON'T TOUCH HIM!
HE'S BEEN POSSESSED ...
SHEILA'S SPIRIT HAS GONE INTO CAIN'S BODY!

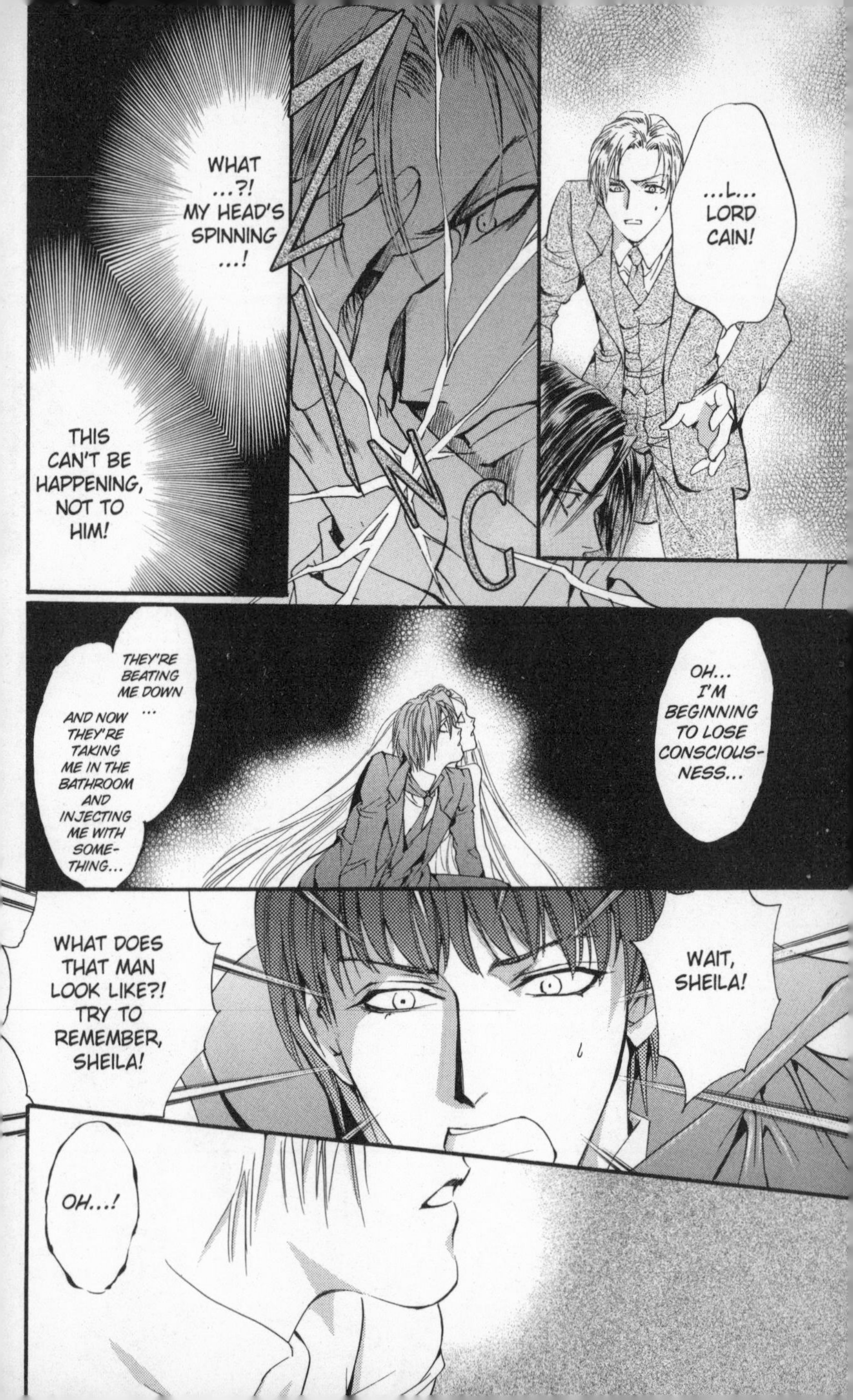
...L... LORD CAIN!
WHAT ...?! MY HEAD'S SPINNING ...!
THIS CAN'T BE HAPPENING, NOT TO HIM!
OH... I'M BEGINNING TO LOSE CONSCIOUS-NESS...
THEY'RE BEATING ME DOWN ...
AND NOW THEY'RE TAKING ME IN THE BATHROOM AND INJECTING ME WITH SOME-THING...
WAIT, SHEILA!
WHAT DOES THAT MAN LOOK LIKE?! TRY TO REMEMBER, SHEILA!
OH...!

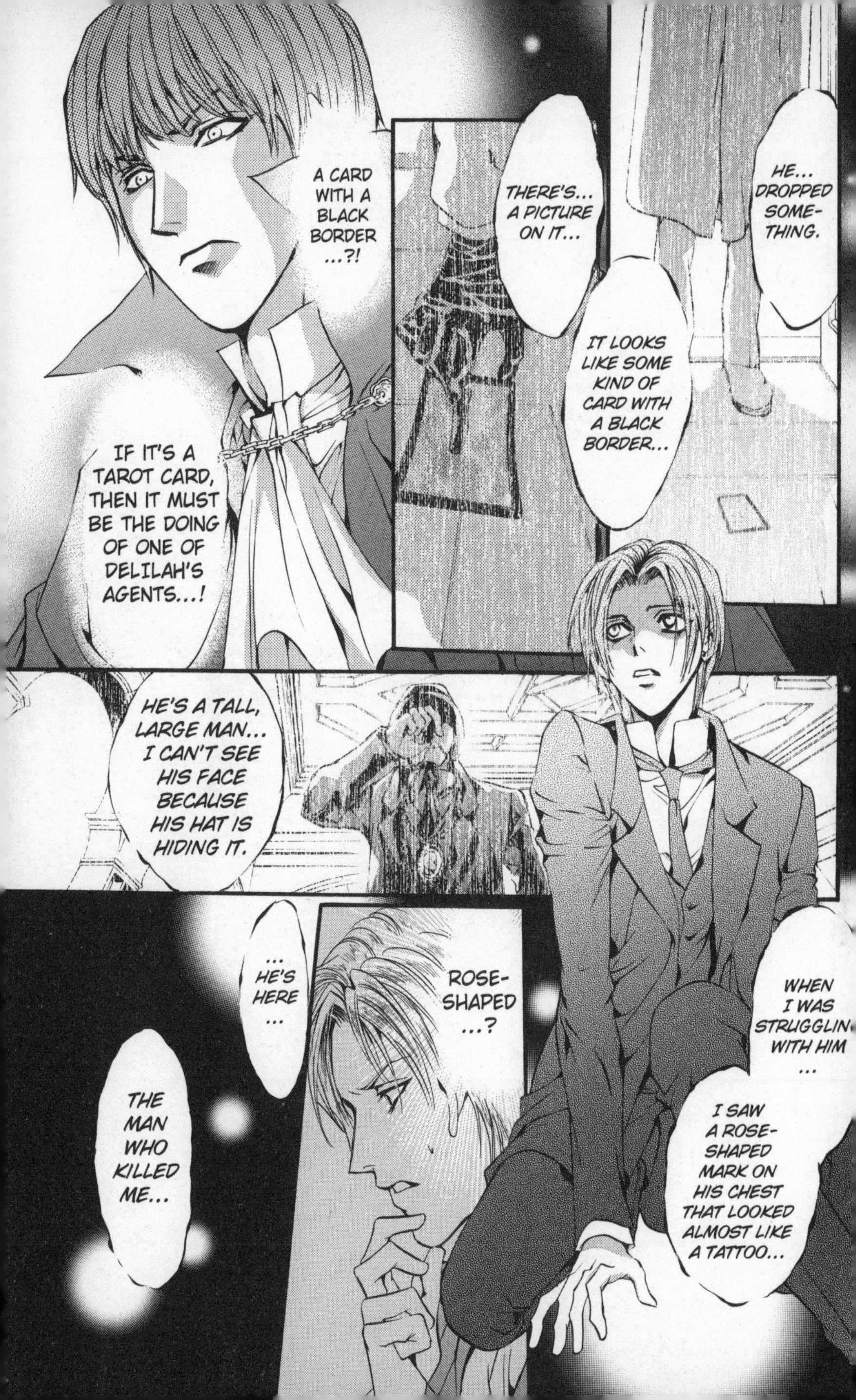
HE... DROPPED SOME-THING.
IT LOOKS LIKE SOME KIND OF CARD WITH A BLACK BORDER...
THERE'S... A PICTURE ON IT...
A CARD WITH A BLACK BORDER ...?!
IF IT'S A TAROT CARD, THEN IT MUST BE THE DOING OF ONE OF DELILAH'S AGENTS...!
HE'S A TALL, LARGE MAN... I CAN'T SEE HIS FACE BECAUSE HIS HAT IS HIDING IT.
WHEN I WAS STRUGGLIN WITH HIM ...
I SAW A ROSE-SHAPED MARK ON HIS CHEST THAT LOOKED ALMOST LIKE A TATTOO...
ROSE-SHAPED ...?
... HE'S HERE ...
THE MAN WHO KILLED ME...

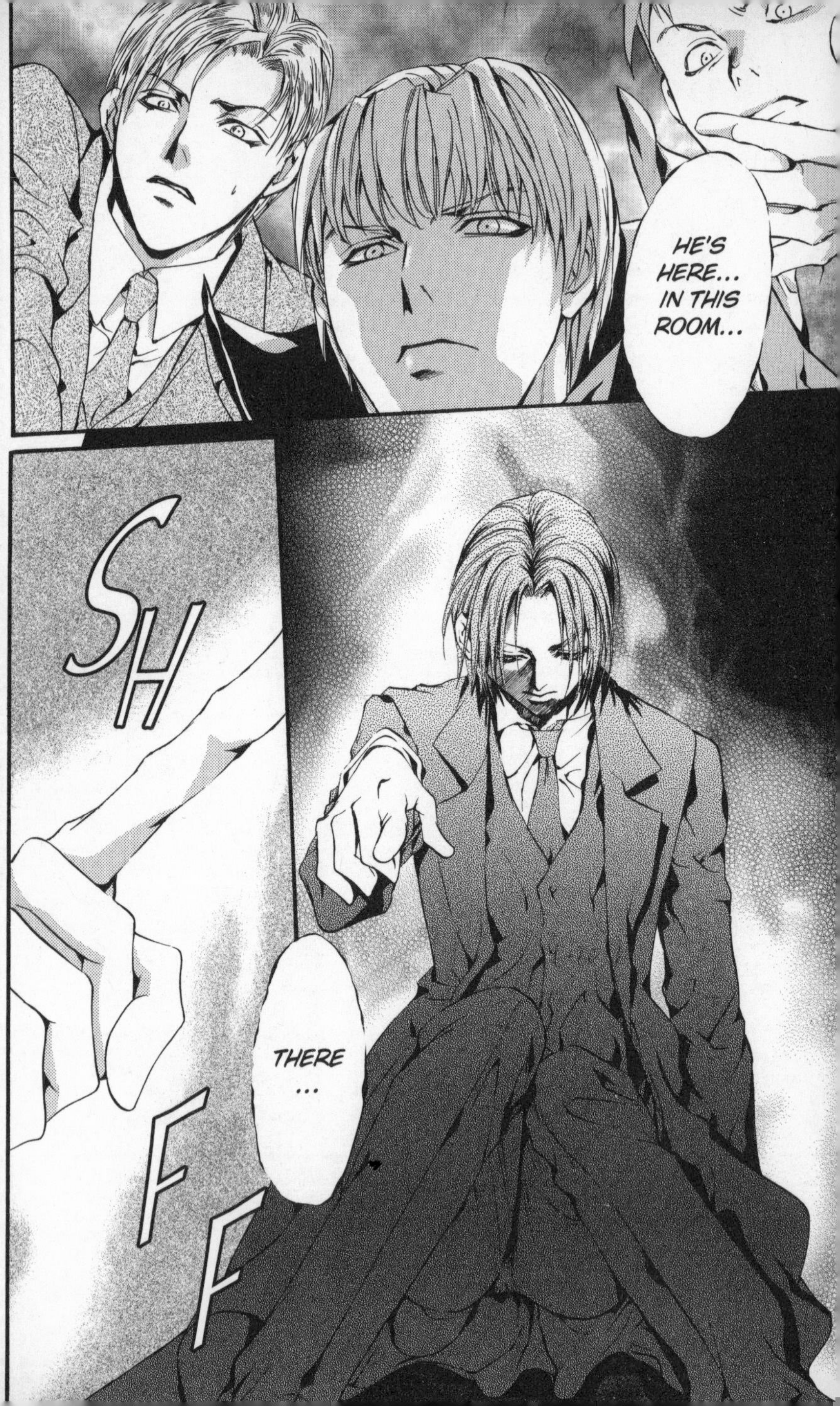
HE'S HERE... IN THIS ROOM...
SHFF
THERE ...

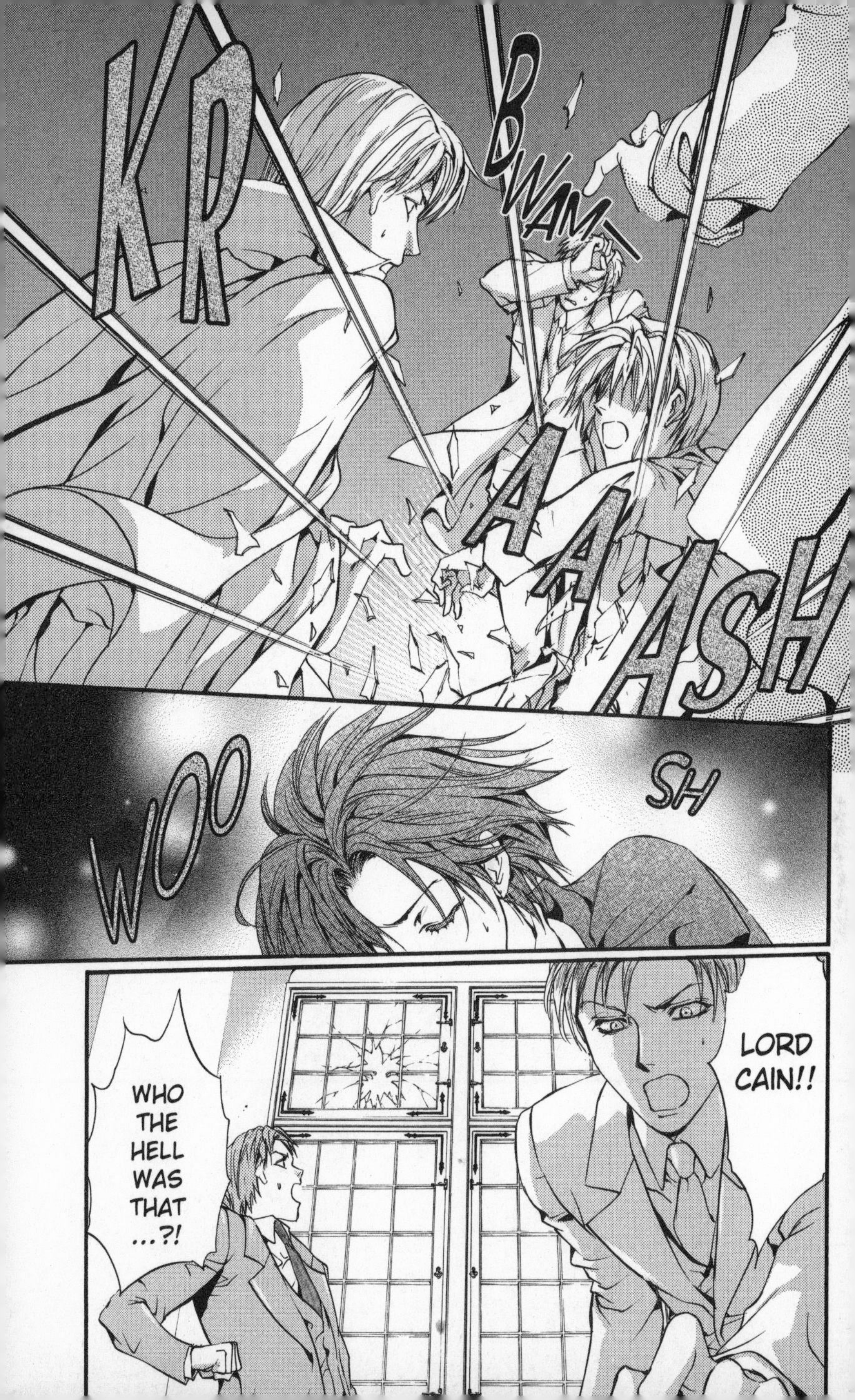
BWAM
KRAAASH
WOOSH
LORD CAIN!!
WHO THE HELL WAS THAT ...?!

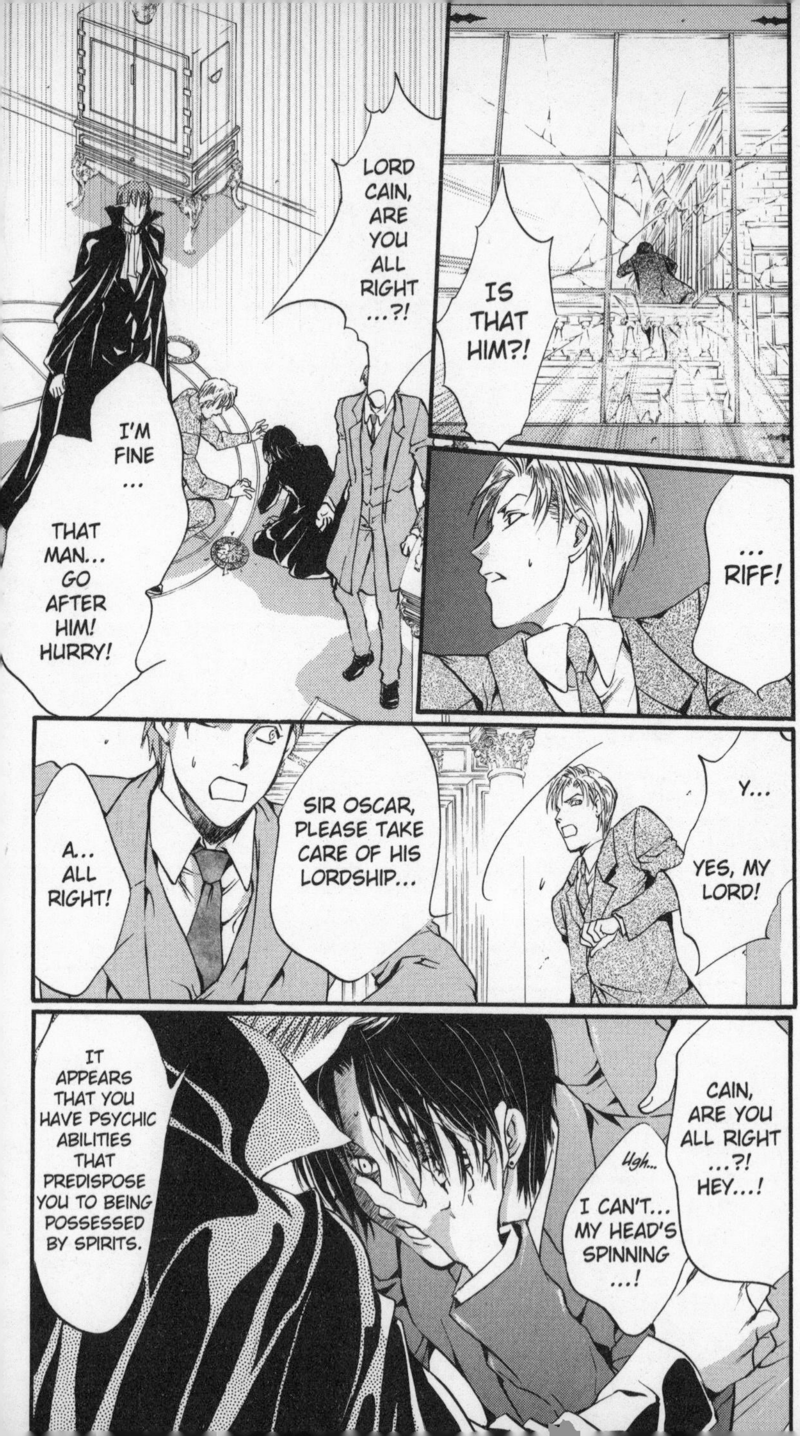
LORD CAIN, ARE YOU ALL RIGHT ...?!
IS THAT HIM?!
I'M FINE ...
THAT MAN... GO AFTER HIM! HURRY!
... RIFF!
Y...
YES, MY LORD!
SIR OSCAR, PLEASE TAKE CARE OF HIS LORDSHIP...
A... ALL RIGHT!
CAIN, ARE YOU ALL RIGHT ...?! HEY...!
Ugh...
I CAN'T... MY HEAD'S SPINNING ...!
IT APPEARS THAT YOU HAVE PSYCHIC ABILITIES THAT PREDISPOSE YOU TO BEING POSSESSED BY SPIRITS.

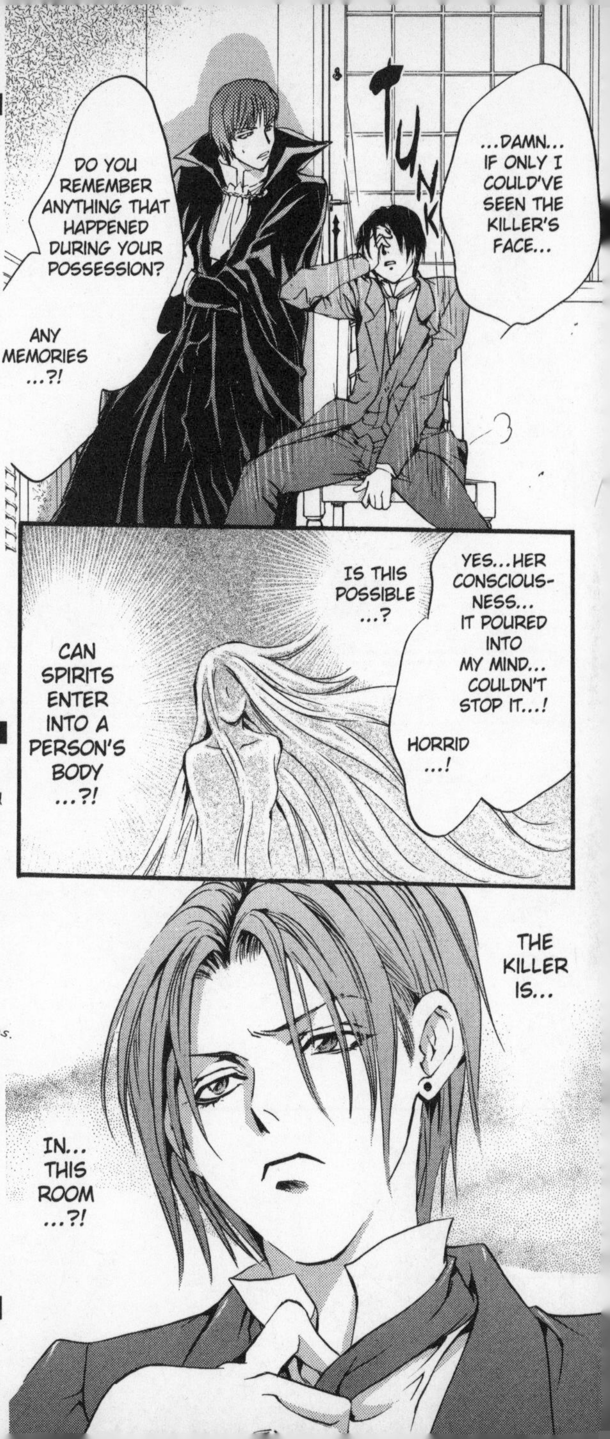
...DAMN... IF ONLY I COULD'VE SEEN THE KILLER'S FACE...
TUNK
DO YOU REMEMBER ANYTHING THAT HAPPENED DURING YOUR POSSESSION?
ANY MEMORIES ...?!
YES...HER CONSCIOUS-NESS... IT POURED INTO MY MIND... COULDN'T STOP IT...!
HORRID ...!
IS THIS POSSIBLE ...?
CAN SPIRITS ENTER INTO A PERSON'S BODY ...?!
THE KILLER IS...
IN... THIS ROOM ...?!

So, that's how the events are unfolding. I really liked Sheila so I didn't want to kill her but I had no choice...♥ I really didn't want her to die, because I like girls with big breasts.♥ I had to laugh when Cain starts acting feminine when he is possessed by Sheila's spirit... Even though I'm the one writing the story. Crehador has a bit of German blood in him. He comes from an aristocratic French family so his name is kind of long. I'm sure he's saved up quite a bit of money up till now.

Crehador as a kid. There was a time when he still looked like this. ↓

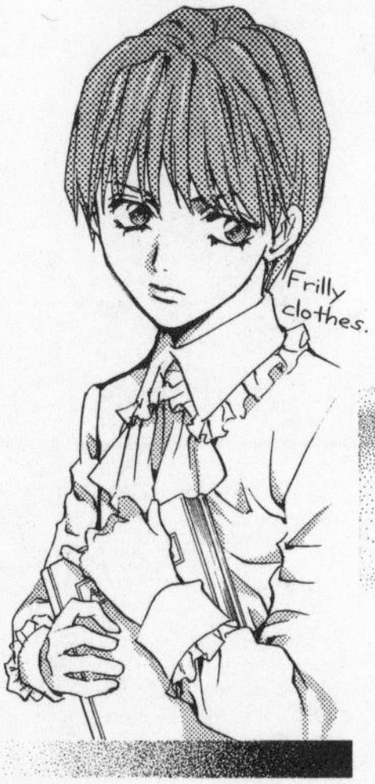
Frilly clothes.

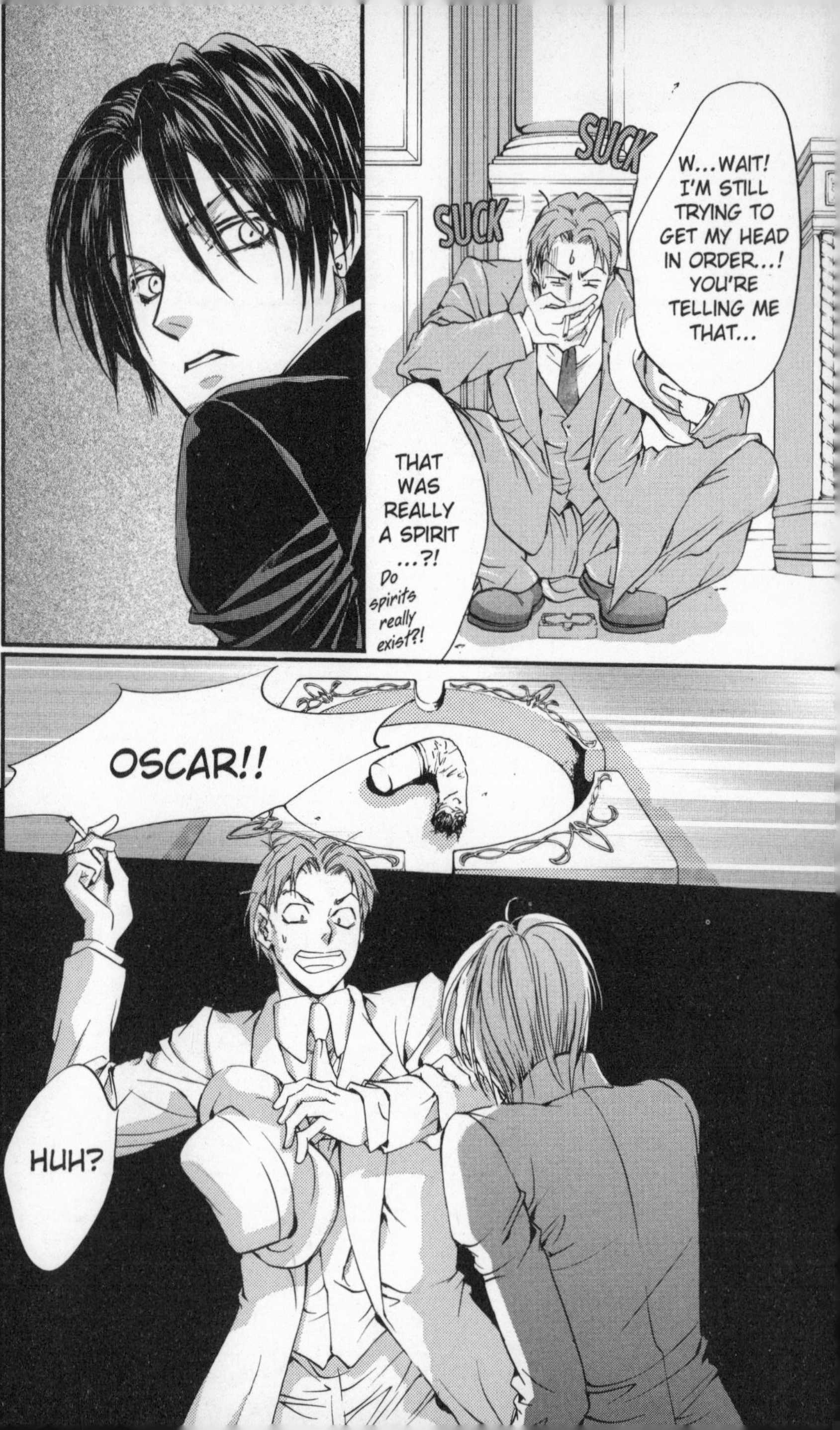
SUCK
SUCK
W...WAIT! I'M STILL TRYING TO GET MY HEAD IN ORDER...! YOU'RE TELLING ME THAT...
THAT WAS REALLY A SPIRIT ...?!
Do spirits really exist?!
OSCAR!!
HUH?

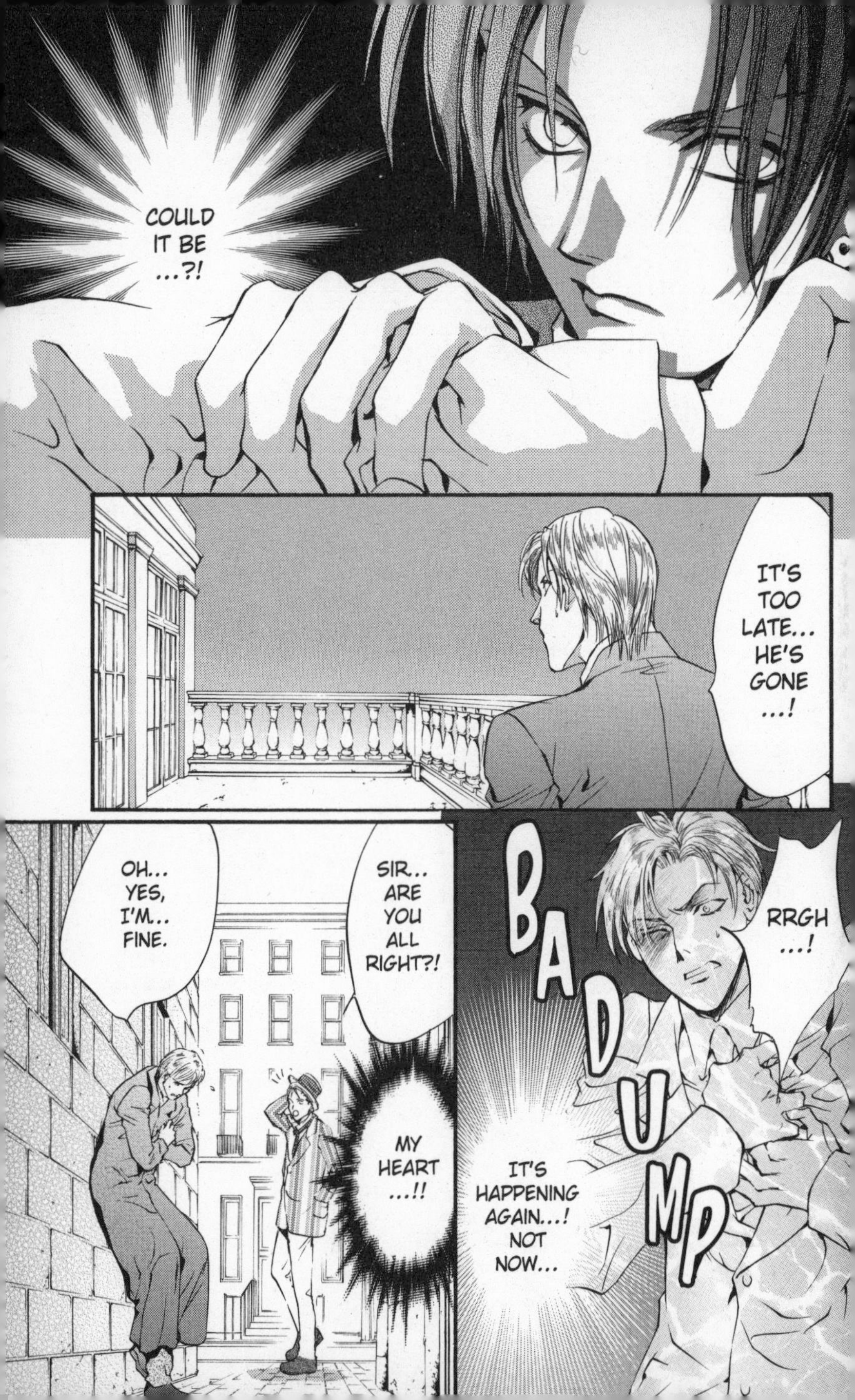
COULD IT BE ...?!
IT'S TOO LATE... HE'S GONE ...!
RRGH ...!
BADUMP
IT'S HAPPENING AGAIN...! NOT NOW...
SIR... ARE YOU ALL RIGHT?!
OH... YES, I'M... FINE.
MY HEART ...!!

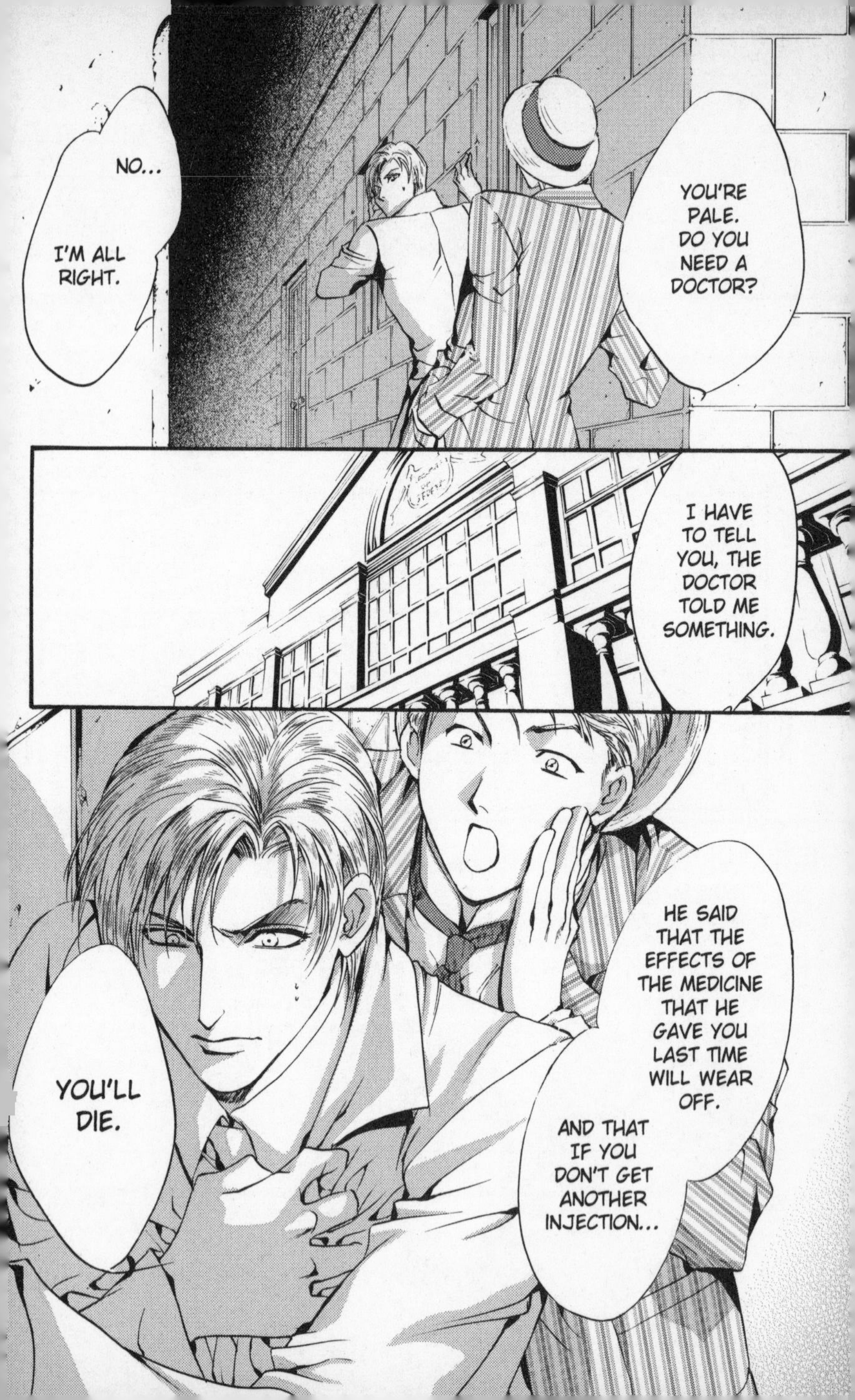
YOU'RE PALE. DO YOU NEED A DOCTOR?
NO...
I'M ALL RIGHT.
I HAVE TO TELL YOU, THE DOCTOR TOLD ME SOMETHING.
HE SAID THAT THE EFFECTS OF THE MEDICINE THAT HE GAVE YOU LAST TIME WILL WEAR OFF.
AND THAT IF YOU DON'T GET ANOTHER INJECTION...
YOU'LL DIE.

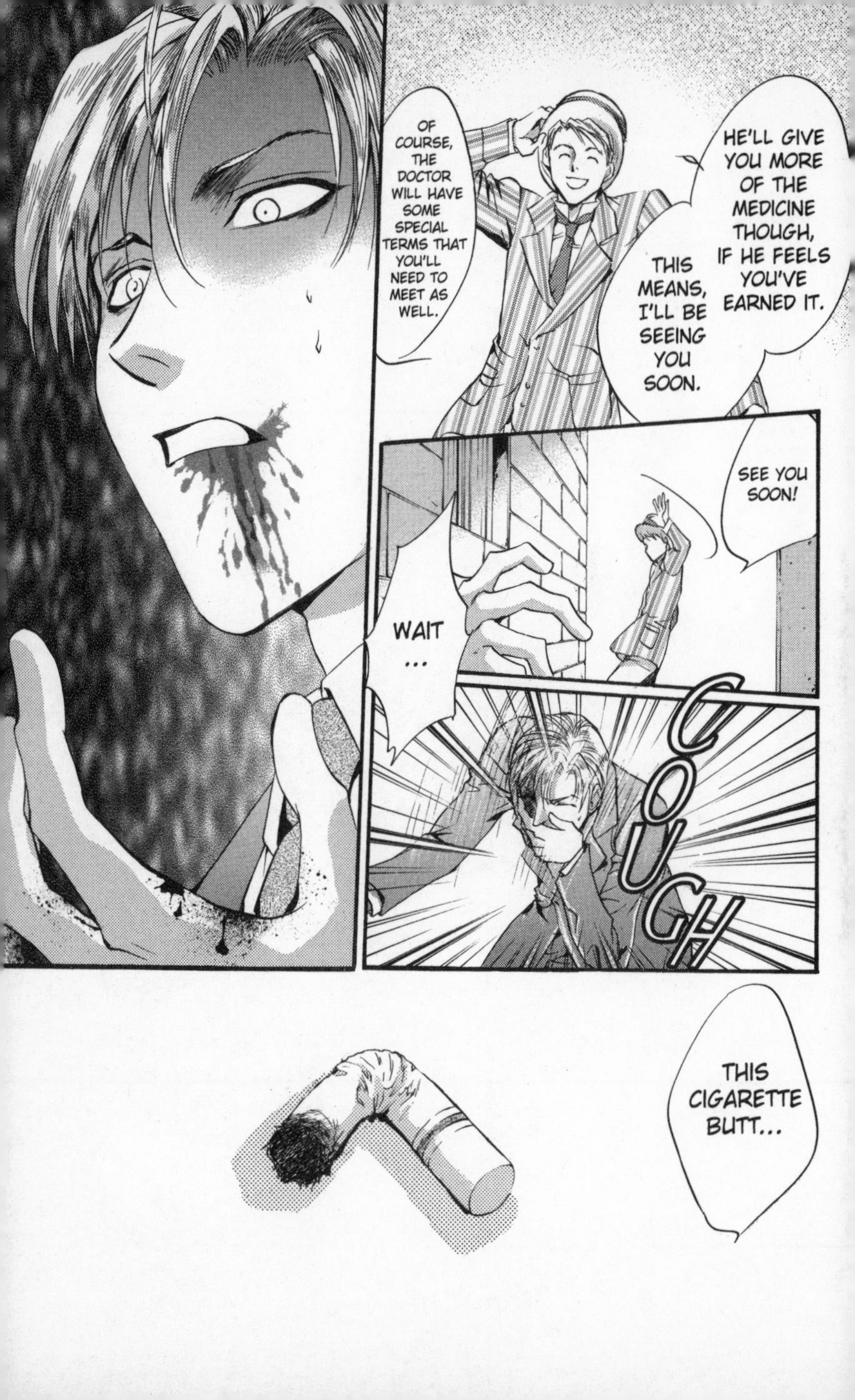
OF COURSE, THE DOCTOR WILL HAVE SOME SPECIAL TERMS THAT YOU'LL NEED TO MEET AS WELL.
HE'LL GIVE YOU MORE OF THE MEDICINE THOUGH, IF HE FEELS YOU'VE EARNED IT.
THIS MEANS, I'LL BE SEEING YOU SOON.
SEE YOU SOON!
WAIT ...
COUGH
THIS CIGARETTE BUTT...

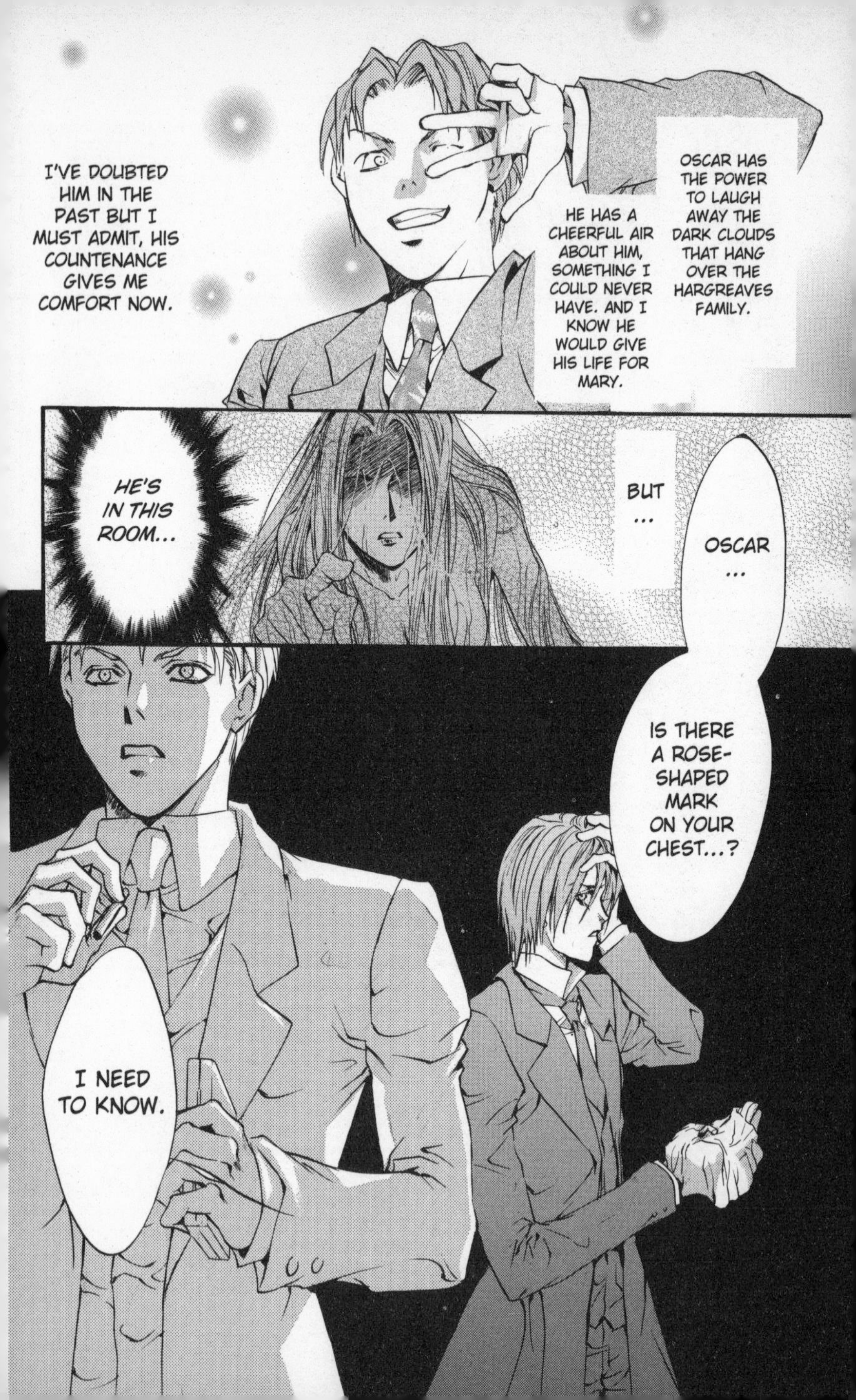
OSCAR HAS THE POWER TO LAUGH AWAY THE DARK CLOUDS THAT HANG OVER THE HARGREAVES FAMILY.
HE HAS A CHEERFUL AIR ABOUT HIM, SOMETHING I COULD NEVER HAVE. AND I KNOW HE WOULD GIVE HIS LIFE FOR MARY.
I'VE DOUBTED HIM IN THE PAST BUT I MUST ADMIT, HIS COUNTENANCE GIVES ME COMFORT NOW.
BUT ...
HE'S IN THIS ROOM...
OSCAR ... IS THERE A ROSE-SHAPED MARK ON YOUR CHEST...?
I NEED TO KNOW.

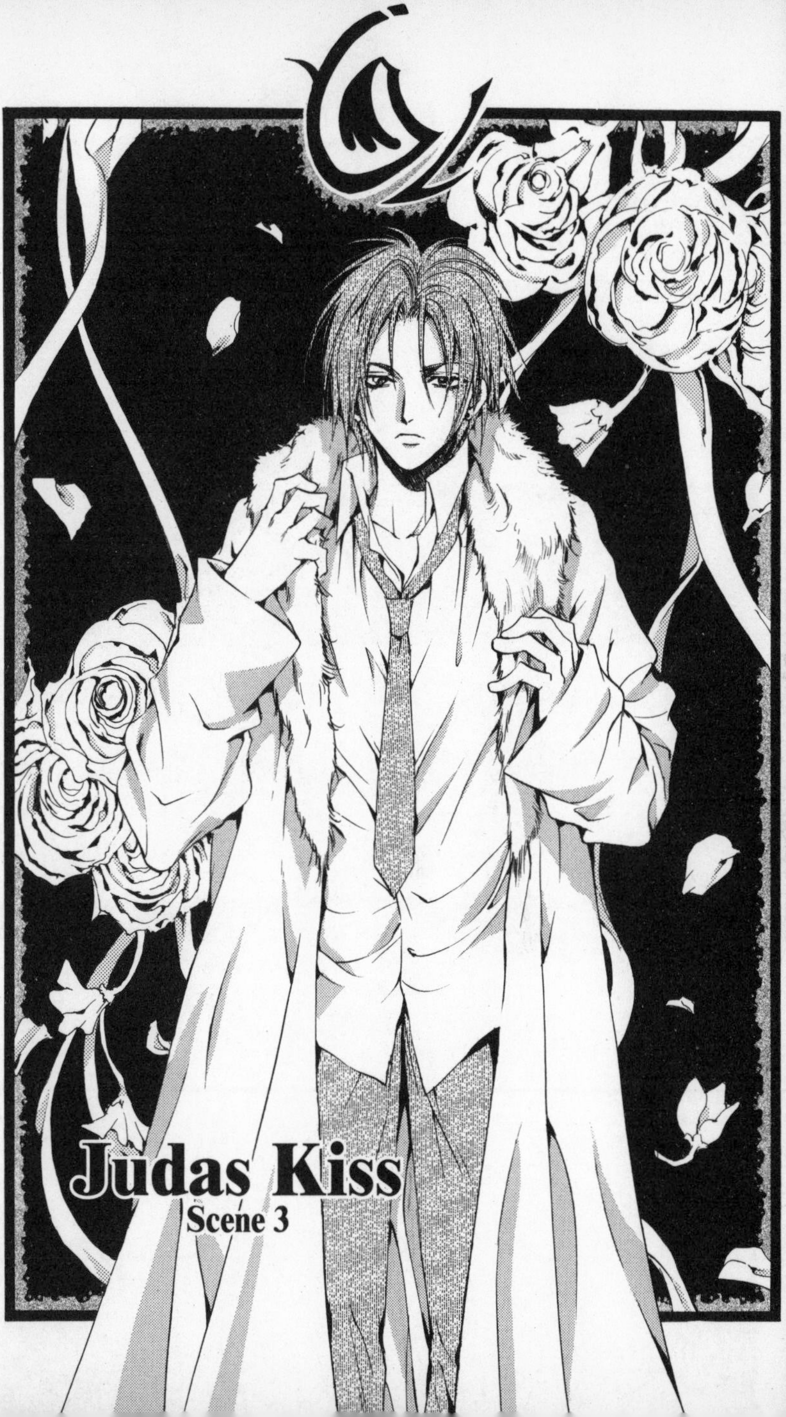
Judas Kiss
Scene 3

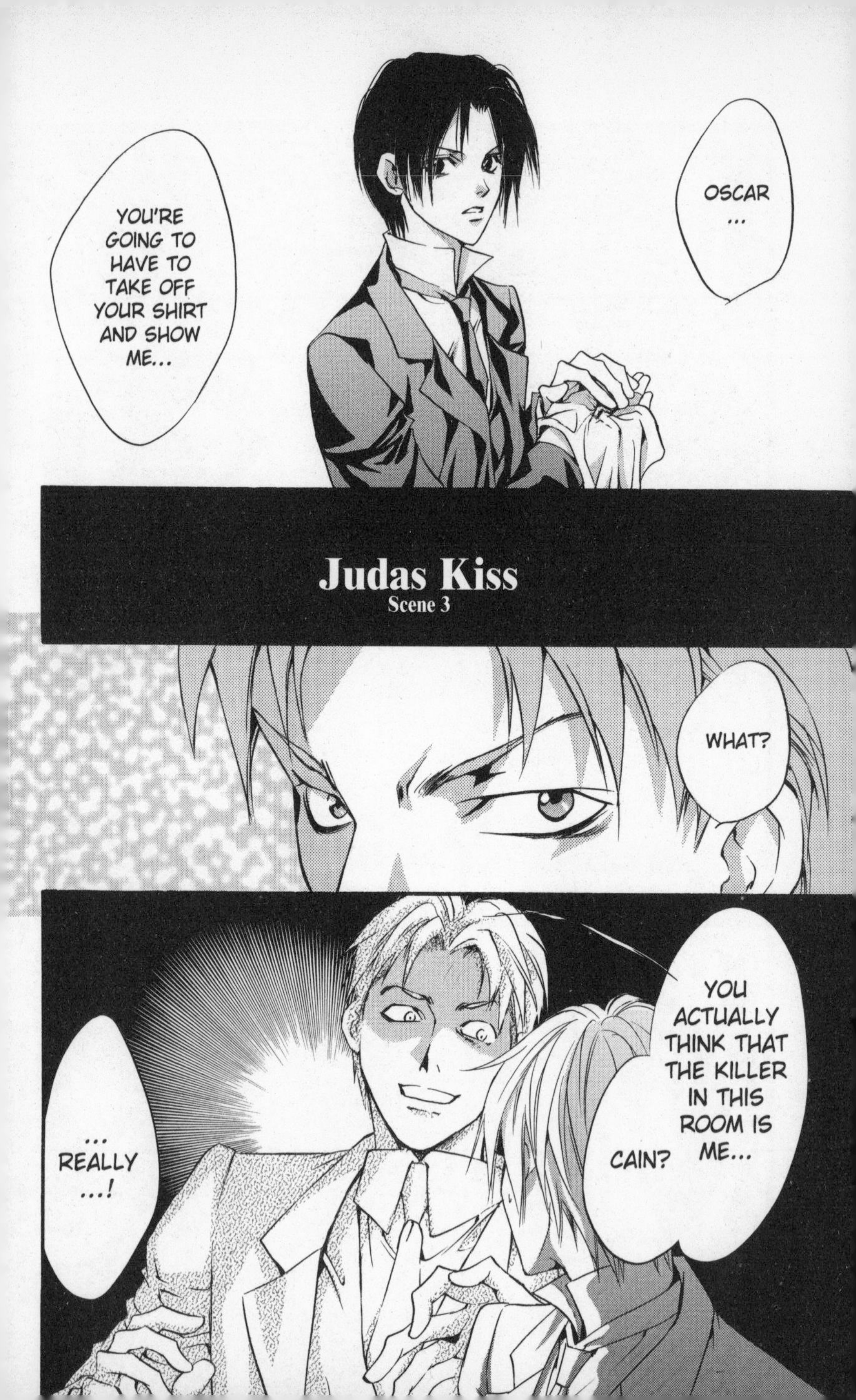
OSCAR ...
YOU'RE GOING TO HAVE TO TAKE OFF YOUR SHIRT AND SHOW ME...
Judas Kiss
Scene 3
WHAT?
YOU ACTUALLY THINK THAT THE KILLER IN THIS ROOM IS ME...
CAIN?
... REALLY ...!

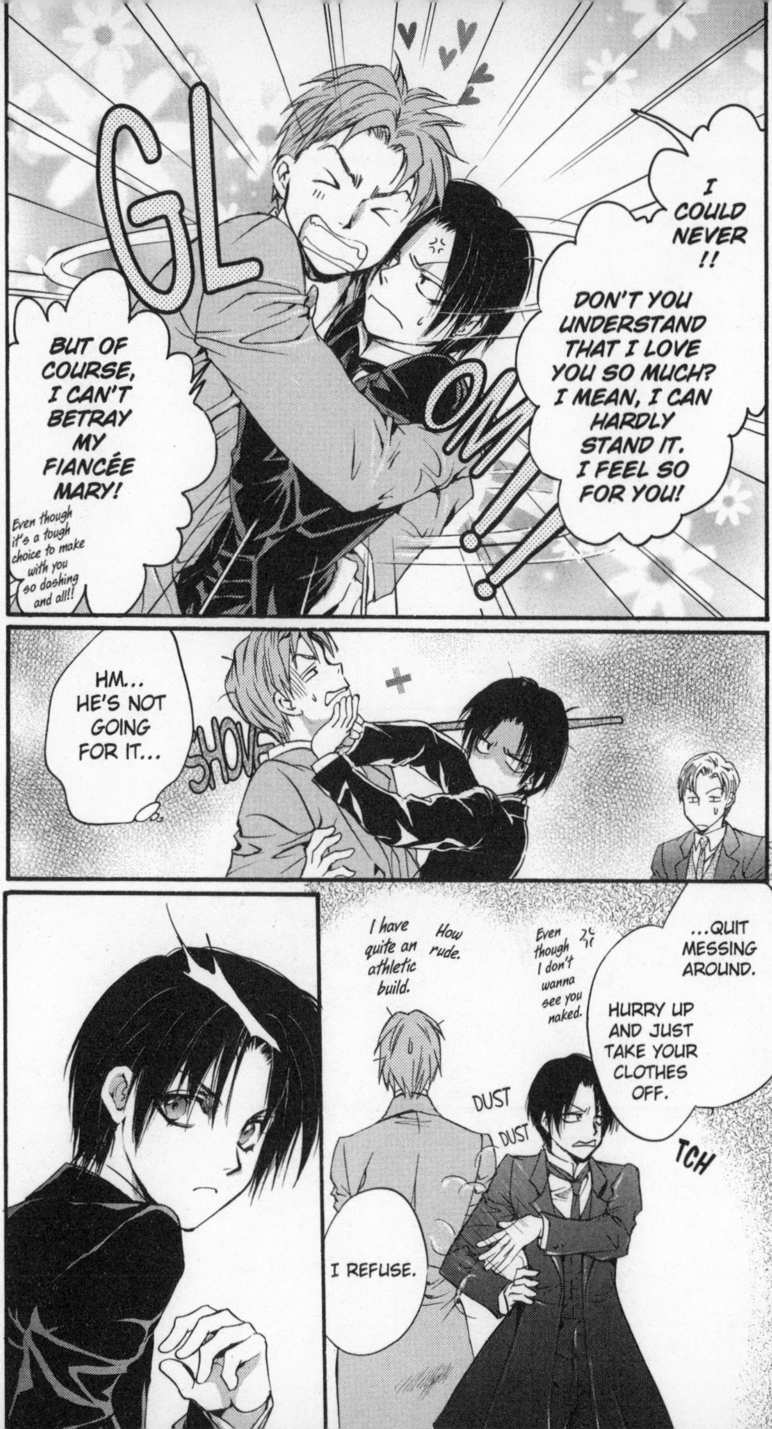
I COULD NEVER!!
DON'T YOU UNDERSTAND THAT I LOVE YOU SO MUCH? I MEAN, I CAN HARDLY STAND IT. I FEEL SO FOR YOU!
GLOM!!
BUT OF COURSE, I CAN'T BETRAY MY FIANCÉE MARY!
Even though it's a tough choice to make with you so dashing and all!!
HM... HE'S NOT GOING FOR IT...
SHOVE
...QUIT MESSING AROUND.
HURRY UP AND JUST TAKE YOUR CLOTHES OFF.
TCH
Even though I don't wanna see you naked.
How rude.
I have quite an athletic build.
DUST
DUST
I REFUSE.

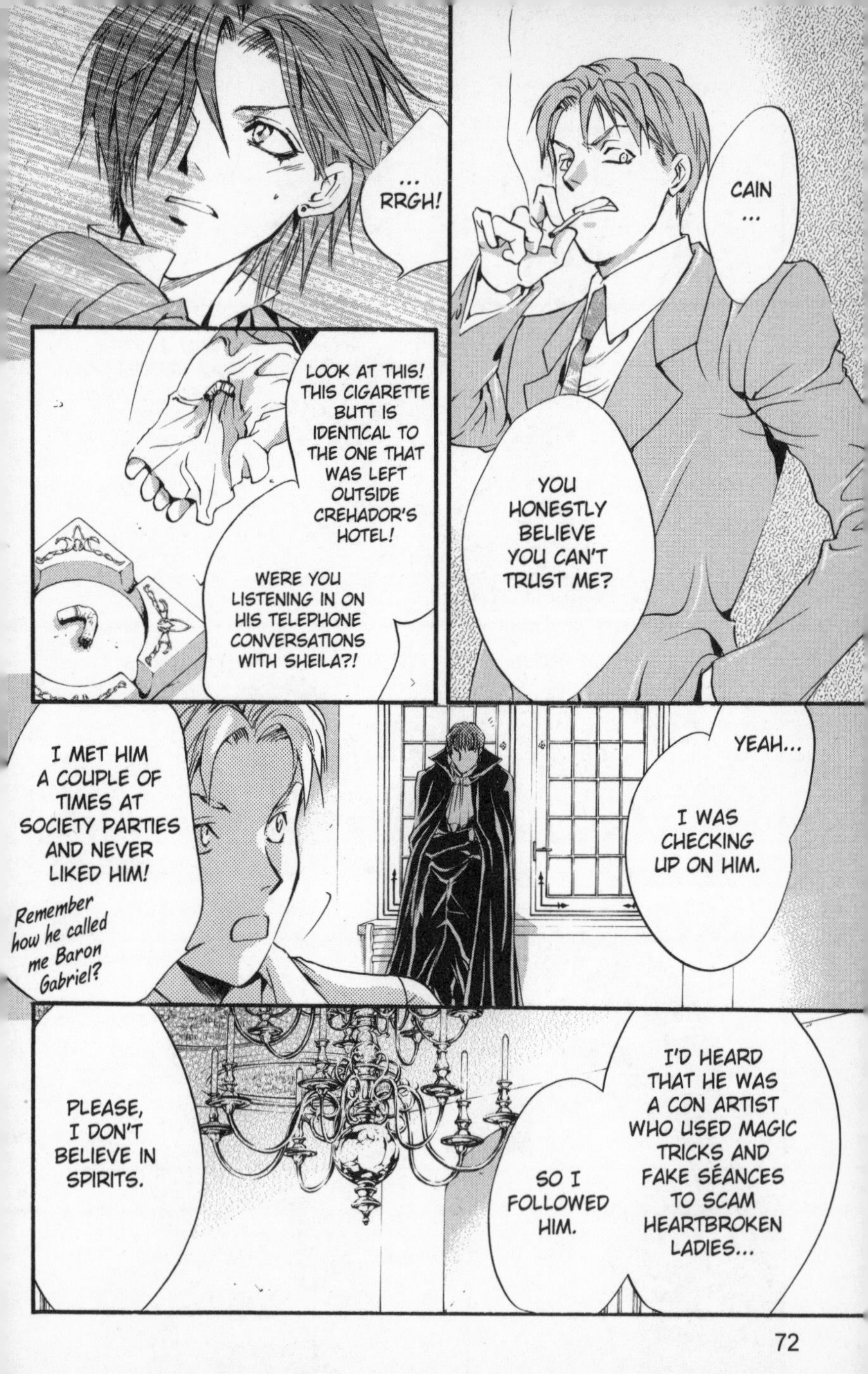

CAIN ...
YOU HONESTLY BELIEVE YOU CAN'T TRUST ME?
... RRGH!
LOOK AT THIS! THIS CIGARETTE BUTT IS IDENTICAL TO THE ONE THAT WAS LEFT OUTSIDE CREHADOR'S HOTEL!
WERE YOU LISTENING IN ON HIS TELEPHONE CONVERSATIONS WITH SHEILA?!
YEAH...
I WAS CHECKING UP ON HIM.
I MET HIM A COUPLE OF TIMES AT SOCIETY PARTIES AND NEVER LIKED HIM!
Remember how he called me Baron Gabriel?
I'D HEARD THAT HE WAS A CON ARTIST WHO USED MAGIC TRICKS AND FAKE SÉANCES TO SCAM HEARTBROKEN LADIES...
SO I FOLLOWED HIM.
PLEASE, I DON'T BELIEVE IN SPIRITS.

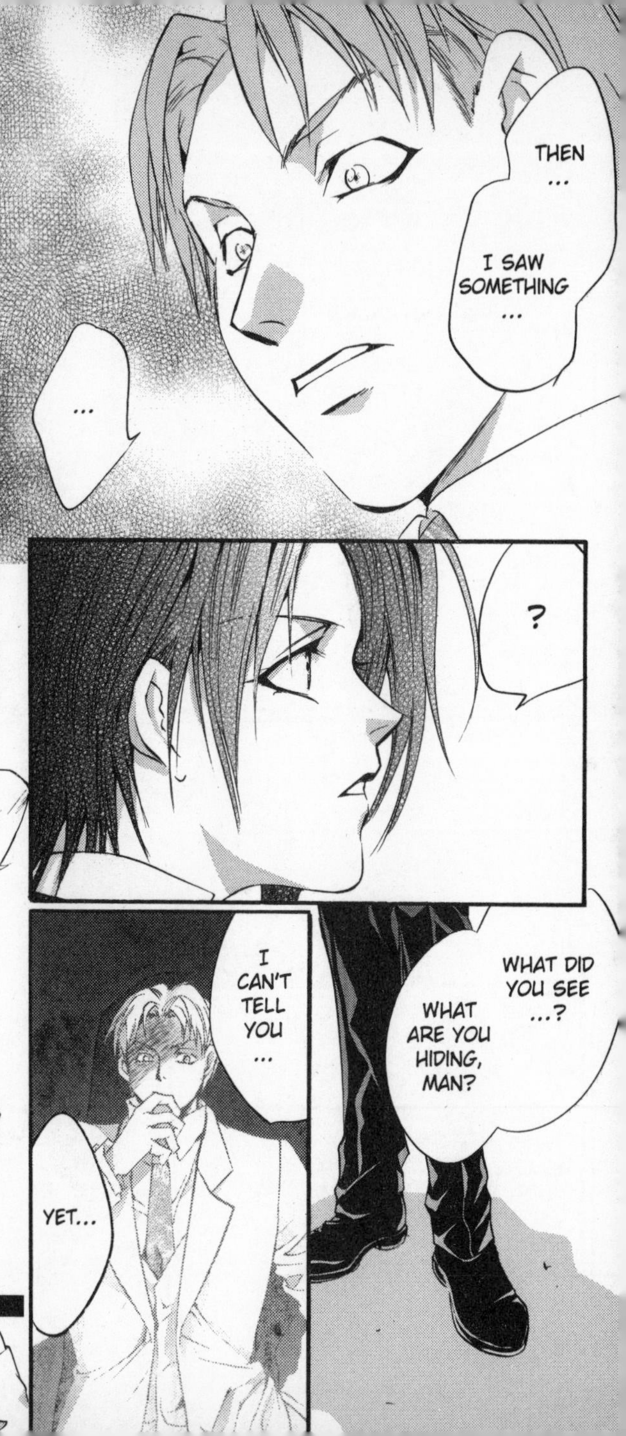
THEN ...
I SAW SOMETHING ...
...
?
WHAT DID YOU SEE ...?
WHAT ARE YOU HIDING, MAN?
I CAN'T TELL YOU ...
YET...

In between my manga series, I did this story. It had a crazy title called "Nighttime Lover Specialists." It was a one-off short story and was extremely well received. I was really surprised. Thanks everyone.♡ I guess I had no cause to worry.

The vampire host.

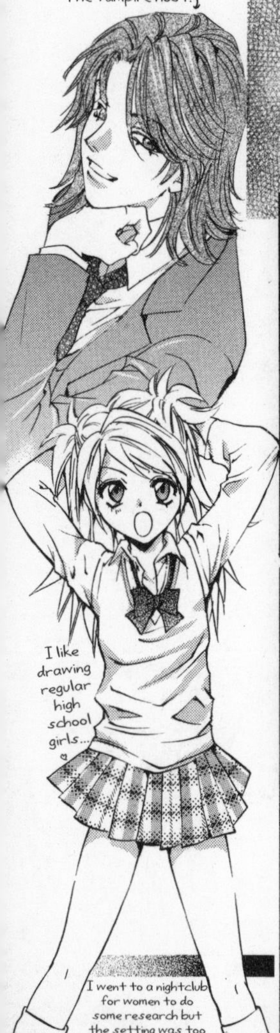
I like drawing regular high school girls...♡

I went to a nightclub for women to do some research but the setting was too abnormal so I couldn't use it...

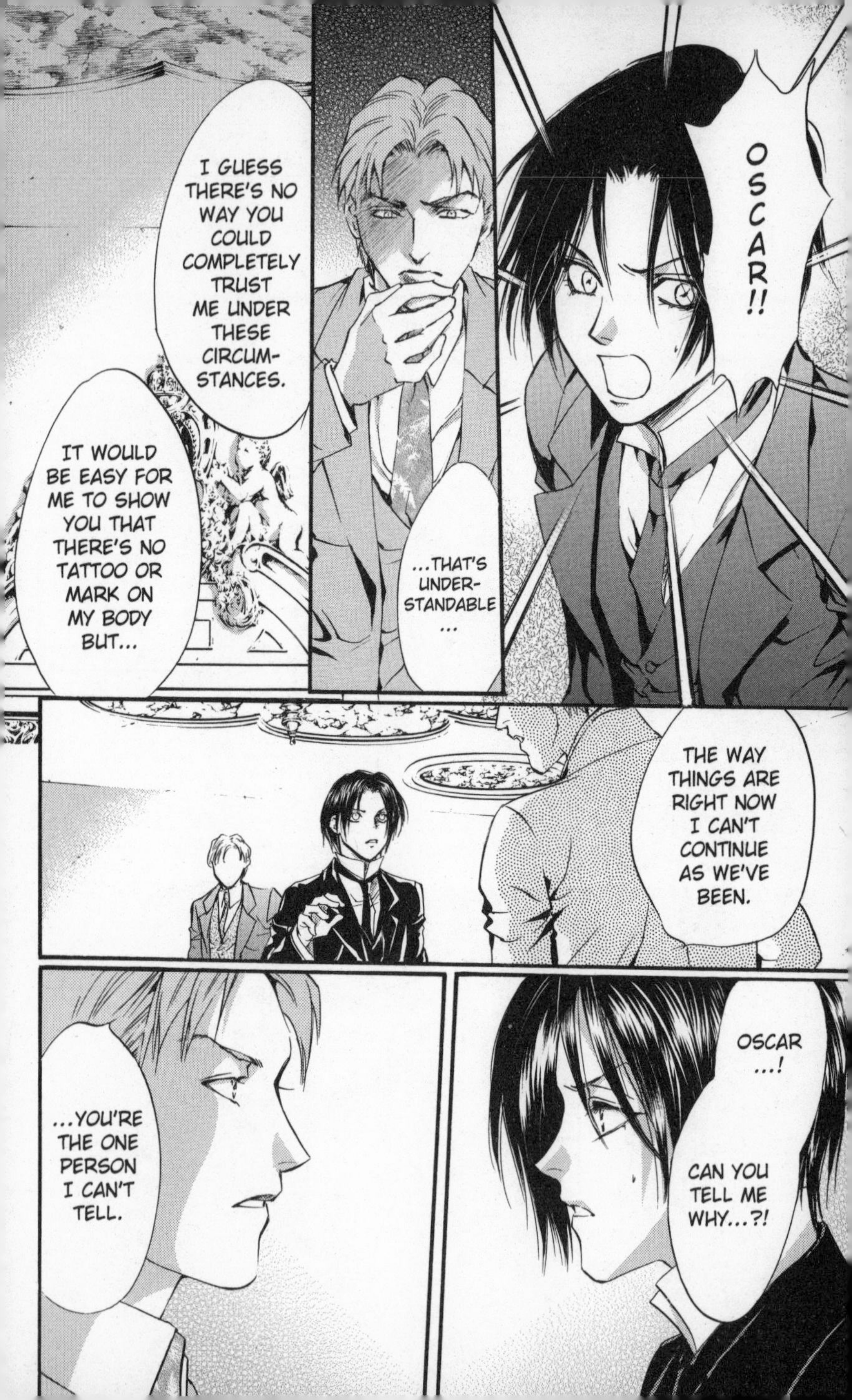
OSCAR!!
...THAT'S UNDERSTANDABLE...
I GUESS THERE'S NO WAY YOU COULD COMPLETELY TRUST ME UNDER THESE CIRCUMSTANCES.
IT WOULD BE EASY FOR ME TO SHOW YOU THAT THERE'S NO TATTOO OR MARK ON MY BODY BUT...
THE WAY THINGS ARE RIGHT NOW I CAN'T CONTINUE AS WE'VE BEEN.
OSCAR...!
CAN YOU TELL ME WHY...?!
...YOU'RE THE ONE PERSON I CAN'T TELL.

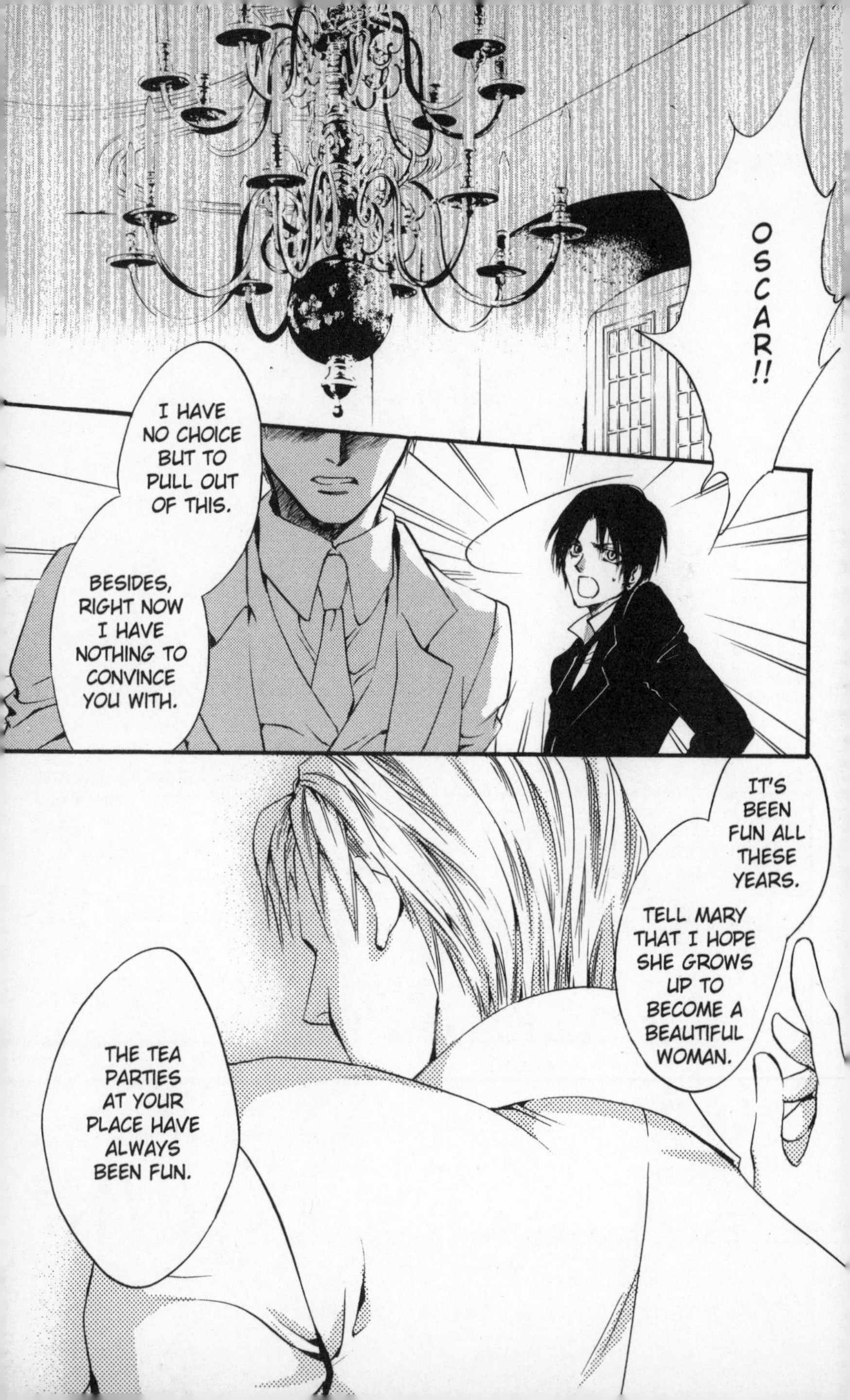
OSCAR!!
I HAVE NO CHOICE BUT TO PULL OUT OF THIS.
BESIDES, RIGHT NOW I HAVE NOTHING TO CONVINCE YOU WITH.
IT'S BEEN FUN ALL THESE YEARS.
TELL MARY THAT I HOPE SHE GROWS UP TO BECOME A BEAUTIFUL WOMAN.
THE TEA PARTIES AT YOUR PLACE HAVE ALWAYS BEEN FUN.

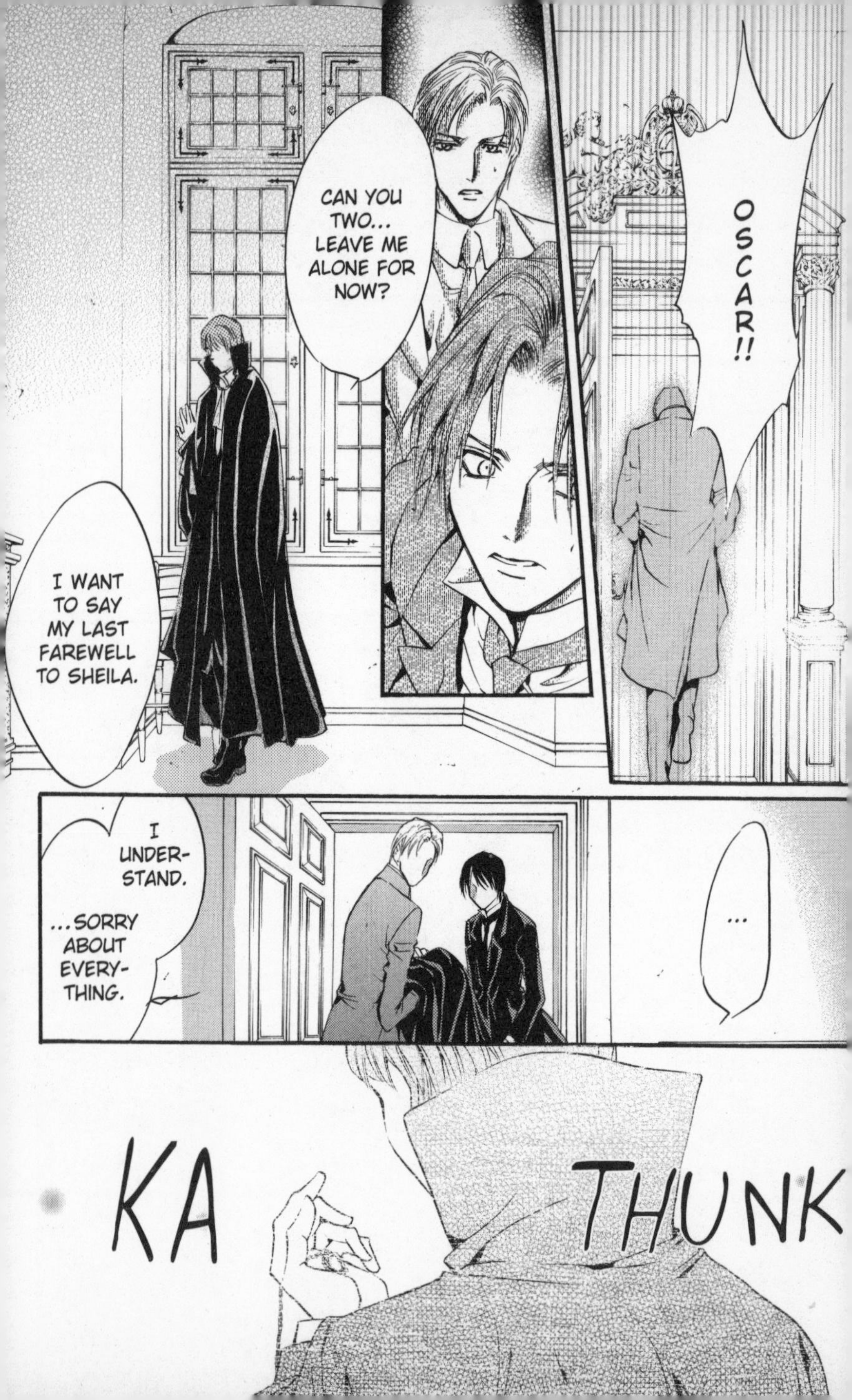
OSCAR!!
CAN YOU TWO... LEAVE ME ALONE FOR NOW?
I WANT TO SAY MY LAST FAREWELL TO SHEILA.
...
I UNDER-STAND.
...SORRY ABOUT EVERY-THING.
KA THUNK

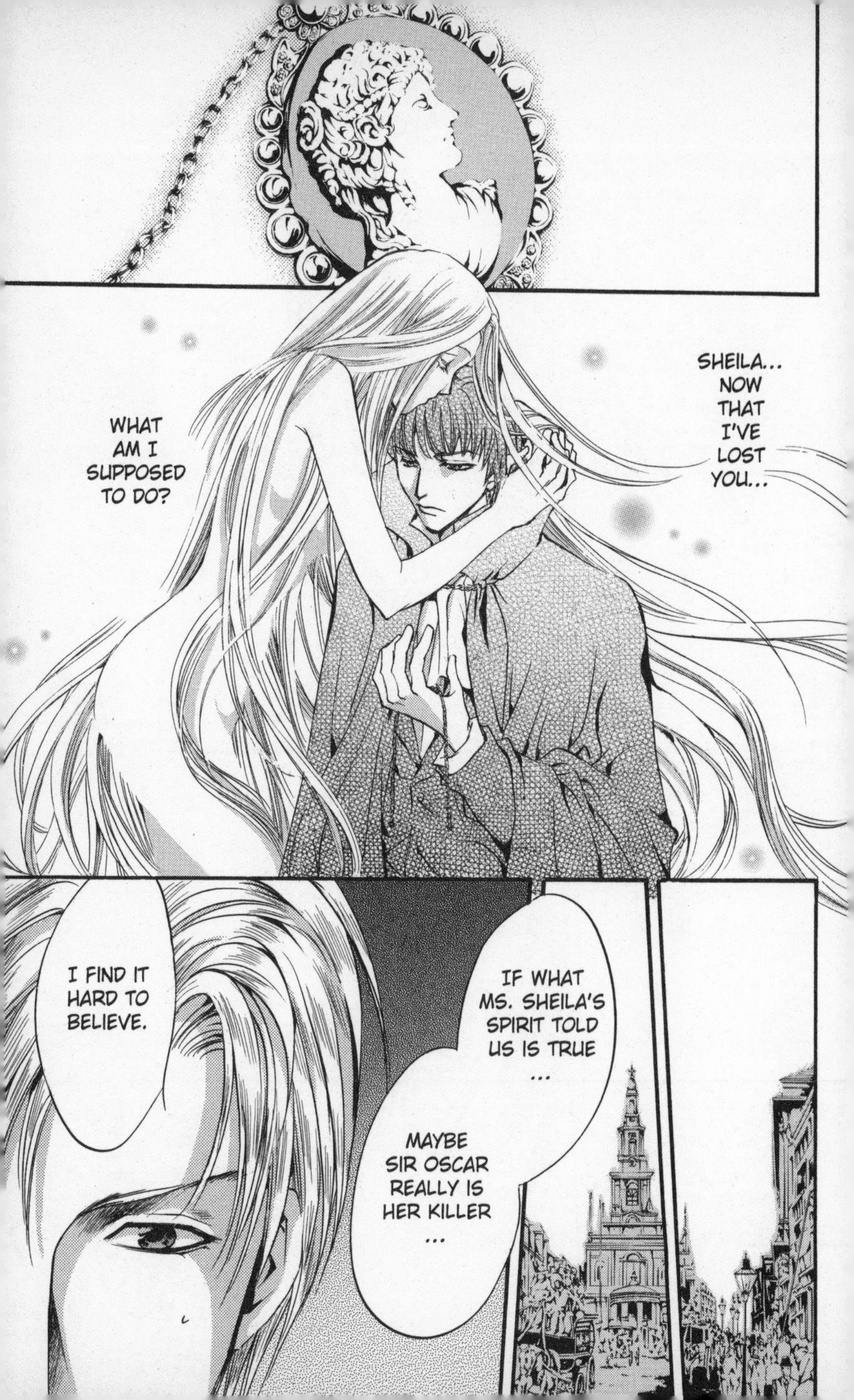
SHEILA... NOW THAT I'VE LOST YOU...
WHAT AM I SUPPOSED TO DO?
IF WHAT MS. SHEILA'S SPIRIT TOLD US IS TRUE...
MAYBE SIR OSCAR REALLY IS HER KILLER...
I FIND IT HARD TO BELIEVE.

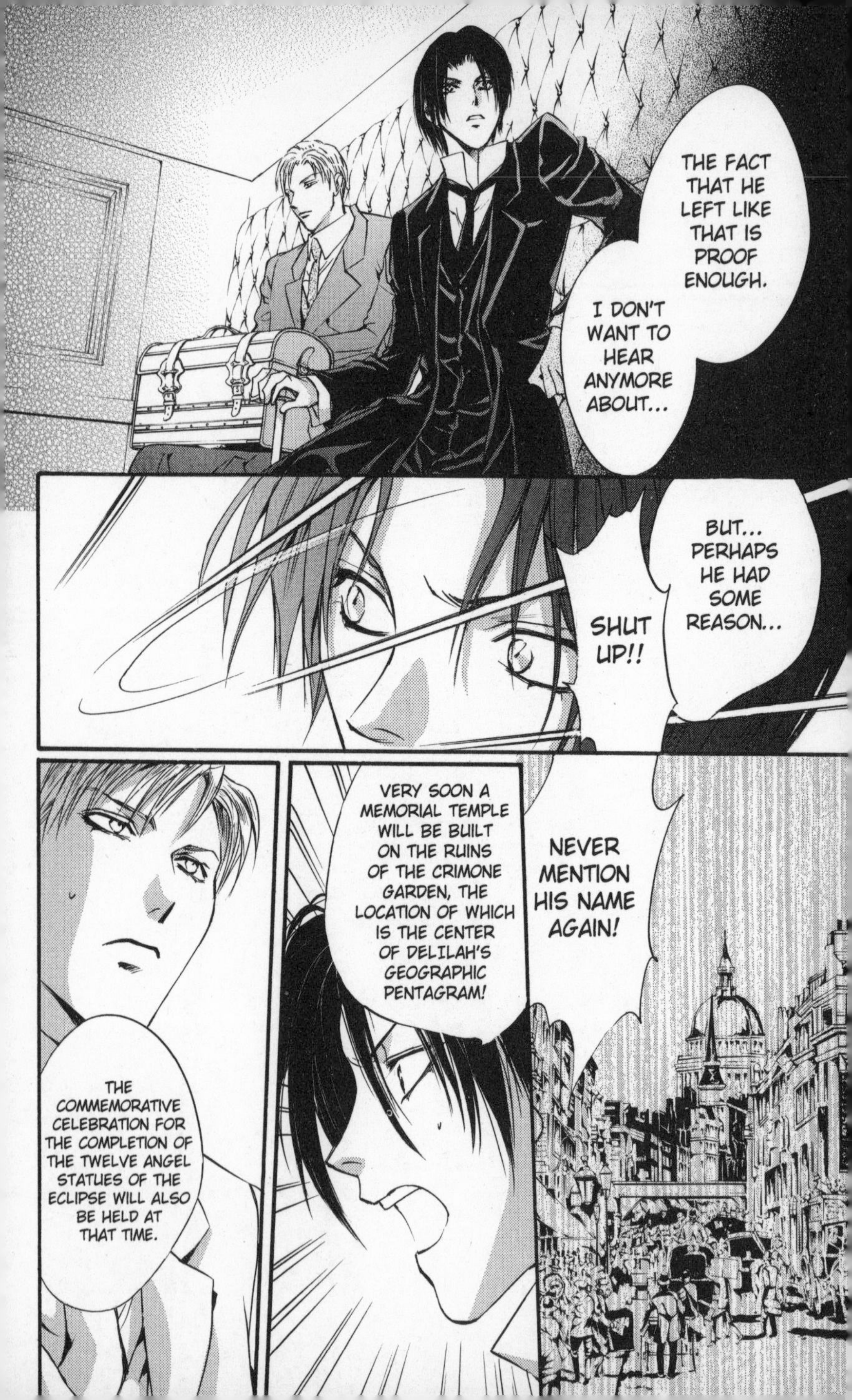
THE FACT THAT HE LEFT LIKE THAT IS PROOF ENOUGH.
I DON'T WANT TO HEAR ANYMORE ABOUT...
BUT... PERHAPS HE HAD SOME REASON...
SHUT UP!!
NEVER MENTION HIS NAME AGAIN!
VERY SOON A MEMORIAL TEMPLE WILL BE BUILT ON THE RUINS OF THE CRIMONE GARDEN, THE LOCATION OF WHICH IS THE CENTER OF DELILAH'S GEOGRAPHIC PENTAGRAM!
THE COMMEMORATIVE CELEBRATION FOR THE COMPLETION OF THE TWELVE ANGEL STATUES OF THE ECLIPSE WILL ALSO BE HELD AT THAT TIME.

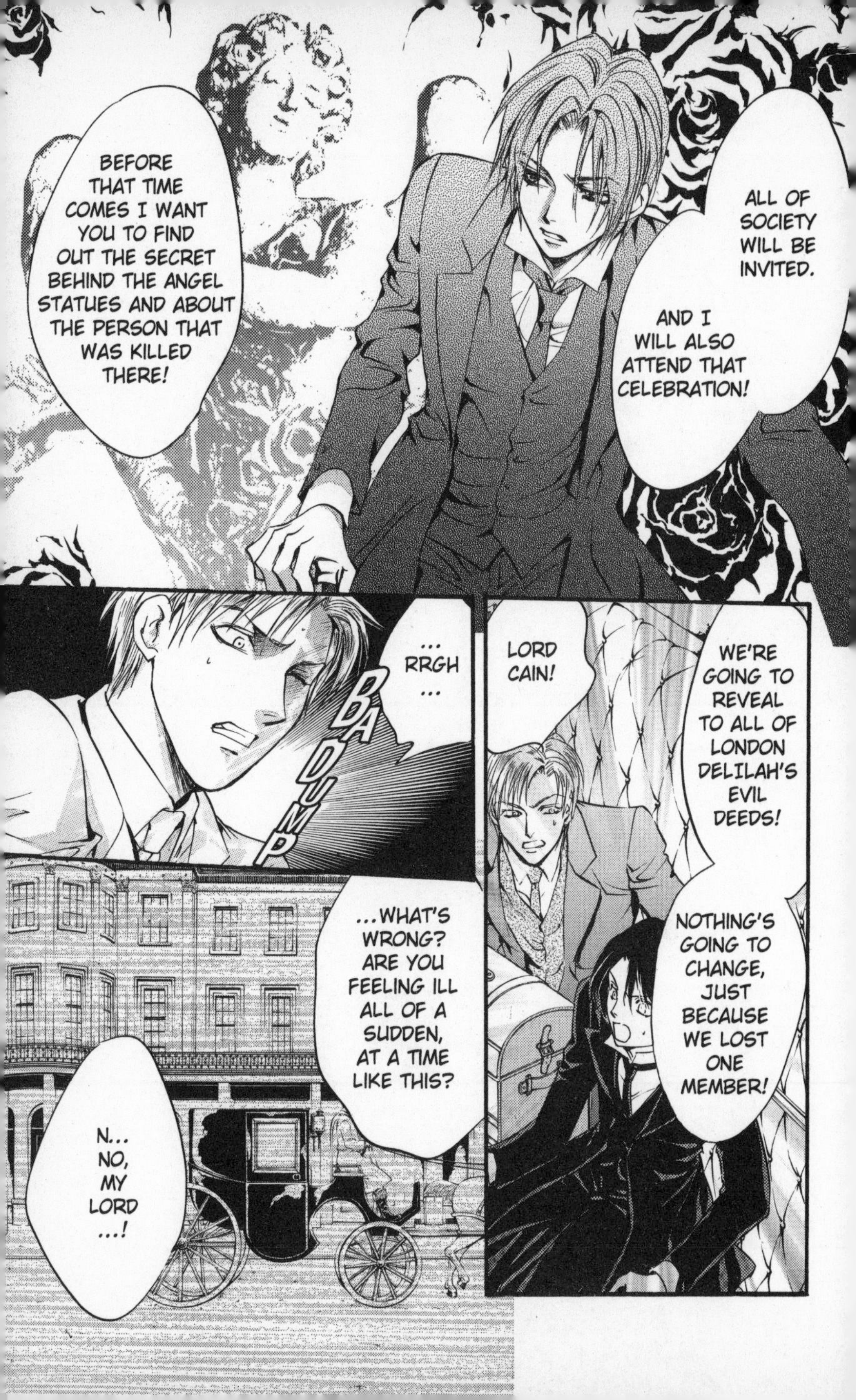
ALL OF SOCIETY WILL BE INVITED.
AND I WILL ALSO ATTEND THAT CELEBRATION!
BEFORE THAT TIME COMES I WANT YOU TO FIND OUT THE SECRET BEHIND THE ANGEL STATUES AND ABOUT THE PERSON THAT WAS KILLED THERE!
WE'RE GOING TO REVEAL TO ALL OF LONDON DELILAH'S EVIL DEEDS!
LORD CAIN!
NOTHING'S GOING TO CHANGE, JUST BECAUSE WE LOST ONE MEMBER!
... RRGH ...
BADUMP
...WHAT'S WRONG? ARE YOU FEELING ILL ALL OF A SUDDEN, AT A TIME LIKE THIS?
N... NO, MY LORD ...!

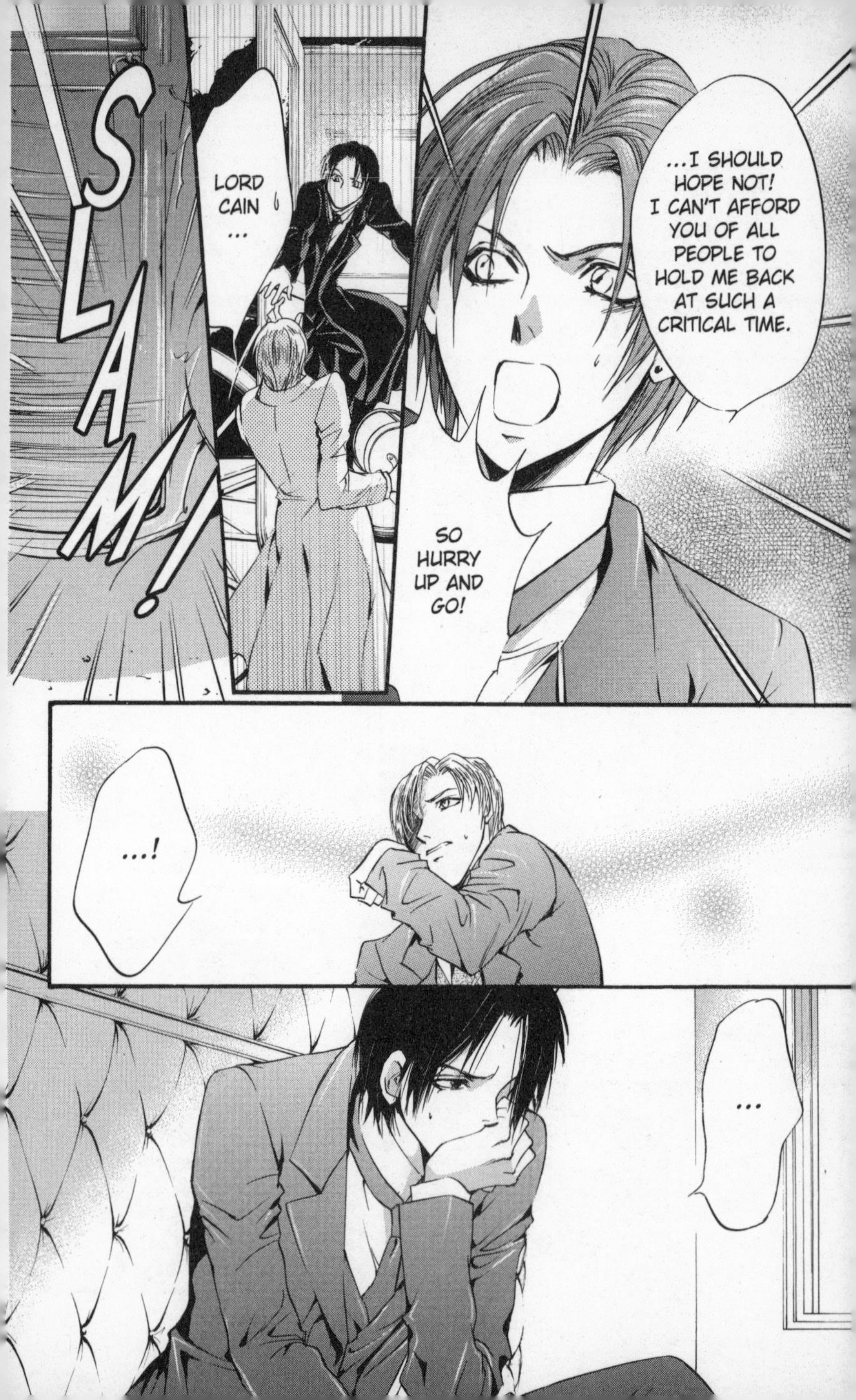
...I SHOULD HOPE NOT! I CAN'T AFFORD YOU OF ALL PEOPLE TO HOLD ME BACK AT SUCH A CRITICAL TIME.
SO HURRY UP AND GO!
LORD CAIN ...
SLAM!
...!
...

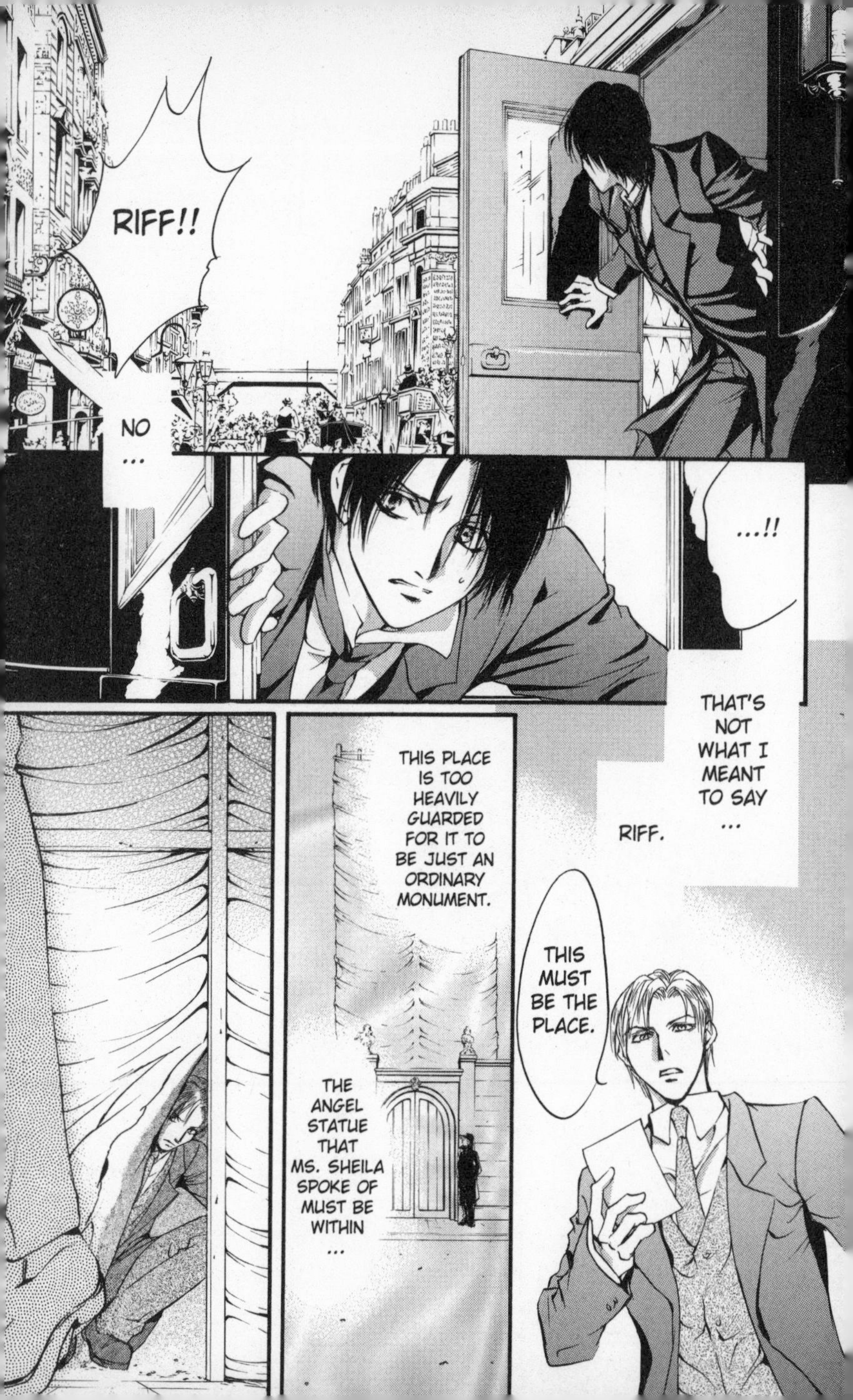
RIFF!!
NO ...
...!!
THAT'S NOT WHAT I MEANT TO SAY ...
RIFF.
THIS MUST BE THE PLACE.
THIS PLACE IS TOO HEAVILY GUARDED FOR IT TO BE JUST AN ORDINARY MONUMENT.
THE ANGEL STATUE THAT MS. SHEILA SPOKE OF MUST BE WITHIN ...

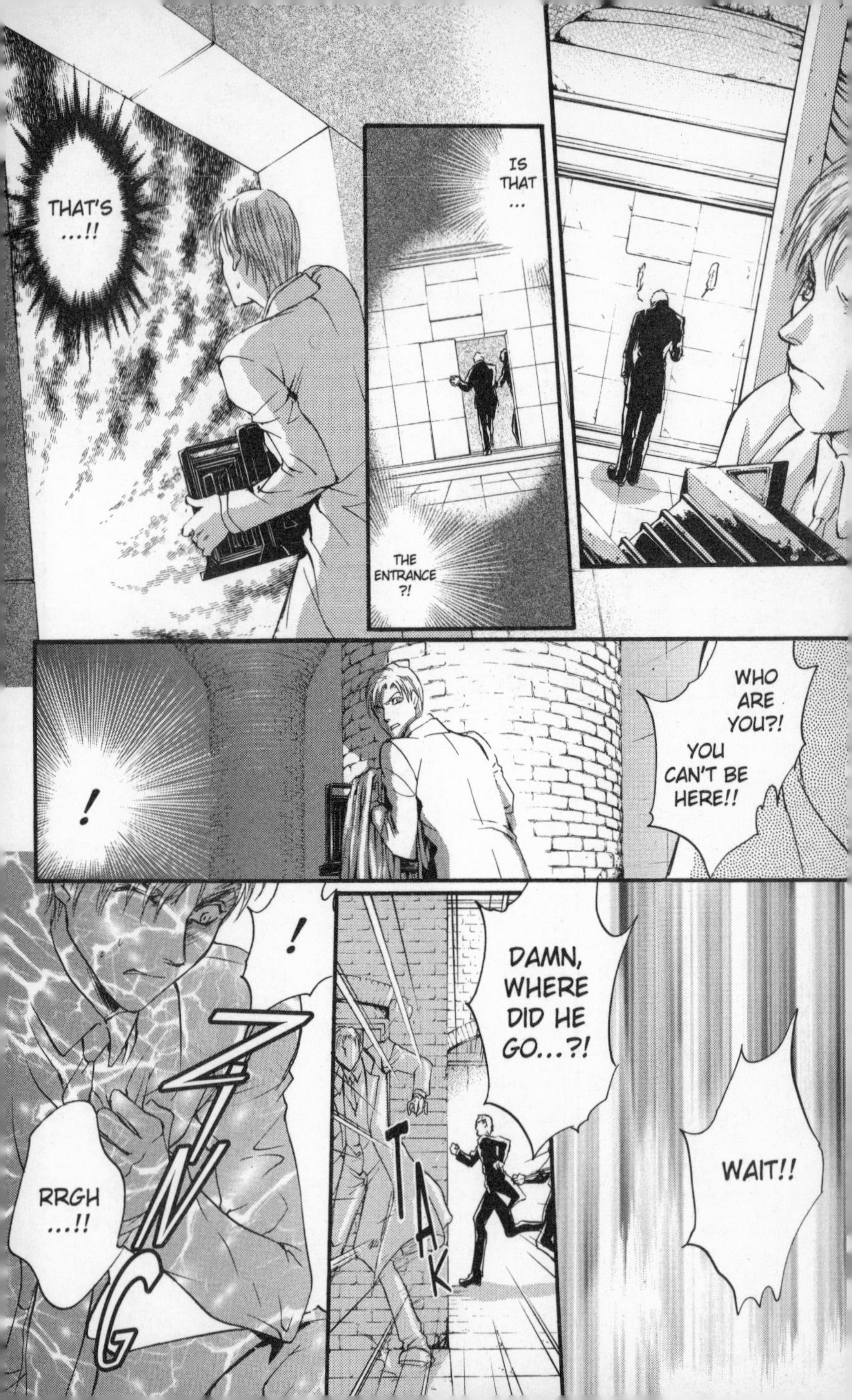
IS THAT ...
THE ENTRANCE ?!
THAT'S ...!!
WHO ARE YOU?!
YOU CAN'T BE HERE!!
!
WAIT!!
DAMN, WHERE DID HE GO...?!
TAK
!
ZZNG
RRGH ...!!

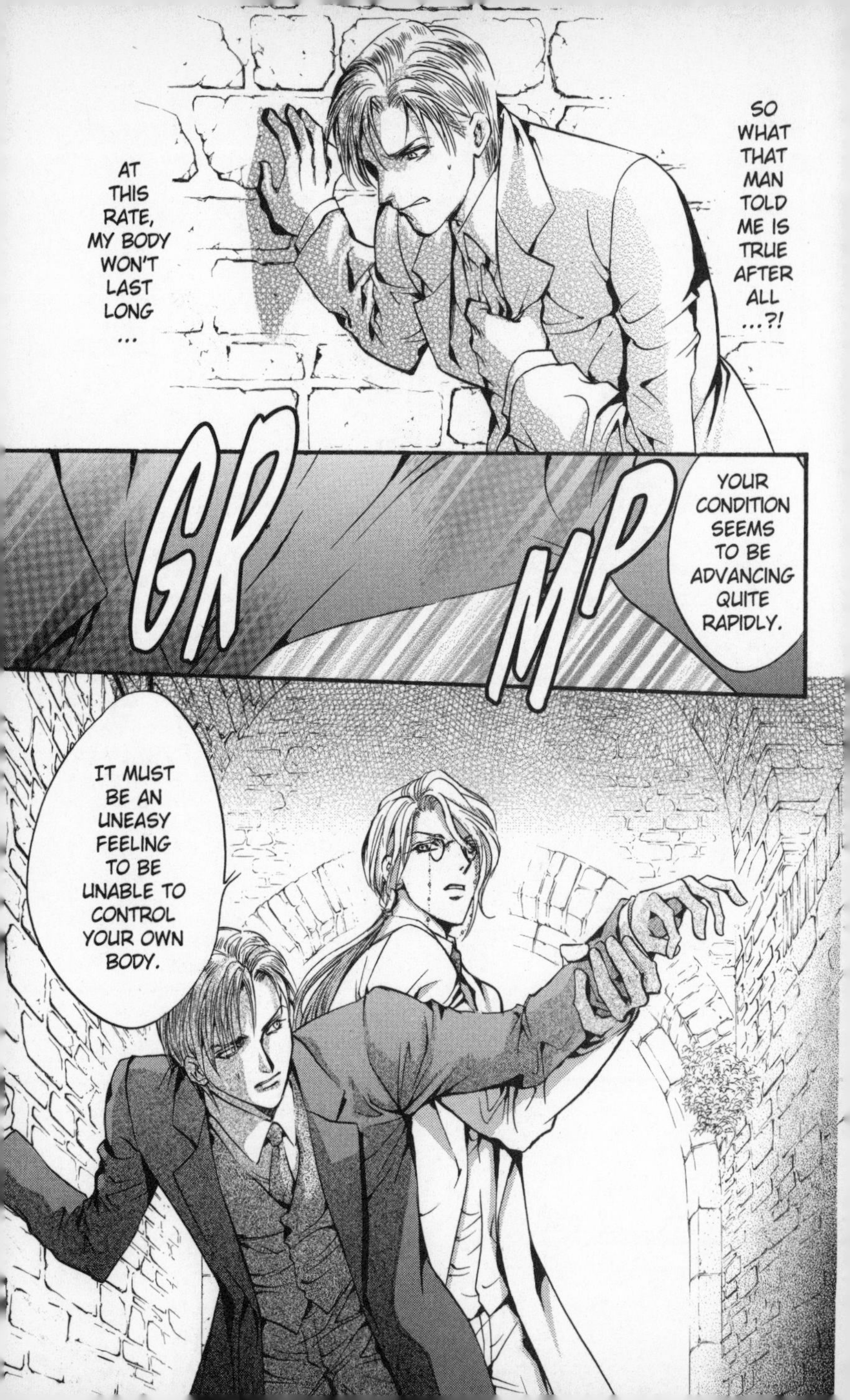
SO WHAT THAT MAN TOLD ME IS TRUE AFTER ALL ...?!
AT THIS RATE, MY BODY WON'T LAST LONG ...
YOUR CONDITION SEEMS TO BE ADVANCING QUITE RAPIDLY.
GRMP
IT MUST BE AN UNEASY FEELING TO BE UNABLE TO CONTROL YOUR OWN BODY.

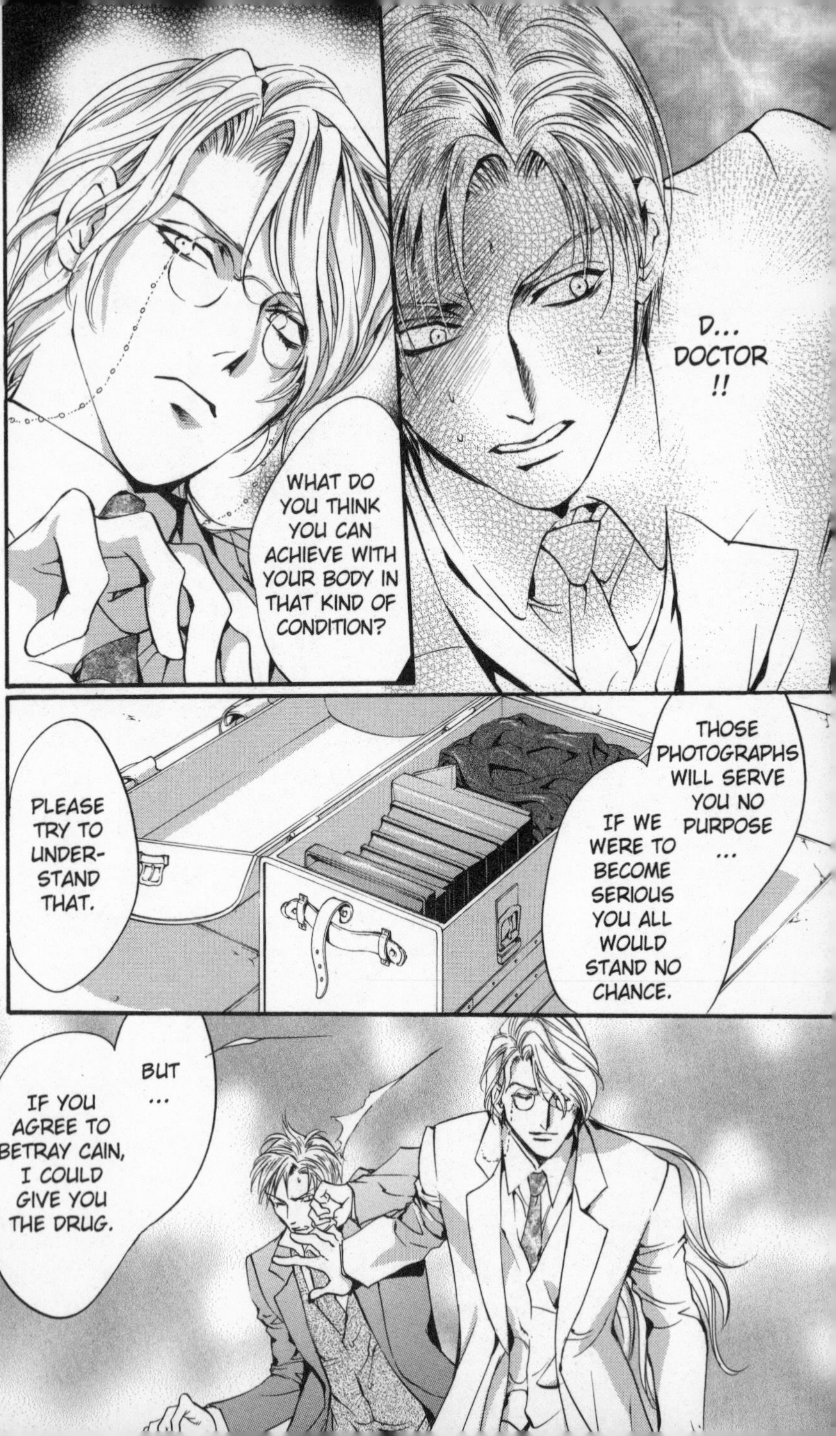
D... DOCTOR !!
WHAT DO YOU THINK YOU CAN ACHIEVE WITH YOUR BODY IN THAT KIND OF CONDITION?
THOSE PHOTOGRAPHS WILL SERVE YOU NO PURPOSE ...
IF WE WERE TO BECOME SERIOUS YOU ALL WOULD STAND NO CHANCE.
PLEASE TRY TO UNDER-STAND THAT.
BUT ...
IF YOU AGREE TO BETRAY CAIN, I COULD GIVE YOU THE DRUG.

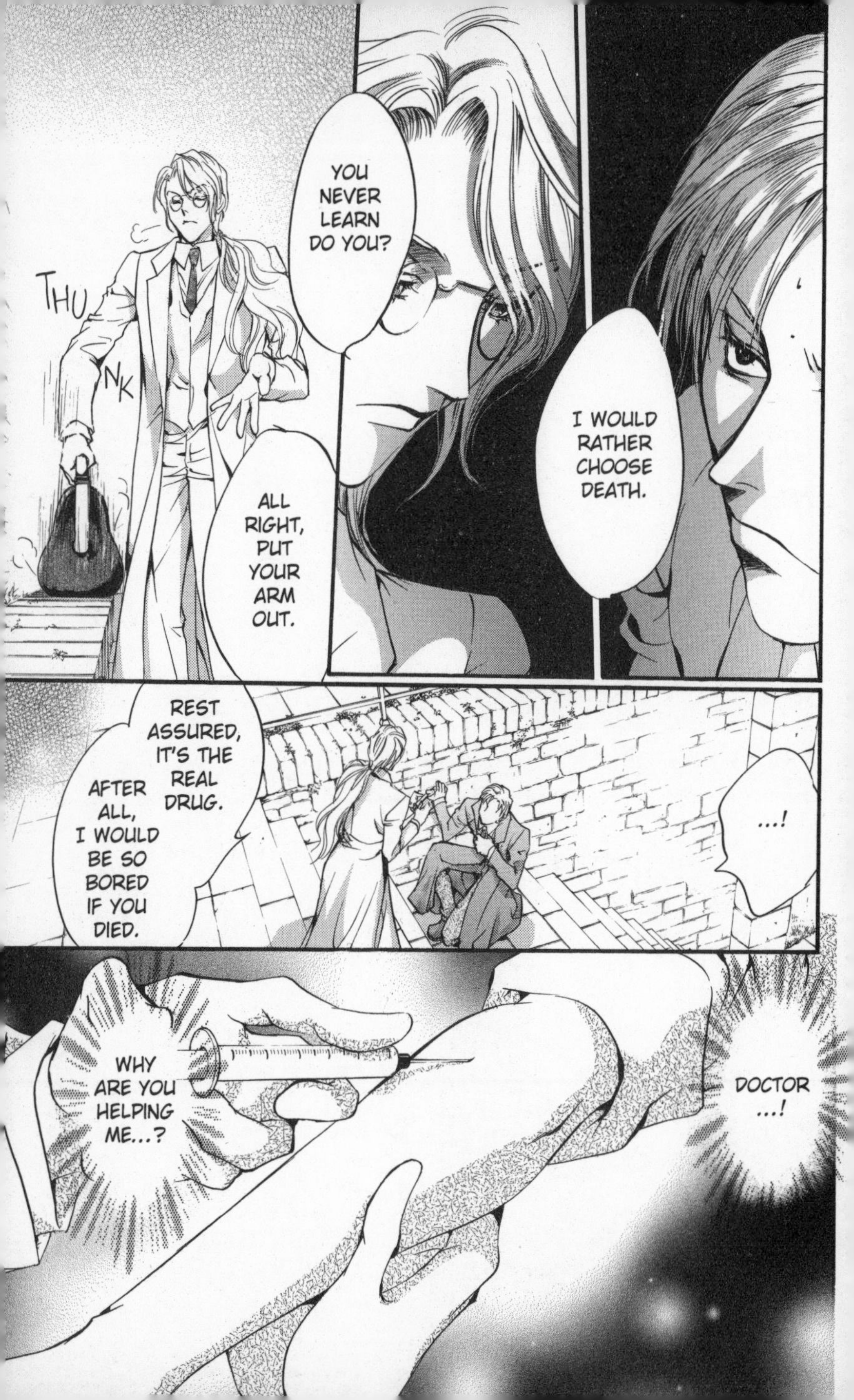
I WOULD RATHER CHOOSE DEATH.
YOU NEVER LEARN DO YOU?
THUNK
ALL RIGHT, PUT YOUR ARM OUT.
...!
REST ASSURED, IT'S THE REAL DRUG.
AFTER ALL, I WOULD BE SO BORED IF YOU DIED.
DOCTOR ...!
WHY ARE YOU HELPING ME...?

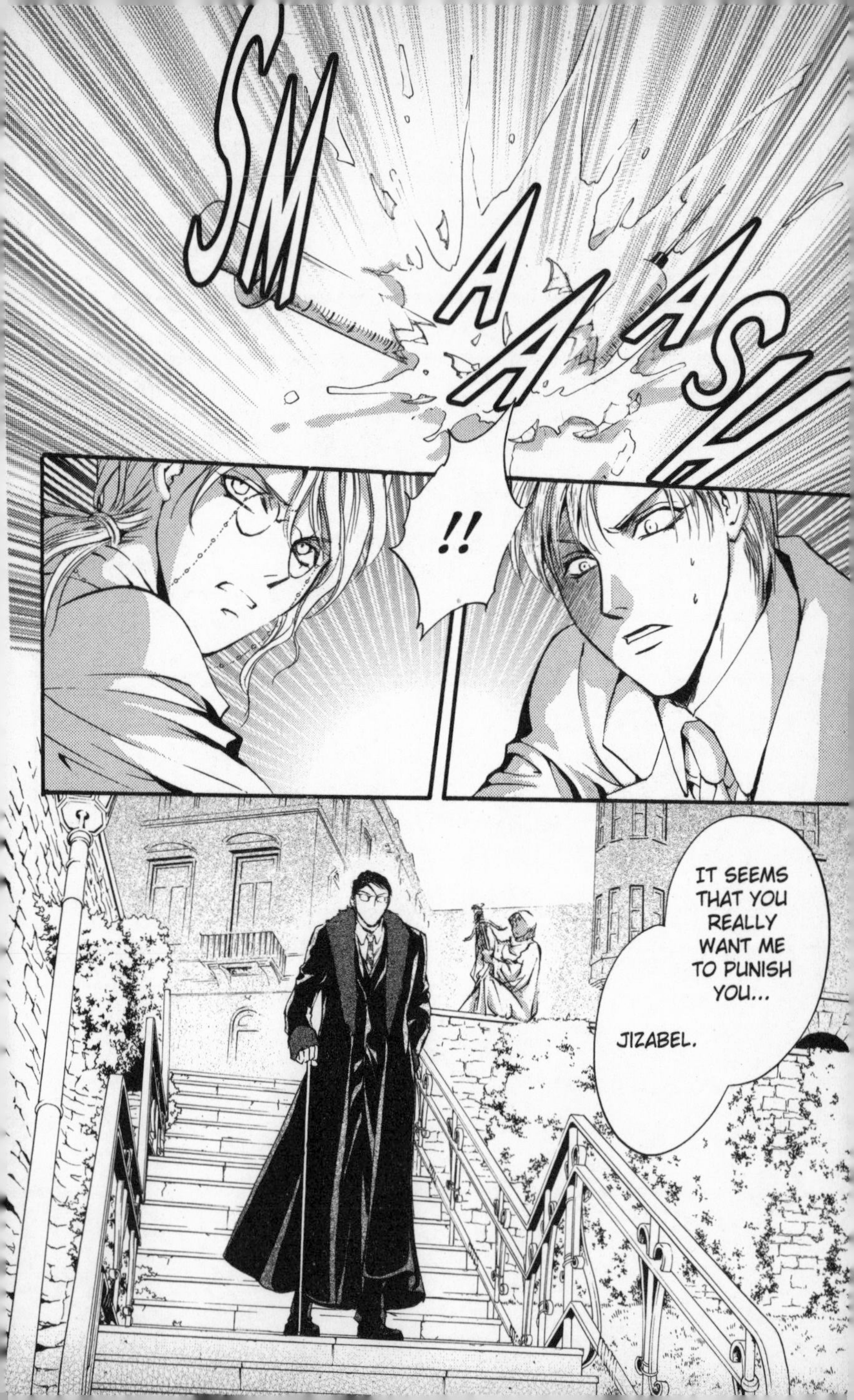
SMAAASH
!!
IT SEEMS THAT YOU REALLY WANT ME TO PUNISH YOU...
JIZABEL.

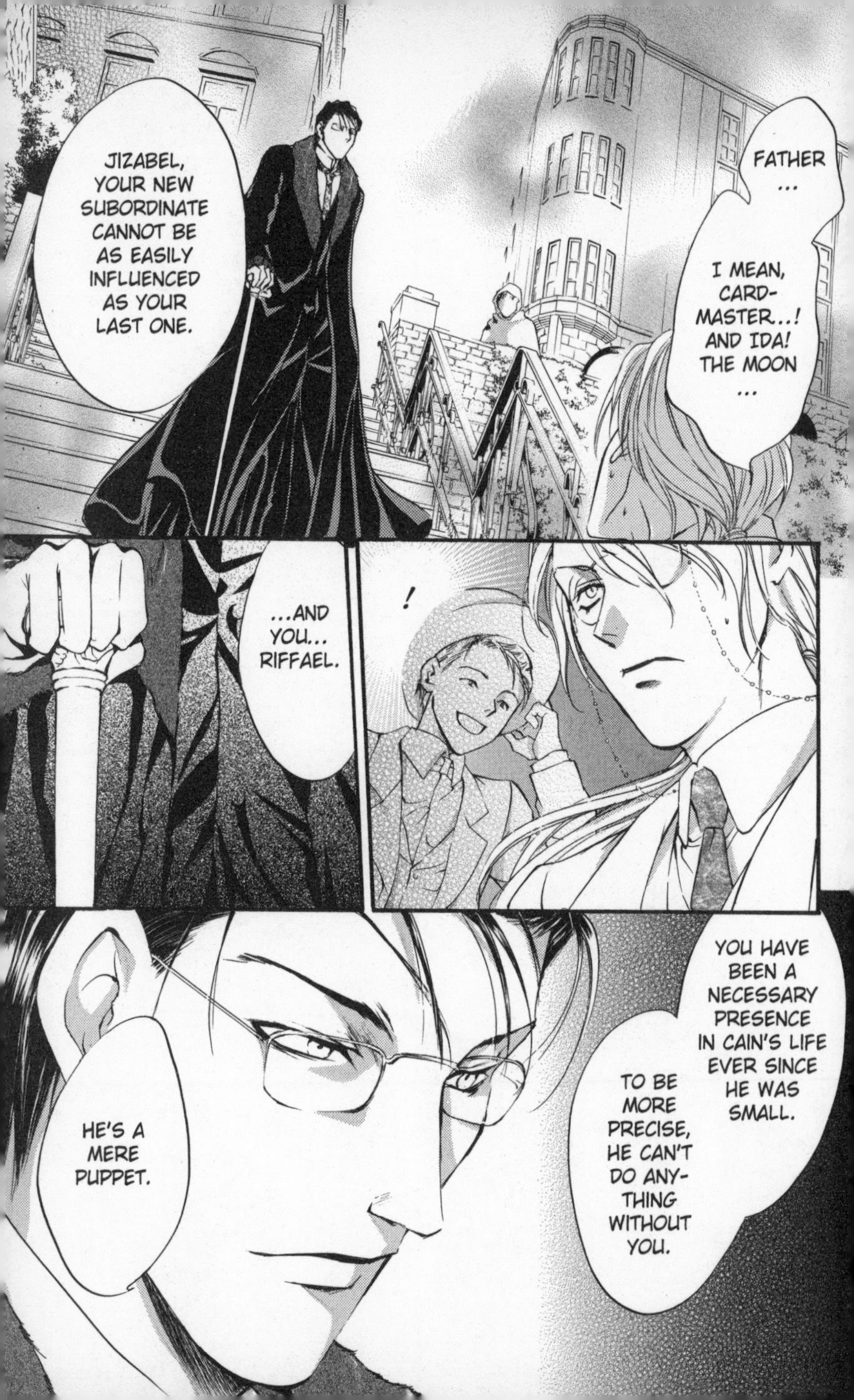
FATHER ...
I MEAN, CARD-MASTER...! AND IDA! THE MOON ...
JIZABEL, YOUR NEW SUBORDINATE CANNOT BE AS EASILY INFLUENCED AS YOUR LAST ONE.
!
...AND YOU... RIFFAEL.
YOU HAVE BEEN A NECESSARY PRESENCE IN CAIN'S LIFE EVER SINCE HE WAS SMALL.
TO BE MORE PRECISE, HE CAN'T DO ANY-THING WITHOUT YOU.
HE'S A MERE PUPPET.

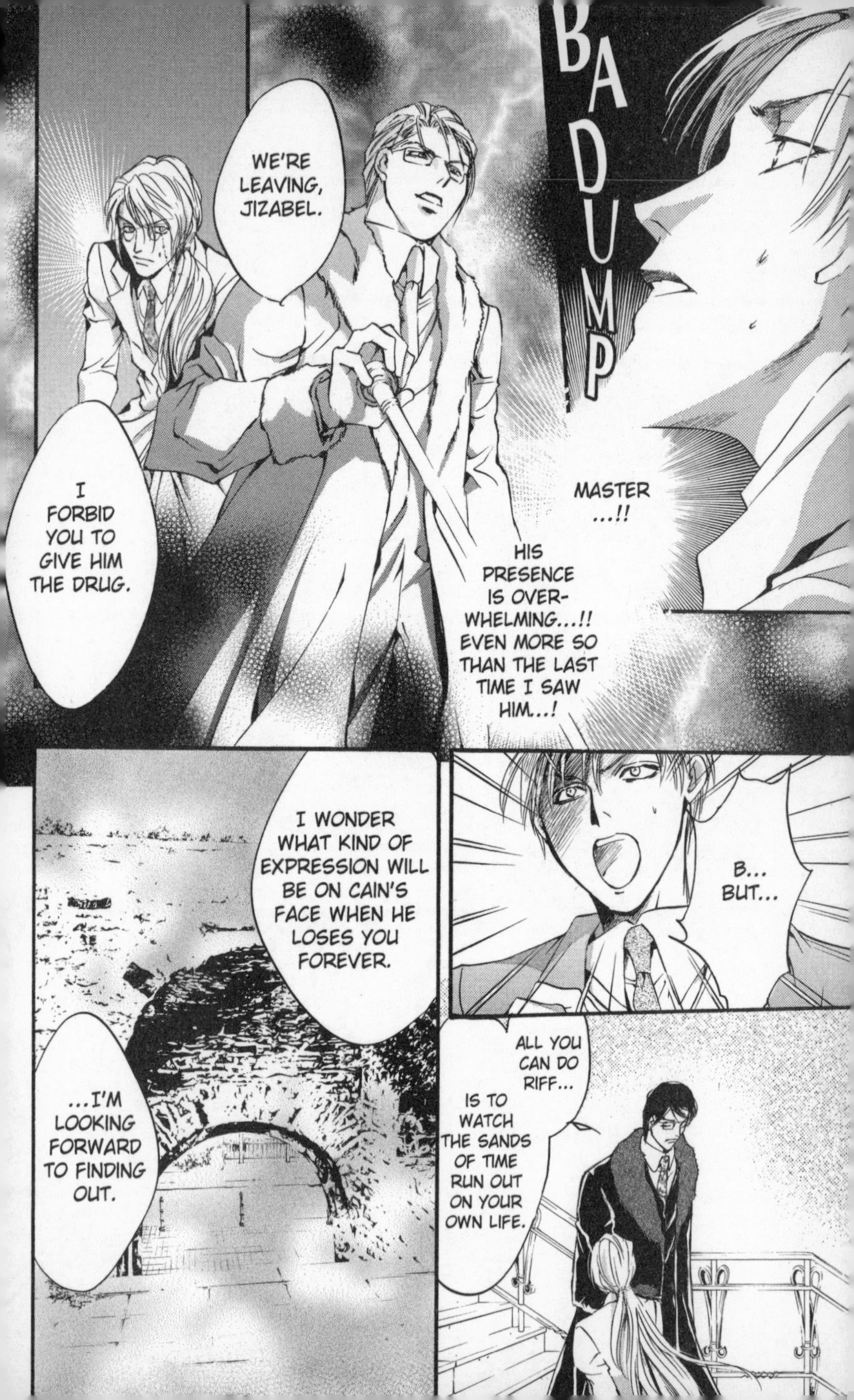
BADUMP
WE'RE LEAVING, JIZABEL.
I FORBID YOU TO GIVE HIM THE DRUG.
MASTER ...!!
HIS PRESENCE IS OVER-WHELMING...!! EVEN MORE SO THAN THE LAST TIME I SAW HIM...!
B... BUT...
ALL YOU CAN DO RIFF...
IS TO WATCH THE SANDS OF TIME RUN OUT ON YOUR OWN LIFE.
I WONDER WHAT KIND OF EXPRESSION WILL BE ON CAIN'S FACE WHEN HE LOSES YOU FOREVER.
...I'M LOOKING FORWARD TO FINDING OUT.

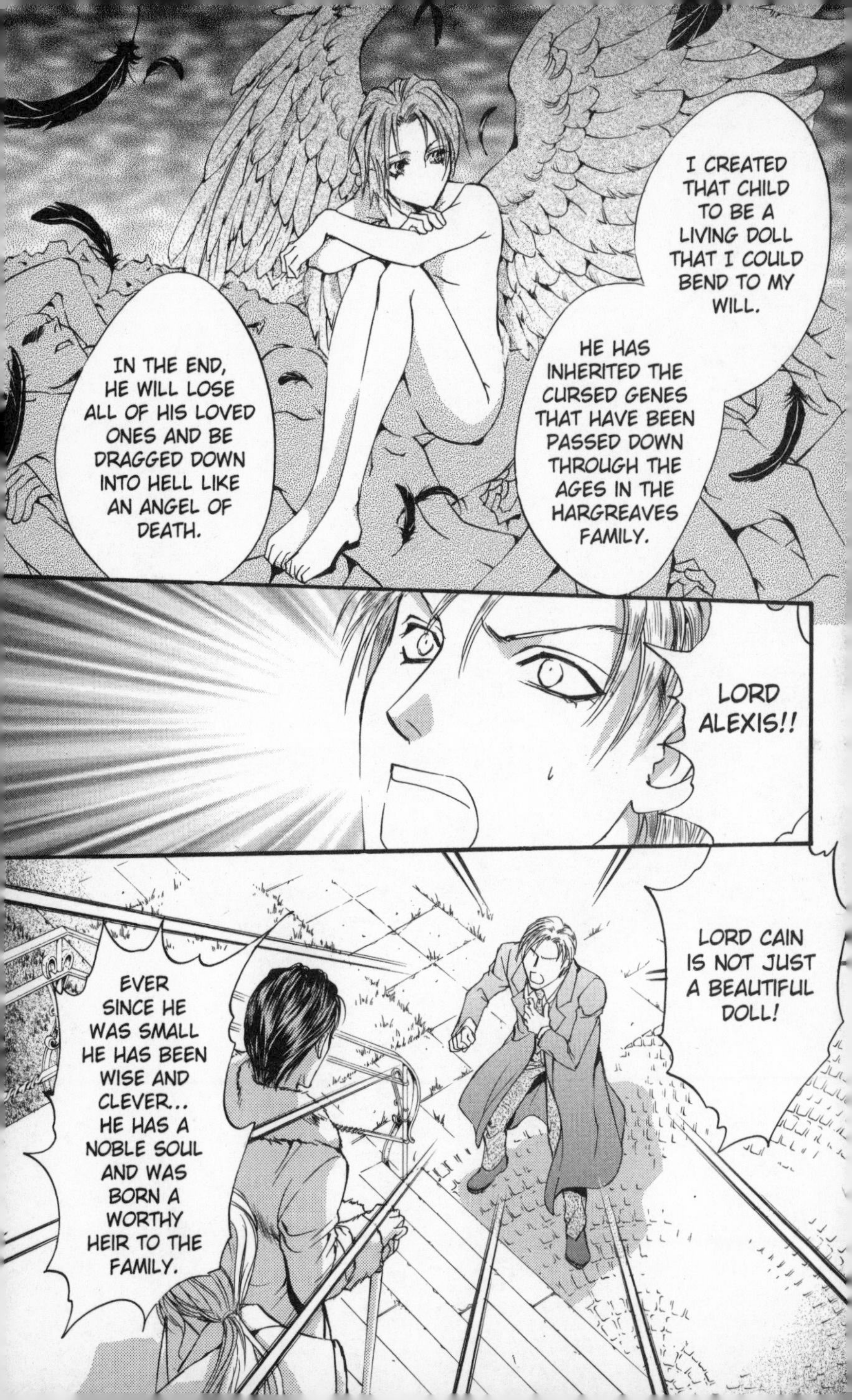
I CREATED THAT CHILD TO BE A LIVING DOLL THAT I COULD BEND TO MY WILL.
HE HAS INHERITED THE CURSED GENES THAT HAVE BEEN PASSED DOWN THROUGH THE AGES IN THE HARGREAVES FAMILY.
IN THE END, HE WILL LOSE ALL OF HIS LOVED ONES AND BE DRAGGED DOWN INTO HELL LIKE AN ANGEL OF DEATH.
LORD ALEXIS!!
LORD CAIN IS NOT JUST A BEAUTIFUL DOLL!
EVER SINCE HE WAS SMALL HE HAS BEEN WISE AND CLEVER... HE HAS A NOBLE SOUL AND WAS BORN A WORTHY HEIR TO THE FAMILY.

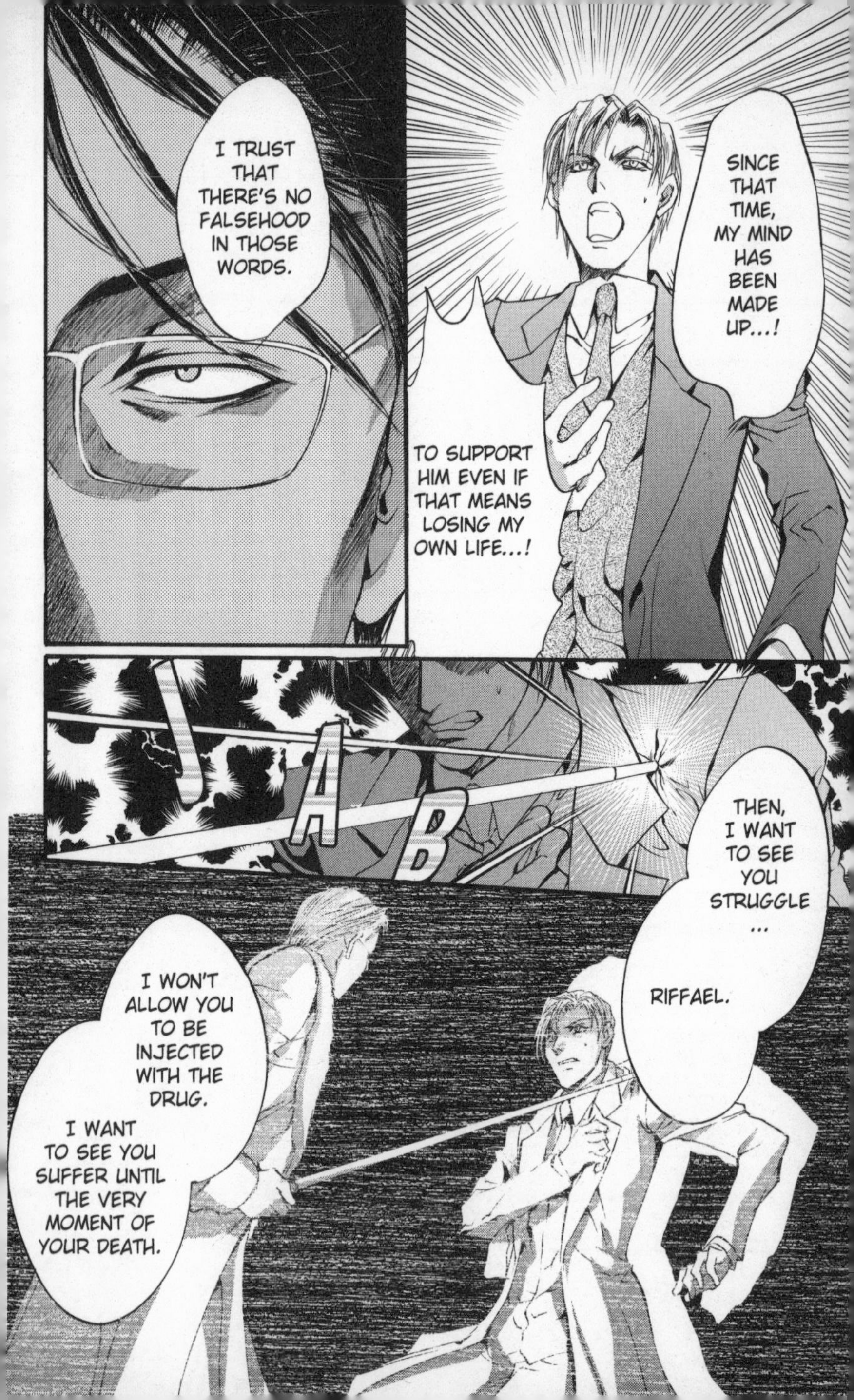
SINCE THAT TIME, MY MIND HAS BEEN MADE UP...!
TO SUPPORT HIM EVEN IF THAT MEANS LOSING MY OWN LIFE...!
I TRUST THAT THERE'S NO FALSEHOOD IN THOSE WORDS.
JAB
THEN, I WANT TO SEE YOU STRUGGLE ...
RIFFAEL.
I WON'T ALLOW YOU TO BE INJECTED WITH THE DRUG.
I WANT TO SEE YOU SUFFER UNTIL THE VERY MOMENT OF YOUR DEATH.

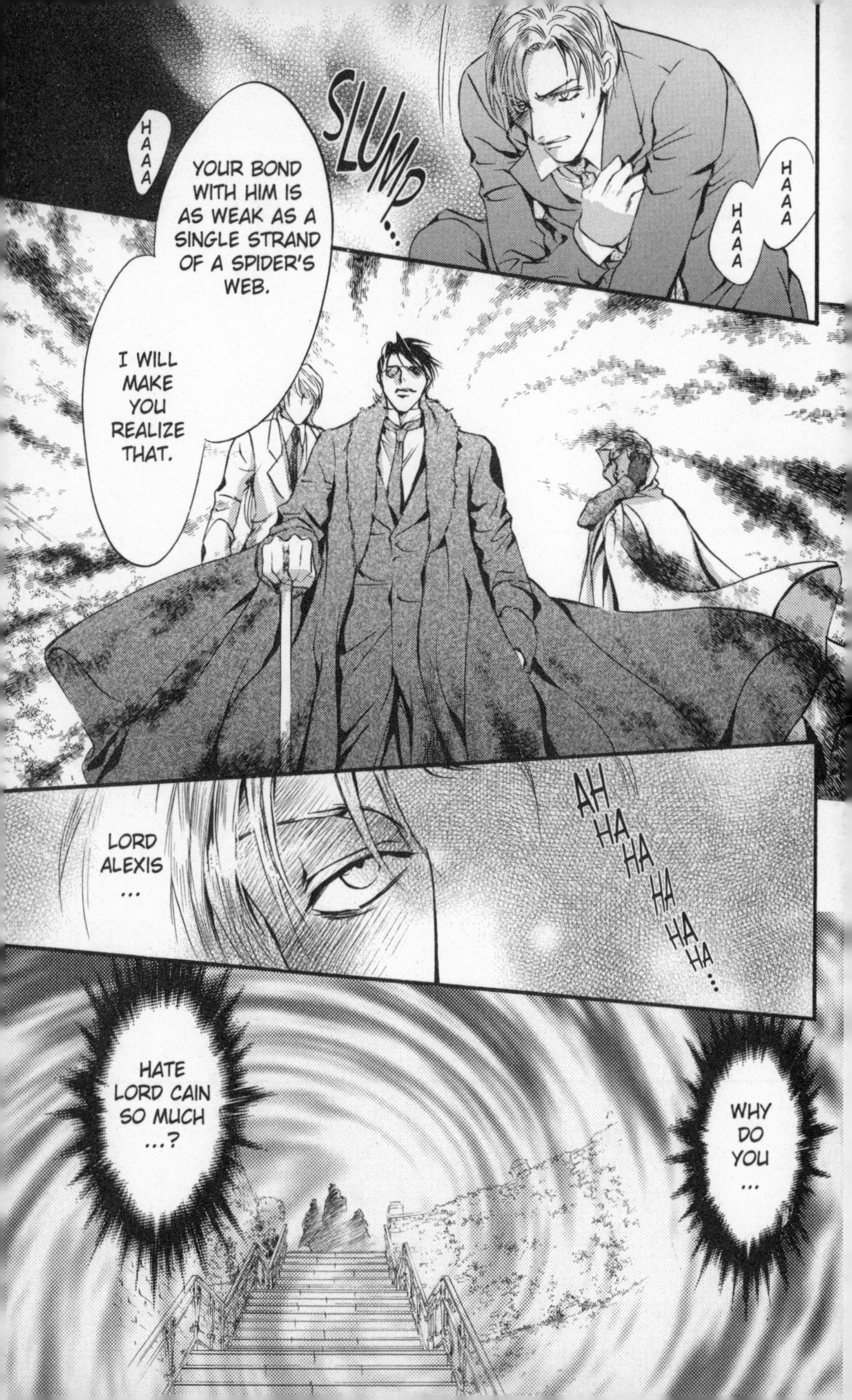
HAAA
HAAA
SLUMP...
HAAA
YOUR BOND WITH HIM IS AS WEAK AS A SINGLE STRAND OF A SPIDER'S WEB.
I WILL MAKE YOU REALIZE THAT.
AH HA HA HA HA HA HA...
LORD ALEXIS ...
WHY DO YOU ...
HATE LORD CAIN SO MUCH ...?

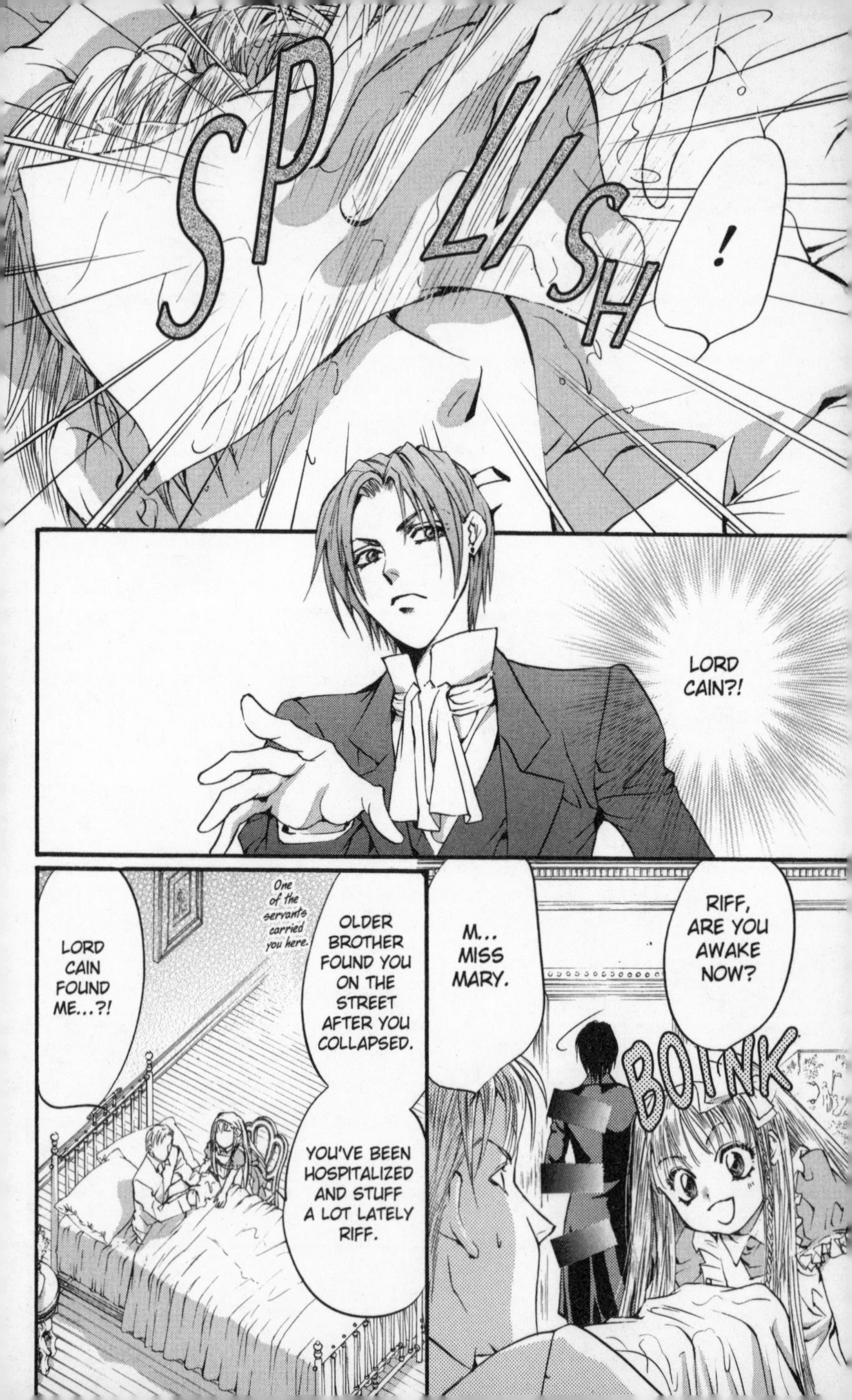
SPLISH
!
LORD CAIN?!
RIFF, ARE YOU AWAKE NOW?
BOINK
M... MISS MARY.
OLDER BROTHER FOUND YOU ON THE STREET AFTER YOU COLLAPSED.
One of the servants carried you here.
LORD CAIN FOUND ME...?!
YOU'VE BEEN HOSPITALIZED AND STUFF A LOT LATELY RIFF.

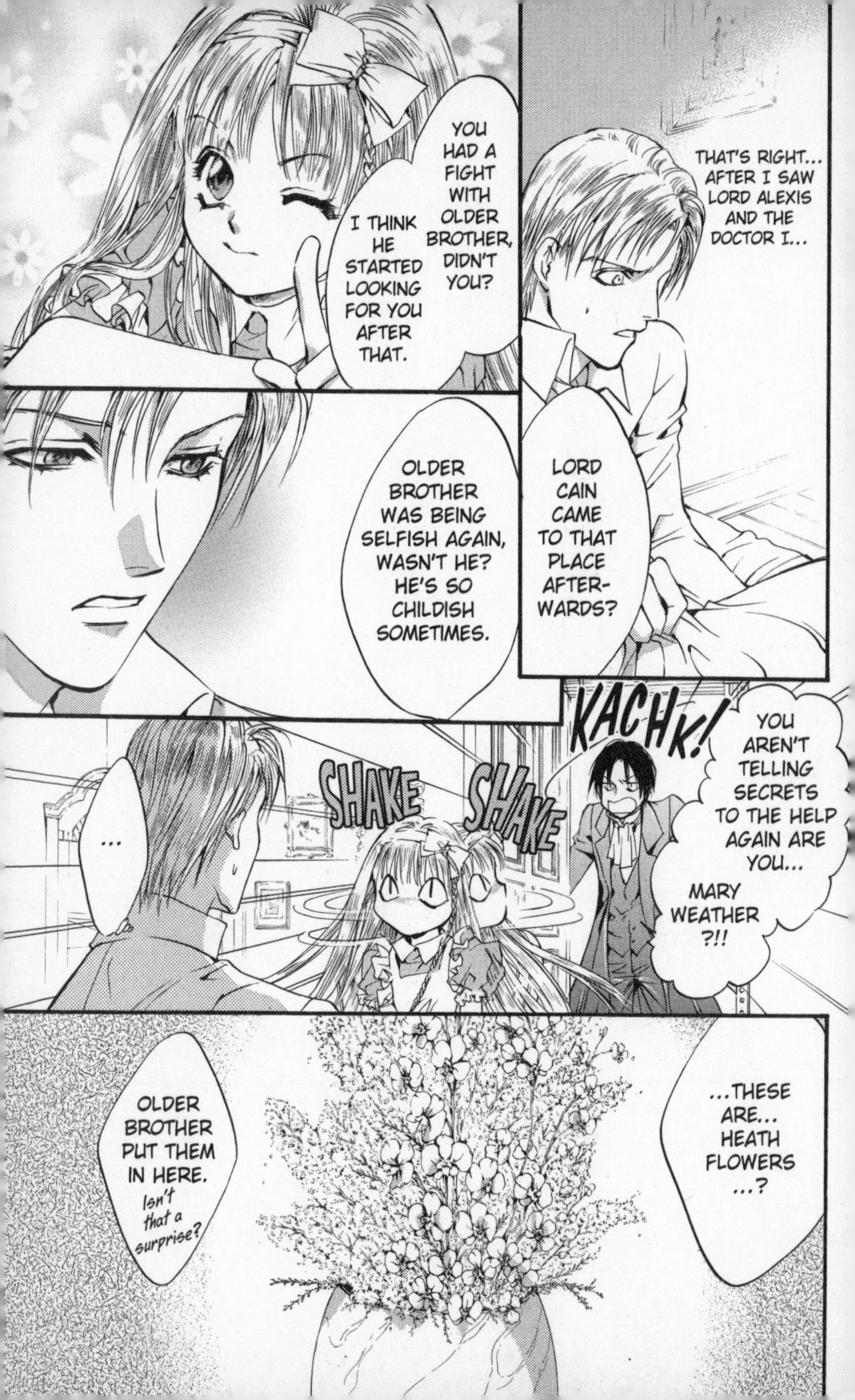
THAT'S RIGHT... AFTER I SAW LORD ALEXIS AND THE DOCTOR I...
LORD CAIN CAME TO THAT PLACE AFTER-WARDS?
YOU HAD A FIGHT WITH OLDER BROTHER, DIDN'T YOU?
I THINK HE STARTED LOOKING FOR YOU AFTER THAT.
OLDER BROTHER WAS BEING SELFISH AGAIN, WASN'T HE? HE'S SO CHILDISH SOMETIMES.
KACHK!
YOU AREN'T TELLING SECRETS TO THE HELP AGAIN ARE YOU...
MARY WEATHER ?!!
SHAKE
SHAKE
...
...THESE ARE... HEATH FLOWERS ...?
OLDER BROTHER PUT THEM IN HERE.
Isn't that a surprise?

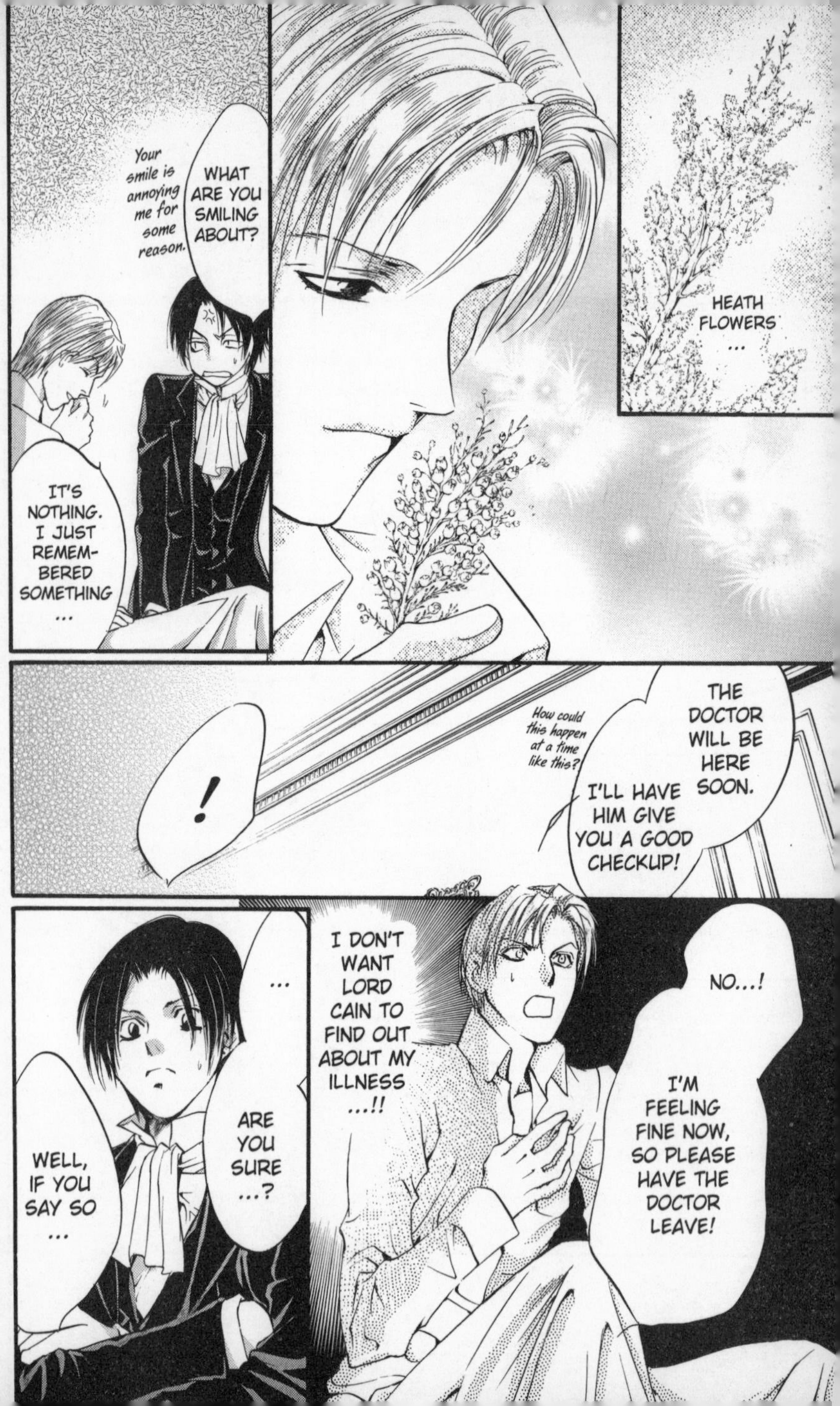
HEATH FLOWERS ...
WHAT ARE YOU SMILING ABOUT?
Your smile is annoying me for some reason.
IT'S NOTHING. I JUST REMEMBERED SOMETHING ...
THE DOCTOR WILL BE HERE SOON.
I'LL HAVE HIM GIVE YOU A GOOD CHECKUP!
How could this happen at a time like this?
!
NO...!
I'M FEELING FINE NOW, SO PLEASE HAVE THE DOCTOR LEAVE!
I DON'T WANT LORD CAIN TO FIND OUT ABOUT MY ILLNESS ...!!
...
ARE YOU SURE ...?
WELL, IF YOU SAY SO ...

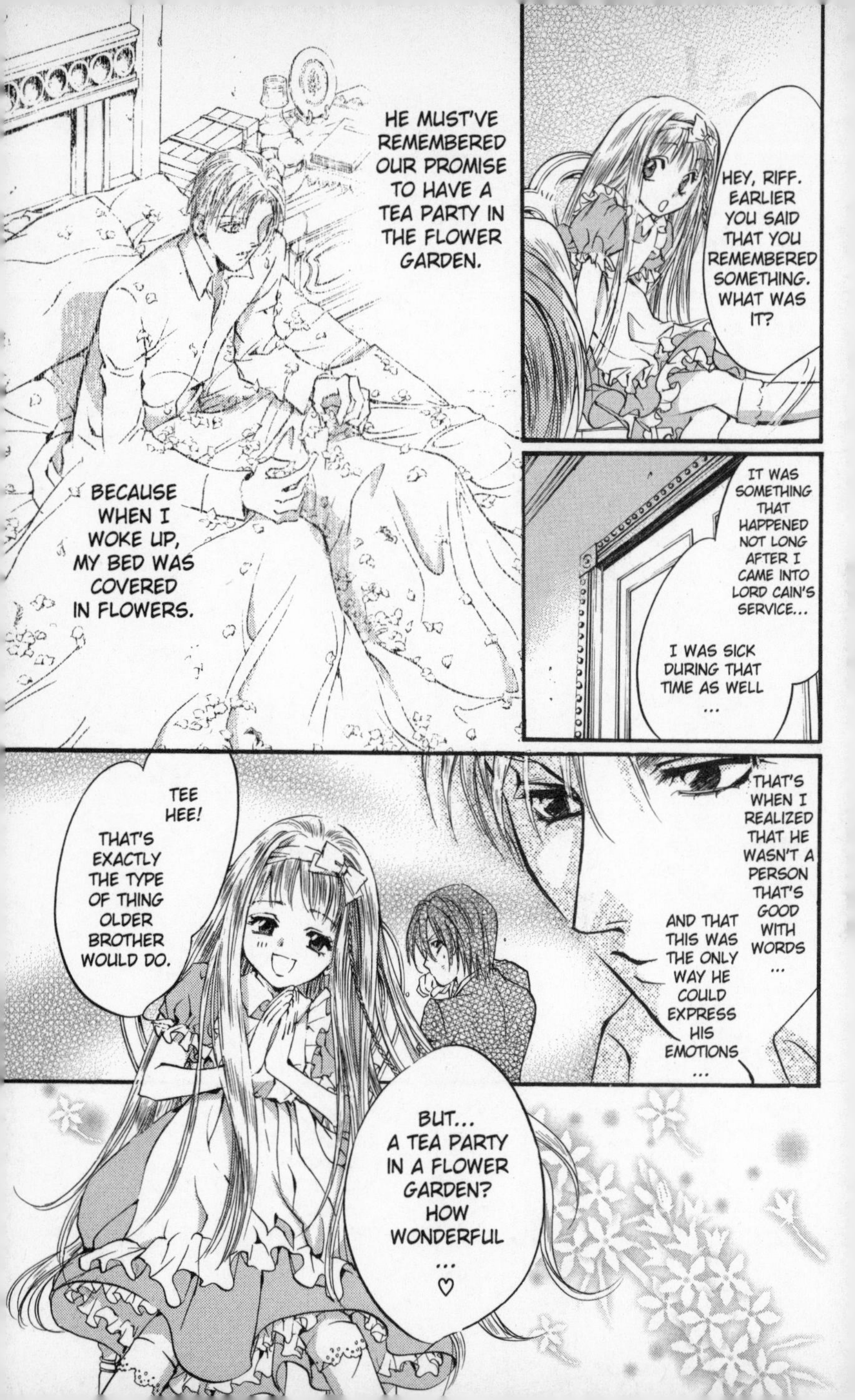
HEY, RIFF. EARLIER YOU SAID THAT YOU REMEMBERED SOMETHING. WHAT WAS IT?
IT WAS SOMETHING THAT HAPPENED NOT LONG AFTER I CAME INTO LORD CAIN'S SERVICE...
I WAS SICK DURING THAT TIME AS WELL...
HE MUST'VE REMEMBERED OUR PROMISE TO HAVE A TEA PARTY IN THE FLOWER GARDEN.
BECAUSE WHEN I WOKE UP, MY BED WAS COVERED IN FLOWERS.
THAT'S WHEN I REALIZED THAT HE WASN'T A PERSON THAT'S GOOD WITH WORDS...
AND THAT THIS WAS THE ONLY WAY HE COULD EXPRESS HIS EMOTIONS...
TEE HEE!
THAT'S EXACTLY THE TYPE OF THING OLDER BROTHER WOULD DO.
BUT... A TEA PARTY IN A FLOWER GARDEN? HOW WONDERFUL... ♡

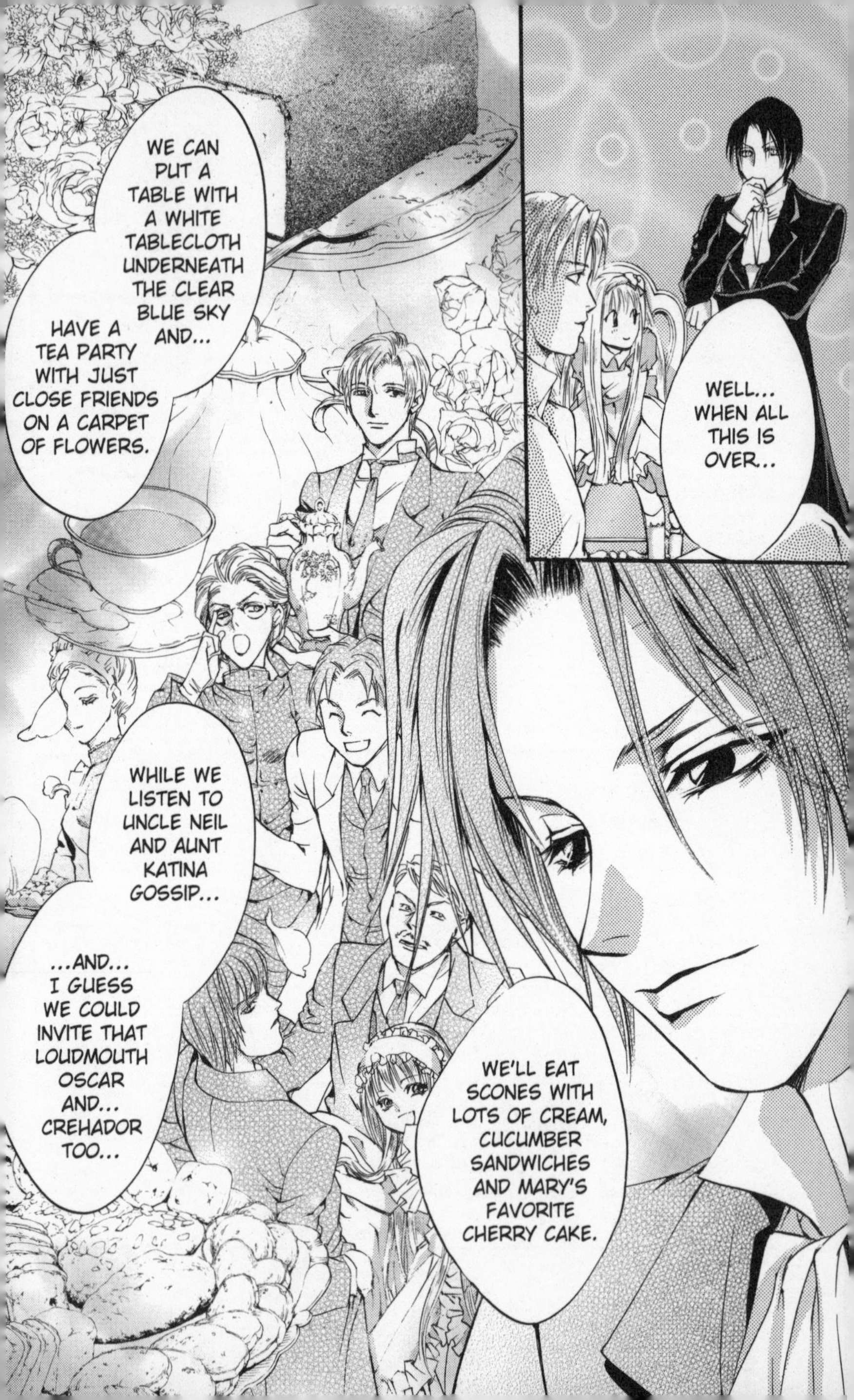
WELL... WHEN ALL THIS IS OVER...
WE CAN PUT A TABLE WITH A WHITE TABLECLOTH UNDERNEATH THE CLEAR BLUE SKY AND...
HAVE A TEA PARTY WITH JUST CLOSE FRIENDS ON A CARPET OF FLOWERS.
WE'LL EAT SCONES WITH LOTS OF CREAM, CUCUMBER SANDWICHES AND MARY'S FAVORITE CHERRY CAKE.
WHILE WE LISTEN TO UNCLE NEIL AND AUNT KATINA GOSSIP...
...AND... I GUESS WE COULD INVITE THAT LOUDMOUTH OSCAR AND... CREHADOR TOO...

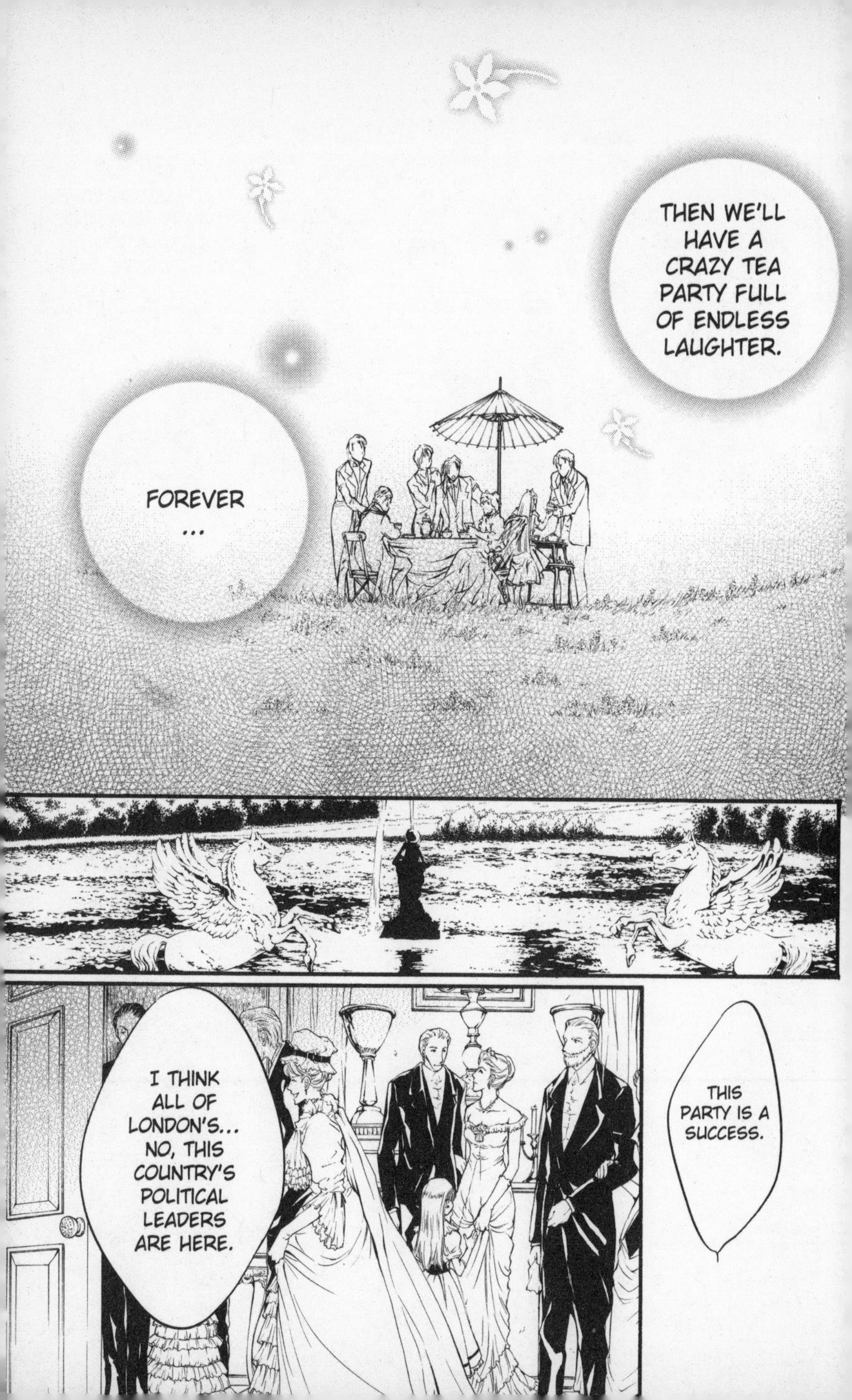
THEN WE'LL HAVE A CRAZY TEA PARTY FULL OF ENDLESS LAUGHTER.
FOREVER ...
THIS PARTY IS A SUCCESS.
I THINK ALL OF LONDON'S... NO, THIS COUNTRY'S POLITICAL LEADERS ARE HERE.

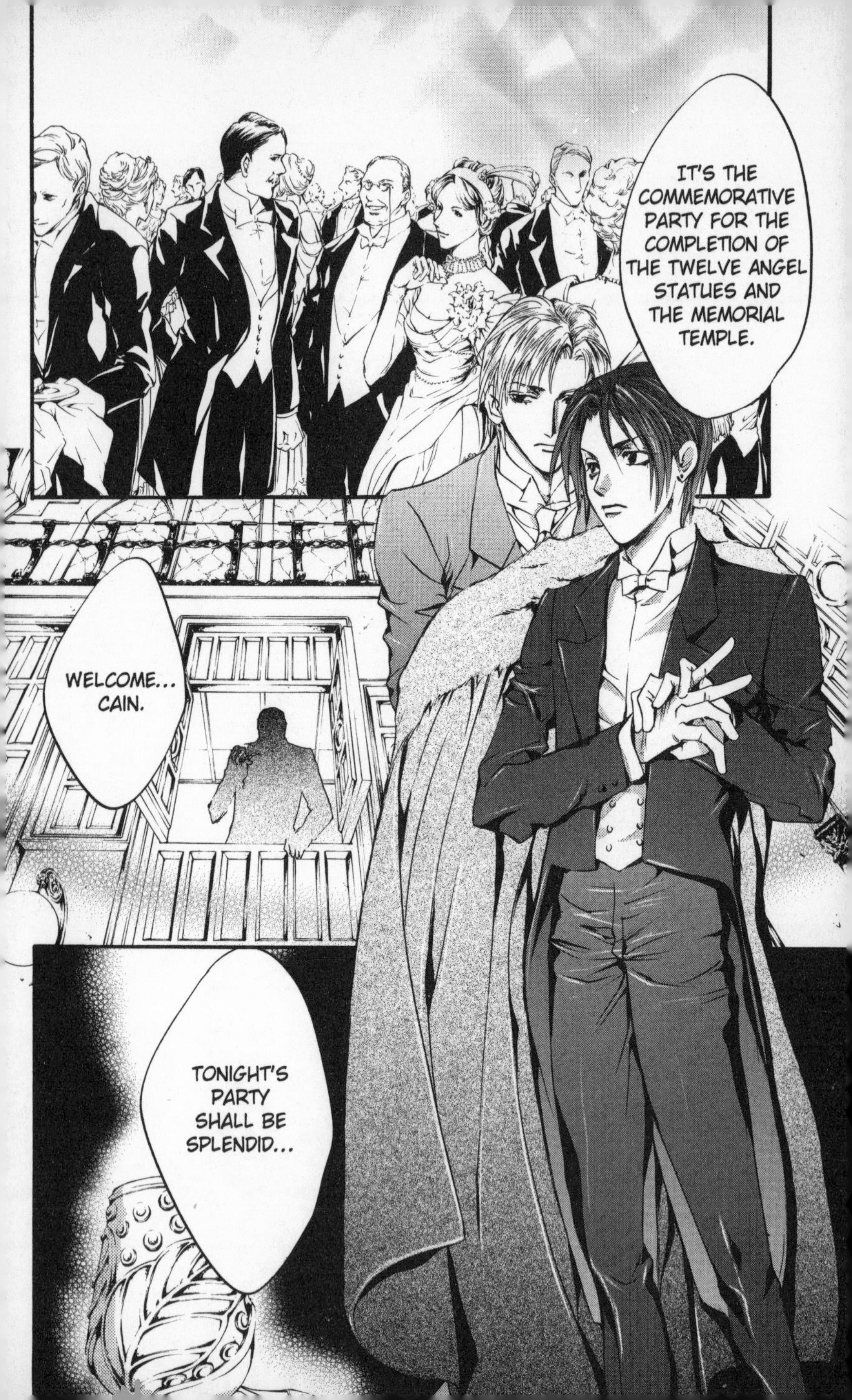
IT'S THE COMMEMORATIVE PARTY FOR THE COMPLETION OF THE TWELVE ANGEL STATUES AND THE MEMORIAL TEMPLE.
WELCOME... CAIN.
TONIGHT'S PARTY SHALL BE SPLENDID...

Judas Kiss
Scene 4

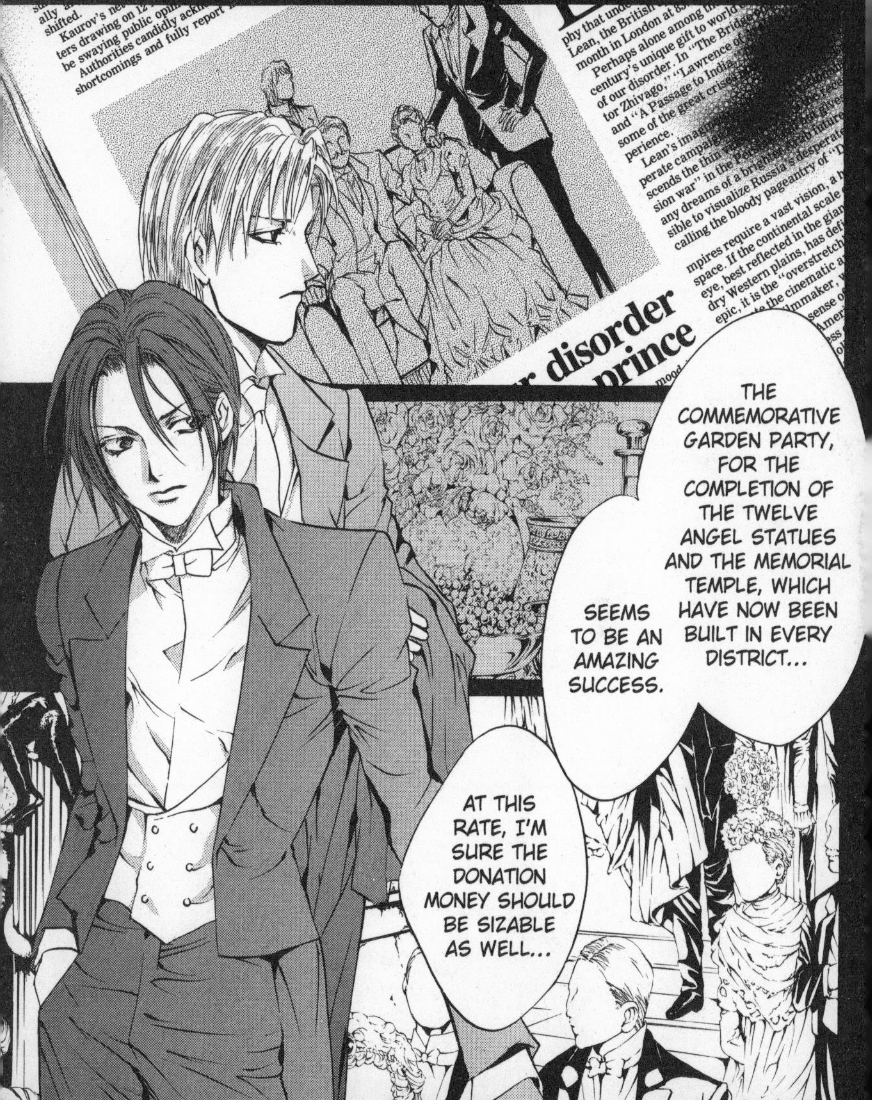
THE COMMEMORATIVE GARDEN PARTY, FOR THE COMPLETION OF THE TWELVE ANGEL STATUES AND THE MEMORIAL TEMPLE, WHICH HAVE NOW BEEN BUILT IN EVERY DISTRICT...
SEEMS TO BE AN AMAZING SUCCESS.
AT THIS RATE, I'M SURE THE DONATION MONEY SHOULD BE SIZABLE AS WELL...

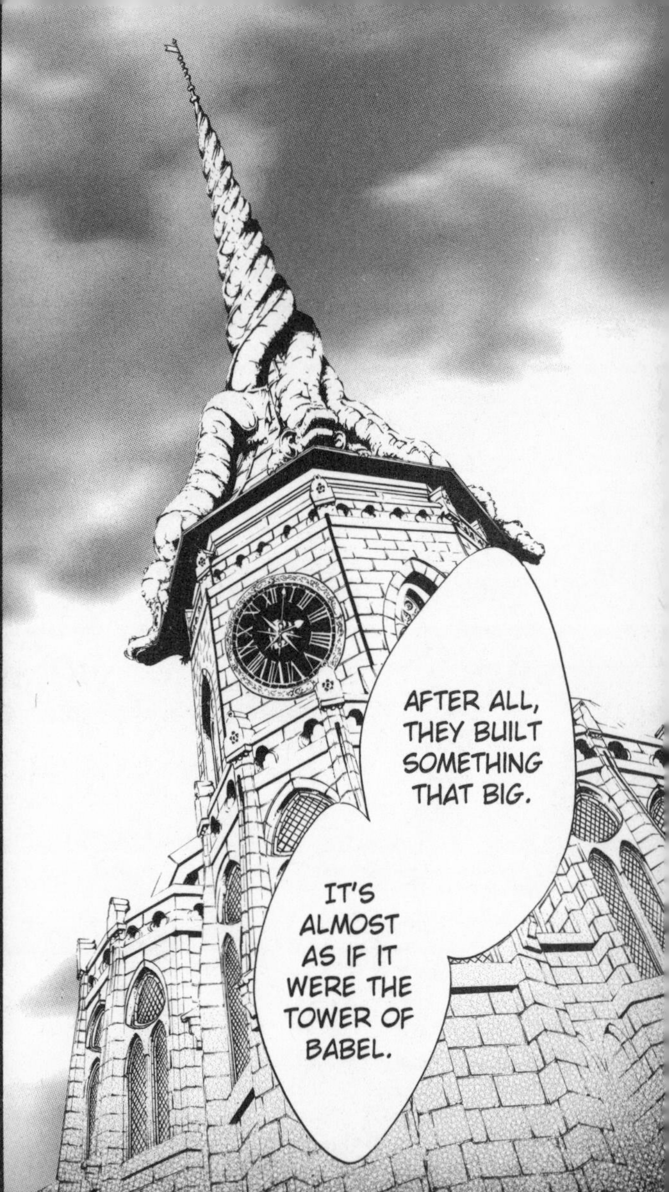
AFTER ALL, THEY BUILT SOMETHING THAT BIG.
IT'S ALMOST AS IF IT WERE THE TOWER OF BABEL.

Judas Kiss

Scene 4

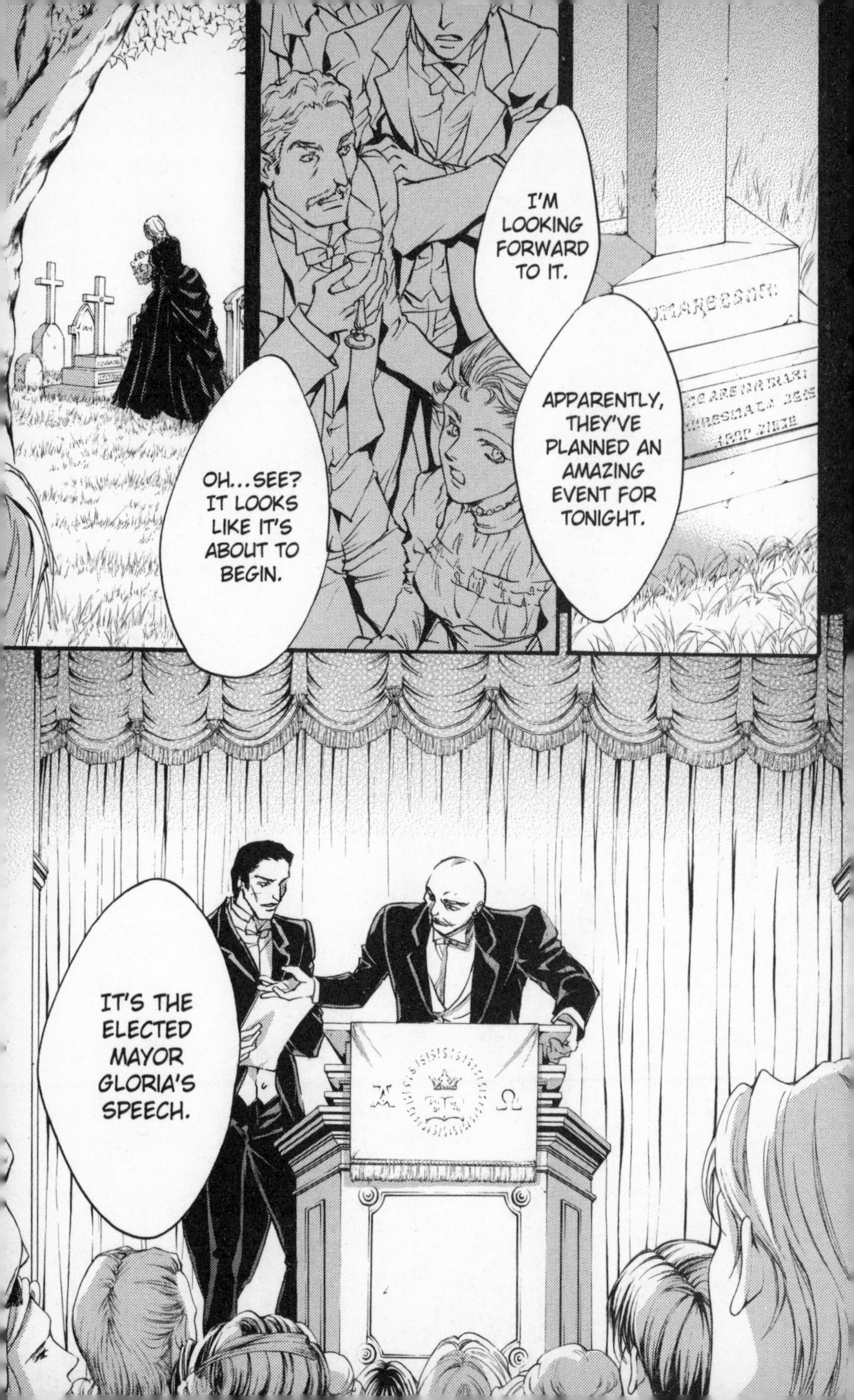
I'M LOOKING FORWARD TO IT.
APPARENTLY, THEY'VE PLANNED AN AMAZING EVENT FOR TONIGHT.
OH...SEE? IT LOOKS LIKE IT'S ABOUT TO BEGIN.
IT'S THE ELECTED MAYOR GLORIA'S SPEECH.

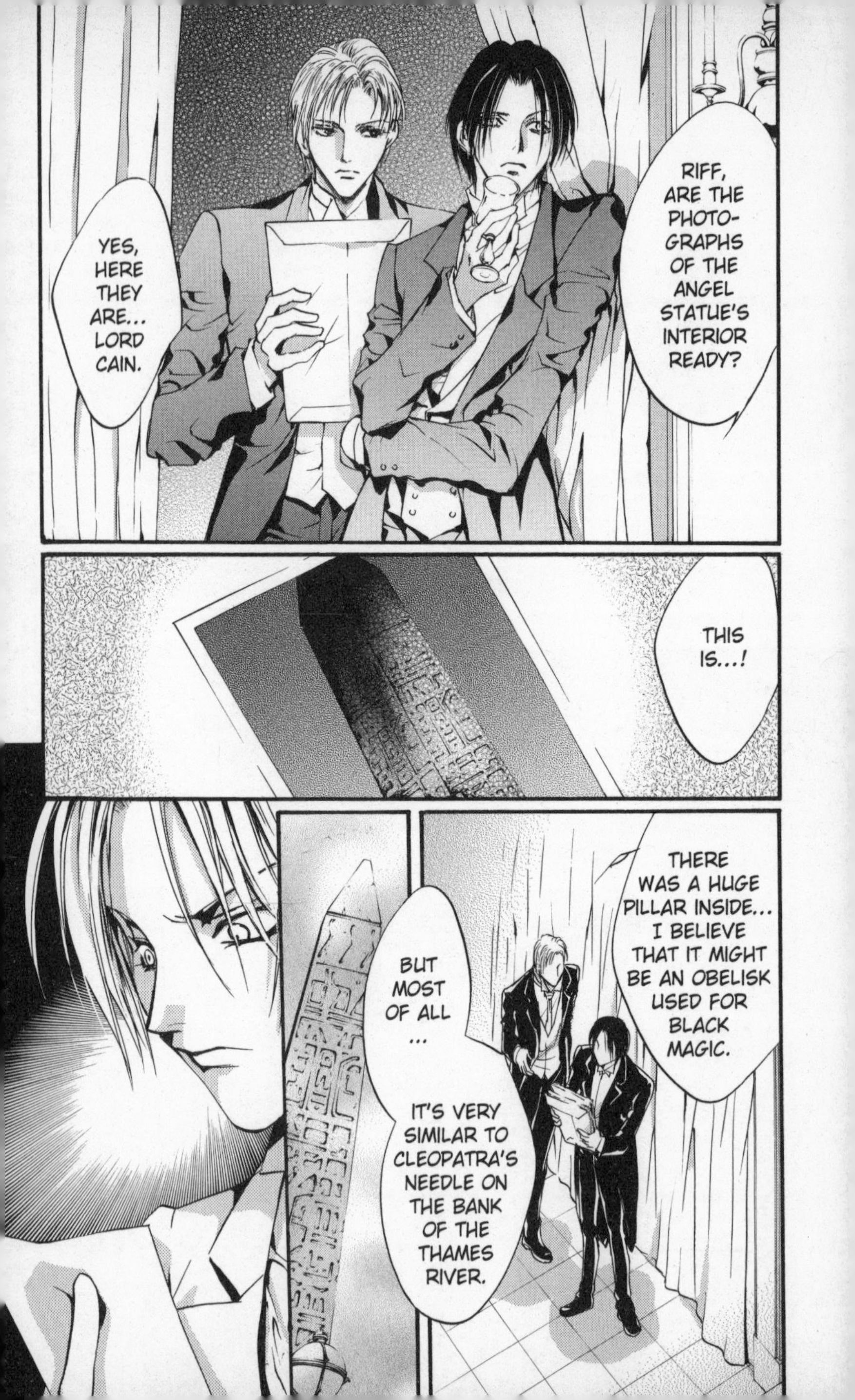
RIFF, ARE THE PHOTOGRAPHS OF THE ANGEL STATUE'S INTERIOR READY?
YES, HERE THEY ARE... LORD CAIN.
THIS IS...!
THERE WAS A HUGE PILLAR INSIDE... I BELIEVE THAT IT MIGHT BE AN OBELISK USED FOR BLACK MAGIC.
BUT MOST OF ALL ...
IT'S VERY SIMILAR TO CLEOPATRA'S NEEDLE ON THE BANK OF THE THAMES RIVER.

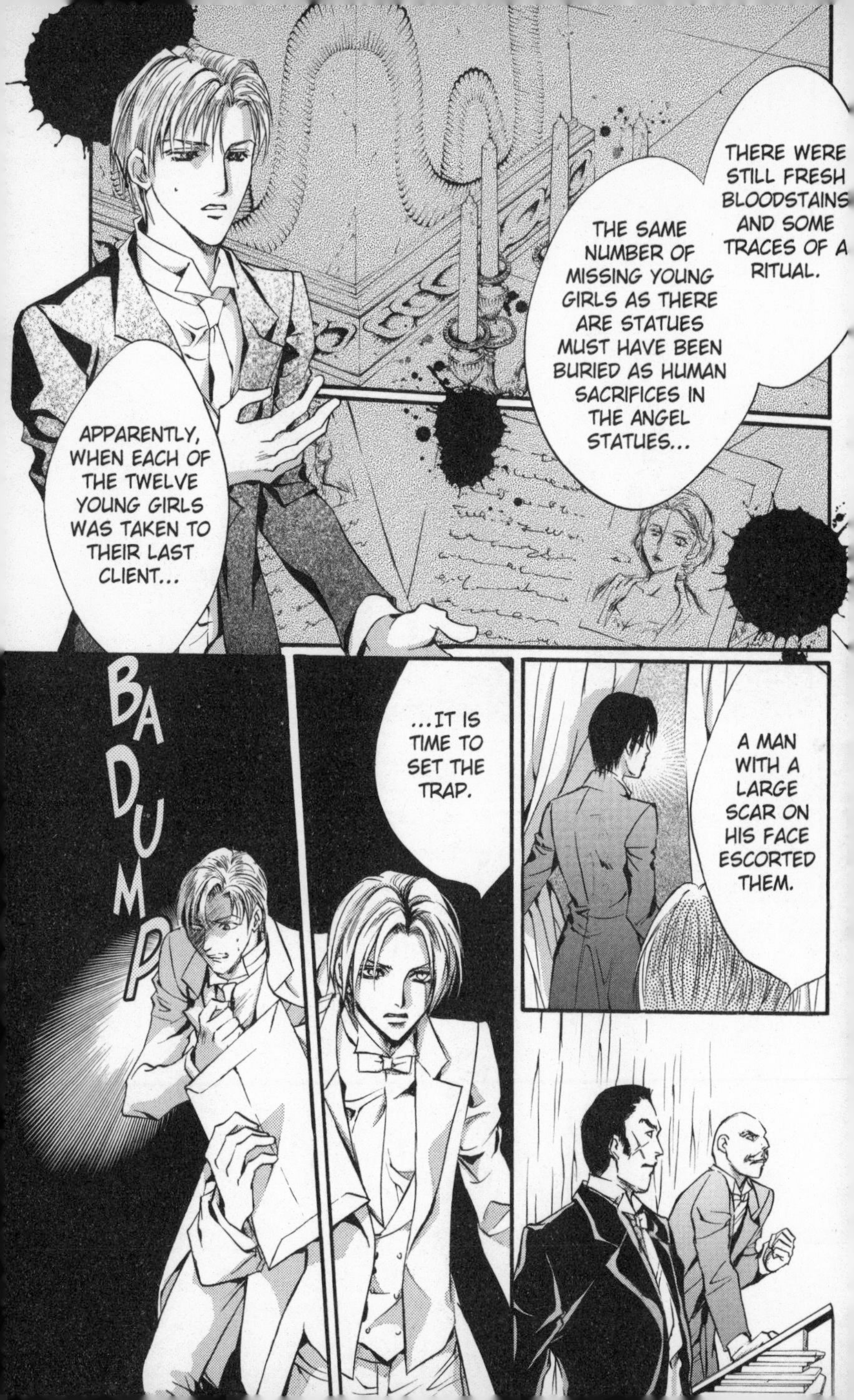
THERE WERE STILL FRESH BLOODSTAINS AND SOME TRACES OF A RITUAL.
THE SAME NUMBER OF MISSING YOUNG GIRLS AS THERE ARE STATUES MUST HAVE BEEN BURIED AS HUMAN SACRIFICES IN THE ANGEL STATUES...
APPARENTLY, WHEN EACH OF THE TWELVE YOUNG GIRLS WAS TAKEN TO THEIR LAST CLIENT...
A MAN WITH A LARGE SCAR ON HIS FACE ESCORTED THEM.
...IT IS TIME TO SET THE TRAP.
BADUMP

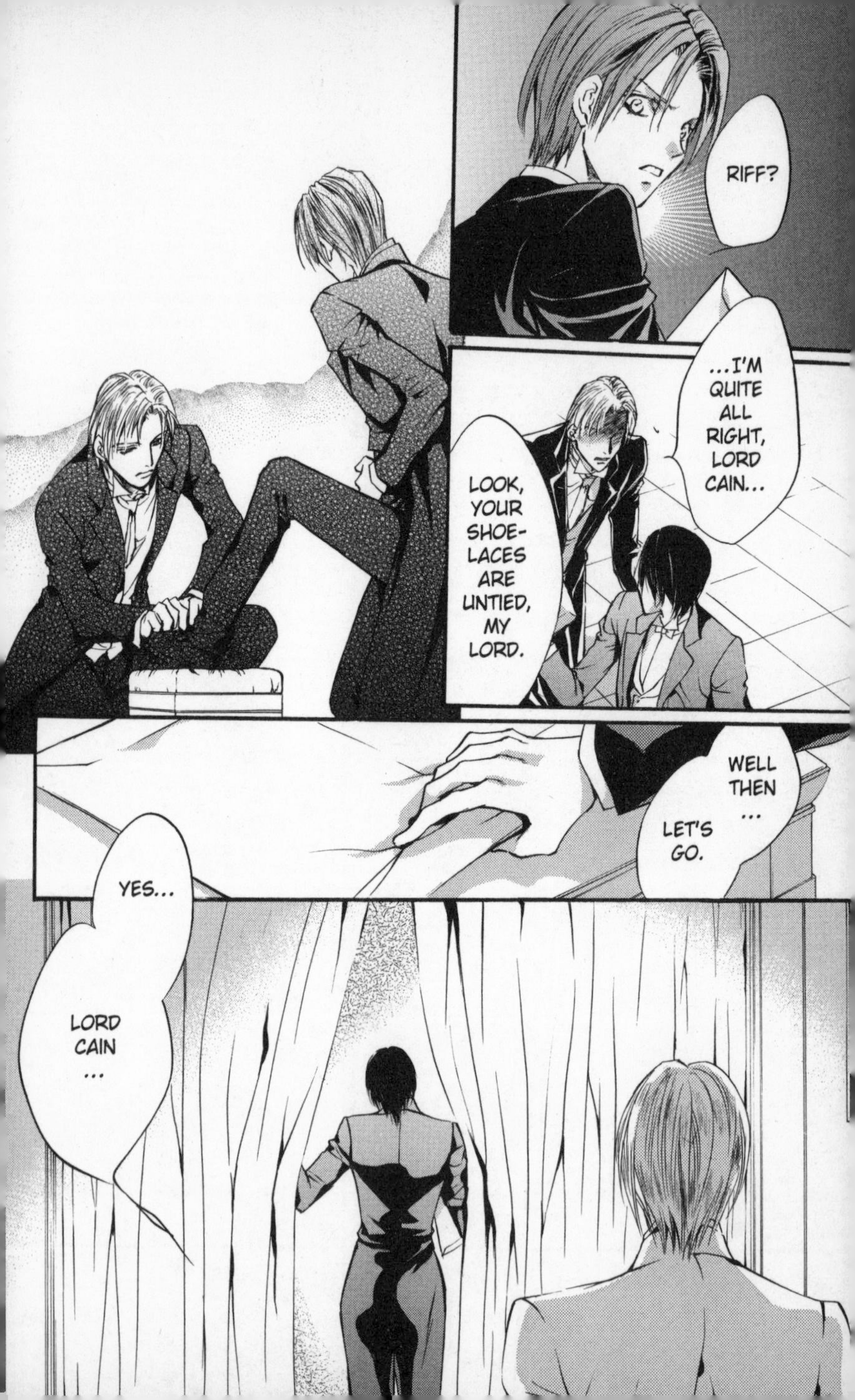
RIFF?
...I'M QUITE ALL RIGHT, LORD CAIN...
LOOK, YOUR SHOE-LACES ARE UNTIED, MY LORD.
WELL THEN ... LET'S GO.
YES...
LORD CAIN ...

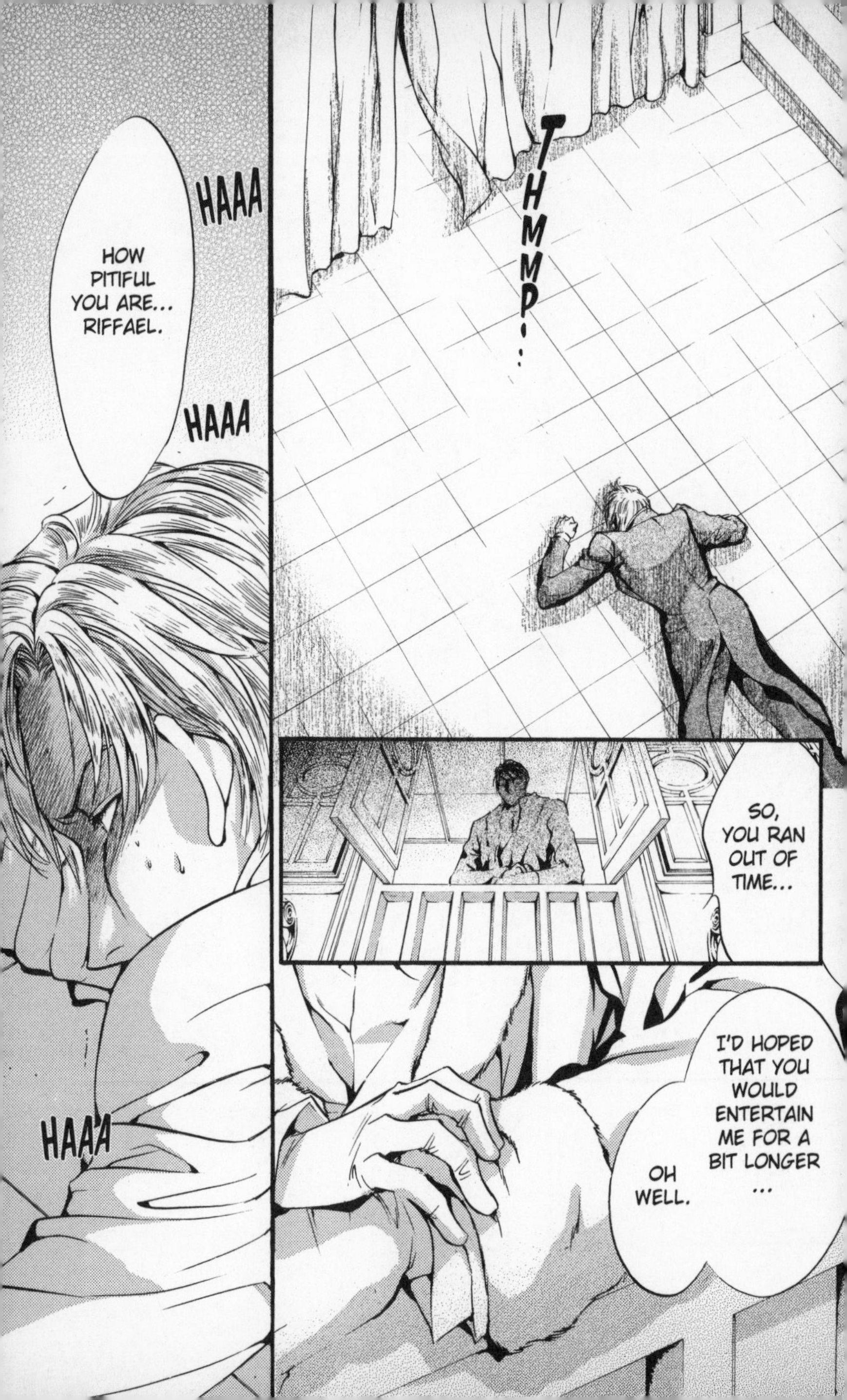
THMMP...
SO, YOU RAN OUT OF TIME...
I'D HOPED THAT YOU WOULD ENTERTAIN ME FOR A BIT LONGER...
OH WELL.
HAAA
HOW PITIFUL YOU ARE... RIFFAEL.
HAAA
HAAA

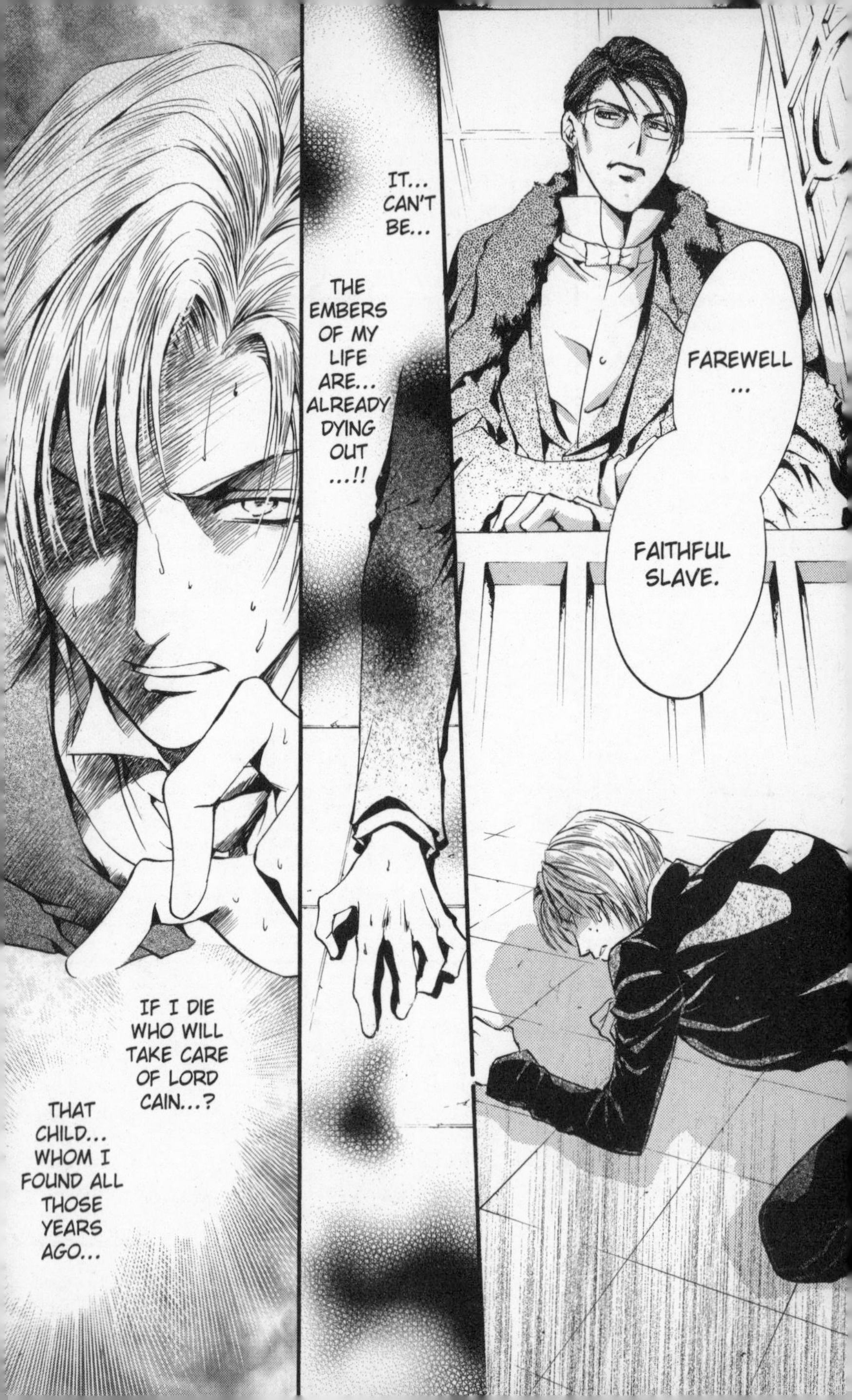
FAREWELL ...
FAITHFUL SLAVE.
IT... CAN'T BE...
THE EMBERS OF MY LIFE ARE... ALREADY DYING OUT ...!!
IF I DIE WHO WILL TAKE CARE OF LORD CAIN...?
THAT CHILD... WHOM I FOUND ALL THOSE YEARS AGO...

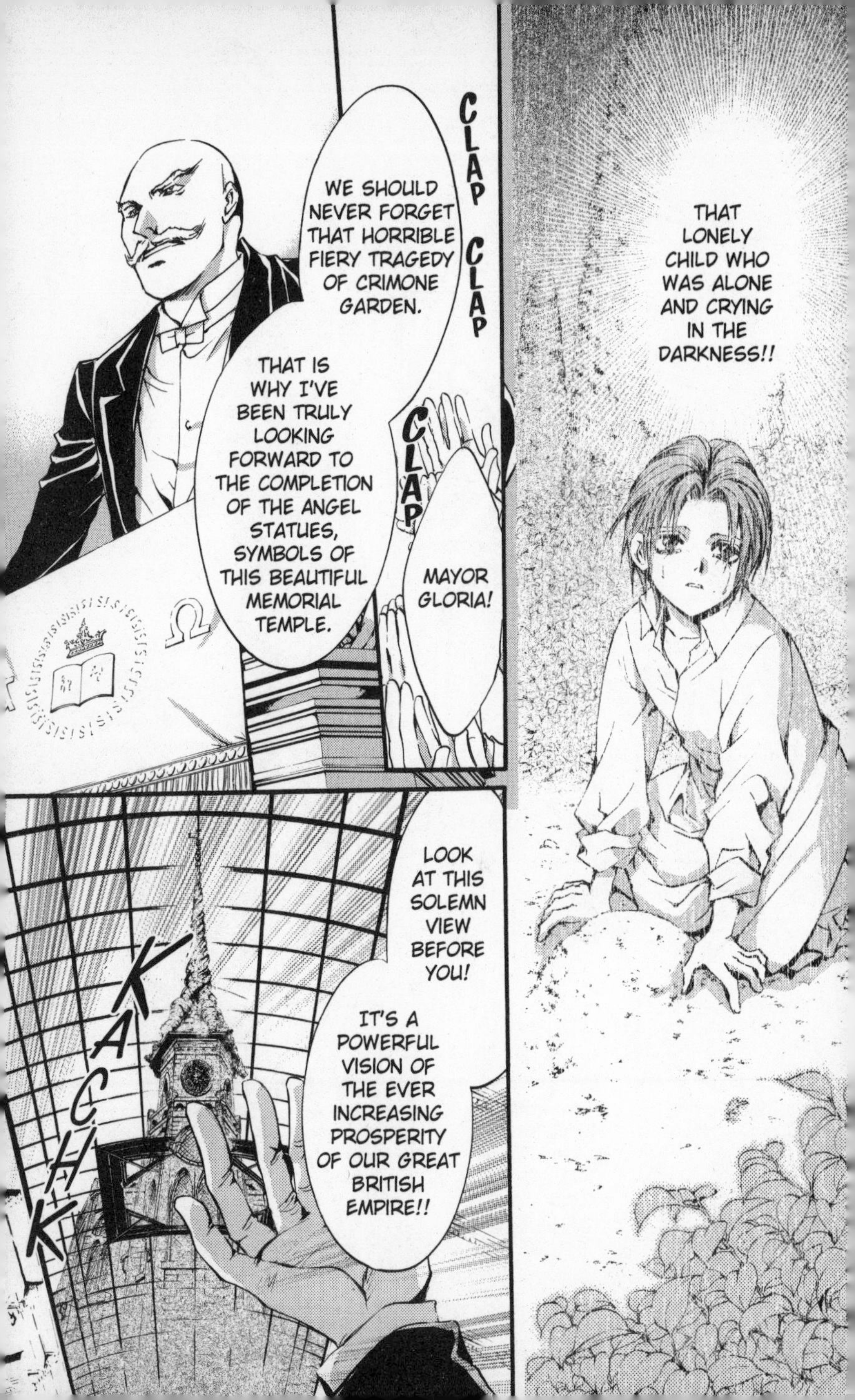
THAT LONELY CHILD WHO WAS ALONE AND CRYING IN THE DARKNESS!!
CLAP CLAP
WE SHOULD NEVER FORGET THAT HORRIBLE FIERY TRAGEDY OF CRIMONE GARDEN.
THAT IS WHY I'VE BEEN TRULY LOOKING FORWARD TO THE COMPLETION OF THE ANGEL STATUES, SYMBOLS OF THIS BEAUTIFUL MEMORIAL TEMPLE.
CLAP
MAYOR GLORIA!
LOOK AT THIS SOLEMN VIEW BEFORE YOU!
IT'S A POWERFUL VISION OF THE EVER INCREASING PROSPERITY OF OUR GREAT BRITISH EMPIRE!!
KACHK

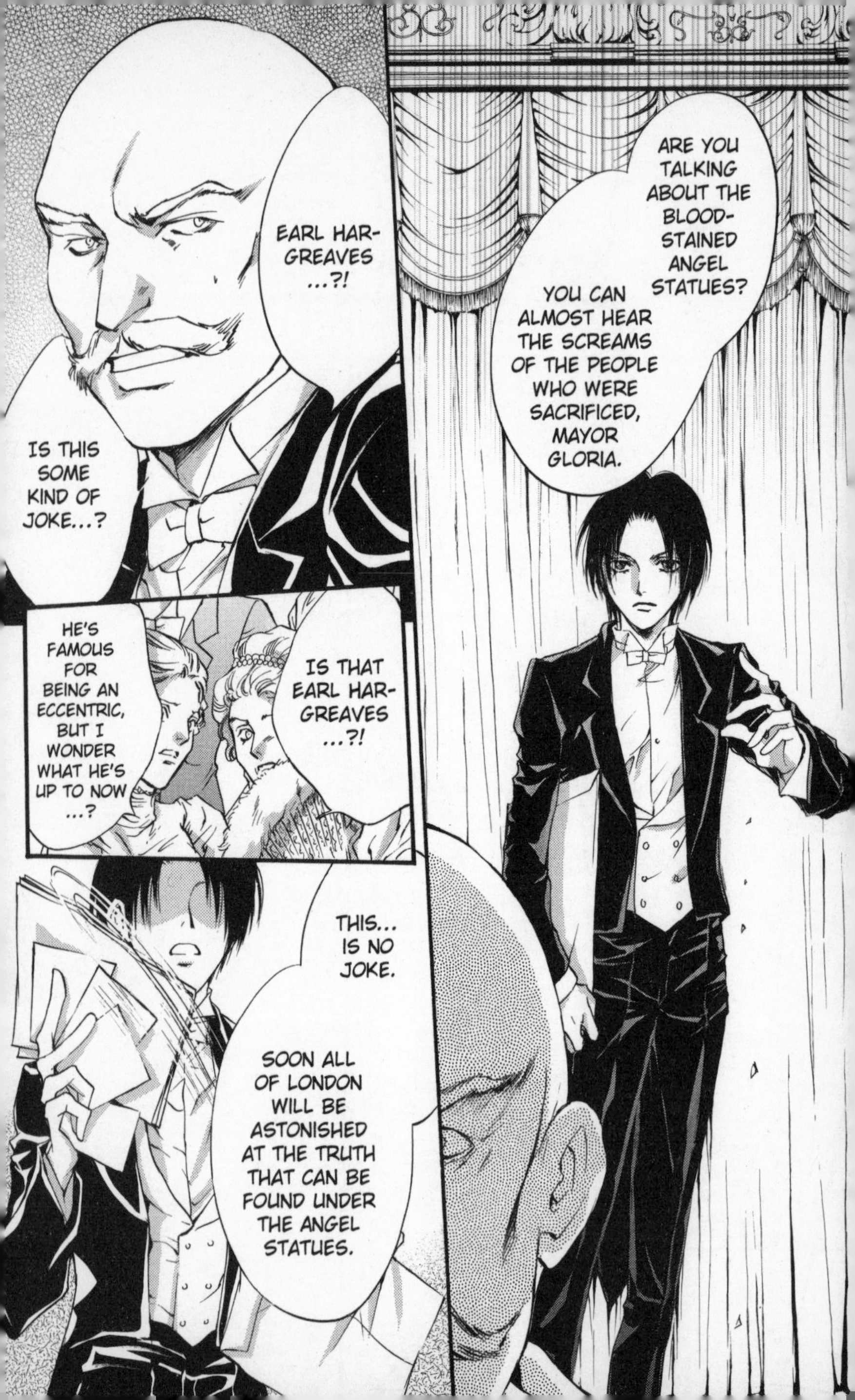
ARE YOU TALKING ABOUT THE BLOOD-STAINED ANGEL STATUES?
YOU CAN ALMOST HEAR THE SCREAMS OF THE PEOPLE WHO WERE SACRIFICED, MAYOR GLORIA.
EARL HARGREAVES ...?!
IS THIS SOME KIND OF JOKE...?
IS THAT EARL HARGREAVES ...?!
HE'S FAMOUS FOR BEING AN ECCENTRIC, BUT I WONDER WHAT HE'S UP TO NOW ...?
THIS... IS NO JOKE.
SOON ALL OF LONDON WILL BE ASTONISHED AT THE TRUTH THAT CAN BE FOUND UNDER THE ANGEL STATUES.

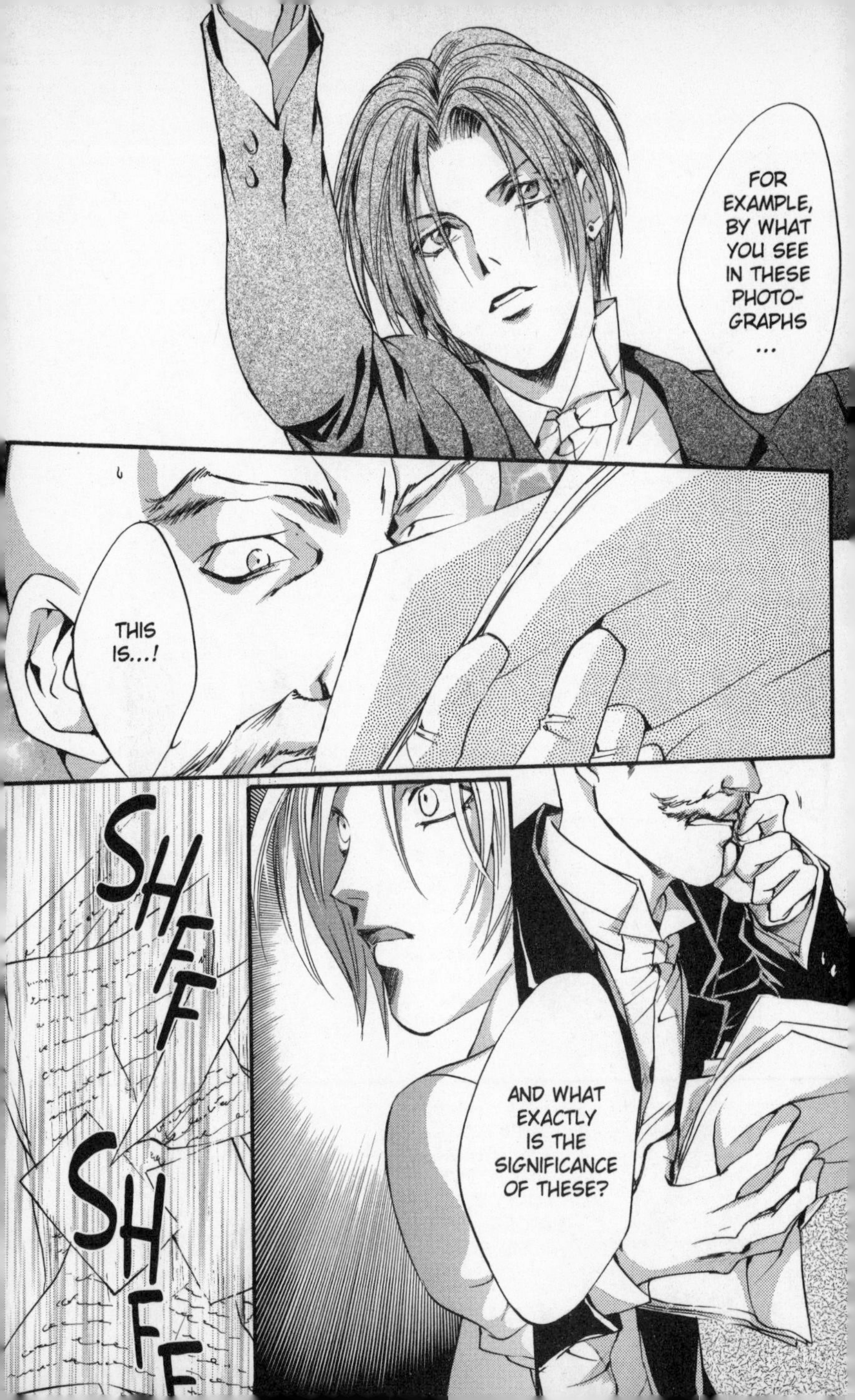
FOR EXAMPLE, BY WHAT YOU SEE IN THESE PHOTO-GRAPHS...
THIS IS...!
AND WHAT EXACTLY IS THE SIGNIFICANCE OF THESE?
SHFF
SHFF

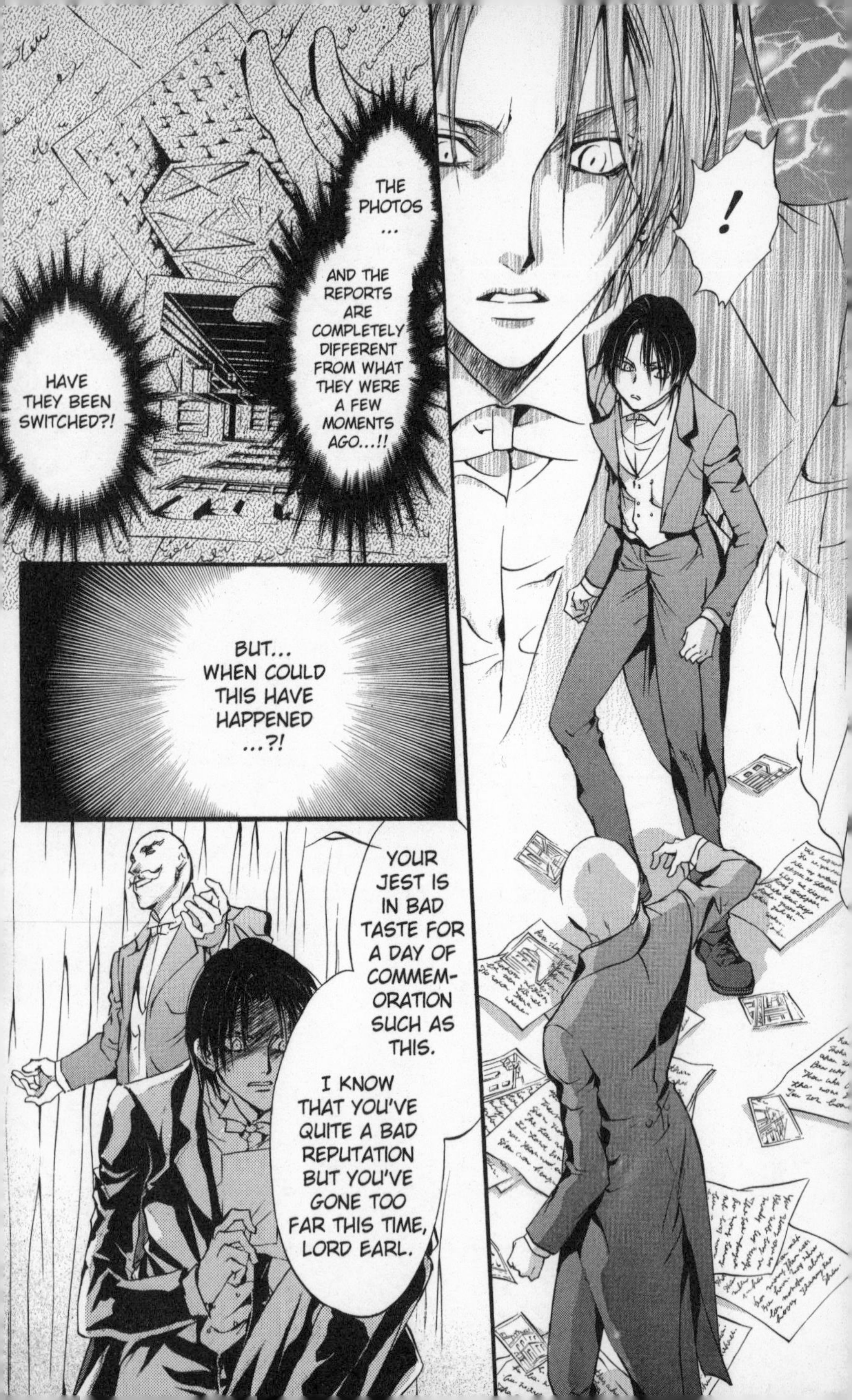
!
THE PHOTOS ...
AND THE REPORTS ARE COMPLETELY DIFFERENT FROM WHAT THEY WERE A FEW MOMENTS AGO...!!
HAVE THEY BEEN SWITCHED?!
BUT... WHEN COULD THIS HAVE HAPPENED ...?!
YOUR JEST IS IN BAD TASTE FOR A DAY OF COMMEM-ORATION SUCH AS THIS.
I KNOW THAT YOU'VE QUITE A BAD REPUTATION BUT YOU'VE GONE TOO FAR THIS TIME, LORD EARL.

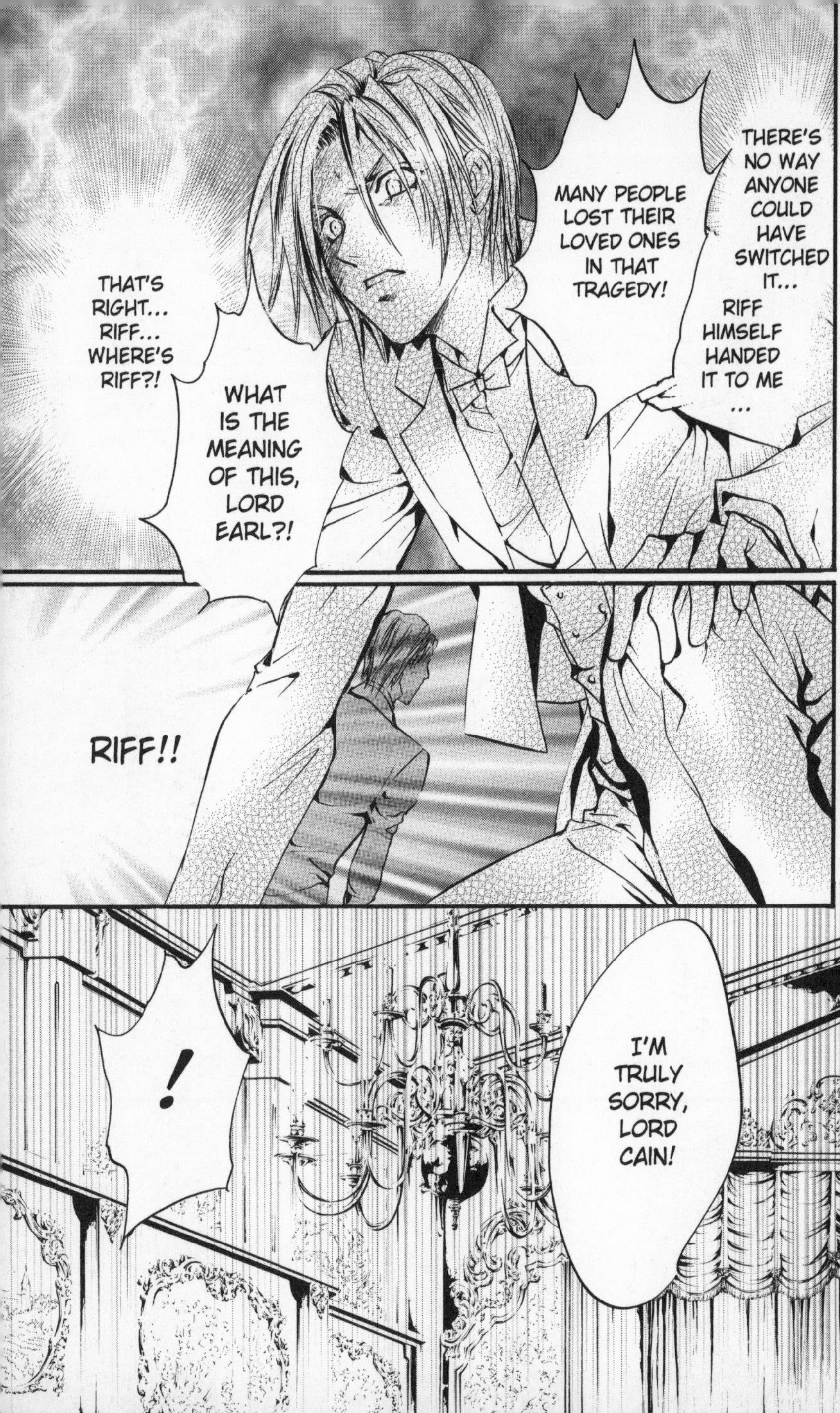
THERE'S NO WAY ANYONE COULD HAVE SWITCHED IT...
RIFF HIMSELF HANDED IT TO ME ...
MANY PEOPLE LOST THEIR LOVED ONES IN THAT TRAGEDY!
WHAT IS THE MEANING OF THIS, LORD EARL?!
THAT'S RIGHT... RIFF... WHERE'S RIFF?!
RIFF!!
I'M TRULY SORRY, LORD CAIN!
!

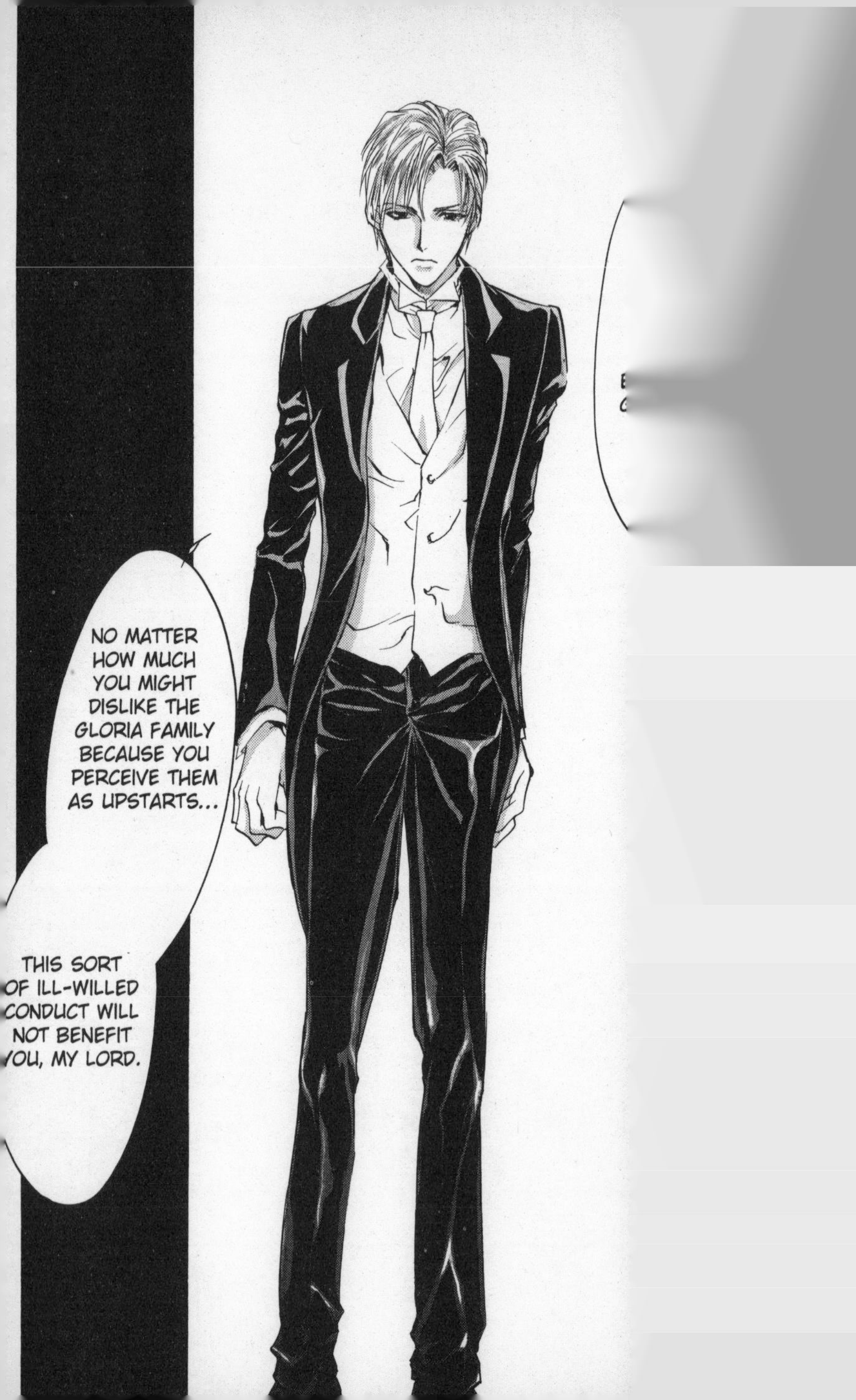
NO MATTER HOW MUCH YOU MIGHT DISLIKE THE GLORIA FAMILY BECAUSE YOU PERCEIVE THEM AS UPSTARTS...
THIS SORT OF ILL-WILLED CONDUCT WILL NOT BENEFIT YOU, MY LORD.

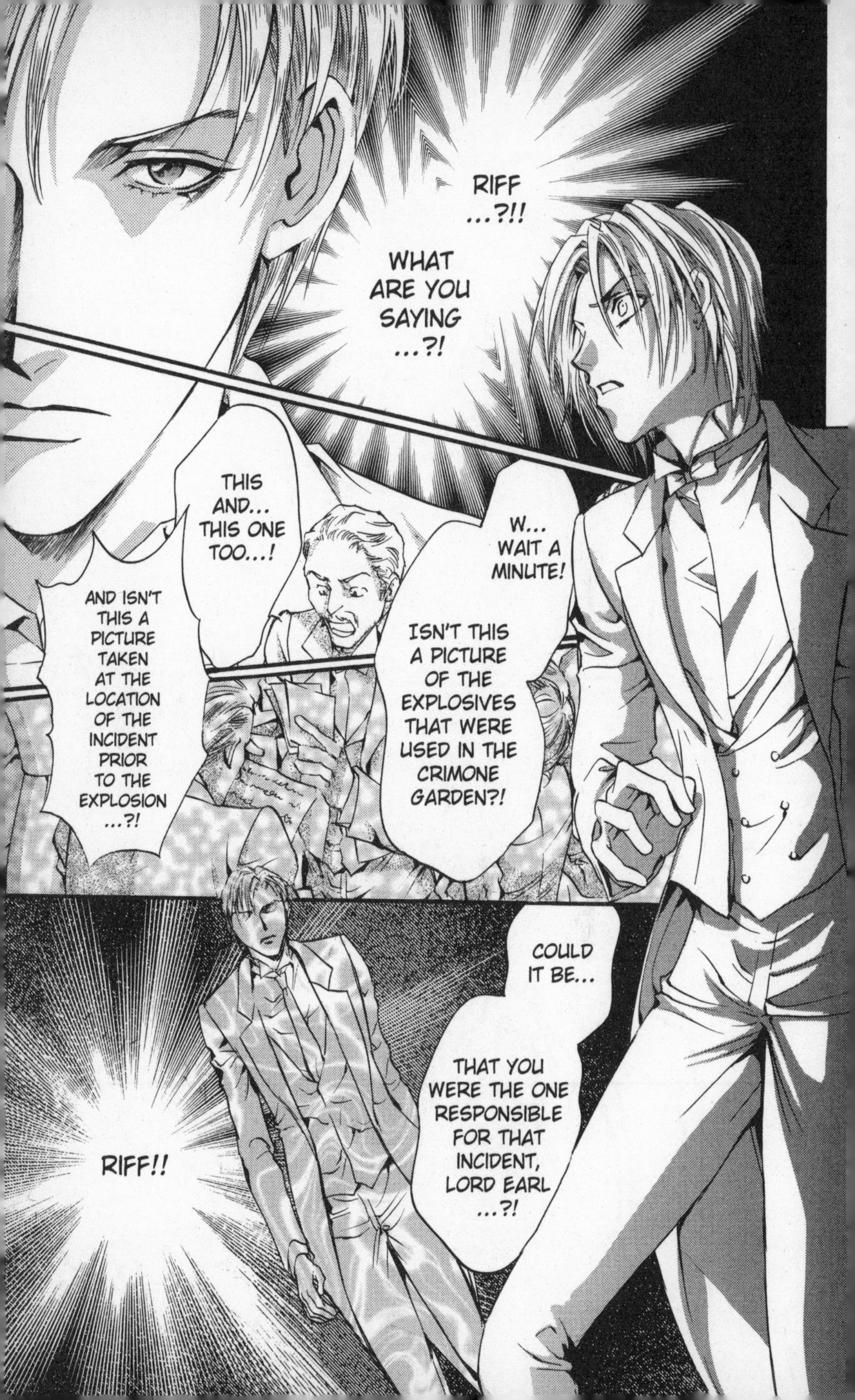
RIFF ...?!!
WHAT ARE YOU SAYING ...?!
W... WAIT A MINUTE!
ISN'T THIS A PICTURE OF THE EXPLOSIVES THAT WERE USED IN THE CRIMONE GARDEN?!
THIS AND... THIS ONE TOO...!
AND ISN'T THIS A PICTURE TAKEN AT THE LOCATION OF THE INCIDENT PRIOR TO THE EXPLOSION ...?!
COULD IT BE...
THAT YOU WERE THE ONE RESPONSIBLE FOR THAT INCIDENT, LORD EARL ...?!
RIFF!!

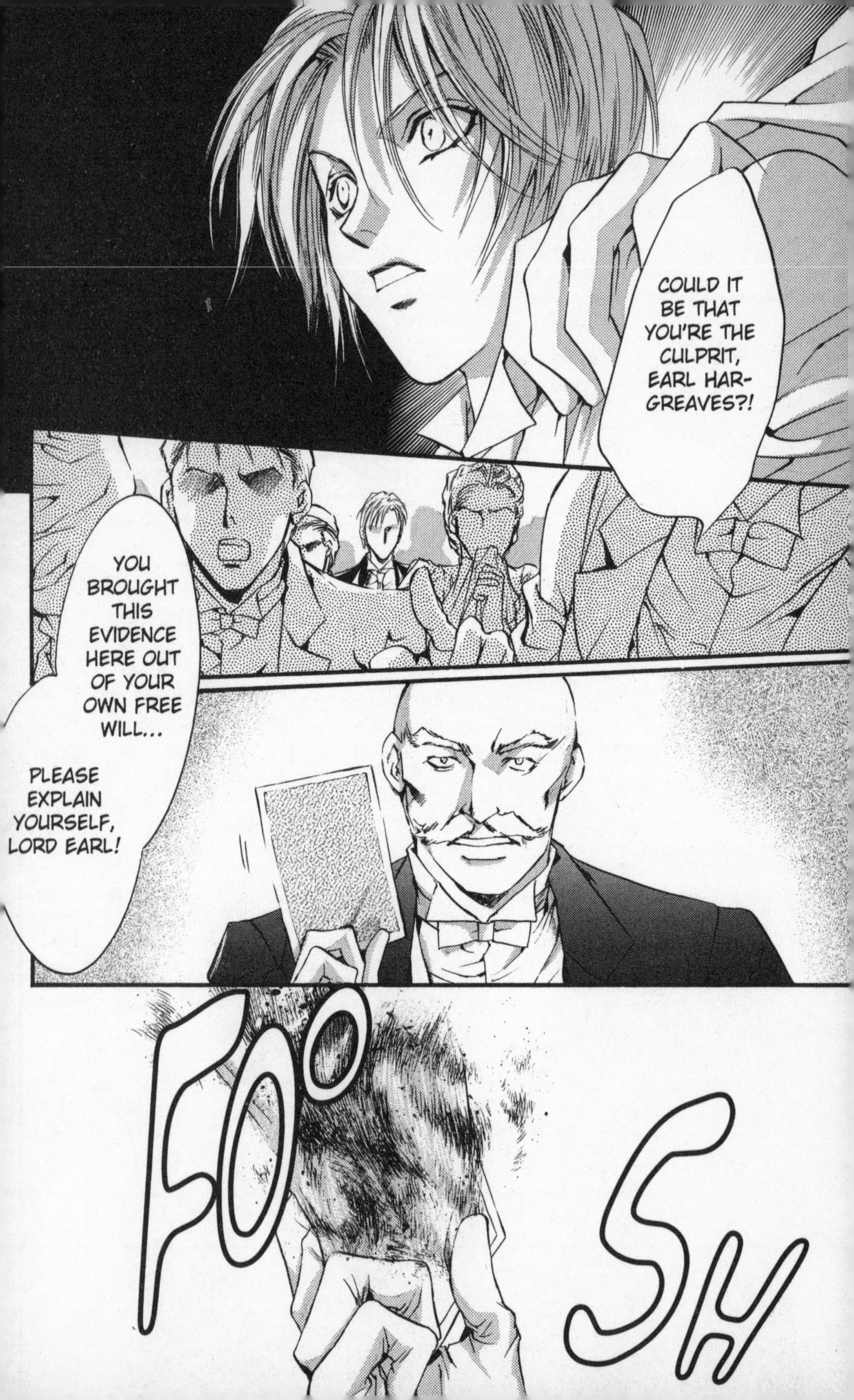
COULD IT BE THAT YOU'RE THE CULPRIT, EARL HAR-GREAVES?!
YOU BROUGHT THIS EVIDENCE HERE OUT OF YOUR OWN FREE WILL...
PLEASE EXPLAIN YOURSELF, LORD EARL!
FOOSH

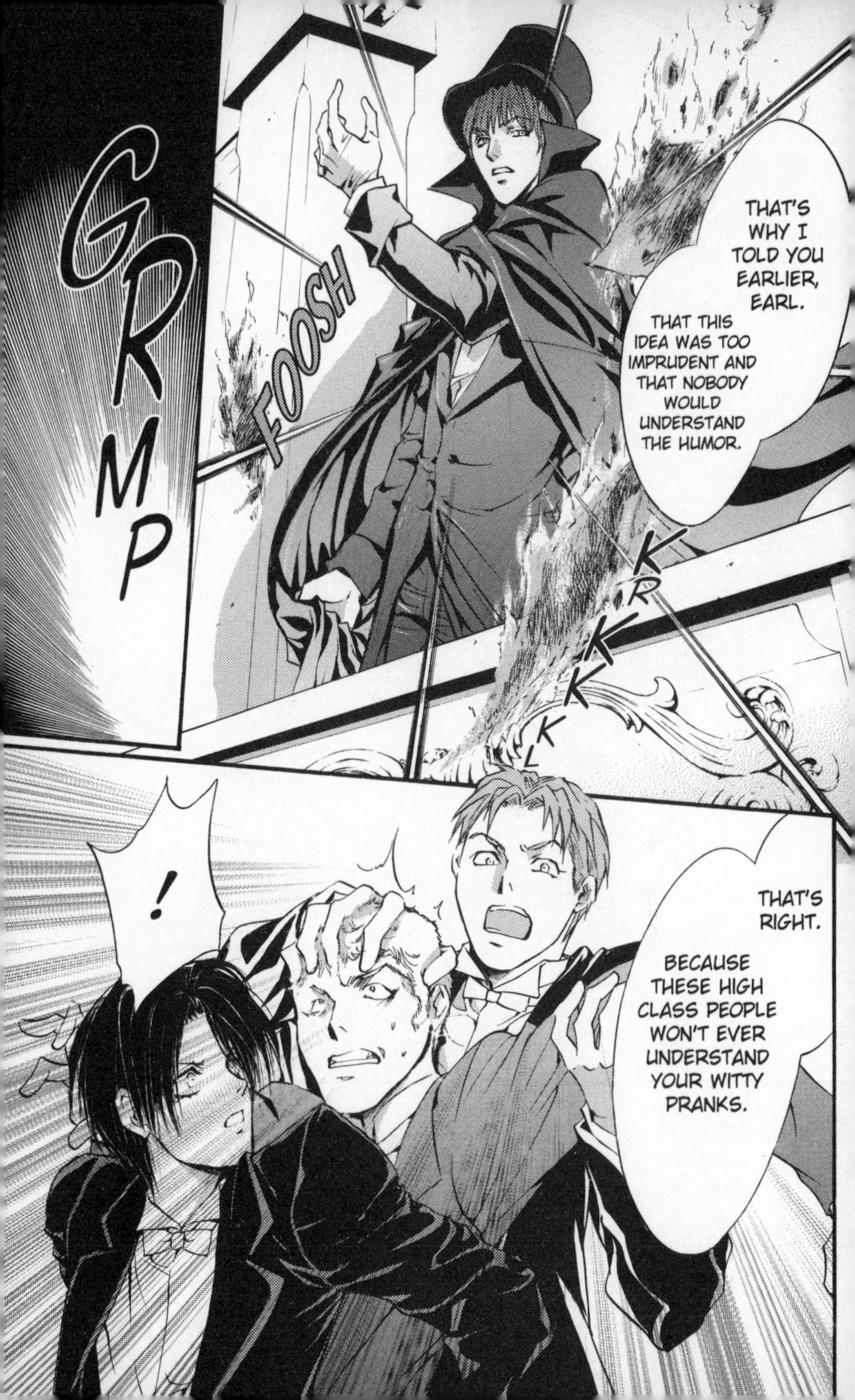
THAT'S WHY I TOLD YOU EARLIER, EARL.
THAT THIS IDEA WAS TOO IMPRUDENT AND THAT NOBODY WOULD UNDERSTAND THE HUMOR.
KRKKKKL
FOOSH
GRMP
THAT'S RIGHT.
BECAUSE THESE HIGH CLASS PEOPLE WON'T EVER UNDERSTAND YOUR WITTY PRANKS.
!

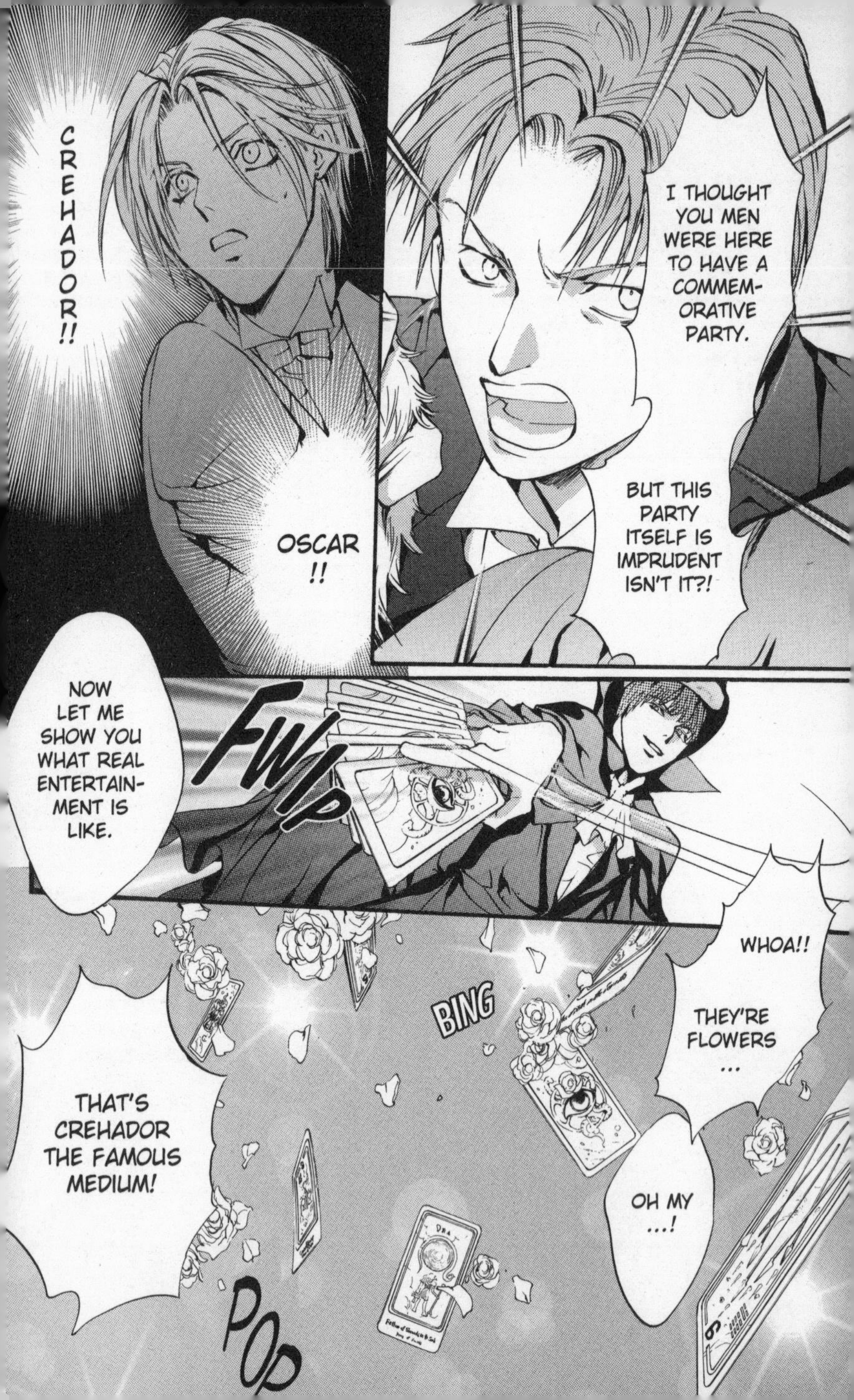
I THOUGHT YOU MEN WERE HERE TO HAVE A COMMEM-ORATIVE PARTY.
BUT THIS PARTY ITSELF IS IMPRUDENT ISN'T IT?!
CREHADOR!!
OSCAR !!
NOW LET ME SHOW YOU WHAT REAL ENTERTAIN-MENT IS LIKE.
FWIP
WHOA!!
THEY'RE FLOWERS ...
BING
OH MY ...!
THAT'S CREHADOR THE FAMOUS MEDIUM!
POP

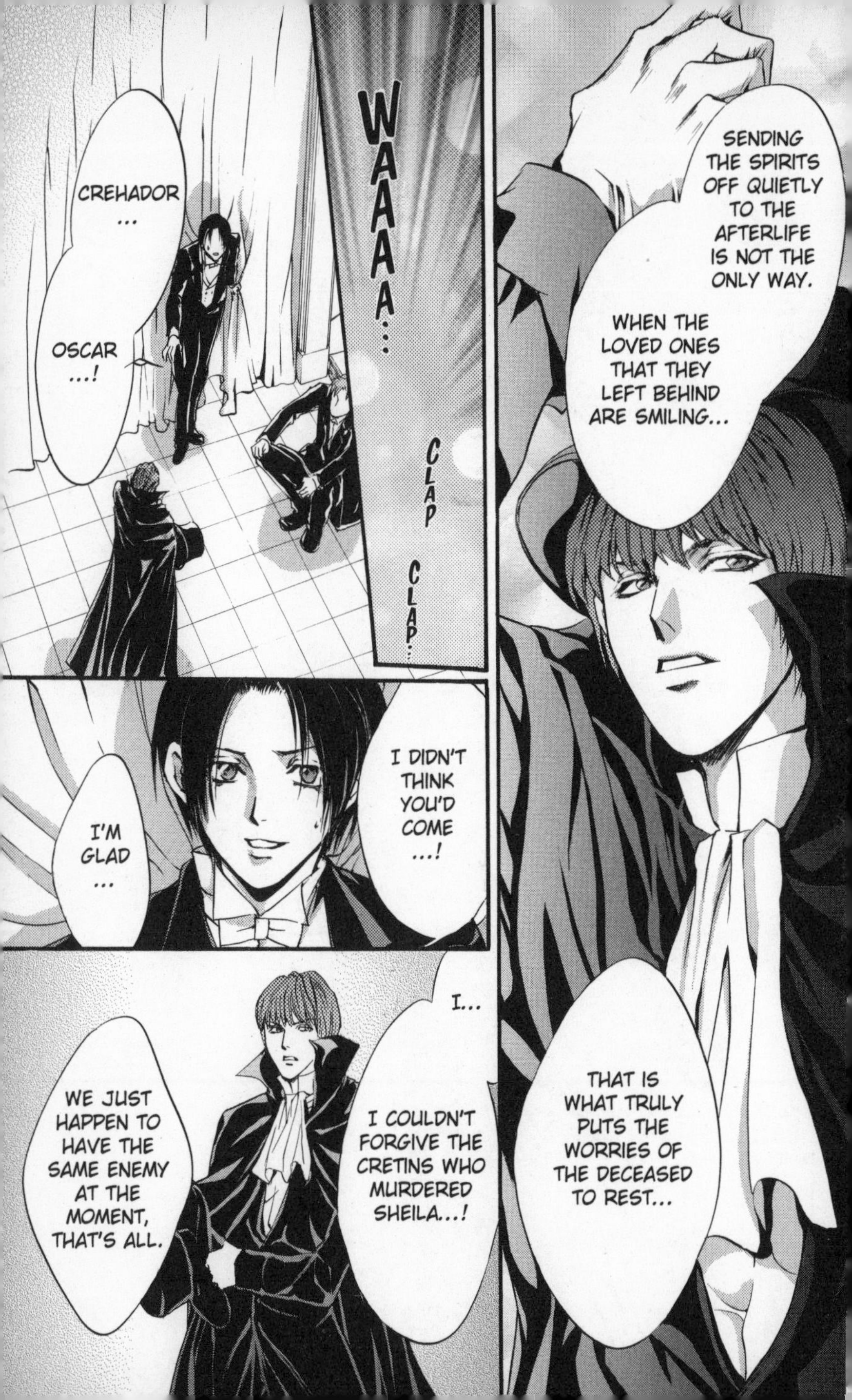
SENDING THE SPIRITS OFF QUIETLY TO THE AFTERLIFE IS NOT THE ONLY WAY.
WHEN THE LOVED ONES THAT THEY LEFT BEHIND ARE SMILING...
THAT IS WHAT TRULY PUTS THE WORRIES OF THE DECEASED TO REST...
WAAAAA...
CREHADOR ...
OSCAR ...!
CLAP CLAP...
I DIDN'T THINK YOU'D COME ...!
I'M GLAD ...
I...
I COULDN'T FORGIVE THE CRETINS WHO MURDERED SHEILA...!
WE JUST HAPPEN TO HAVE THE SAME ENEMY AT THE MOMENT, THAT'S ALL.

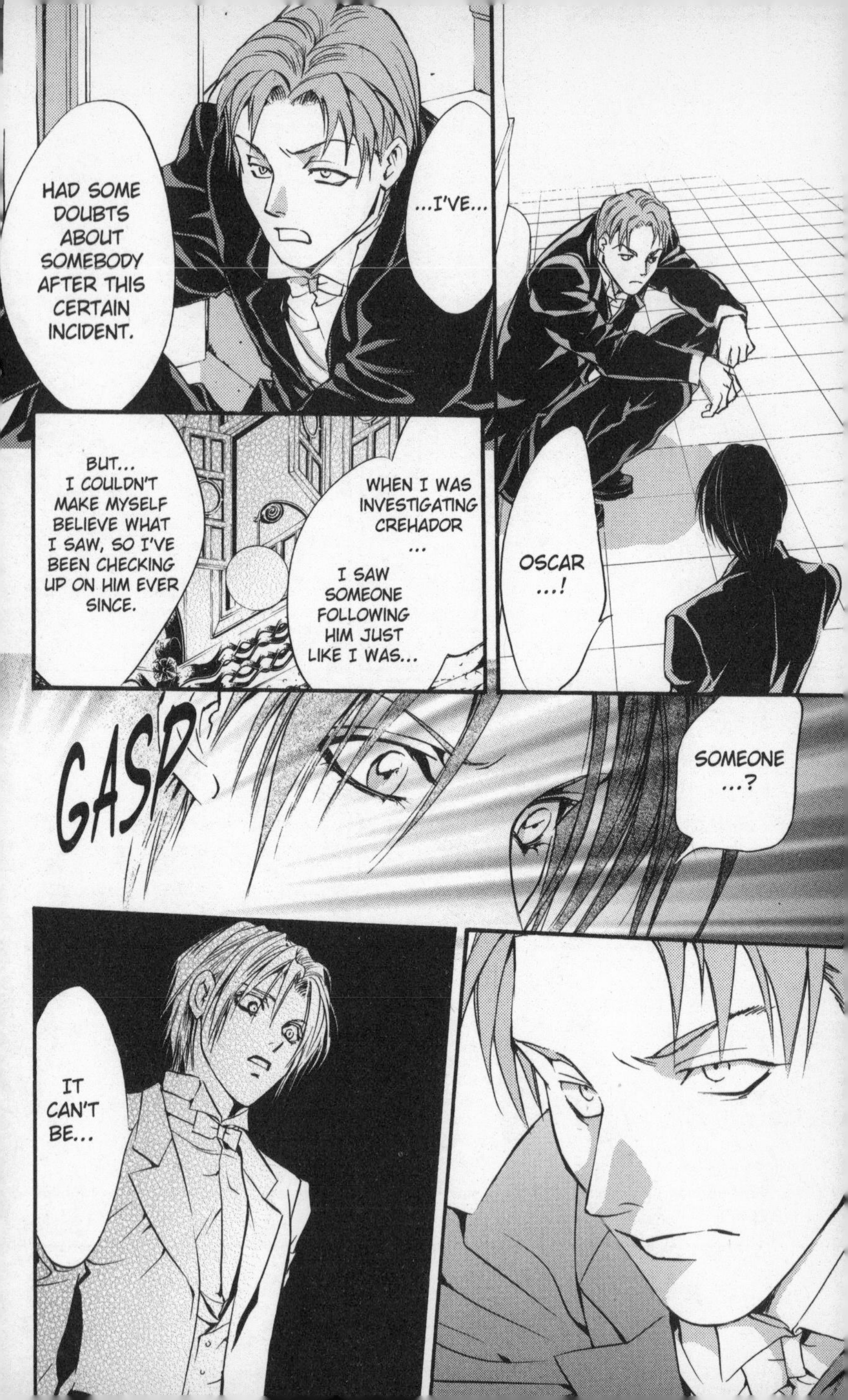
OSCAR ...!
...I'VE...
HAD SOME DOUBTS ABOUT SOMEBODY AFTER THIS CERTAIN INCIDENT.
WHEN I WAS INVESTIGATING CREHADOR ...
I SAW SOMEONE FOLLOWING HIM JUST LIKE I WAS...
BUT... I COULDN'T MAKE MYSELF BELIEVE WHAT I SAW, SO I'VE BEEN CHECKING UP ON HIM EVER SINCE.
SOMEONE ...?
GASP
IT CAN'T BE...

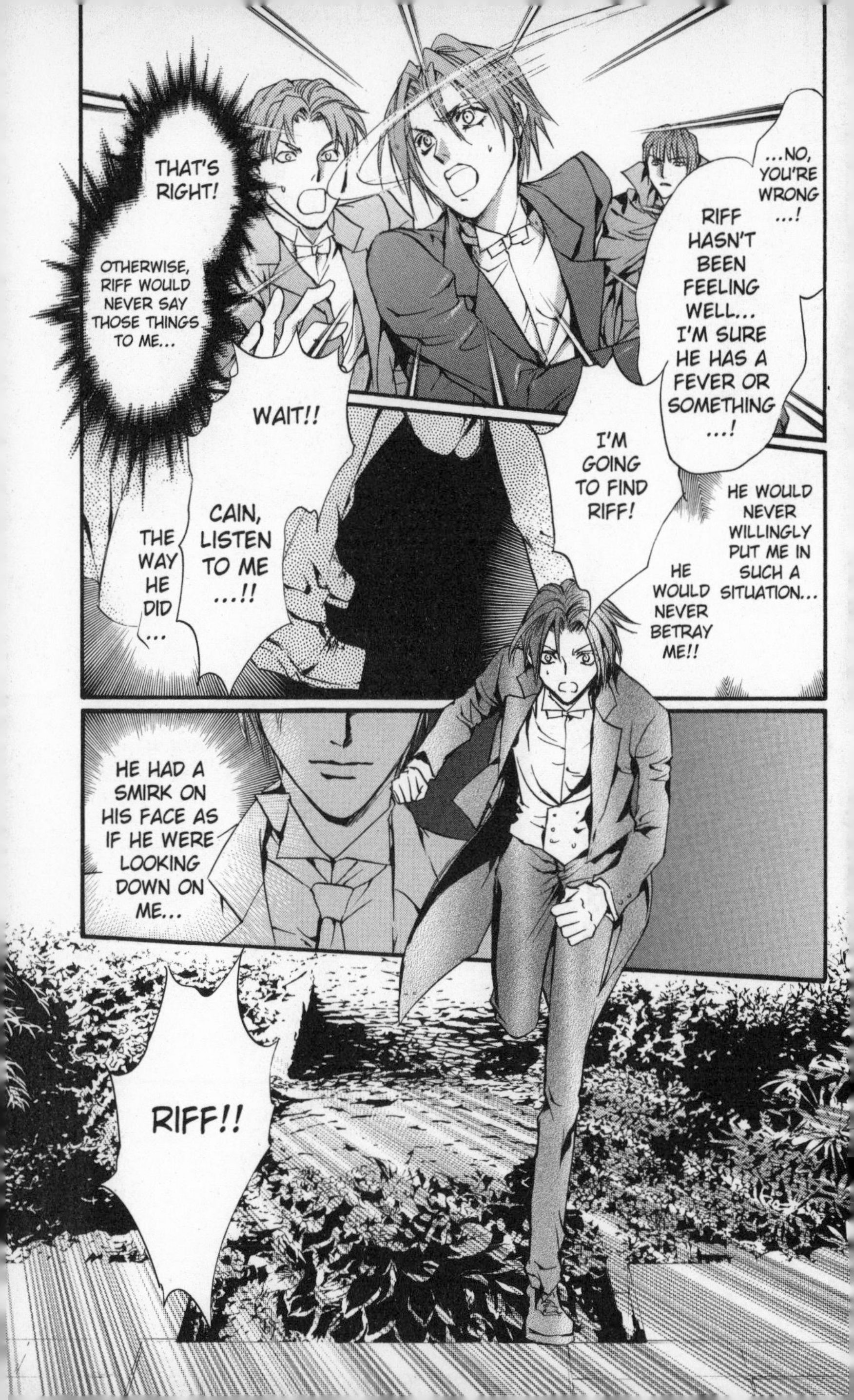
...NO, YOU'RE WRONG ...!
RIFF HASN'T BEEN FEELING WELL... I'M SURE HE HAS A FEVER OR SOMETHING ...!
THAT'S RIGHT!
OTHERWISE, RIFF WOULD NEVER SAY THOSE THINGS TO ME...
HE WOULD NEVER WILLINGLY PUT ME IN SUCH A SITUATION...
HE WOULD NEVER BETRAY ME!!
I'M GOING TO FIND RIFF!
WAIT!!
CAIN, LISTEN TO ME ...!!
THE WAY HE DID ...
HE HAD A SMIRK ON HIS FACE AS IF HE WERE LOOKING DOWN ON ME...
RIFF!!

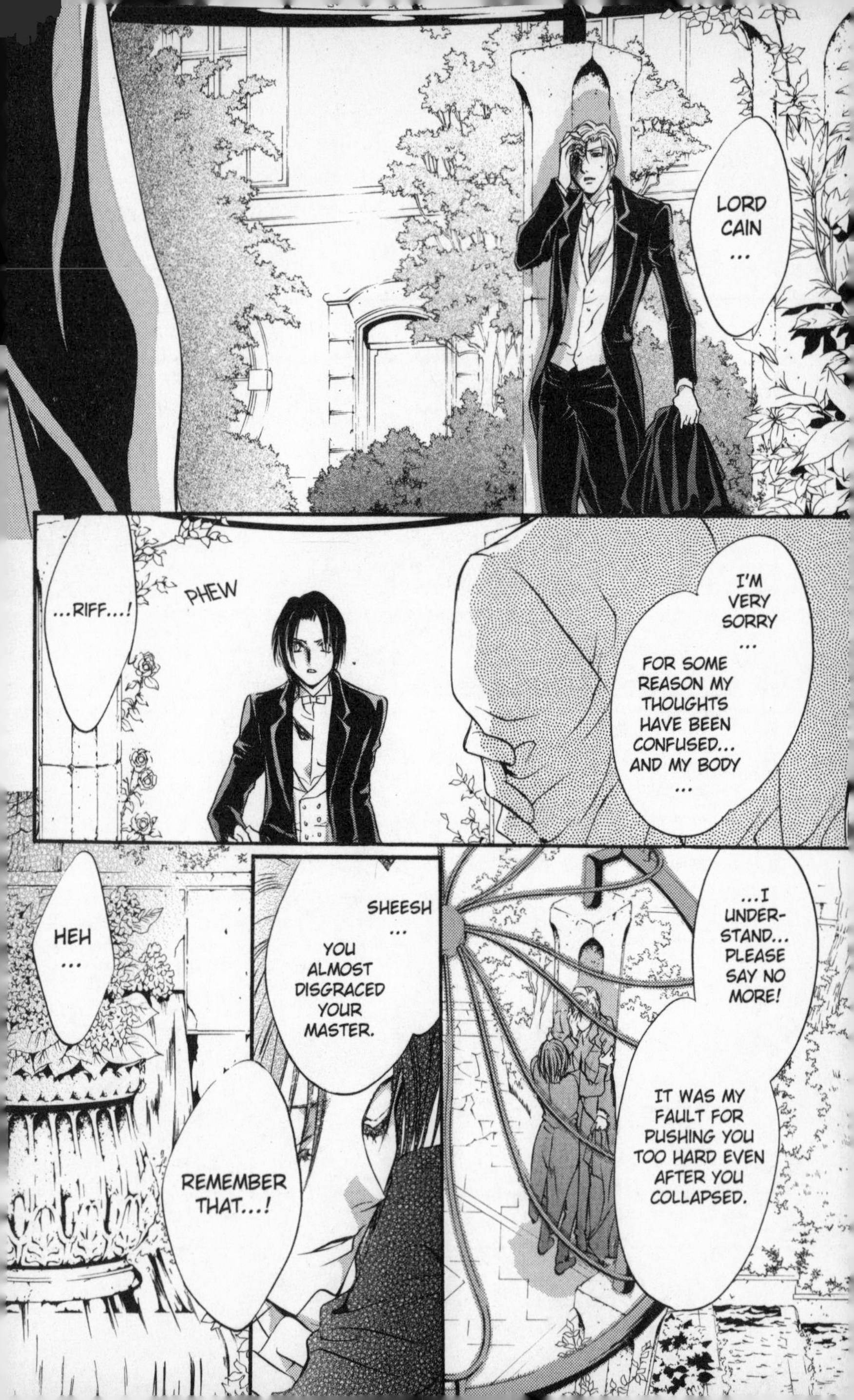
LORD CAIN ...
I'M VERY SORRY ...
FOR SOME REASON MY THOUGHTS HAVE BEEN CONFUSED... AND MY BODY ...
PHEW
...RIFF...!
...I UNDER-STAND... PLEASE SAY NO MORE!
IT WAS MY FAULT FOR PUSHING YOU TOO HARD EVEN AFTER YOU COLLAPSED.
SHEESH ...
YOU ALMOST DISGRACED YOUR MASTER.
REMEMBER THAT...!
HEH ...

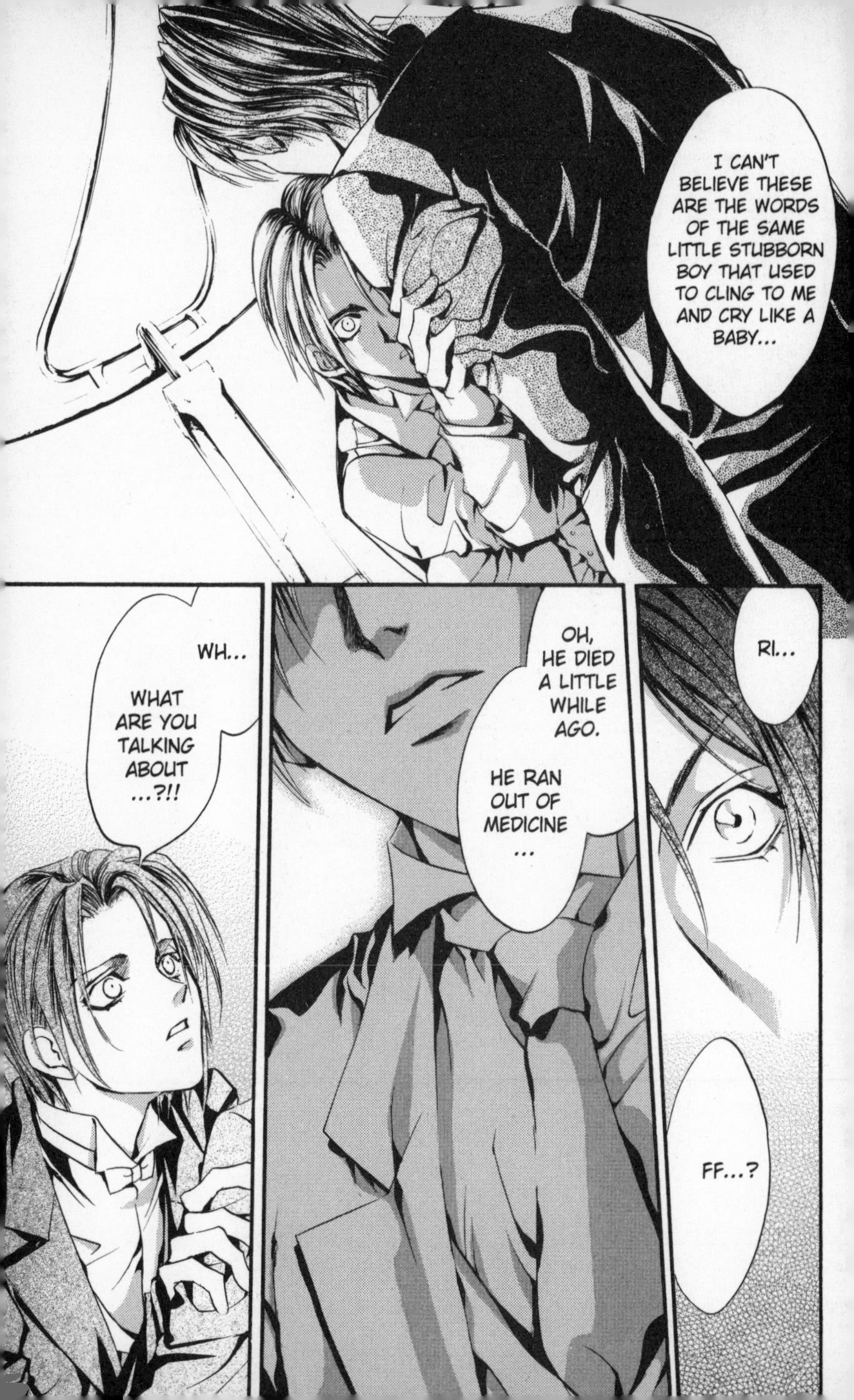
I CAN'T BELIEVE THESE ARE THE WORDS OF THE SAME LITTLE STUBBORN BOY THAT USED TO CLING TO ME AND CRY LIKE A BABY...
RI...
FF...?
OH, HE DIED A LITTLE WHILE AGO.
HE RAN OUT OF MEDICINE ...
WH...
WHAT ARE YOU TALKING ABOUT ...?!!

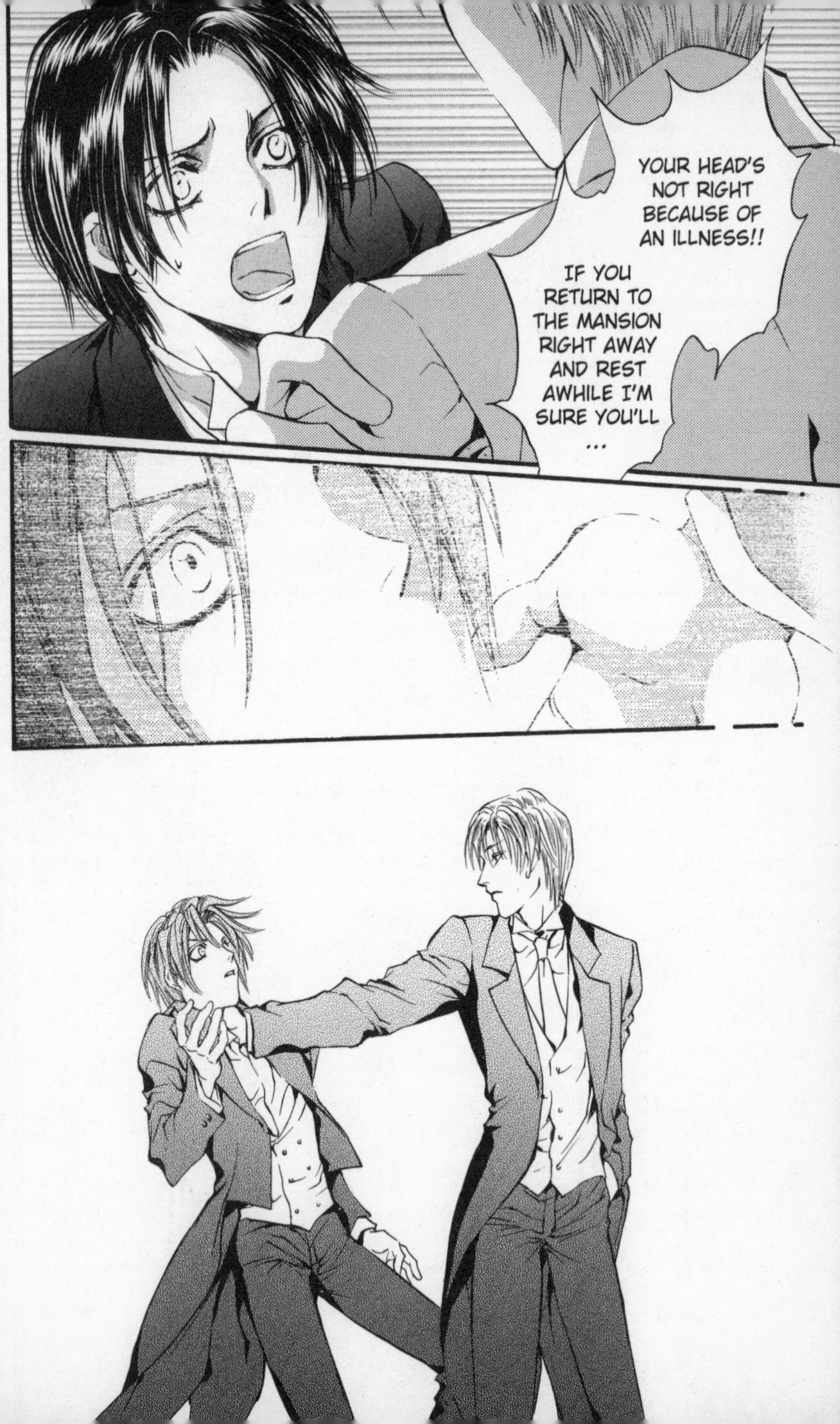
YOUR HEAD'S NOT RIGHT BECAUSE OF AN ILLNESS!!
IF YOU RETURN TO THE MANSION RIGHT AWAY AND REST AWHILE I'M SURE YOU'LL ...

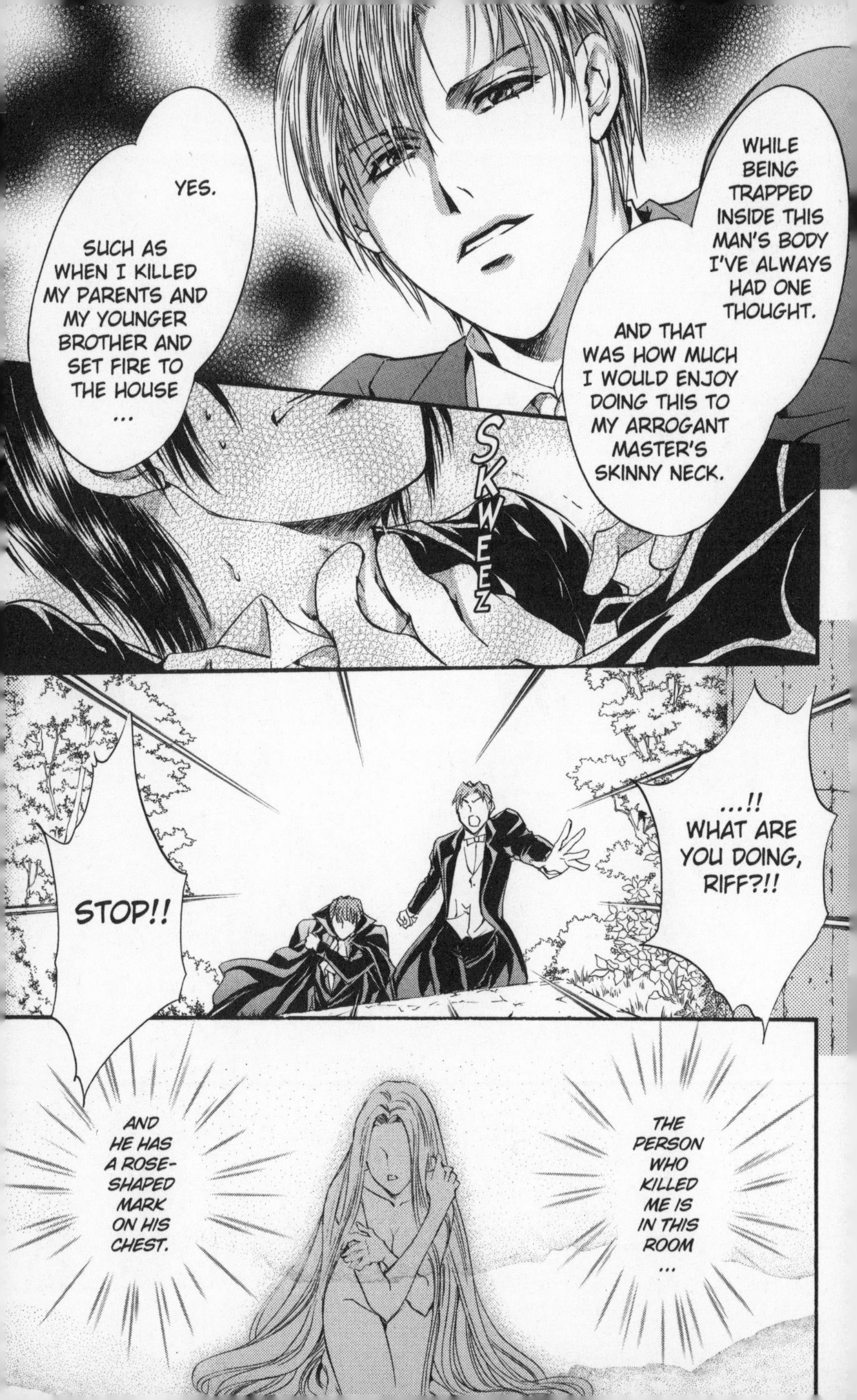
WHILE BEING TRAPPED INSIDE THIS MAN'S BODY I'VE ALWAYS HAD ONE THOUGHT.
AND THAT WAS HOW MUCH I WOULD ENJOY DOING THIS TO MY ARROGANT MASTER'S SKINNY NECK.
YES.
SUCH AS WHEN I KILLED MY PARENTS AND MY YOUNGER BROTHER AND SET FIRE TO THE HOUSE ...
SKWEEZ
...!! WHAT ARE YOU DOING, RIFF?!!
STOP!!
THE PERSON WHO KILLED ME IS IN THIS ROOM ...
AND HE HAS A ROSE-SHAPED MARK ON HIS CHEST.

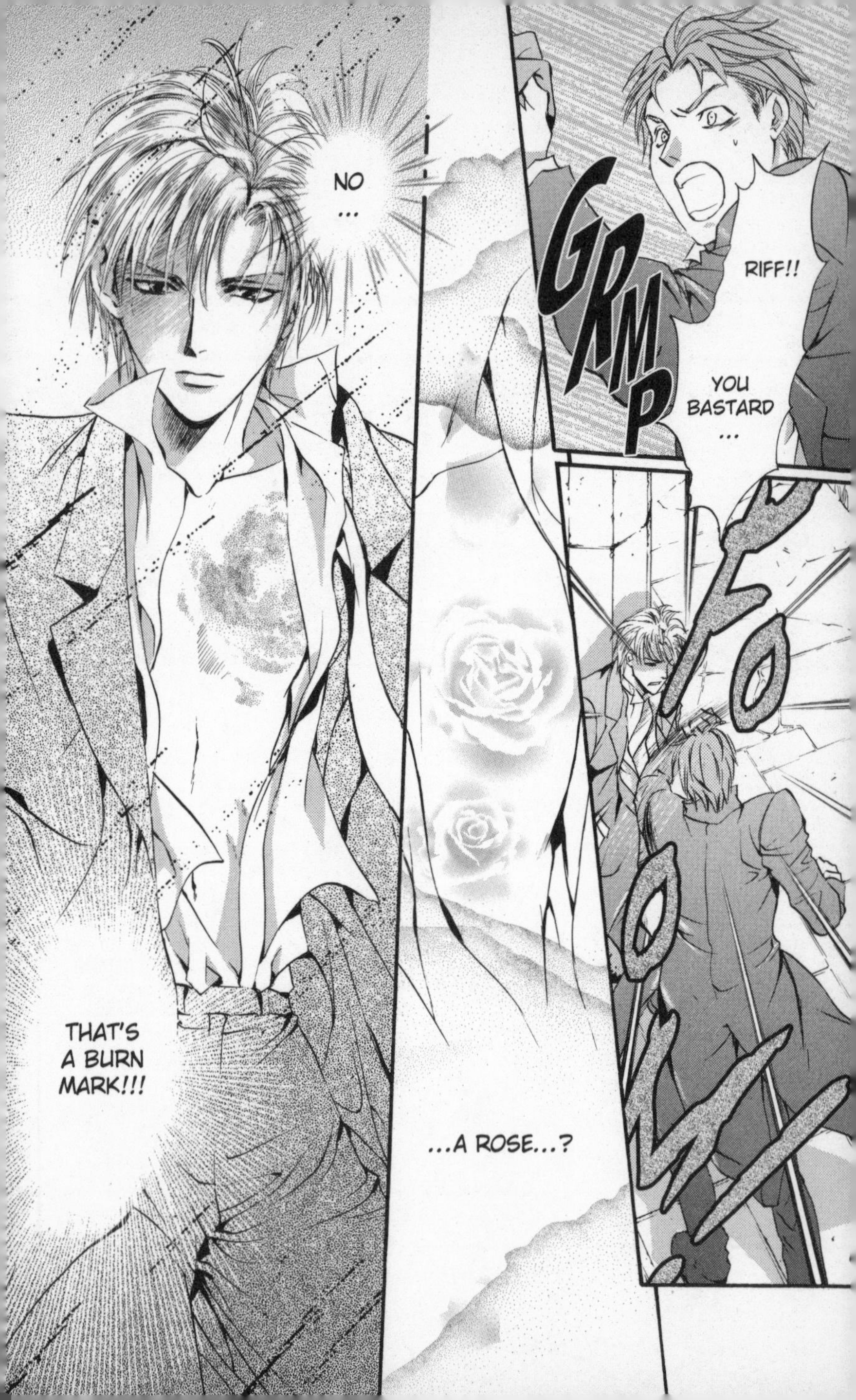
GRMP
RIFF!!
YOU BASTARD ...
...A ROSE...?
NO ...
THAT'S A BURN MARK!!!

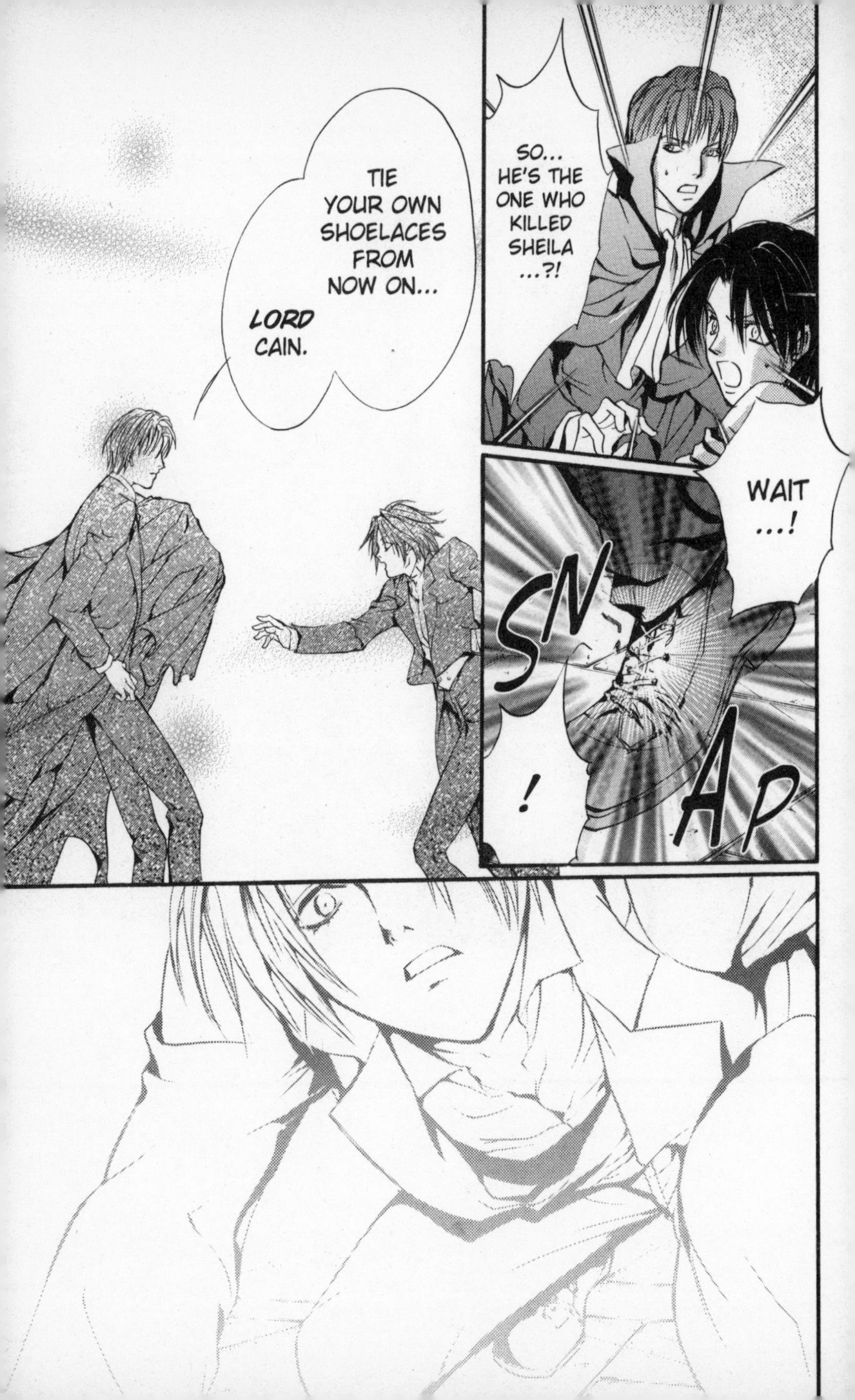
SO... HE'S THE ONE WHO KILLED SHEILA ...?!
WAIT ...!
SNAP
!
TIE YOUR OWN SHOELACES FROM NOW ON...
LORD CAIN.

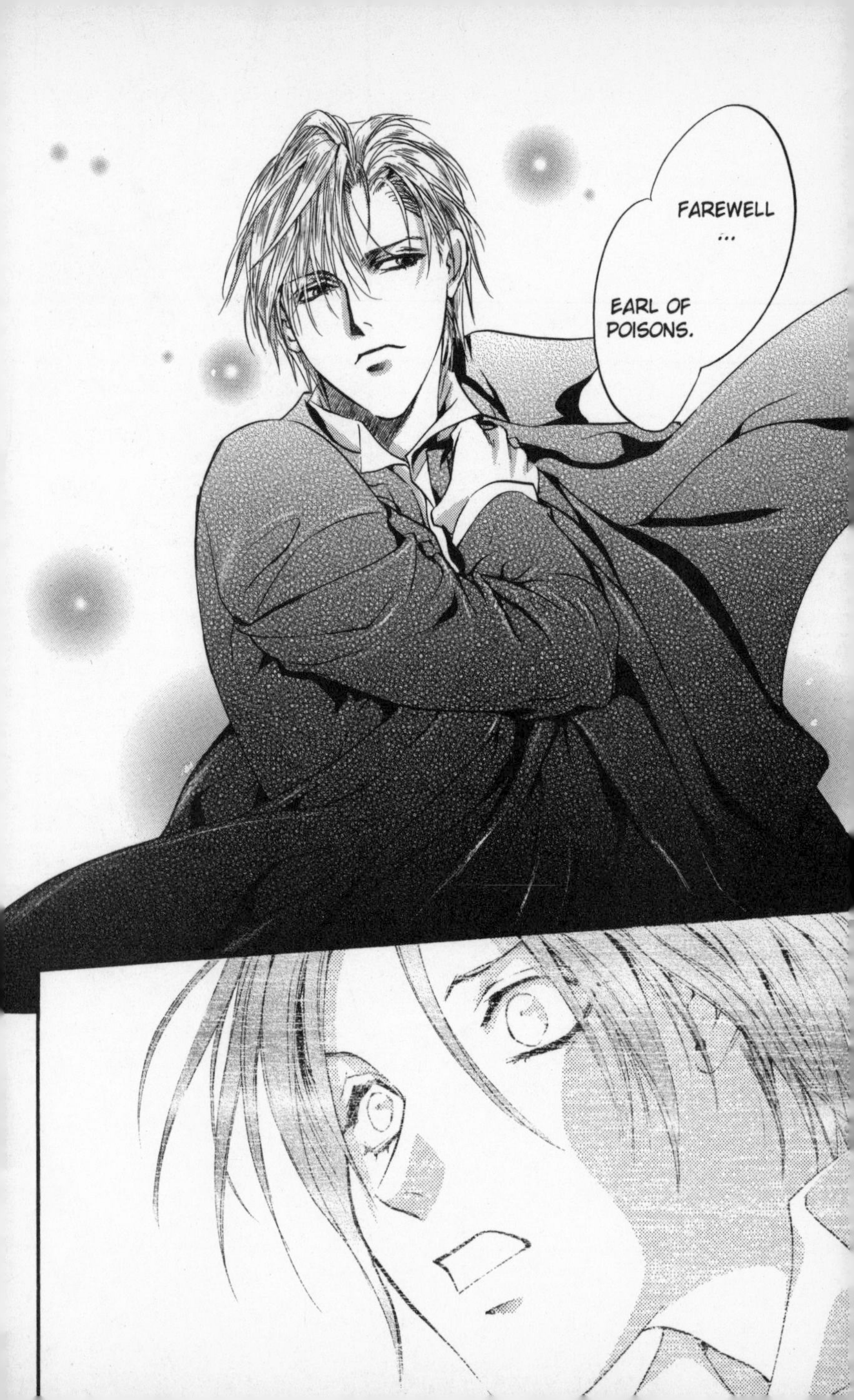
FAREWELL ... EARL OF POISONS.

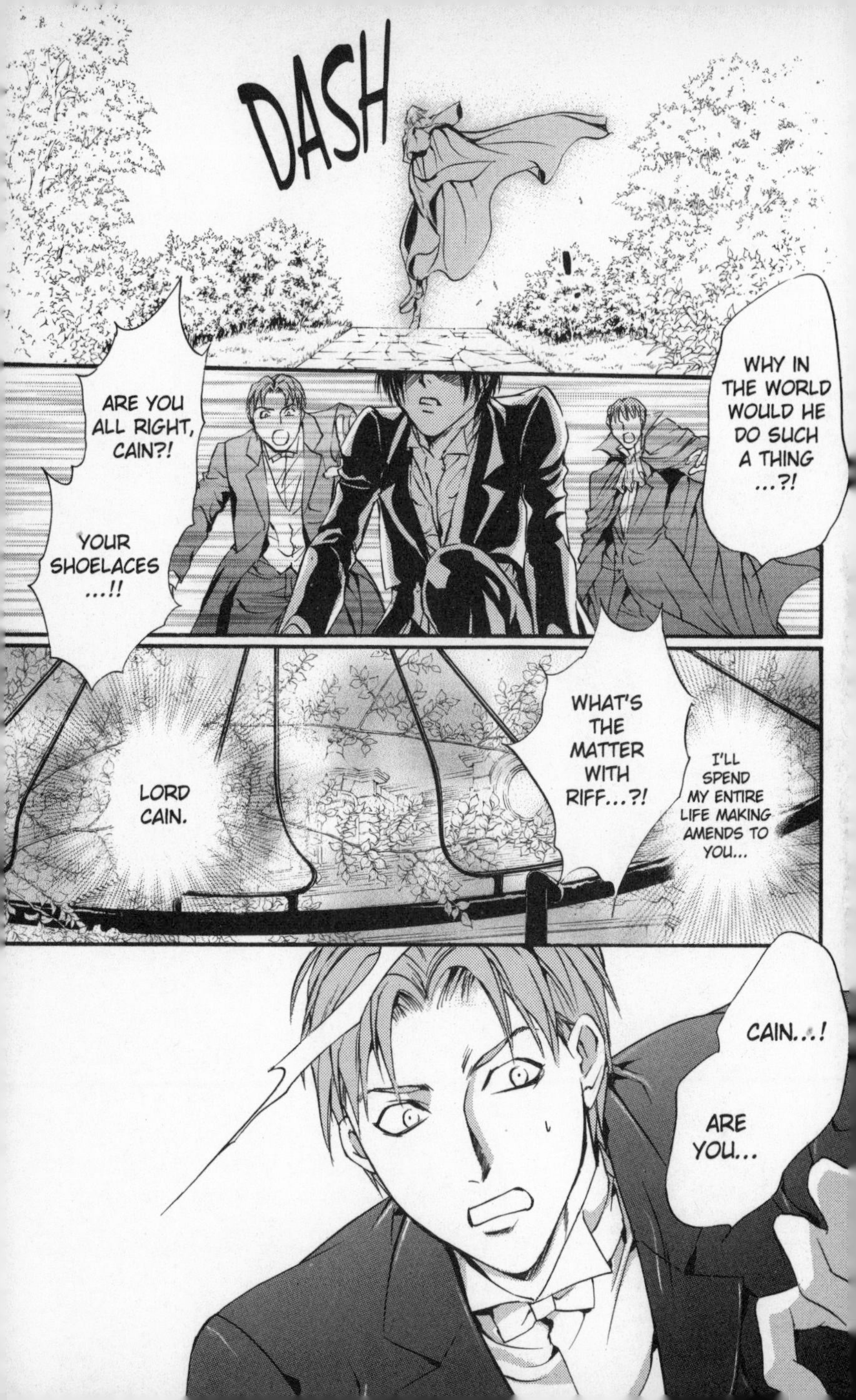
DASH
!
WHY IN THE WORLD WOULD HE DO SUCH A THING ...?!
ARE YOU ALL RIGHT, CAIN?!
YOUR SHOELACES ...!!
I'LL SPEND MY ENTIRE LIFE MAKING AMENDS TO YOU...
WHAT'S THE MATTER WITH RIFF...?!
LORD CAIN.
CAIN...!
ARE YOU...

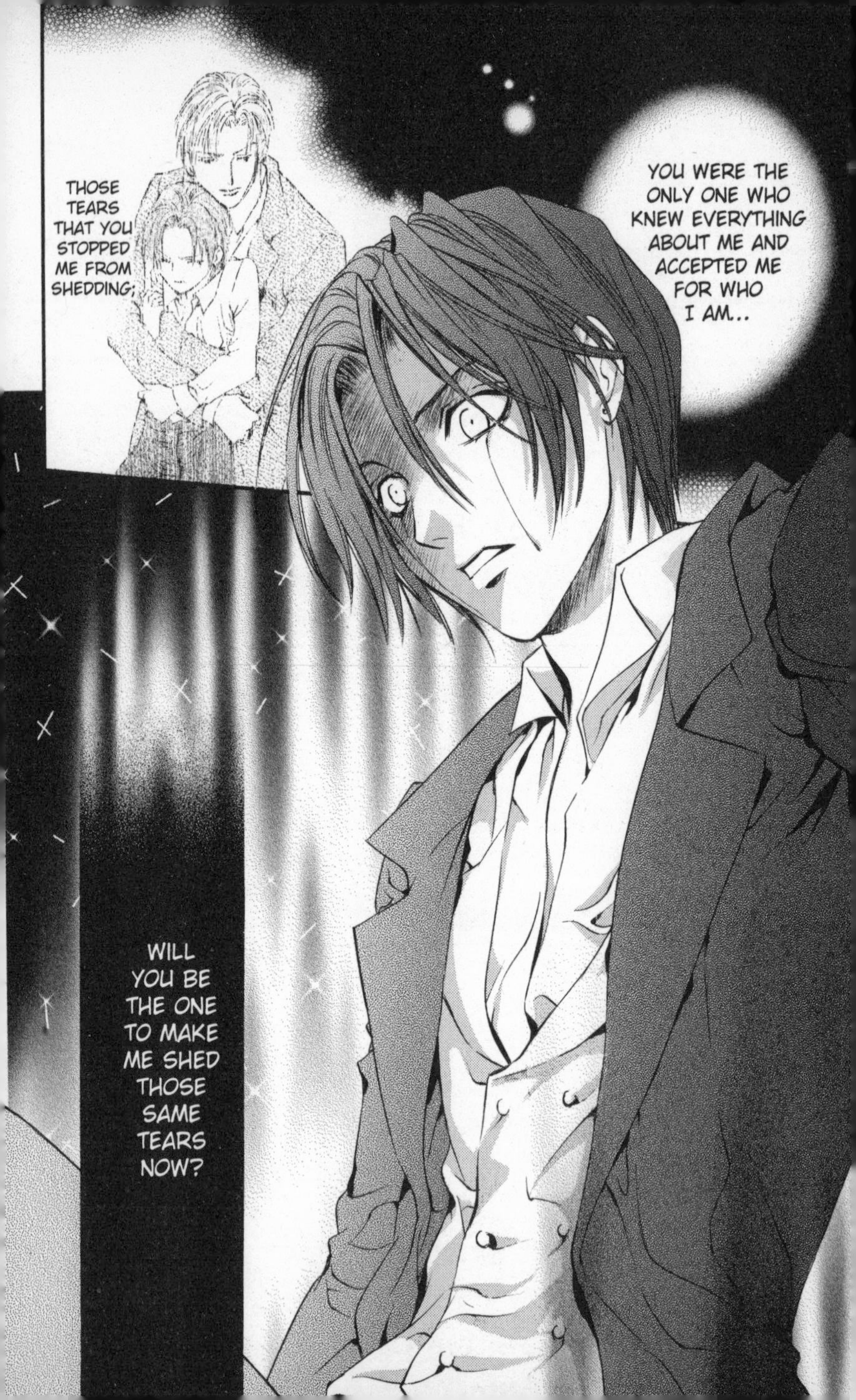
YOU WERE THE ONLY ONE WHO KNEW EVERYTHING ABOUT ME AND ACCEPTED ME FOR WHO I AM...
THOSE TEARS THAT YOU STOPPED ME FROM SHEDDING;
WILL YOU BE THE ONE TO MAKE ME SHED THOSE SAME TEARS NOW?

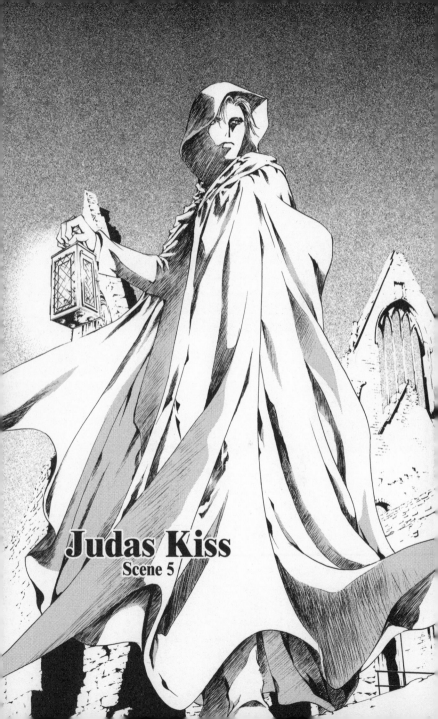

Judas Kiss
Scene 5

EVER SINCE I MET YOU AT CORNWALL CASTLE ...
YOU'VE ALWAYS BELONGED TO ME ALONE.

Judas Kiss
Scene 5

NO MATTER WHERE YOU ARE I CAN ALWAYS FIND YOU, LORD CAIN.

RIFF WOULD NEVER BETRAY ME.

YOU WERE THE ONLY THING THAT WAS ETERNAL IN THIS WORLD.

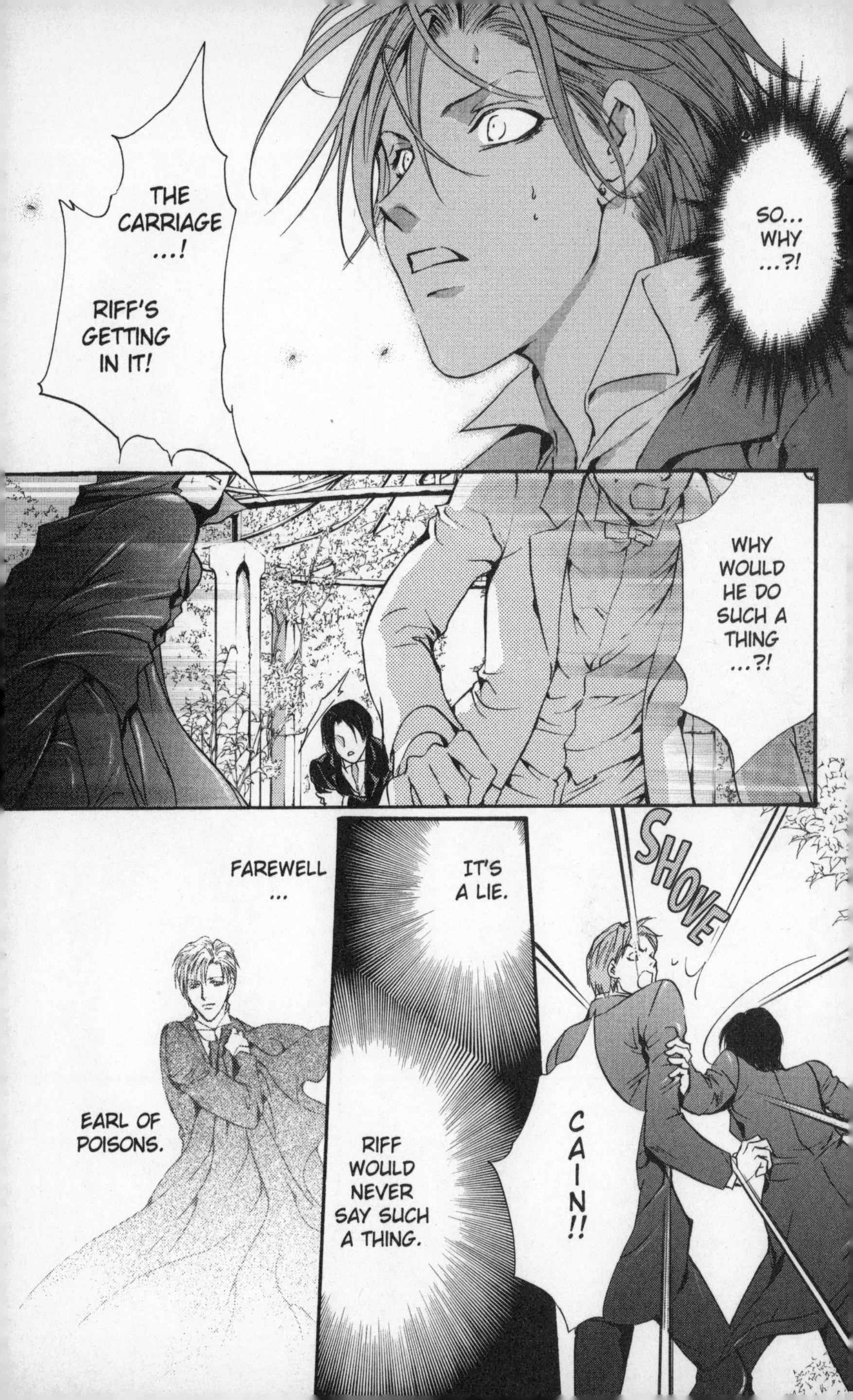
SO... WHY ...?!
THE CARRIAGE ...!
RIFF'S GETTING IN IT!
WHY WOULD HE DO SUCH A THING ...?!
SHOVE
CAIN!!
IT'S A LIE.
RIFF WOULD NEVER SAY SUCH A THING.
FAREWELL ...
EARL OF POISONS.

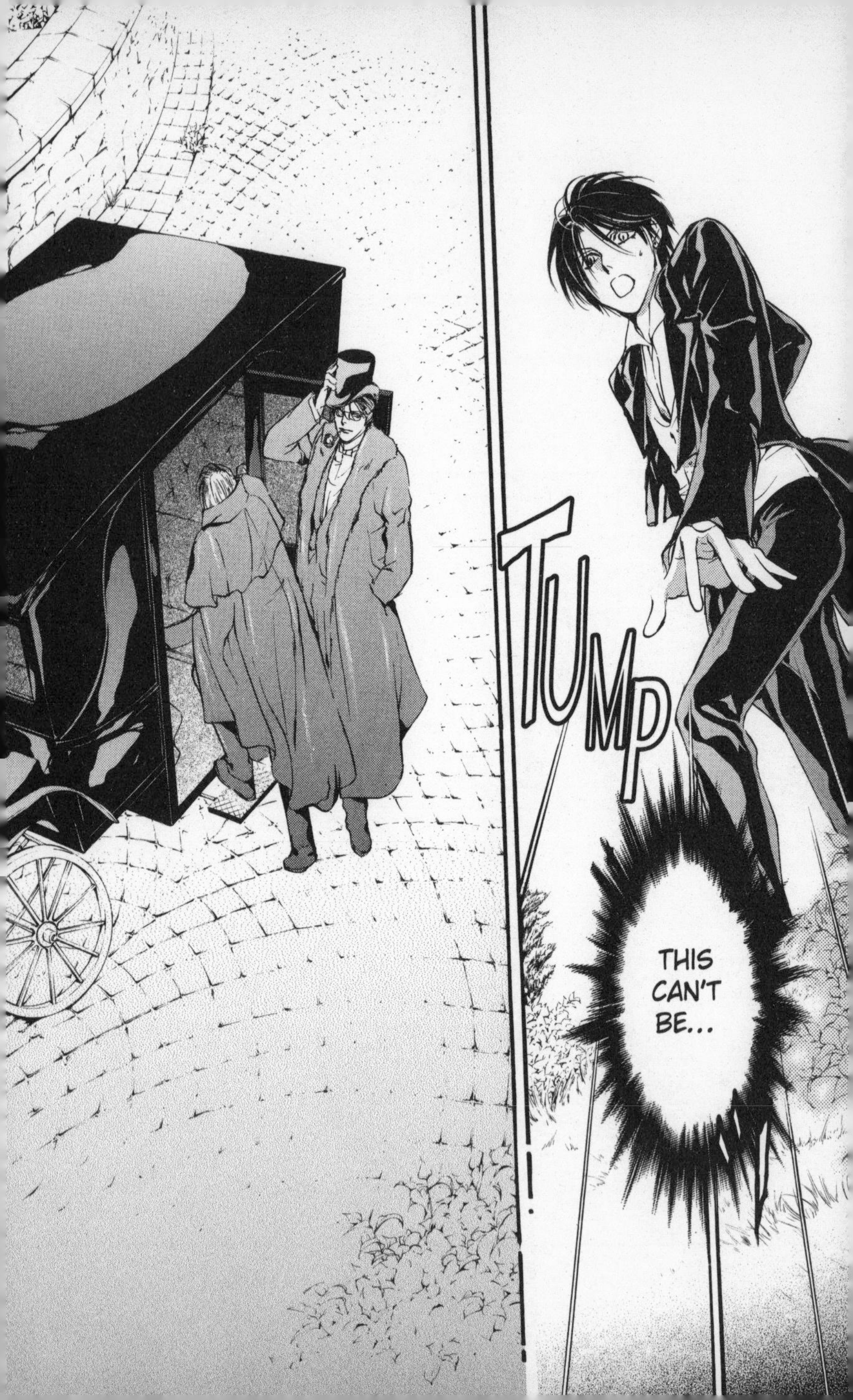
TUMP
THIS CAN'T BE...

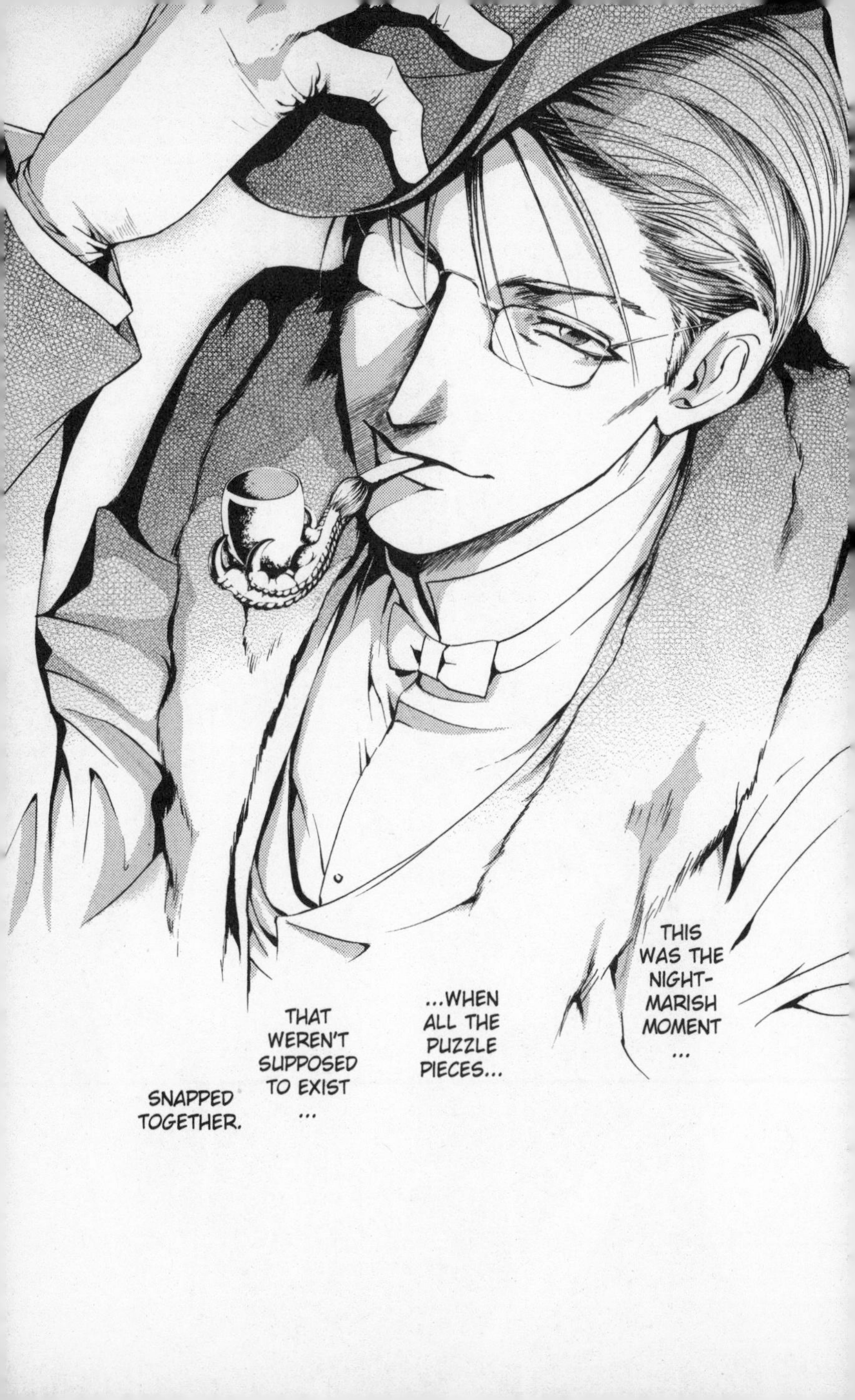
THIS WAS THE NIGHT-MARISH MOMENT ...
...WHEN ALL THE PUZZLE PIECES...
THAT WEREN'T SUPPOSED TO EXIST ...
SNAPPED TOGETHER.

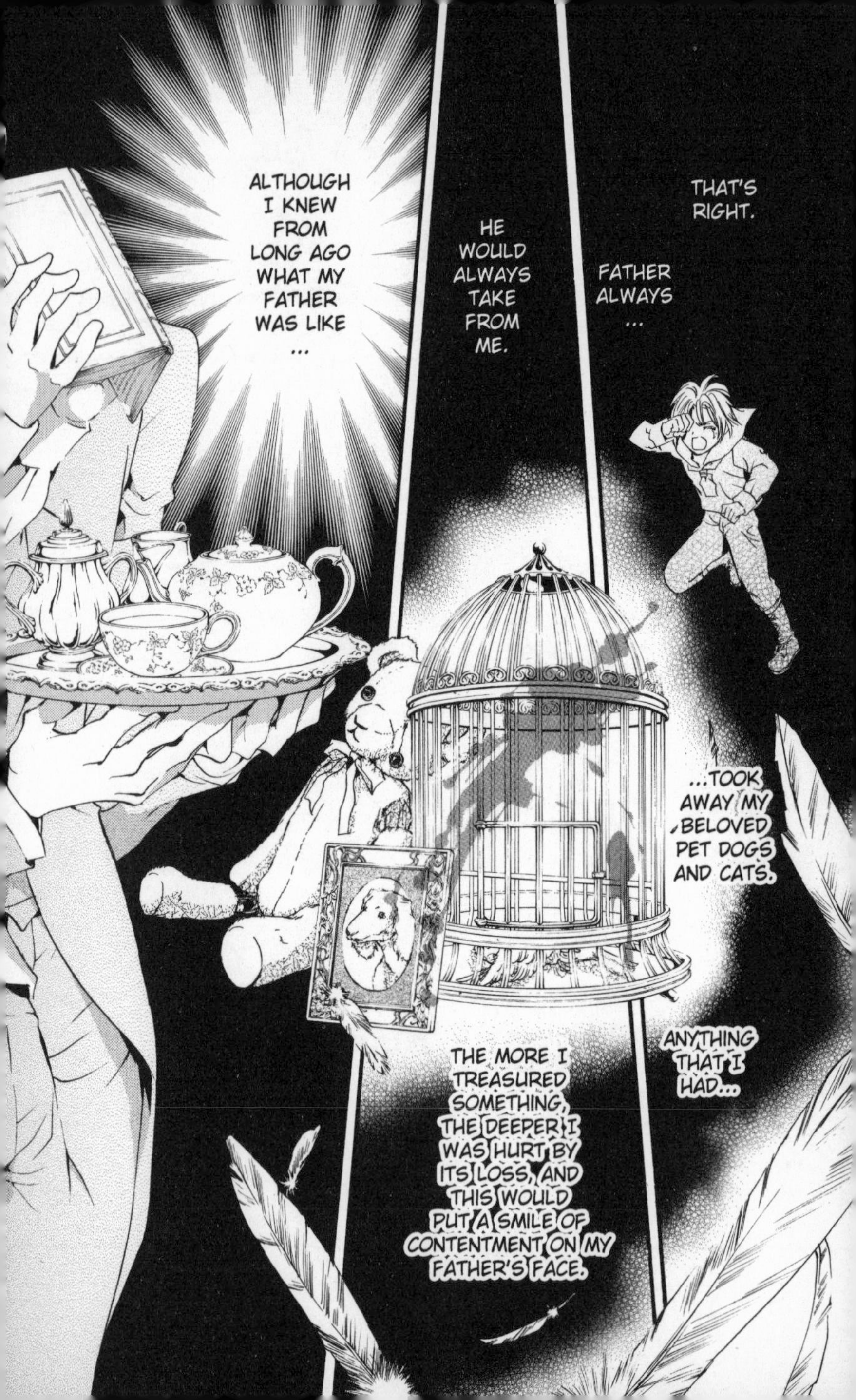
THAT'S RIGHT.
FATHER ALWAYS...
...TOOK AWAY MY BELOVED PET DOGS AND CATS.
ANYTHING THAT I HAD...
HE WOULD ALWAYS TAKE FROM ME.
THE MORE I TREASURED SOMETHING, THE DEEPER I WAS HURT BY ITS LOSS, AND THIS WOULD PUT A SMILE OF CONTENTMENT ON MY FATHER'S FACE.
ALTHOUGH I KNEW FROM LONG AGO WHAT MY FATHER WAS LIKE...

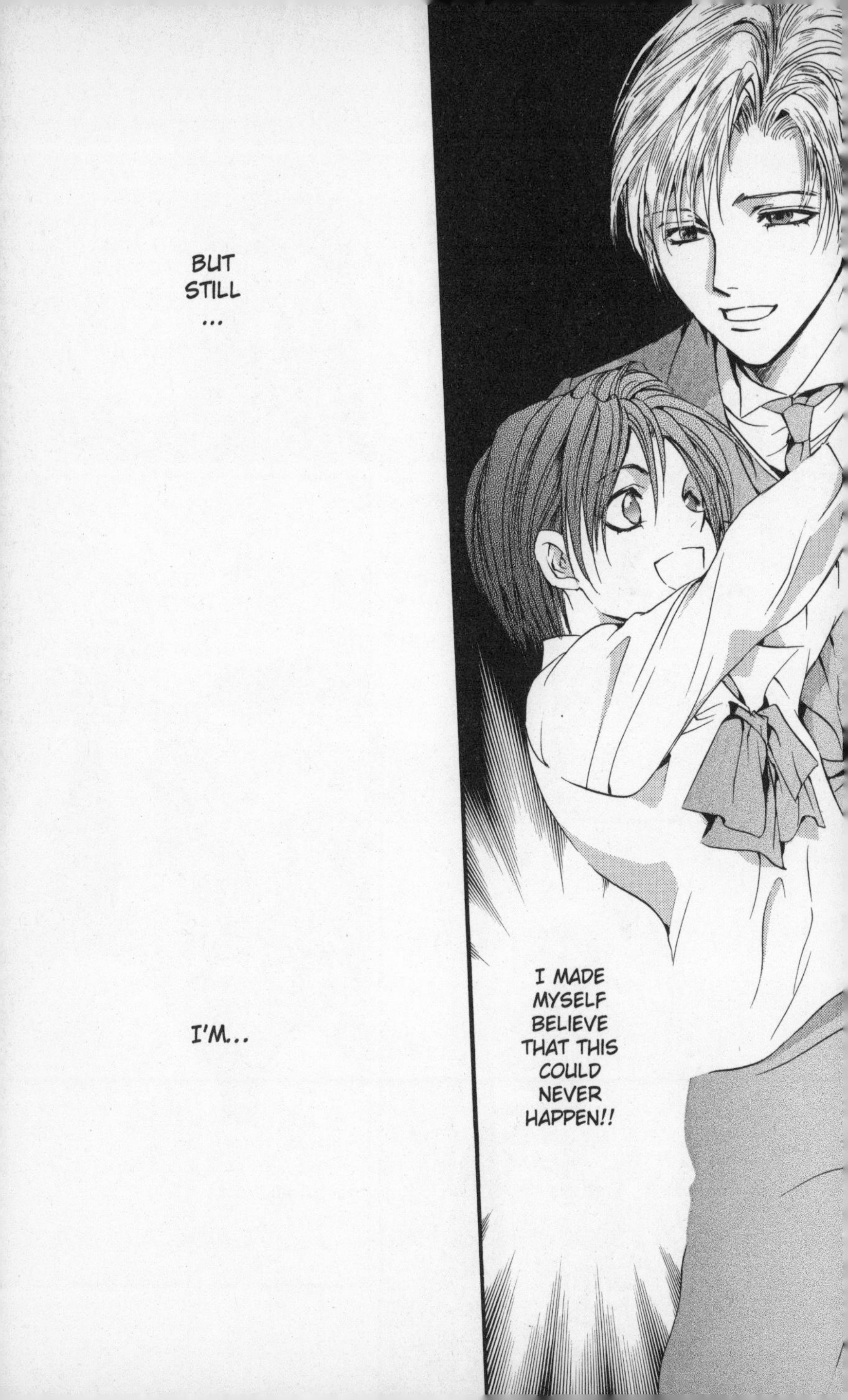
I MADE MYSELF BELIEVE THAT THIS COULD NEVER HAPPEN!!
BUT STILL...
I'M...

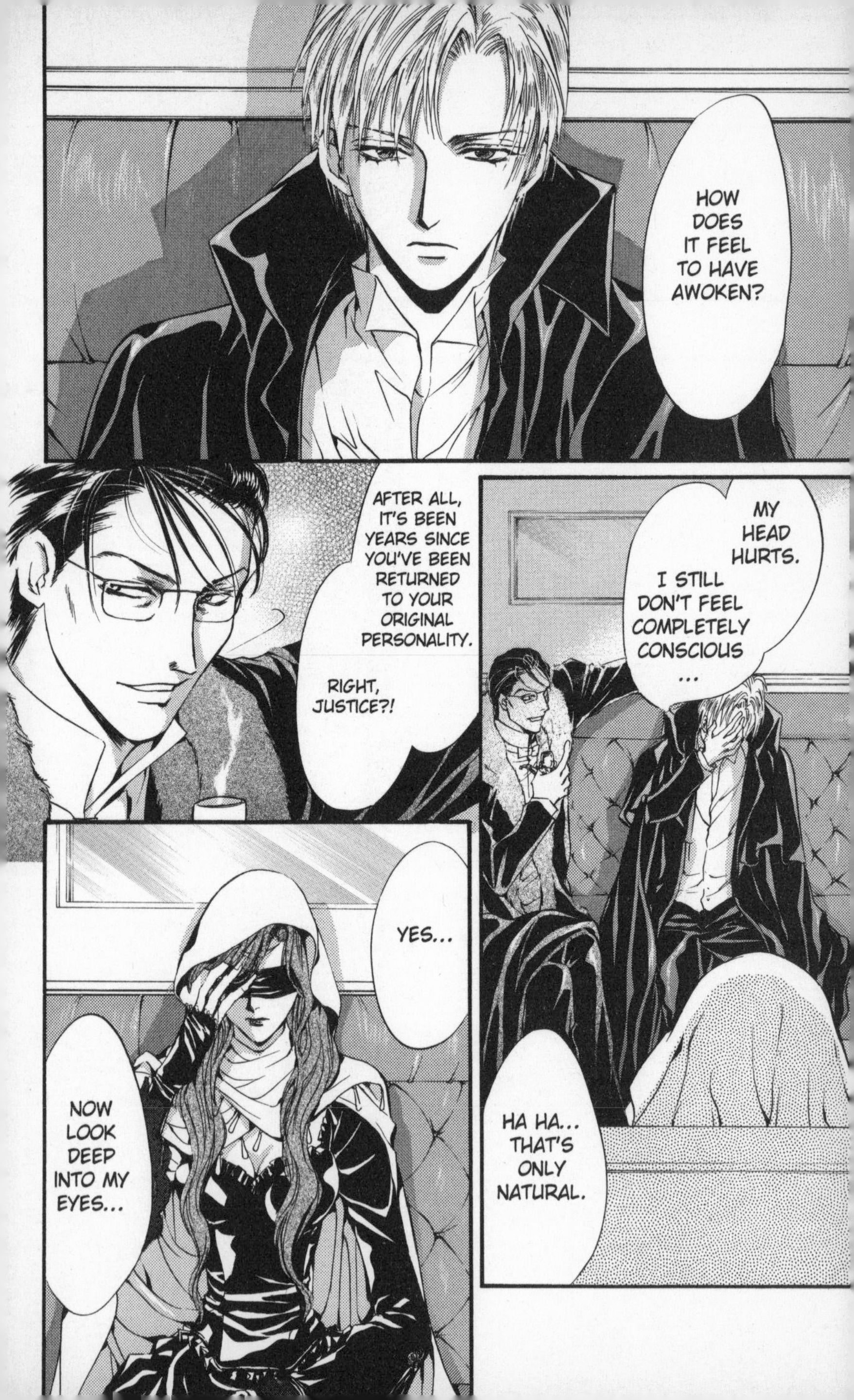
HOW DOES IT FEEL TO HAVE AWOKEN?
MY HEAD HURTS.
I STILL DON'T FEEL COMPLETELY CONSCIOUS...
HA HA... THAT'S ONLY NATURAL.
AFTER ALL, IT'S BEEN YEARS SINCE YOU'VE BEEN RETURNED TO YOUR ORIGINAL PERSONALITY.
RIGHT, JUSTICE?!
YES...
NOW LOOK DEEP INTO MY EYES...

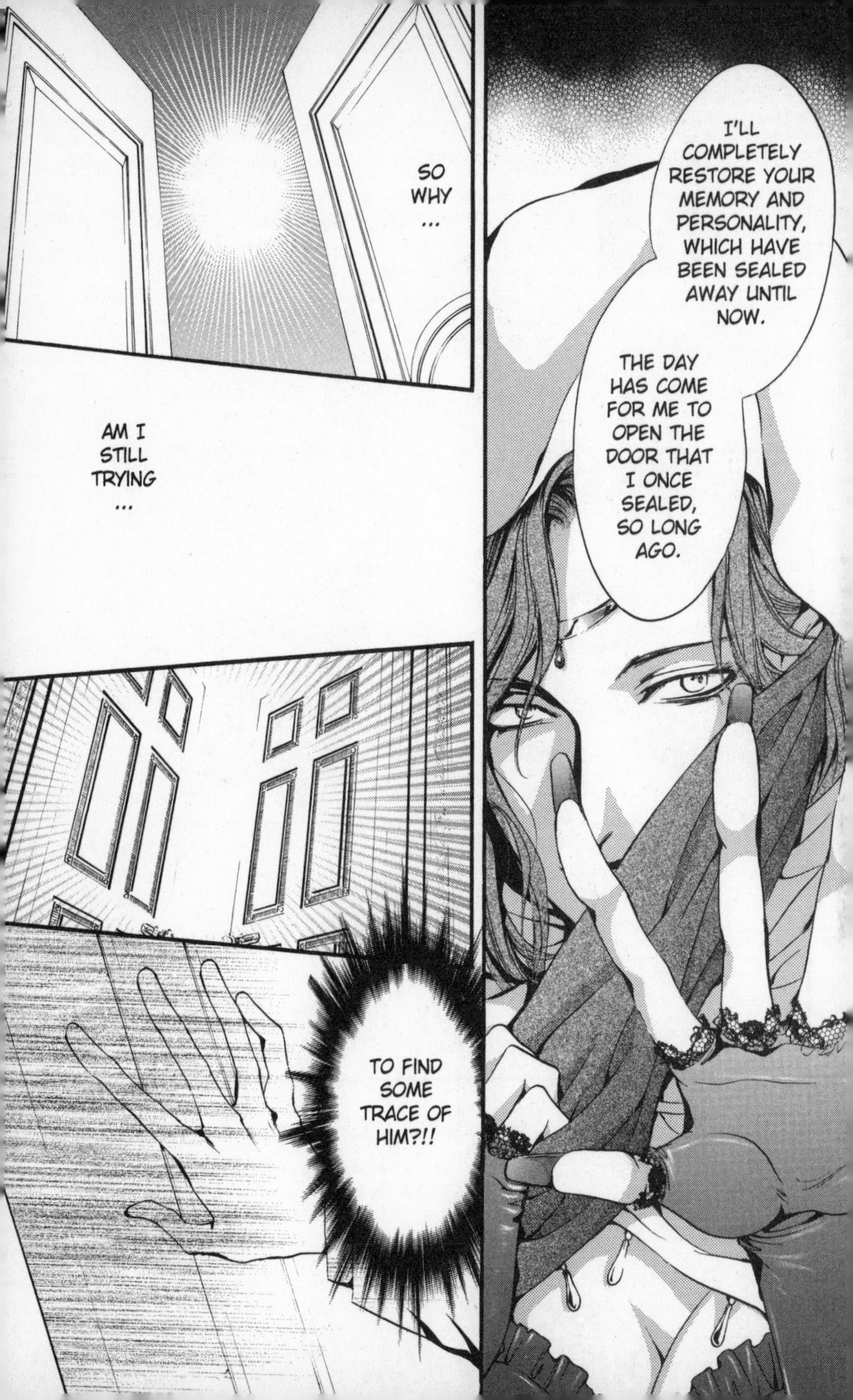
I'LL COMPLETELY RESTORE YOUR MEMORY AND PERSONALITY, WHICH HAVE BEEN SEALED AWAY UNTIL NOW.
THE DAY HAS COME FOR ME TO OPEN THE DOOR THAT I ONCE SEALED, SO LONG AGO.
SO WHY ...
AM I STILL TRYING ...
TO FIND SOME TRACE OF HIM?!!

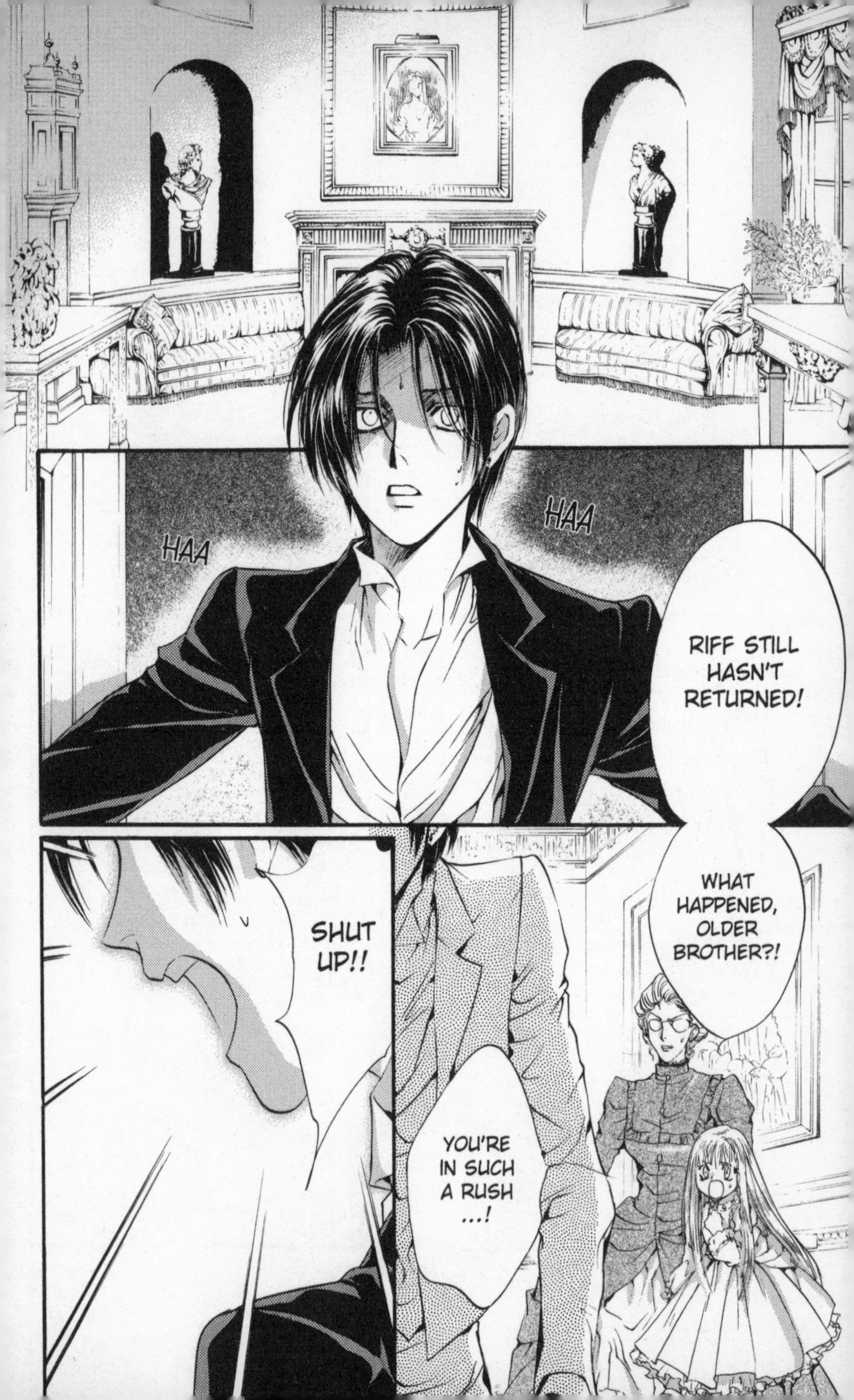
HAA
HAA
RIFF STILL HASN'T RETURNED!
WHAT HAPPENED, OLDER BROTHER?!
YOU'RE IN SUCH A RUSH ...!
SHUT UP!!

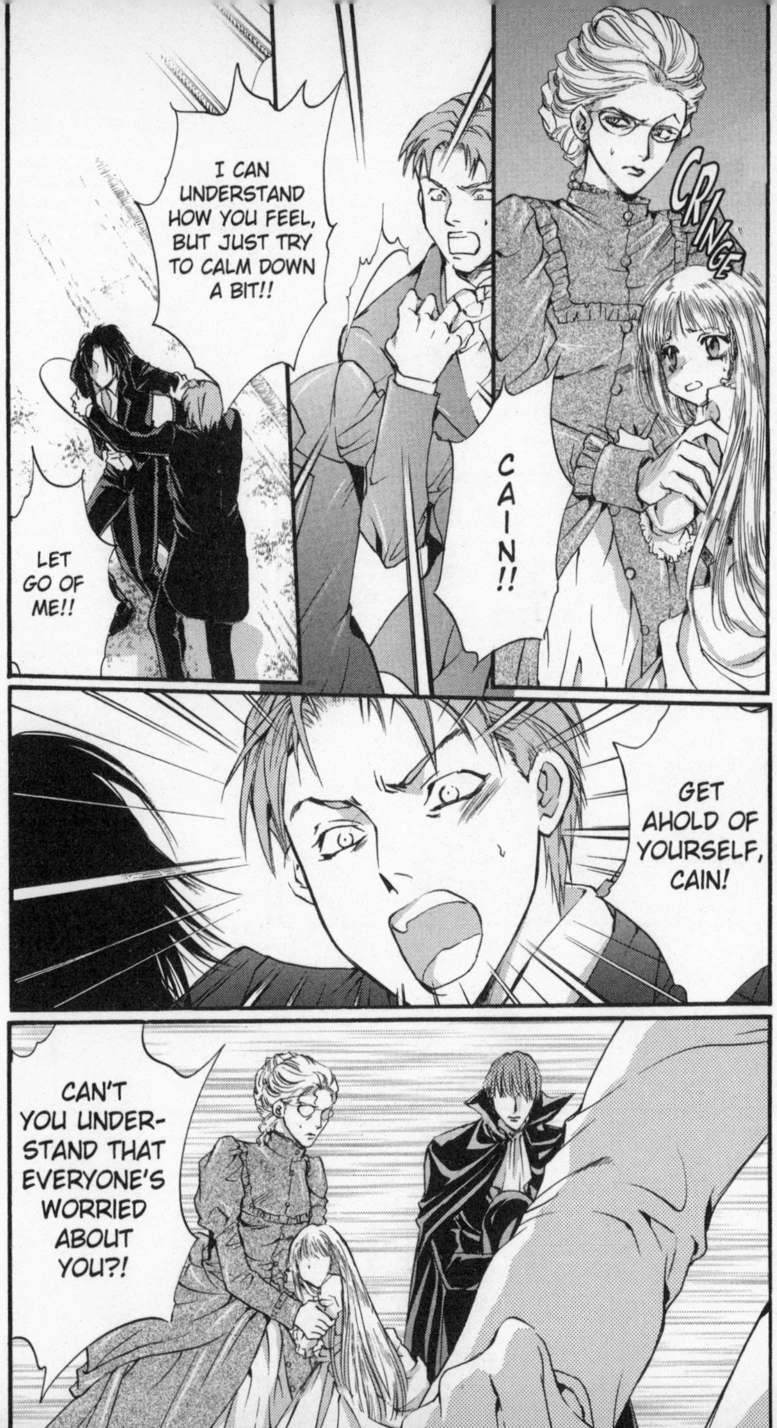
CRINGE
CAIN!!
I CAN UNDERSTAND HOW YOU FEEL, BUT JUST TRY TO CALM DOWN A BIT!!
LET GO OF ME!!
GET AHOLD OF YOURSELF, CAIN!
CAN'T YOU UNDER-STAND THAT EVERYONE'S WORRIED ABOUT YOU?!

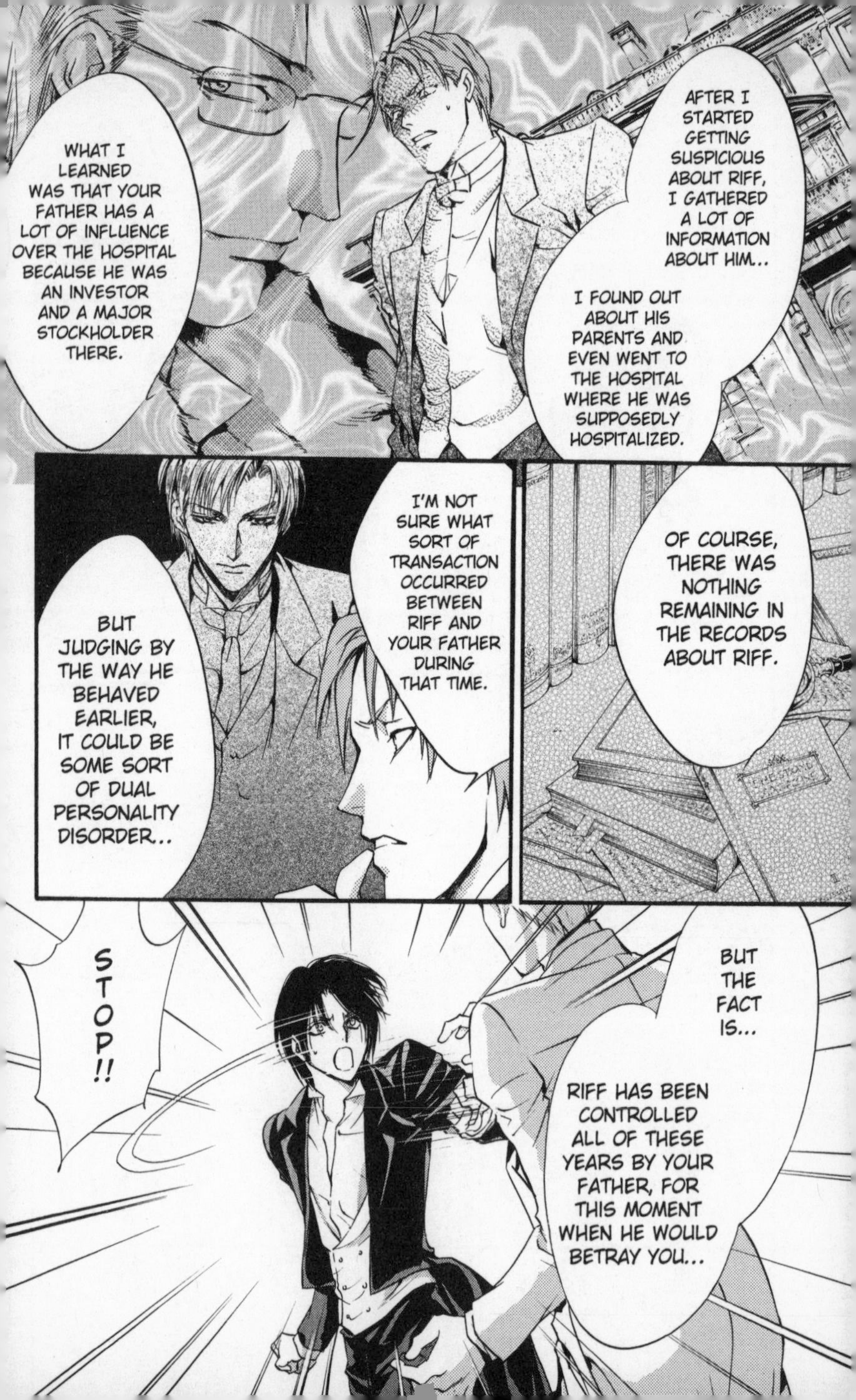
AFTER I STARTED GETTING SUSPICIOUS ABOUT RIFF, I GATHERED A LOT OF INFORMATION ABOUT HIM...
I FOUND OUT ABOUT HIS PARENTS AND EVEN WENT TO THE HOSPITAL WHERE HE WAS SUPPOSEDLY HOSPITALIZED.
WHAT I LEARNED WAS THAT YOUR FATHER HAS A LOT OF INFLUENCE OVER THE HOSPITAL BECAUSE HE WAS AN INVESTOR AND A MAJOR STOCKHOLDER THERE.
OF COURSE, THERE WAS NOTHING REMAINING IN THE RECORDS ABOUT RIFF.
I'M NOT SURE WHAT SORT OF TRANSACTION OCCURRED BETWEEN RIFF AND YOUR FATHER DURING THAT TIME.
BUT JUDGING BY THE WAY HE BEHAVED EARLIER, IT COULD BE SOME SORT OF DUAL PERSONALITY DISORDER...
BUT THE FACT IS...
RIFF HAS BEEN CONTROLLED ALL OF THESE YEARS BY YOUR FATHER, FOR THIS MOMENT WHEN HE WOULD BETRAY YOU...
STOP!!

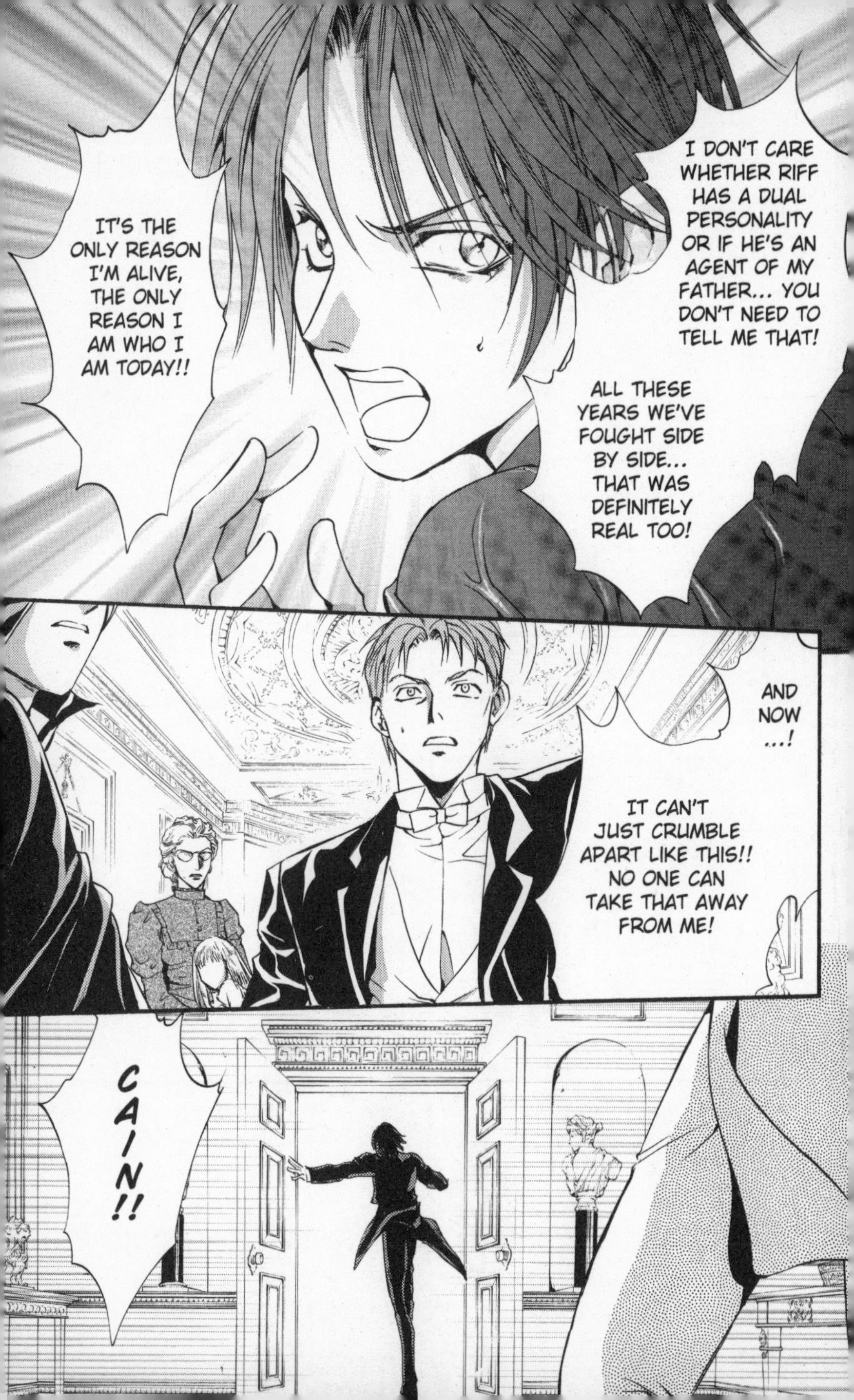
I DON'T CARE WHETHER RIFF HAS A DUAL PERSONALITY OR IF HE'S AN AGENT OF MY FATHER... YOU DON'T NEED TO TELL ME THAT!
IT'S THE ONLY REASON I'M ALIVE, THE ONLY REASON I AM WHO I AM TODAY!!
ALL THESE YEARS WE'VE FOUGHT SIDE BY SIDE... THAT WAS DEFINITELY REAL TOO!
AND NOW ...!
IT CAN'T JUST CRUMBLE APART LIKE THIS!! NO ONE CAN TAKE THAT AWAY FROM ME!
CAIN!!

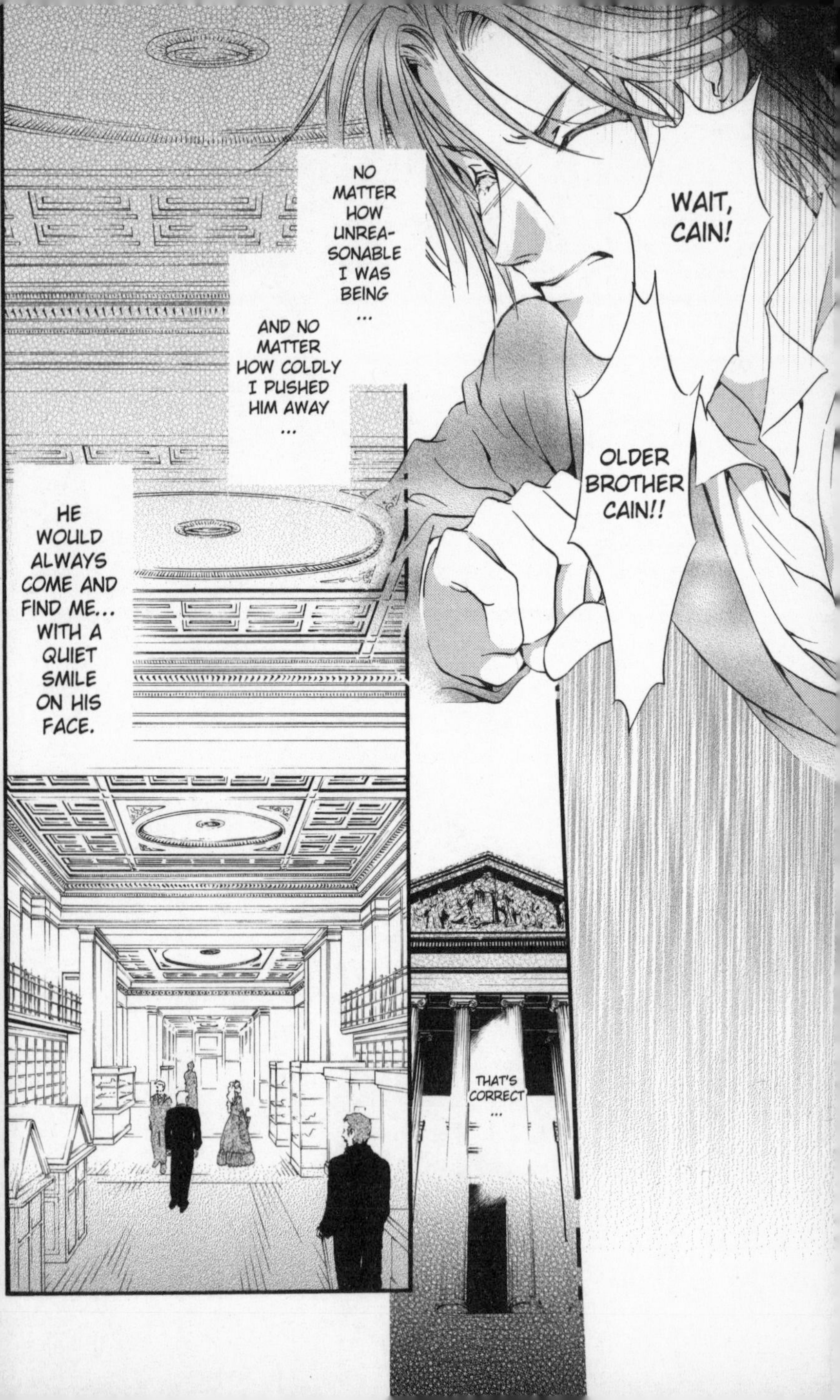
WAIT, CAIN!
OLDER BROTHER CAIN!!
NO MATTER HOW UNREASONABLE I WAS BEING...
AND NO MATTER HOW COLDLY I PUSHED HIM AWAY...
HE WOULD ALWAYS COME AND FIND ME... WITH A QUIET SMILE ON HIS FACE.
THAT'S CORRECT...

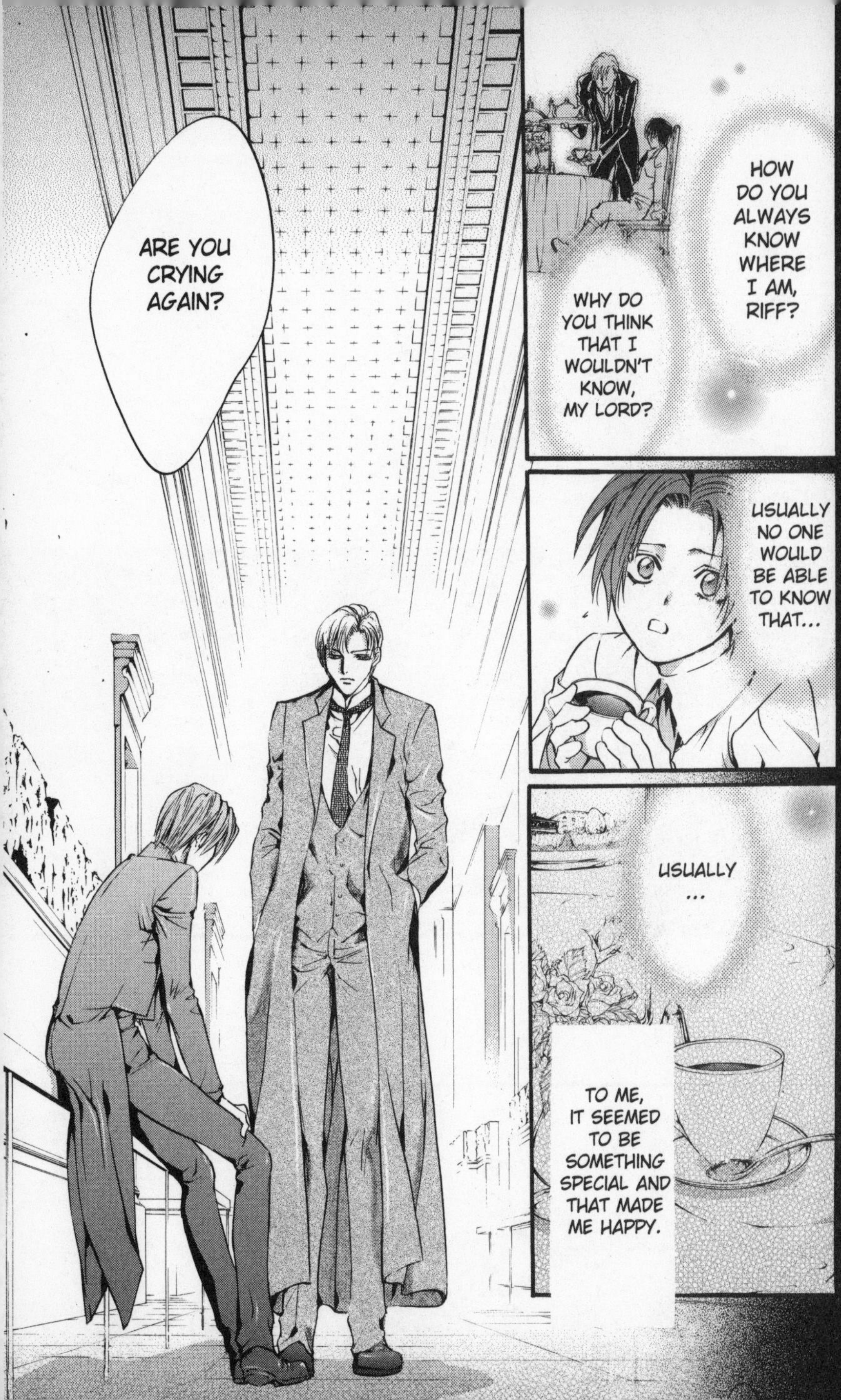
HOW DO YOU ALWAYS KNOW WHERE I AM, RIFF?
WHY DO YOU THINK THAT I WOULDN'T KNOW, MY LORD?
USUALLY NO ONE WOULD BE ABLE TO KNOW THAT...
USUALLY...
TO ME, IT SEEMED TO BE SOMETHING SPECIAL AND THAT MADE ME HAPPY.
ARE YOU CRYING AGAIN?

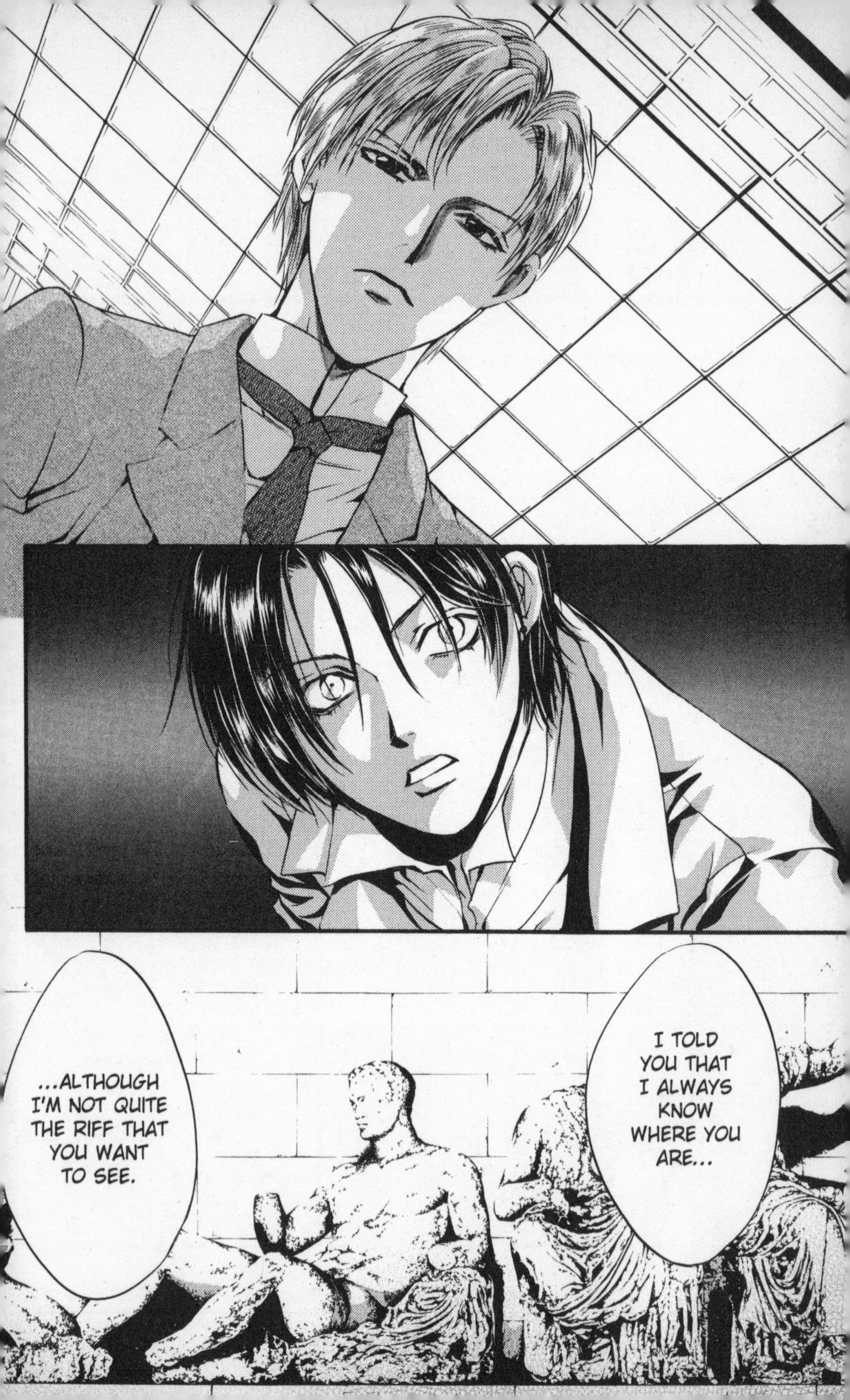
I TOLD YOU THAT I ALWAYS KNOW WHERE YOU ARE...
...ALTHOUGH I'M NOT QUITE THE RIFF THAT YOU WANT TO SEE.

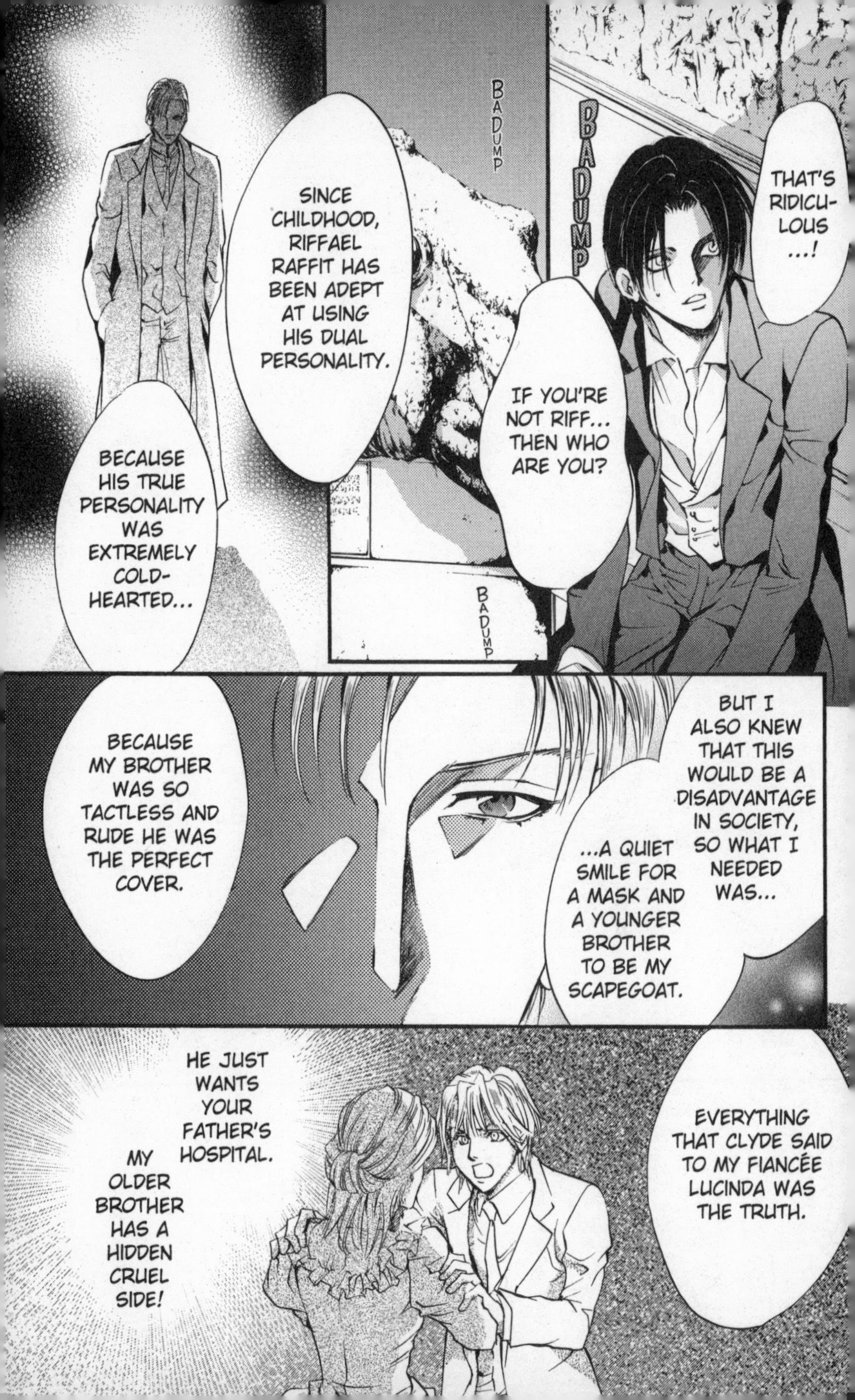

THAT'S RIDICULOUS ...!
BADUMP
IF YOU'RE NOT RIFF... THEN WHO ARE YOU?
BADUMP
SINCE CHILDHOOD, RIFFAEL RAFFIT HAS BEEN ADEPT AT USING HIS DUAL PERSONALITY.
BADUMP
BECAUSE HIS TRUE PERSONALITY WAS EXTREMELY COLD-HEARTED...
BUT I ALSO KNEW THAT THIS WOULD BE A DISADVANTAGE IN SOCIETY, SO WHAT I NEEDED WAS...
...A QUIET SMILE FOR A MASK AND A YOUNGER BROTHER TO BE MY SCAPEGOAT.
BECAUSE MY BROTHER WAS SO TACTLESS AND RUDE HE WAS THE PERFECT COVER.
EVERYTHING THAT CLYDE SAID TO MY FIANCÉE LUCINDA WAS THE TRUTH.
HE JUST WANTS YOUR FATHER'S HOSPITAL.
MY OLDER BROTHER HAS A HIDDEN CRUEL SIDE!

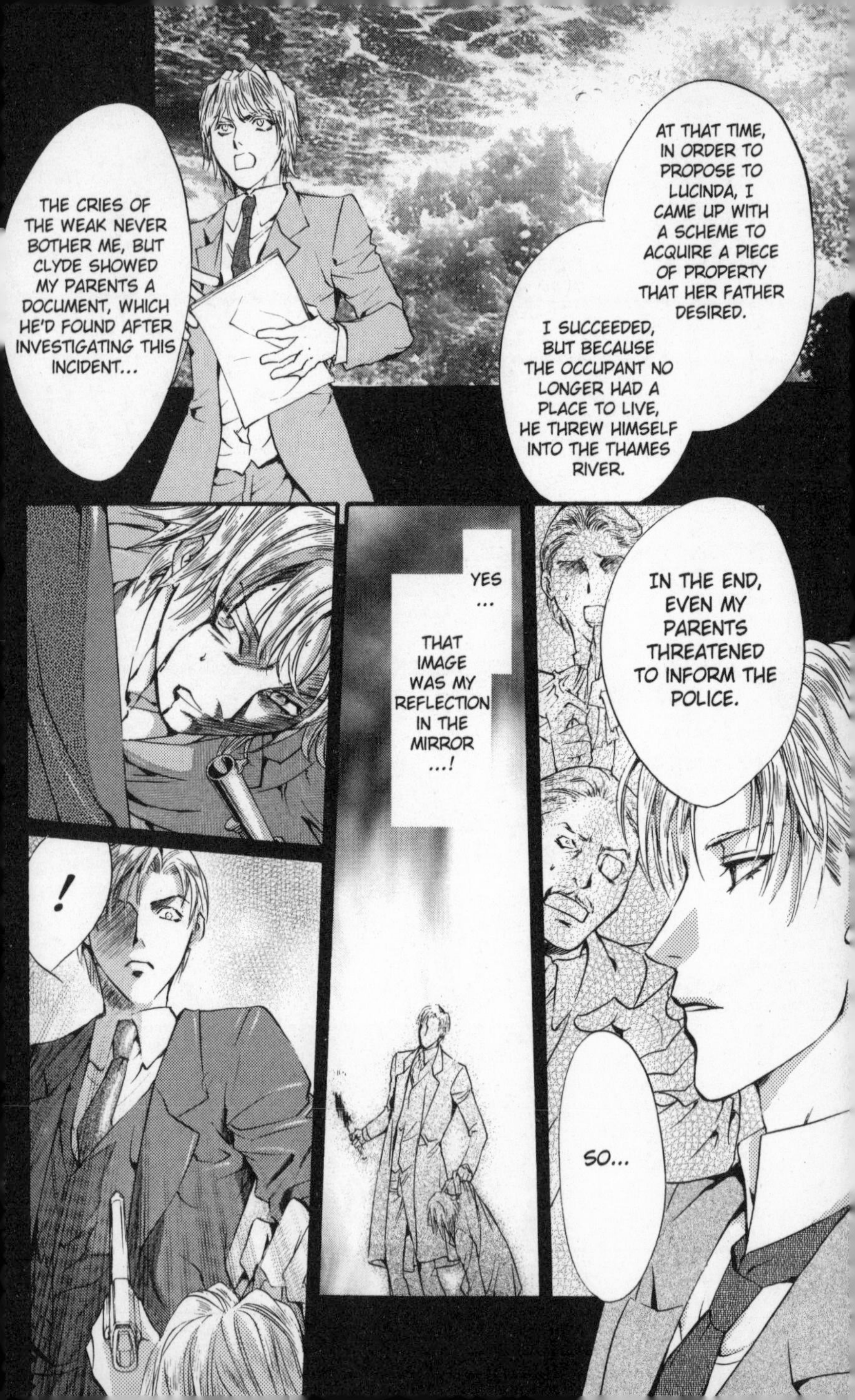
AT THAT TIME, IN ORDER TO PROPOSE TO LUCINDA, I CAME UP WITH A SCHEME TO ACQUIRE A PIECE OF PROPERTY THAT HER FATHER DESIRED.
I SUCCEEDED, BUT BECAUSE THE OCCUPANT NO LONGER HAD A PLACE TO LIVE, HE THREW HIMSELF INTO THE THAMES RIVER.
THE CRIES OF THE WEAK NEVER BOTHER ME, BUT CLYDE SHOWED MY PARENTS A DOCUMENT, WHICH HE'D FOUND AFTER INVESTIGATING THIS INCIDENT...
IN THE END, EVEN MY PARENTS THREATENED TO INFORM THE POLICE.
SO...
YES ...
THAT IMAGE WAS MY REFLECTION IN THE MIRROR ...!
!

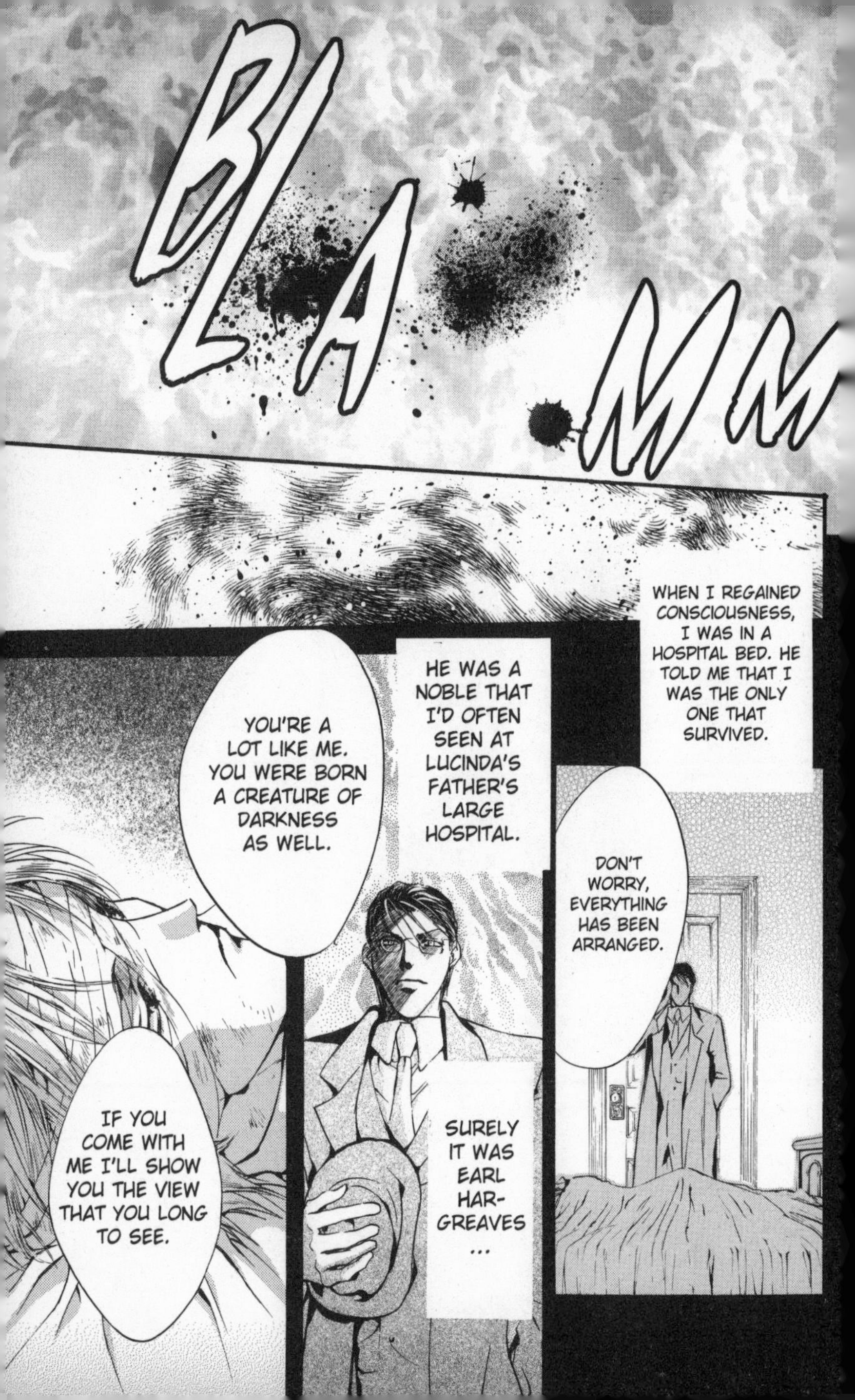
BLAMM
WHEN I REGAINED CONSCIOUSNESS, I WAS IN A HOSPITAL BED. HE TOLD ME THAT I WAS THE ONLY ONE THAT SURVIVED.
DON'T WORRY, EVERYTHING HAS BEEN ARRANGED.
HE WAS A NOBLE THAT I'D OFTEN SEEN AT LUCINDA'S FATHER'S LARGE HOSPITAL.
SURELY IT WAS EARL HAR-GREAVES ...
YOU'RE A LOT LIKE ME. YOU WERE BORN A CREATURE OF DARKNESS AS WELL.
IF YOU COME WITH ME I'LL SHOW YOU THE VIEW THAT YOU LONG TO SEE.

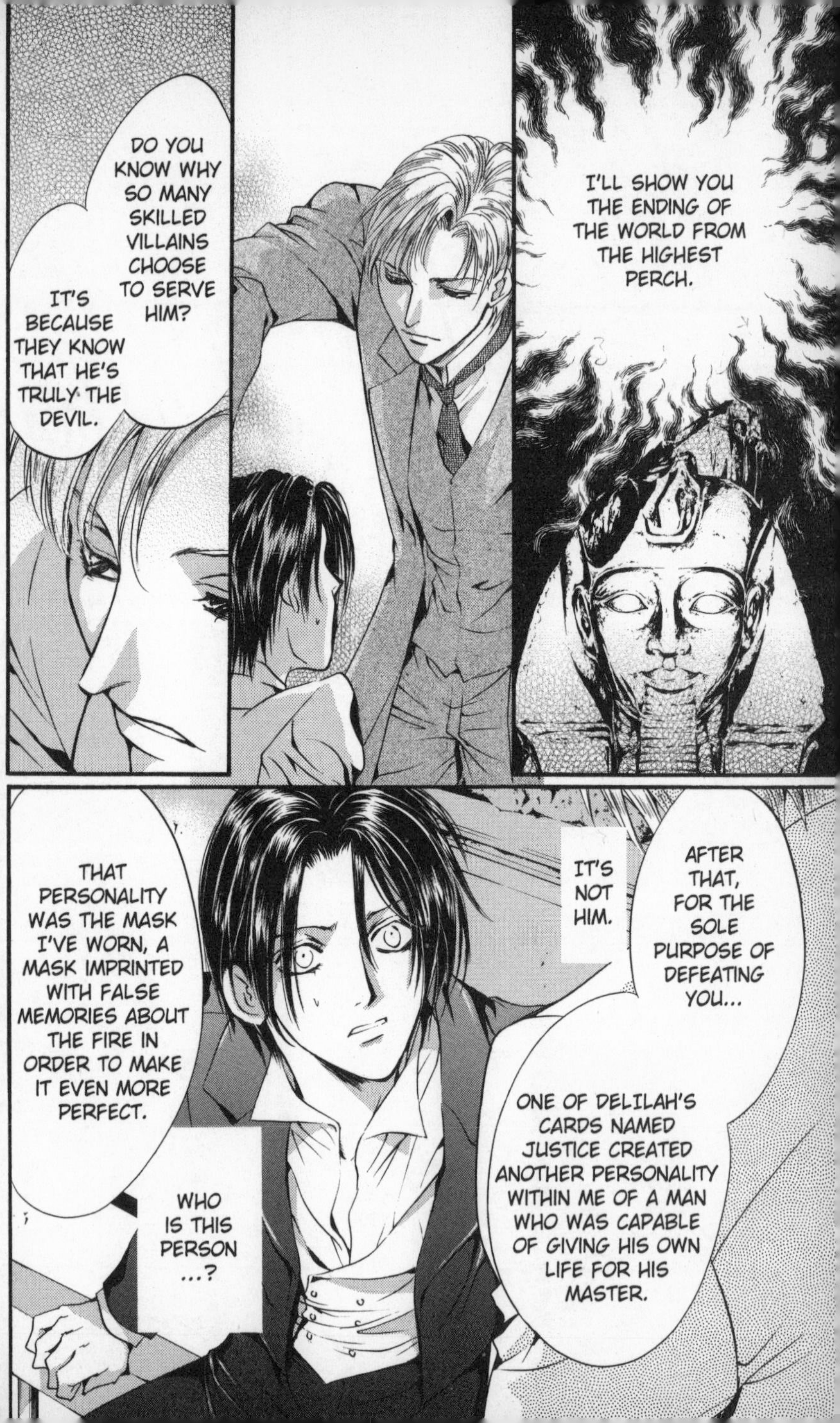
I'LL SHOW YOU THE ENDING OF THE WORLD FROM THE HIGHEST PERCH.
DO YOU KNOW WHY SO MANY SKILLED VILLAINS CHOOSE TO SERVE HIM?
IT'S BECAUSE THEY KNOW THAT HE'S TRULY THE DEVIL.
AFTER THAT, FOR THE SOLE PURPOSE OF DEFEATING YOU...
IT'S NOT HIM.
THAT PERSONALITY WAS THE MASK I'VE WORN, A MASK IMPRINTED WITH FALSE MEMORIES ABOUT THE FIRE IN ORDER TO MAKE IT EVEN MORE PERFECT.
ONE OF DELILAH'S CARDS NAMED JUSTICE CREATED ANOTHER PERSONALITY WITHIN ME OF A MAN WHO WAS CAPABLE OF GIVING HIS OWN LIFE FOR HIS MASTER.
WHO IS THIS PERSON ...?

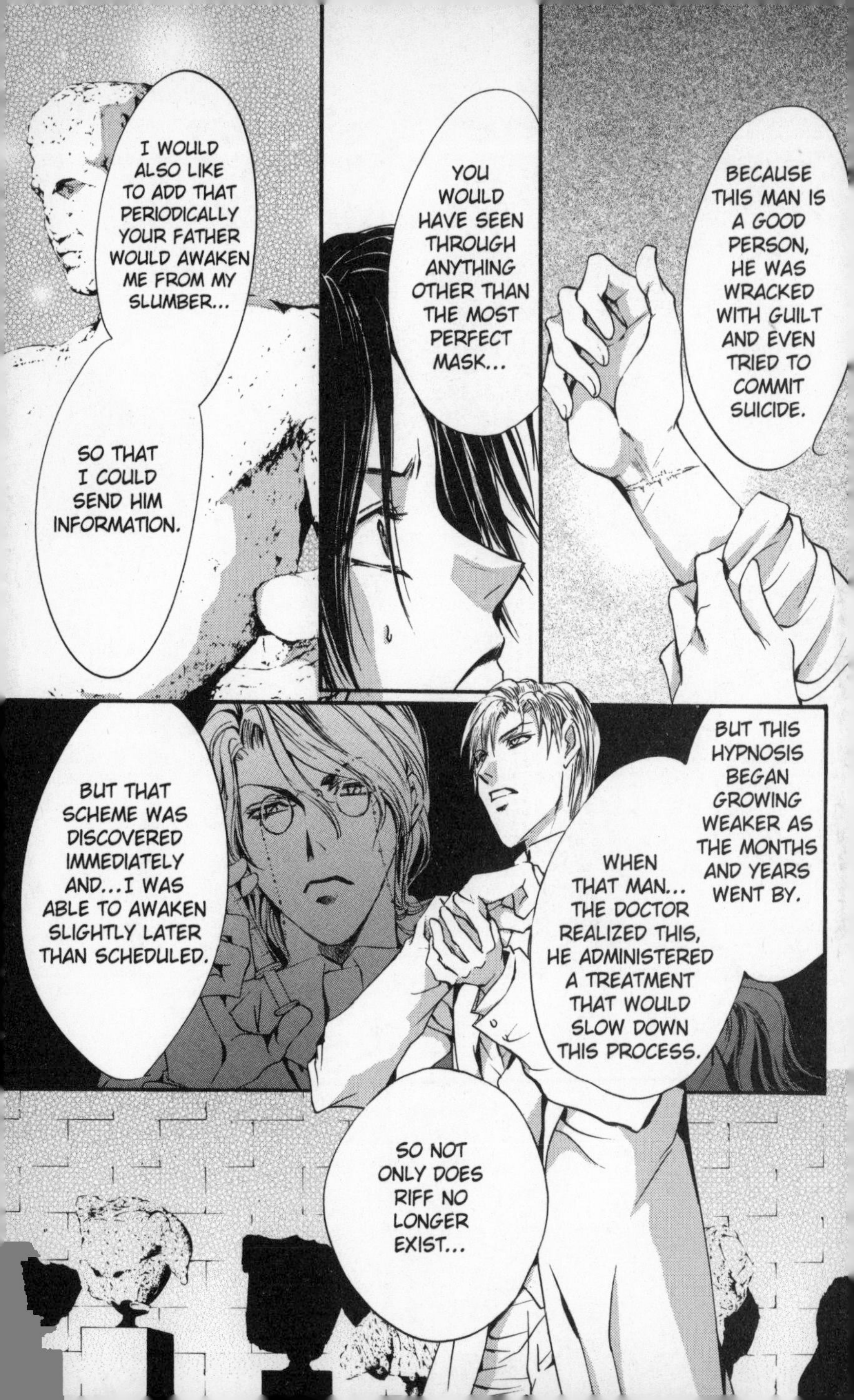
BECAUSE THIS MAN IS A GOOD PERSON, HE WAS WRACKED WITH GUILT AND EVEN TRIED TO COMMIT SUICIDE.
YOU WOULD HAVE SEEN THROUGH ANYTHING OTHER THAN THE MOST PERFECT MASK...
I WOULD ALSO LIKE TO ADD THAT PERIODICALLY YOUR FATHER WOULD AWAKEN ME FROM MY SLUMBER...
SO THAT I COULD SEND HIM INFORMATION.
BUT THIS HYPNOSIS BEGAN GROWING WEAKER AS THE MONTHS AND YEARS WENT BY.
WHEN THAT MAN... THE DOCTOR REALIZED THIS, HE ADMINISTERED A TREATMENT THAT WOULD SLOW DOWN THIS PROCESS.
BUT THAT SCHEME WAS DISCOVERED IMMEDIATELY AND...I WAS ABLE TO AWAKEN SLIGHTLY LATER THAN SCHEDULED.
SO NOT ONLY DOES RIFF NO LONGER EXIST...

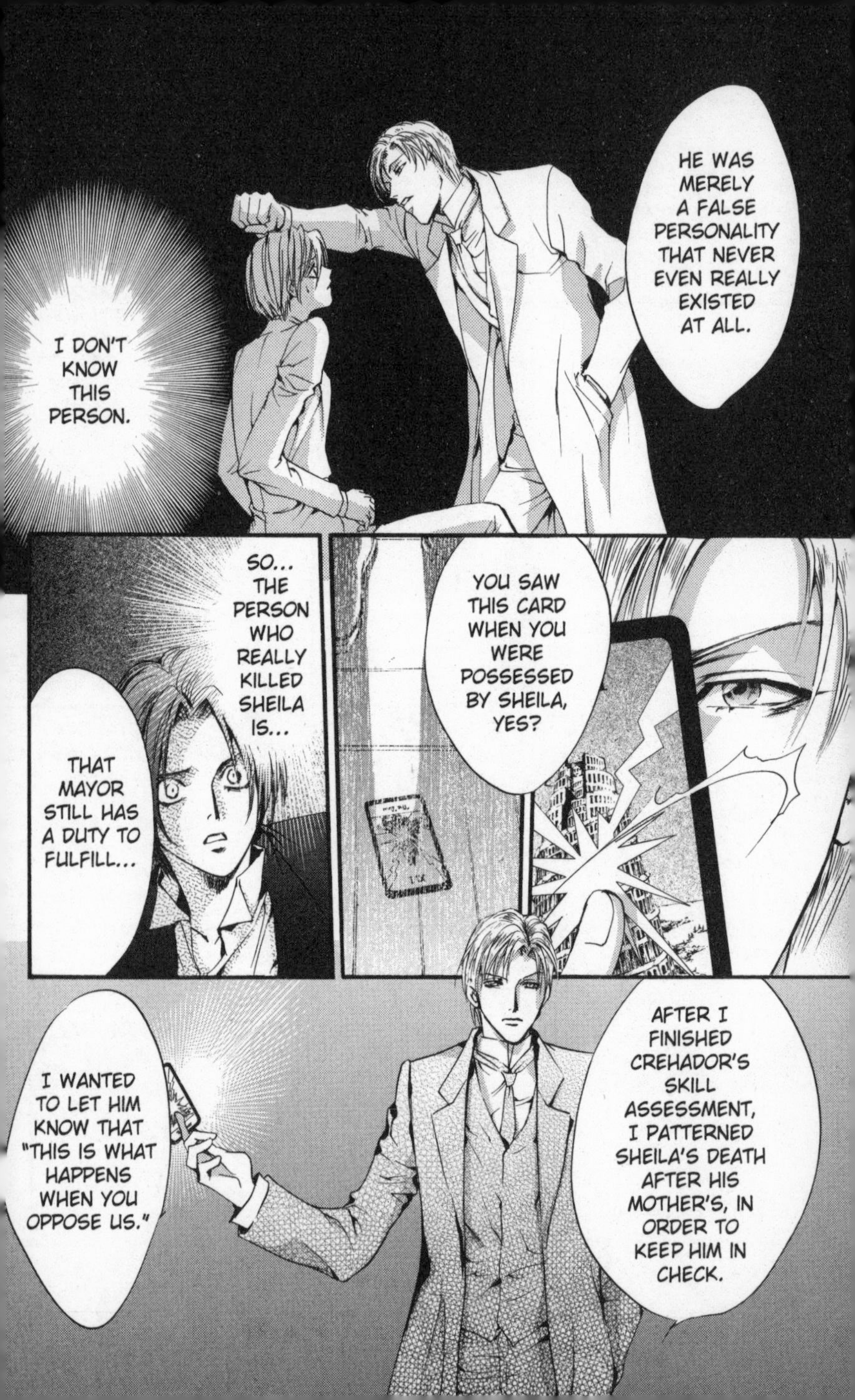
HE WAS MERELY A FALSE PERSONALITY THAT NEVER EVEN REALLY EXISTED AT ALL.
I DON'T KNOW THIS PERSON.
YOU SAW THIS CARD WHEN YOU WERE POSSESSED BY SHEILA, YES?
SO... THE PERSON WHO REALLY KILLED SHEILA IS...
THAT MAYOR STILL HAS A DUTY TO FULFILL...
AFTER I FINISHED CREHADOR'S SKILL ASSESSMENT, I PATTERNED SHEILA'S DEATH AFTER HIS MOTHER'S, IN ORDER TO KEEP HIM IN CHECK.
I WANTED TO LET HIM KNOW THAT "THIS IS WHAT HAPPENS WHEN YOU OPPOSE US."

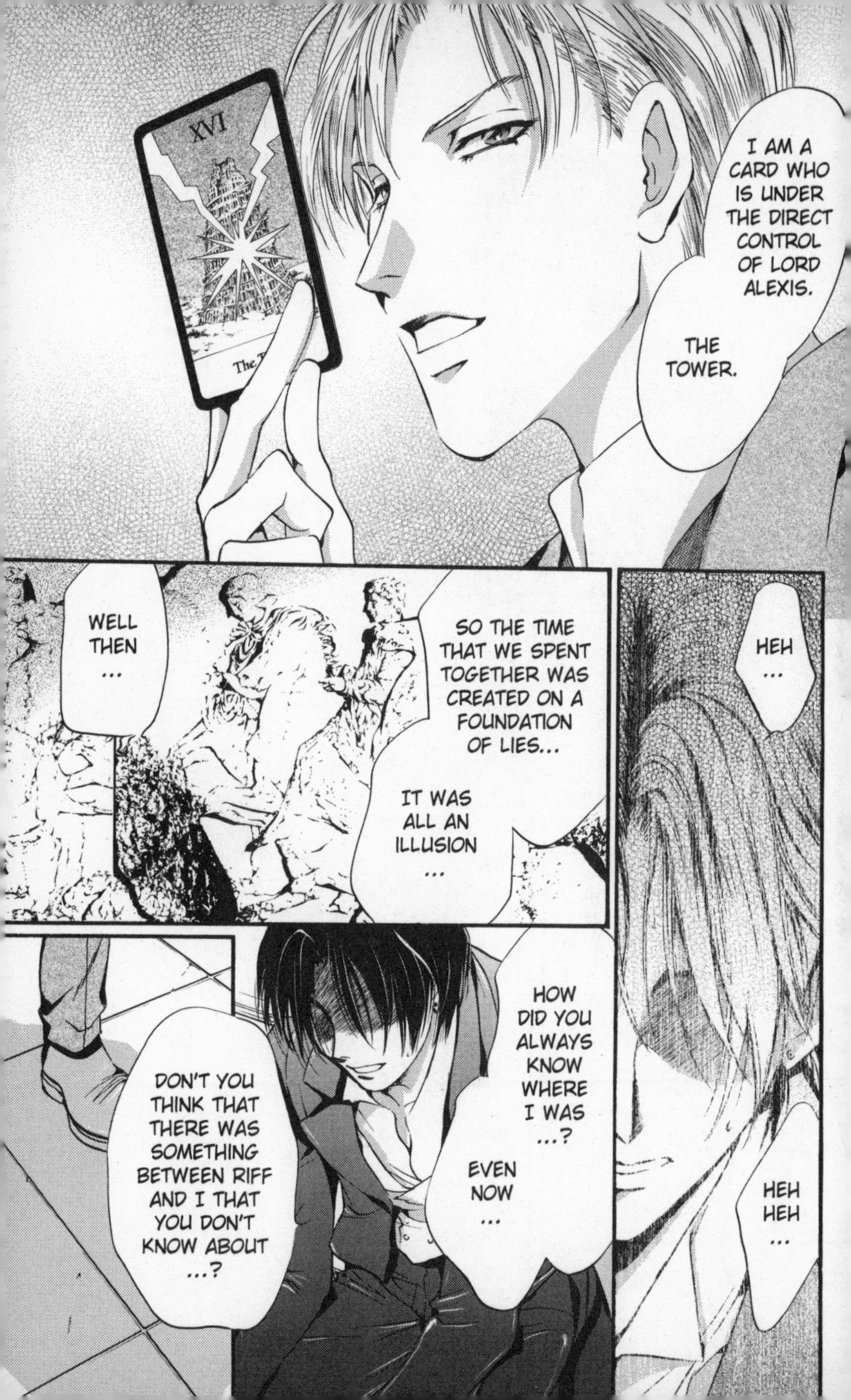
XVI
I AM A CARD WHO IS UNDER THE DIRECT CONTROL OF LORD ALEXIS.
THE TOWER.
HEH ...
SO THE TIME THAT WE SPENT TOGETHER WAS CREATED ON A FOUNDATION OF LIES...
IT WAS ALL AN ILLUSION ...
WELL THEN ...
HEH HEH ...
HOW DID YOU ALWAYS KNOW WHERE I WAS ...?
EVEN NOW ...
DON'T YOU THINK THAT THERE WAS SOMETHING BETWEEN RIFF AND I THAT YOU DON'T KNOW ABOUT ...?

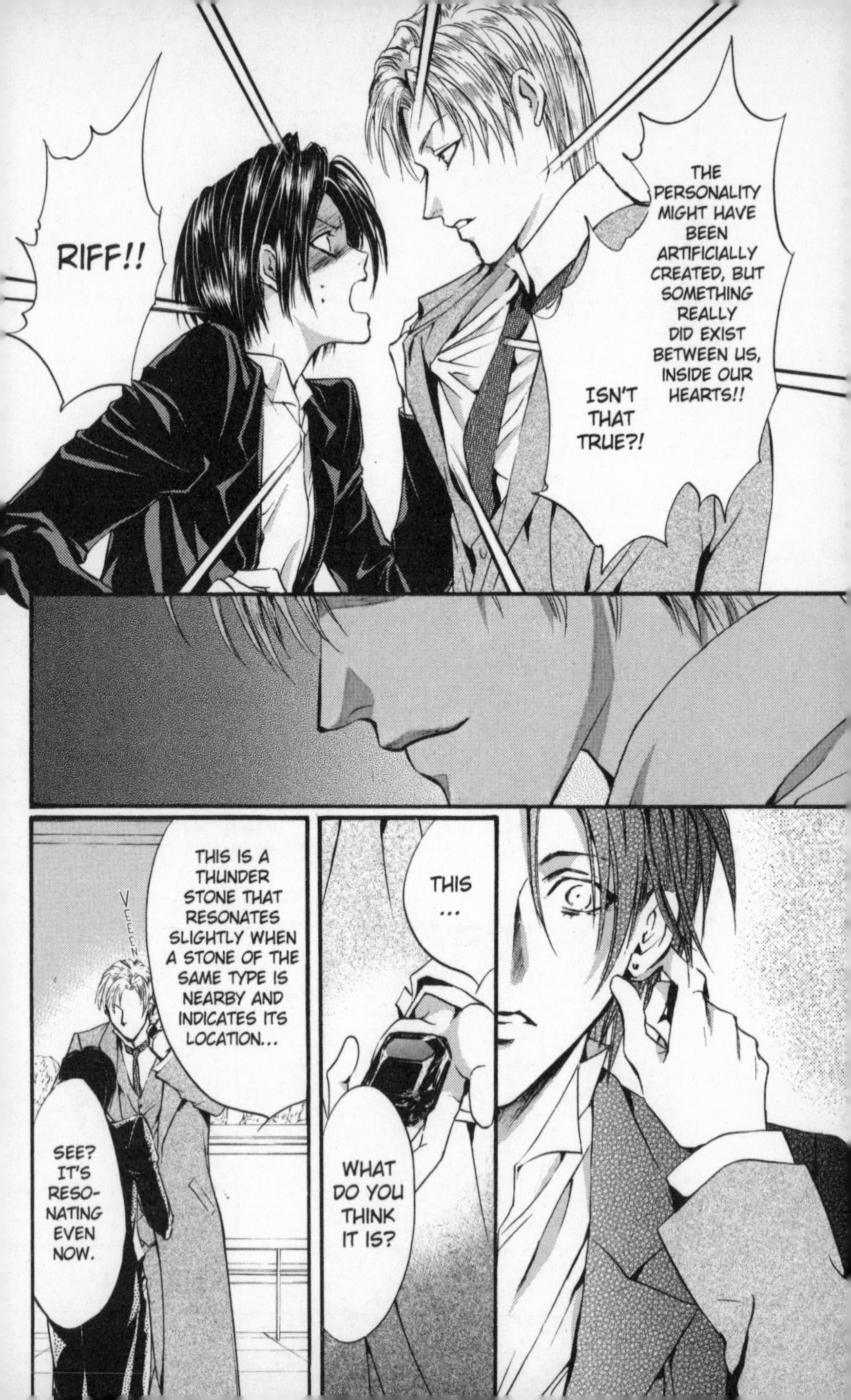
THE PERSONALITY MIGHT HAVE BEEN ARTIFICIALLY CREATED, BUT SOMETHING REALLY DID EXIST BETWEEN US, INSIDE OUR HEARTS!!
ISN'T THAT TRUE?!
RIFF!!
THIS ...
WHAT DO YOU THINK IT IS?
THIS IS A THUNDER STONE THAT RESONATES SLIGHTLY WHEN A STONE OF THE SAME TYPE IS NEARBY AND INDICATES ITS LOCATION...
VEEEN
SEE? IT'S RESO-NATING EVEN NOW.

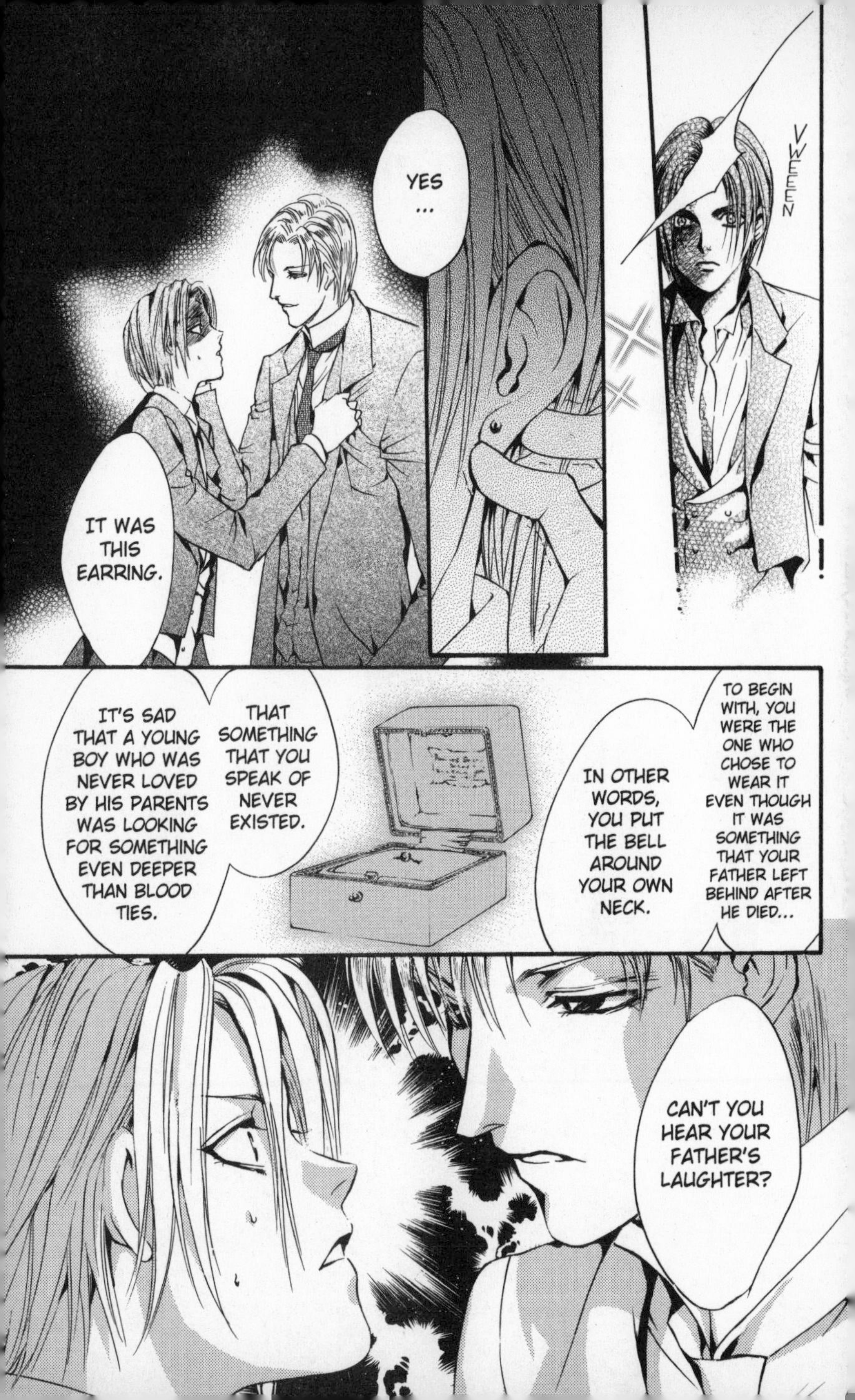
VWEEEN
!
YES ...
IT WAS THIS EARRING.
TO BEGIN WITH, YOU WERE THE ONE WHO CHOSE TO WEAR IT EVEN THOUGH IT WAS SOMETHING THAT YOUR FATHER LEFT BEHIND AFTER HE DIED...
IN OTHER WORDS, YOU PUT THE BELL AROUND YOUR OWN NECK.
IT'S SAD THAT A YOUNG BOY WHO WAS NEVER LOVED BY HIS PARENTS WAS LOOKING FOR SOMETHING EVEN DEEPER THAN BLOOD TIES.
THAT SOMETHING THAT YOU SPEAK OF NEVER EXISTED.
CAN'T YOU HEAR YOUR FATHER'S LAUGHTER?

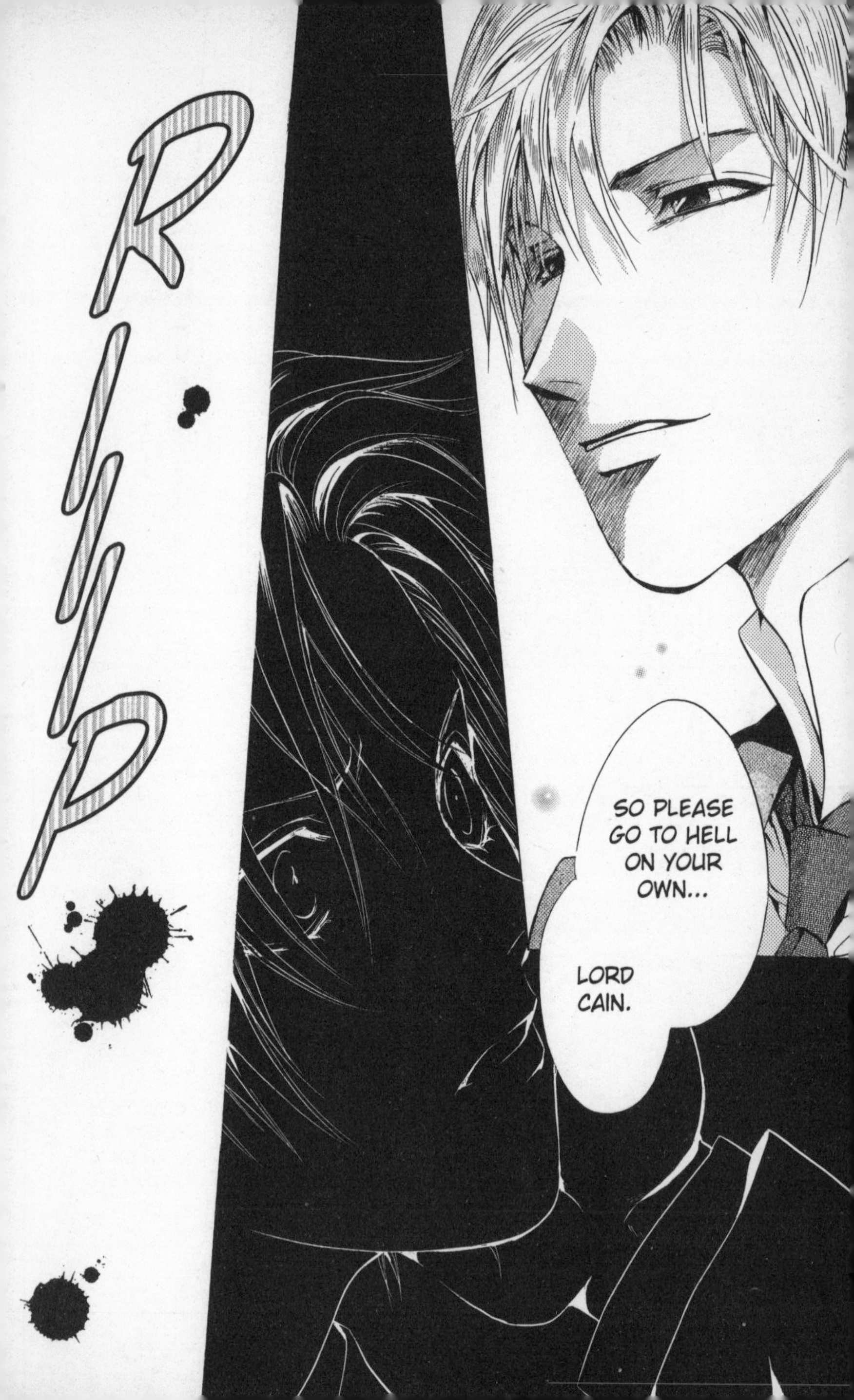
RIIIP
SO PLEASE GO TO HELL ON YOUR OWN...
LORD CAIN.

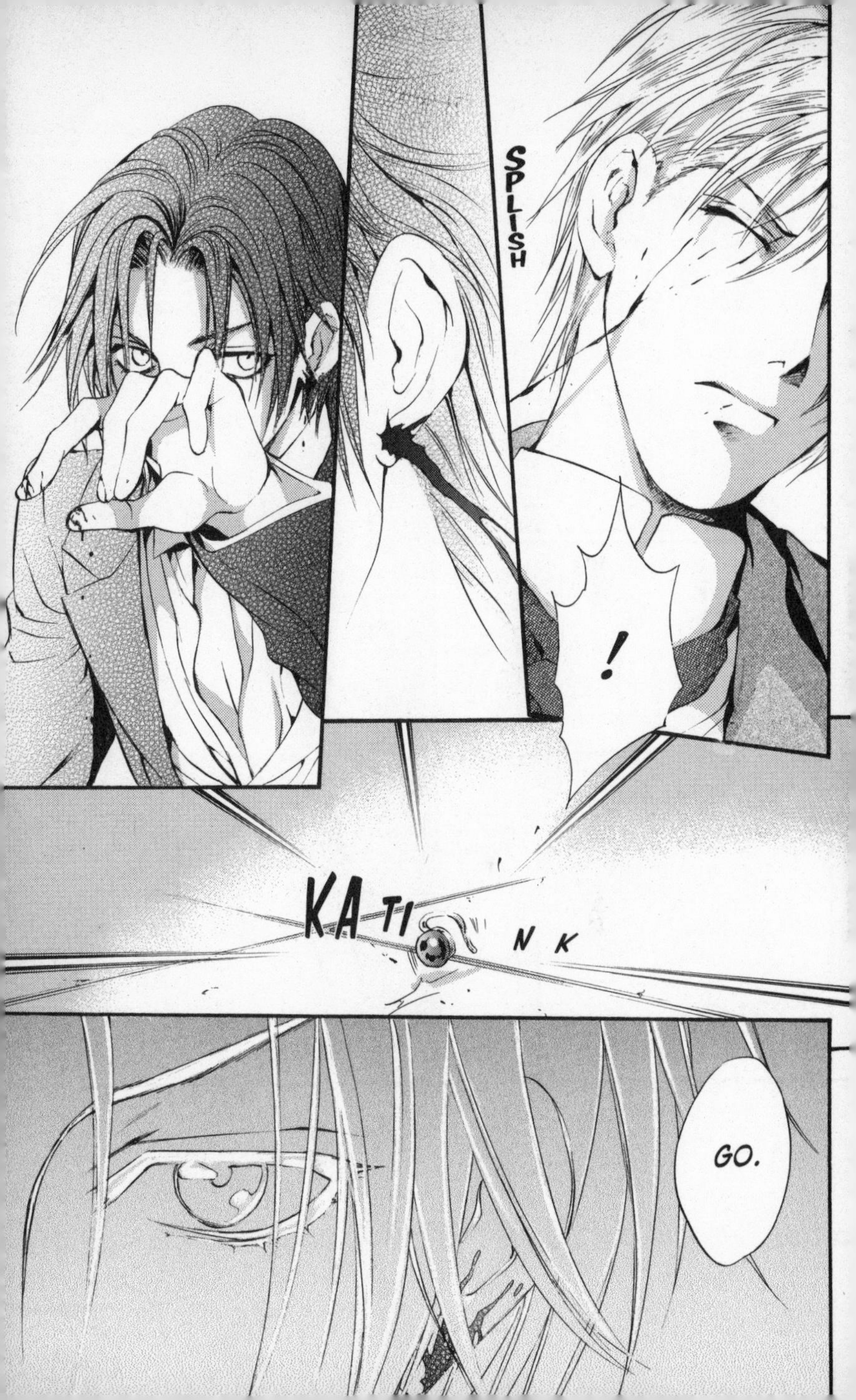
SPLISH
!
KA TI N K
GO.

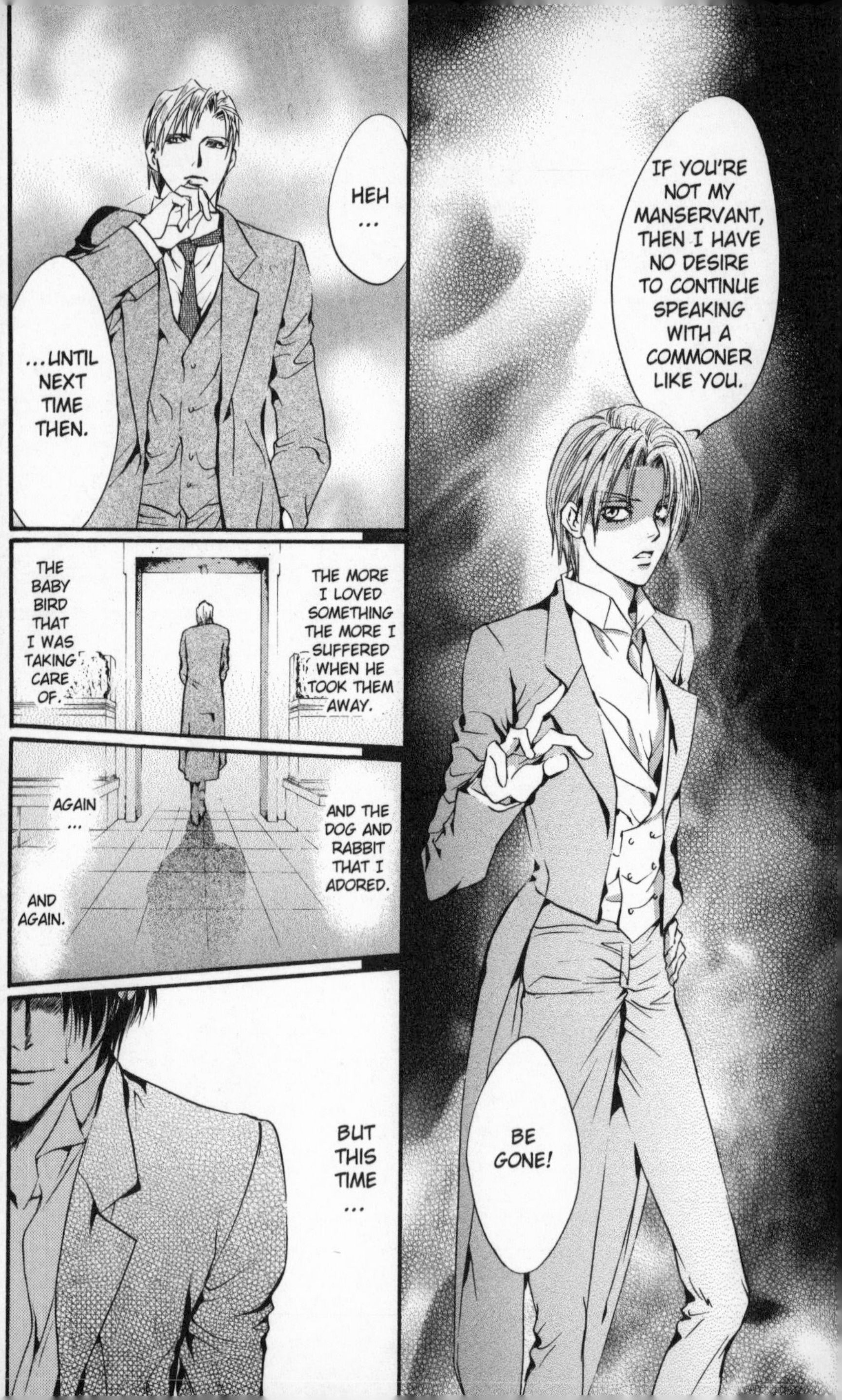
IF YOU'RE NOT MY MANSERVANT, THEN I HAVE NO DESIRE TO CONTINUE SPEAKING WITH A COMMONER LIKE YOU.
BE GONE!
HEH...
...UNTIL NEXT TIME THEN.
THE MORE I LOVED SOMETHING THE MORE I SUFFERED WHEN HE TOOK THEM AWAY.
THE BABY BIRD THAT I WAS TAKING CARE OF.
AND THE DOG AND RABBIT THAT I ADORED.
AGAIN...
AND AGAIN.
BUT THIS TIME...

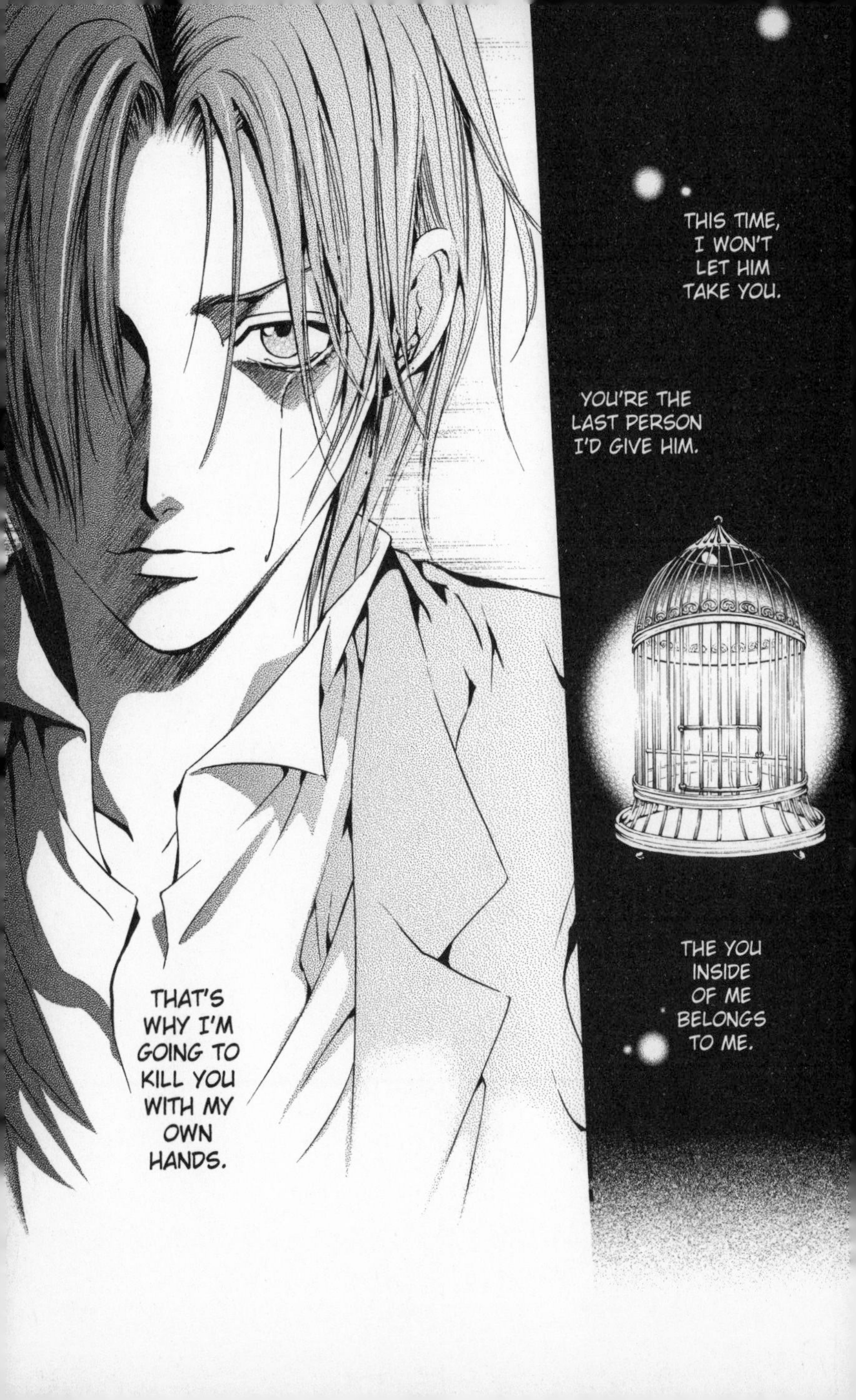
THIS TIME, I WON'T LET HIM TAKE YOU.
YOU'RE THE LAST PERSON I'D GIVE HIM.
THE YOU INSIDE OF ME BELONGS TO ME.
THAT'S WHY I'M GOING TO KILL YOU WITH MY OWN HANDS.

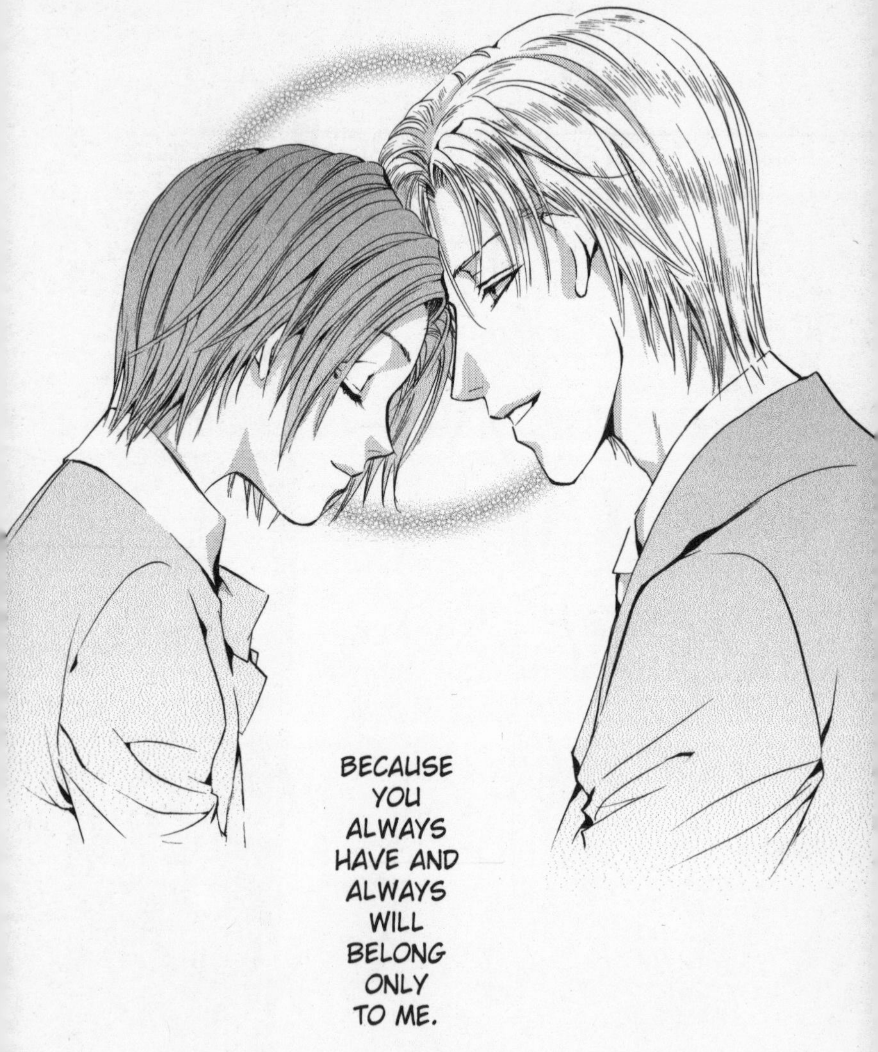
BECAUSE YOU ALWAYS HAVE AND ALWAYS WILL BELONG ONLY TO ME.

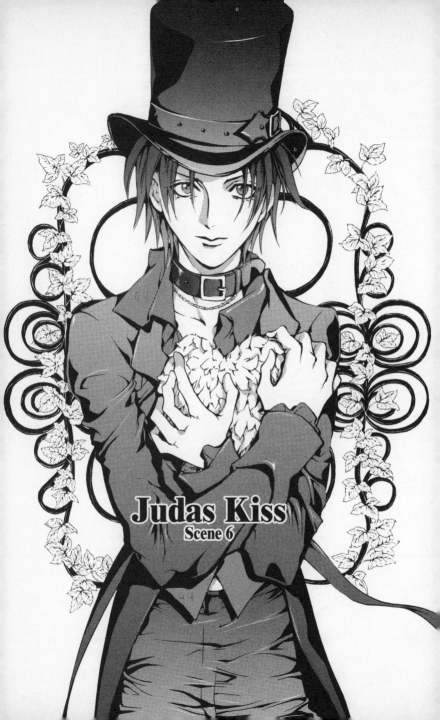

Judas Kiss
Scene 6

Judas Kiss
Scene 6

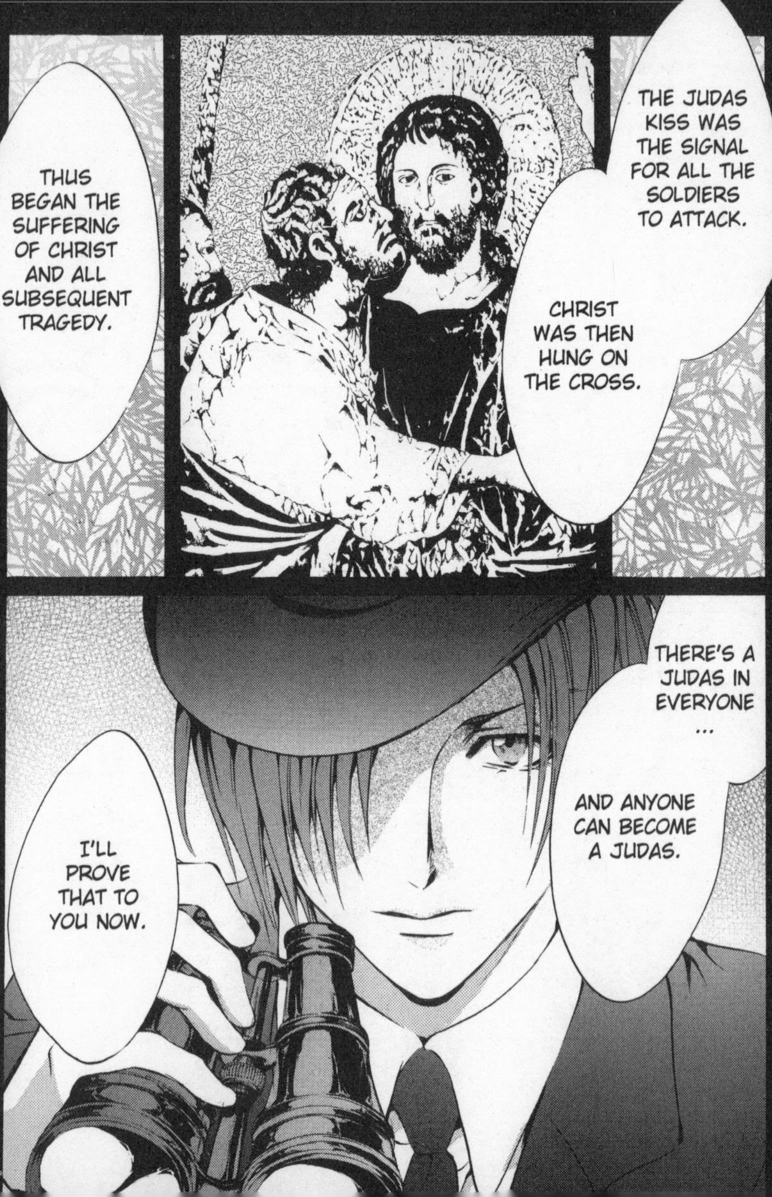
THE JUDAS KISS WAS THE SIGNAL FOR ALL THE SOLDIERS TO ATTACK.
CHRIST WAS THEN HUNG ON THE CROSS.
THUS BEGAN THE SUFFERING OF CHRIST AND ALL SUBSEQUENT TRAGEDY.
THERE'S A JUDAS IN EVERYONE ...
AND ANYONE CAN BECOME A JUDAS.
I'LL PROVE THAT TO YOU NOW.

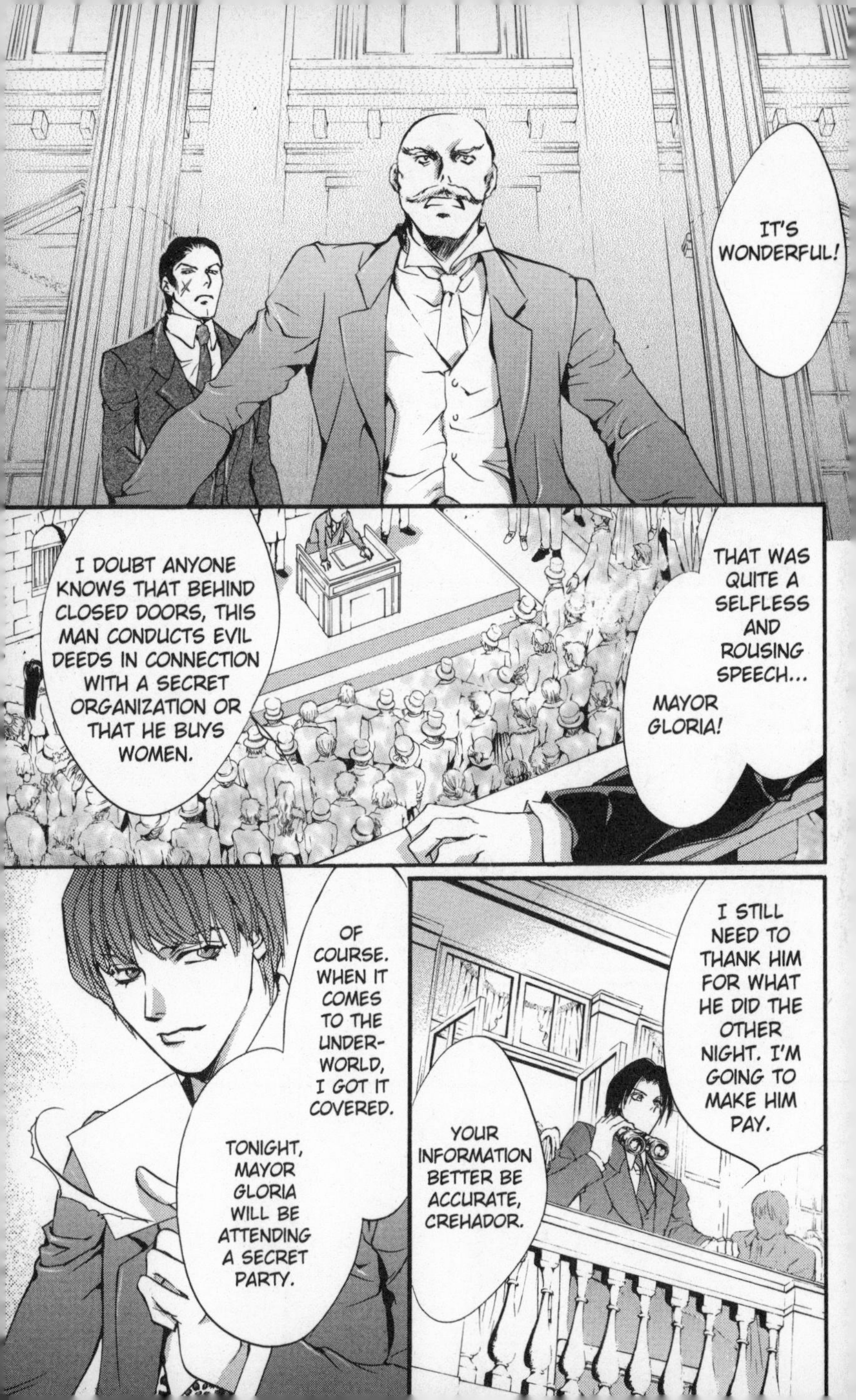
IT'S WONDERFUL!
THAT WAS QUITE A SELFLESS AND ROUSING SPEECH...
MAYOR GLORIA!
I DOUBT ANYONE KNOWS THAT BEHIND CLOSED DOORS, THIS MAN CONDUCTS EVIL DEEDS IN CONNECTION WITH A SECRET ORGANIZATION OR THAT HE BUYS WOMEN.
I STILL NEED TO THANK HIM FOR WHAT HE DID THE OTHER NIGHT. I'M GOING TO MAKE HIM PAY.
YOUR INFORMATION BETTER BE ACCURATE, CREHADOR.
OF COURSE. WHEN IT COMES TO THE UNDER-WORLD, I GOT IT COVERED.
TONIGHT, MAYOR GLORIA WILL BE ATTENDING A SECRET PARTY.

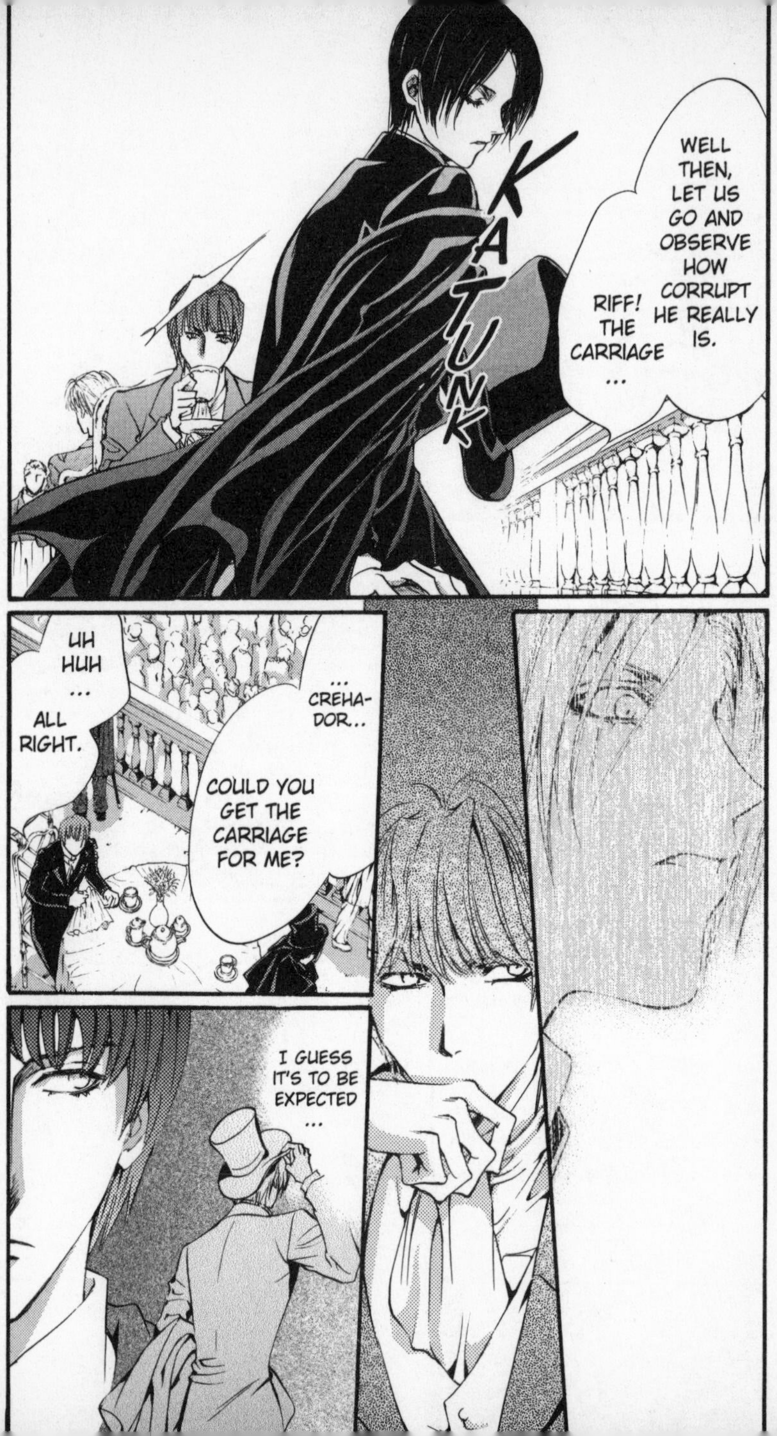
WELL THEN, LET US GO AND OBSERVE HOW CORRUPT HE REALLY IS.
RIFF! THE CARRIAGE ...
KATUNK
... CREHA-DOR...
COULD YOU GET THE CARRIAGE FOR ME?
UH HUH ... ALL RIGHT.
I GUESS IT'S TO BE EXPECTED ...

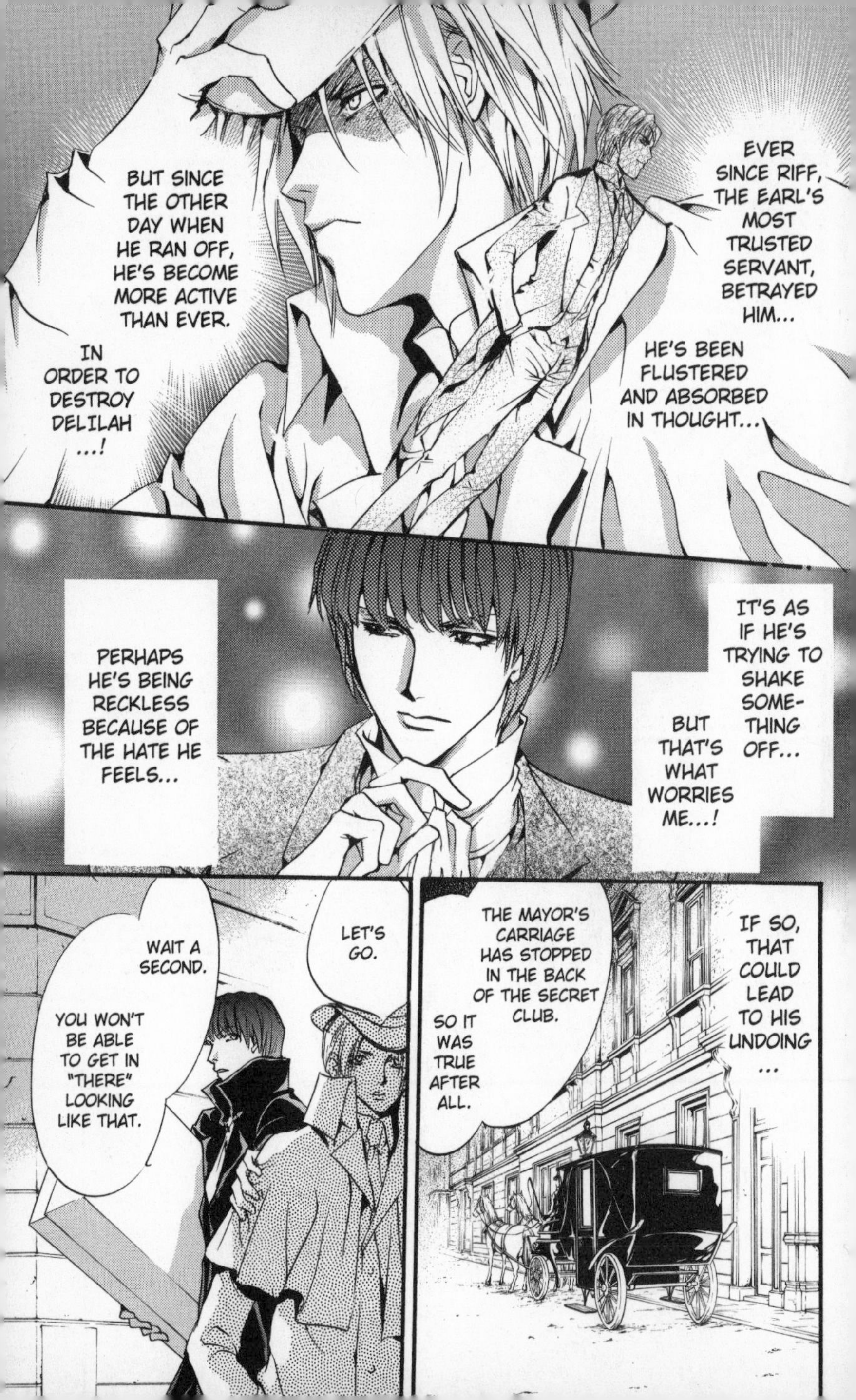
EVER SINCE RIFF, THE EARL'S MOST TRUSTED SERVANT, BETRAYED HIM...
HE'S BEEN FLUSTERED AND ABSORBED IN THOUGHT...
BUT SINCE THE OTHER DAY WHEN HE RAN OFF, HE'S BECOME MORE ACTIVE THAN EVER.
IN ORDER TO DESTROY DELILAH ...!
IT'S AS IF HE'S TRYING TO SHAKE SOME-THING OFF...
BUT THAT'S WHAT WORRIES ME...!
PERHAPS HE'S BEING RECKLESS BECAUSE OF THE HATE HE FEELS...
IF SO, THAT COULD LEAD TO HIS UNDOING ...
THE MAYOR'S CARRIAGE HAS STOPPED IN THE BACK OF THE SECRET CLUB.
SO IT WAS TRUE AFTER ALL.
LET'S GO.
WAIT A SECOND.
YOU WON'T BE ABLE TO GET IN "THERE" LOOKING LIKE THAT.

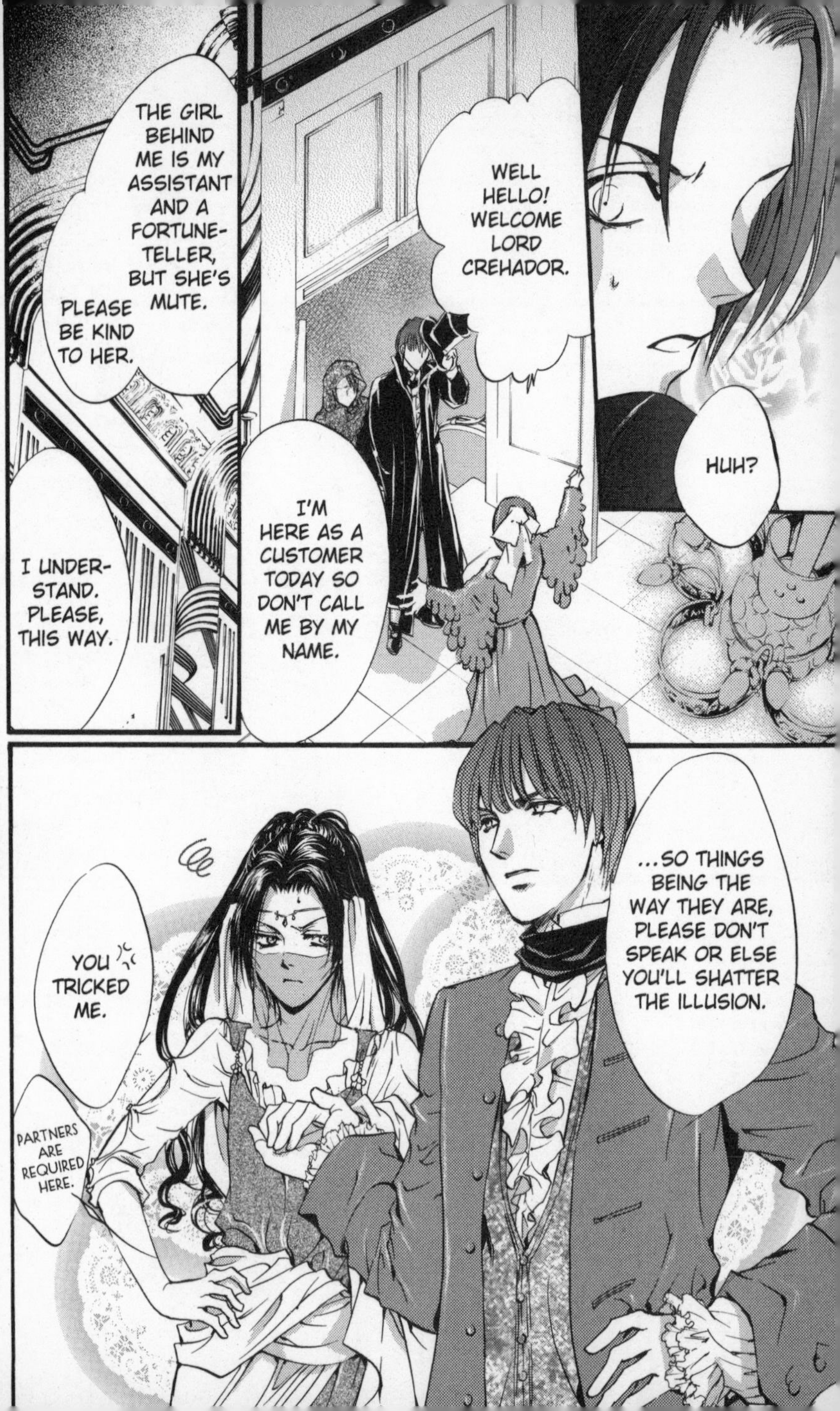
WELL HELLO! WELCOME LORD CREHADOR.
HUH?
I'M HERE AS A CUSTOMER TODAY SO DON'T CALL ME BY MY NAME.
THE GIRL BEHIND ME IS MY ASSISTANT AND A FORTUNE-TELLER, BUT SHE'S MUTE.
PLEASE BE KIND TO HER.
I UNDER-STAND. PLEASE, THIS WAY.
...SO THINGS BEING THE WAY THEY ARE, PLEASE DON'T SPEAK OR ELSE YOU'LL SHATTER THE ILLUSION.
YOU TRICKED ME.
PARTNERS ARE REQUIRED HERE.

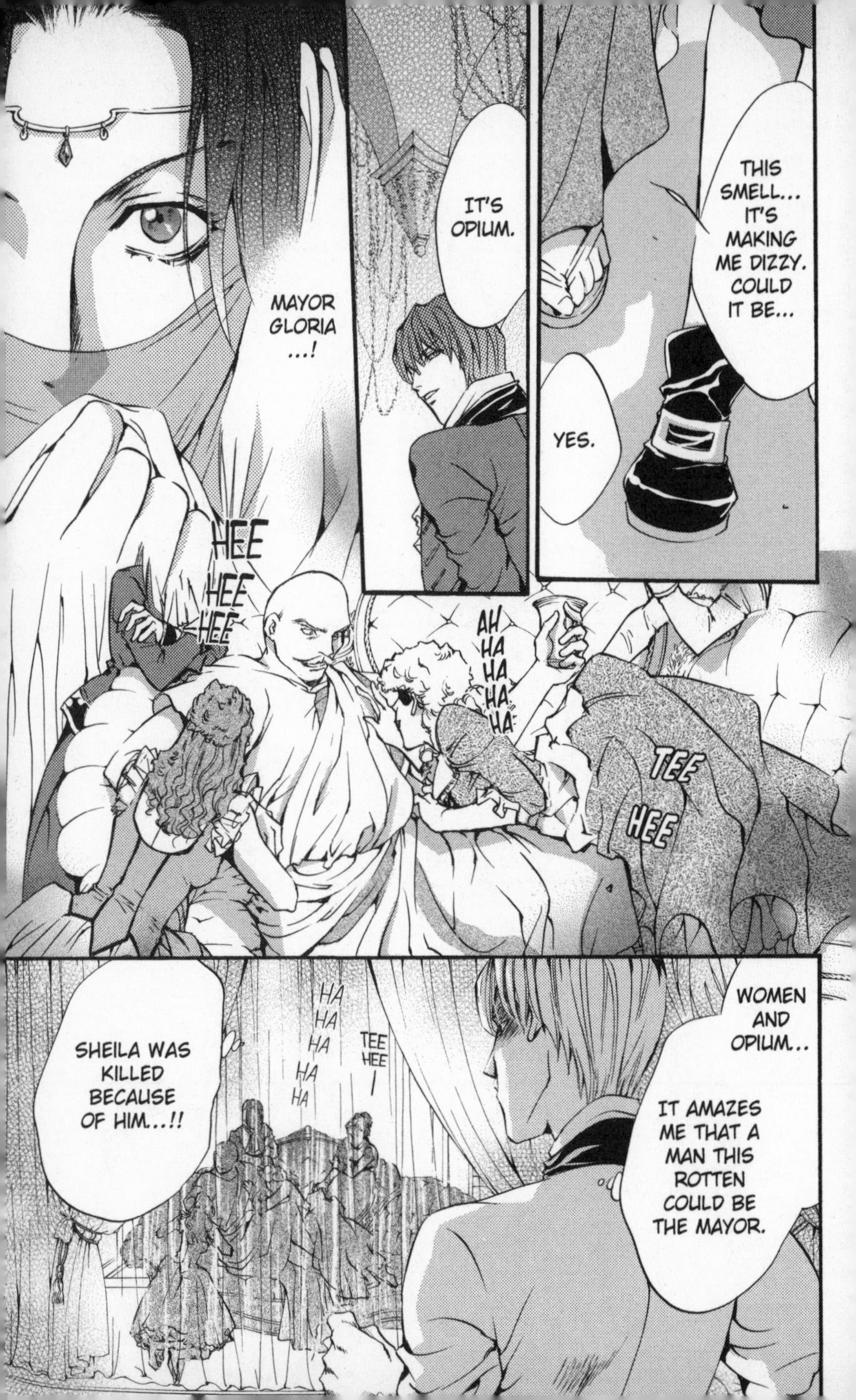
THIS SMELL... IT'S MAKING ME DIZZY. COULD IT BE...
YES.
IT'S OPIUM.
MAYOR GLORIA ...!
TEE HEE
AH HA HA HA HA HA
HEE HEE HEE
WOMEN AND OPIUM...
IT AMAZES ME THAT A MAN THIS ROTTEN COULD BE THE MAYOR.
TEE HEE
HA HA HA HA HA
SHEILA WAS KILLED BECAUSE OF HIM...!!

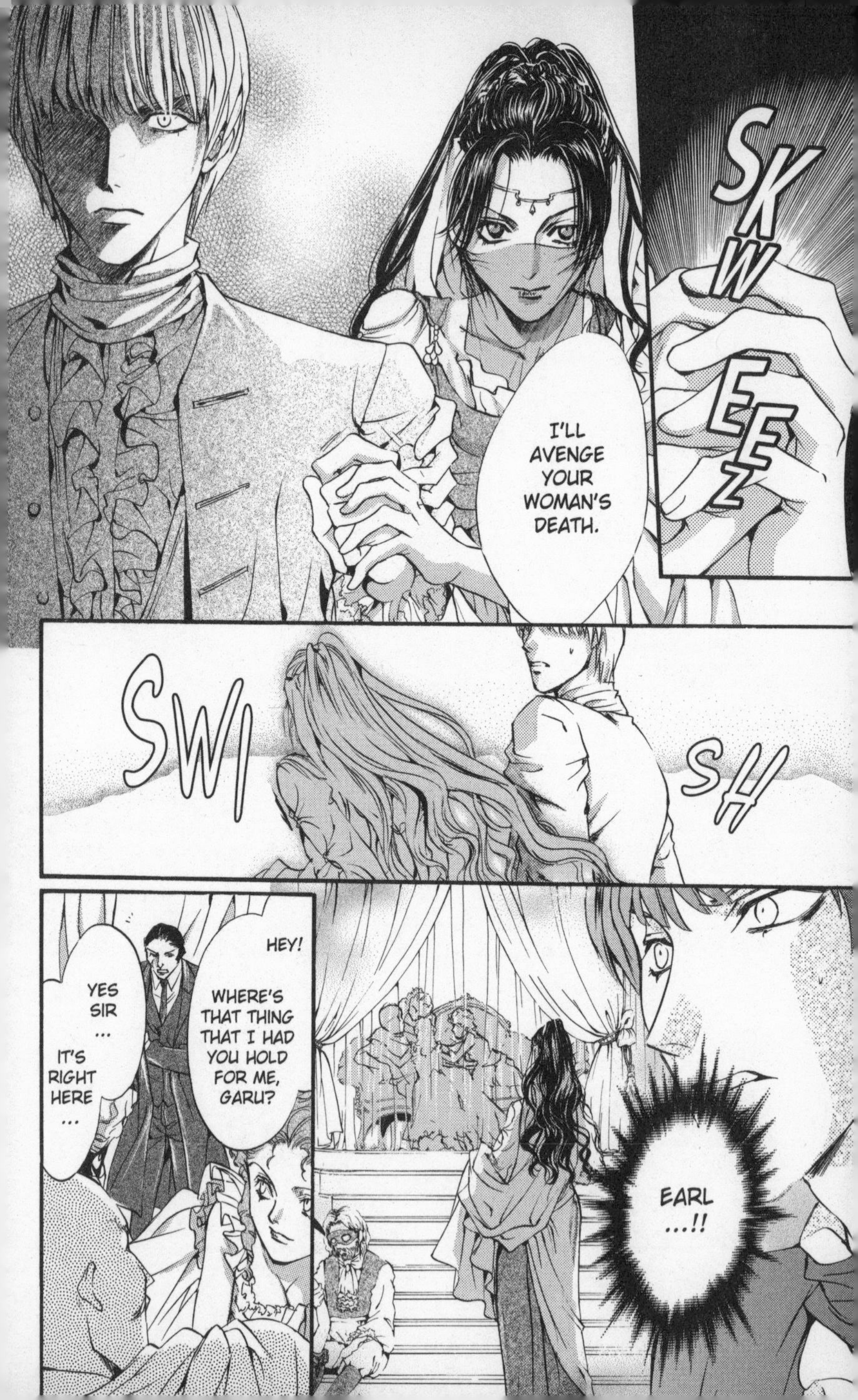
SKWEEZ
I'LL AVENGE YOUR WOMAN'S DEATH.
SWISH
EARL ...!!
HEY!
WHERE'S THAT THING THAT I HAD YOU HOLD FOR ME, GARU?
YES SIR ... IT'S RIGHT HERE ...

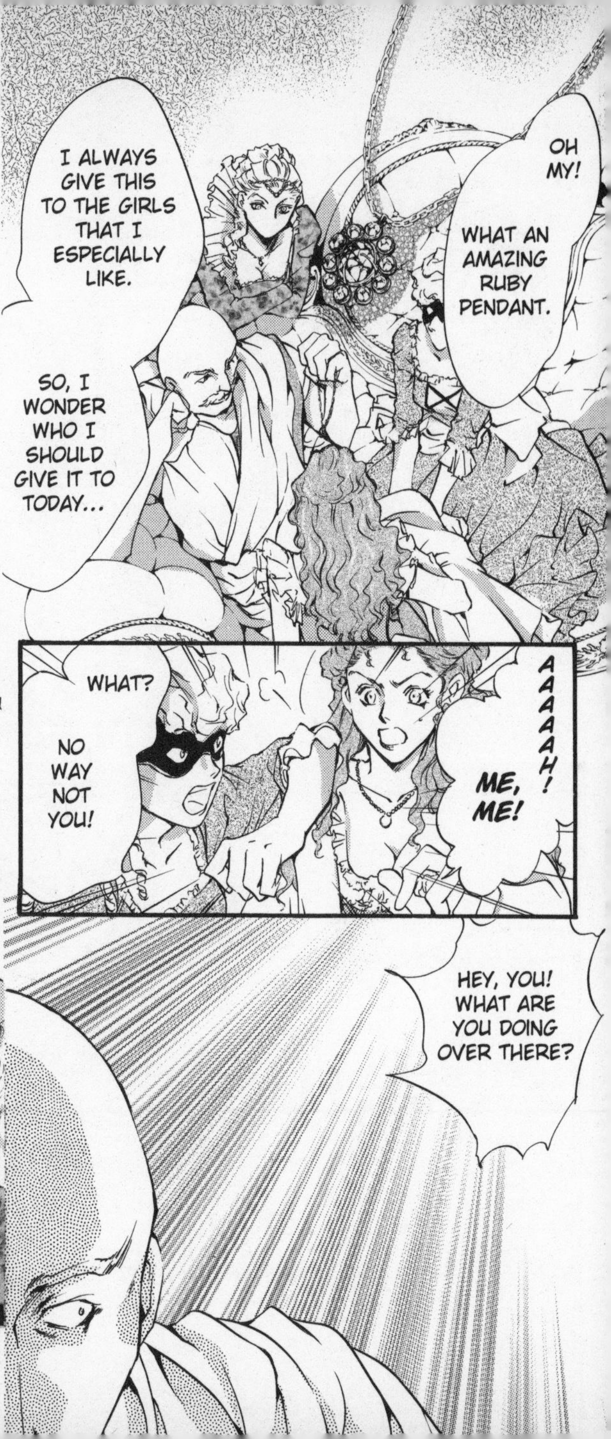
OH MY!
WHAT AN AMAZING RUBY PENDANT.
I ALWAYS GIVE THIS TO THE GIRLS THAT I ESPECIALLY LIKE.
SO, I WONDER WHO I SHOULD GIVE IT TO TODAY...
AAAAAH!
ME, ME!
WHAT?
NO WAY NOT YOU!
HEY, YOU! WHAT ARE YOU DOING OVER THERE?

The place where Cain and Riff were speaking to each other in the last chapter was the British museum. It's an ancient Greek and Roman Parthenon styled gallery. All the sculptures and statues are from there. Such as Ramses the 2nd. The seeds for the episode that reveals Riff is a card for Cain's father had actually already been sewn here and there in the previous series. There was a really big response from everyone so I'm glad I did it... To the people who were really shocked. I'd like to say I'm sorry. It made some people really sad...I feel kind of bad about that... ha ha...

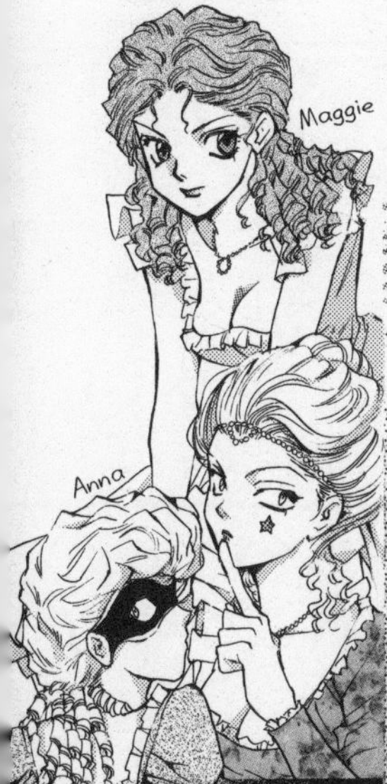
Maggie
Anna
Dixy...
...I just thought of it now.

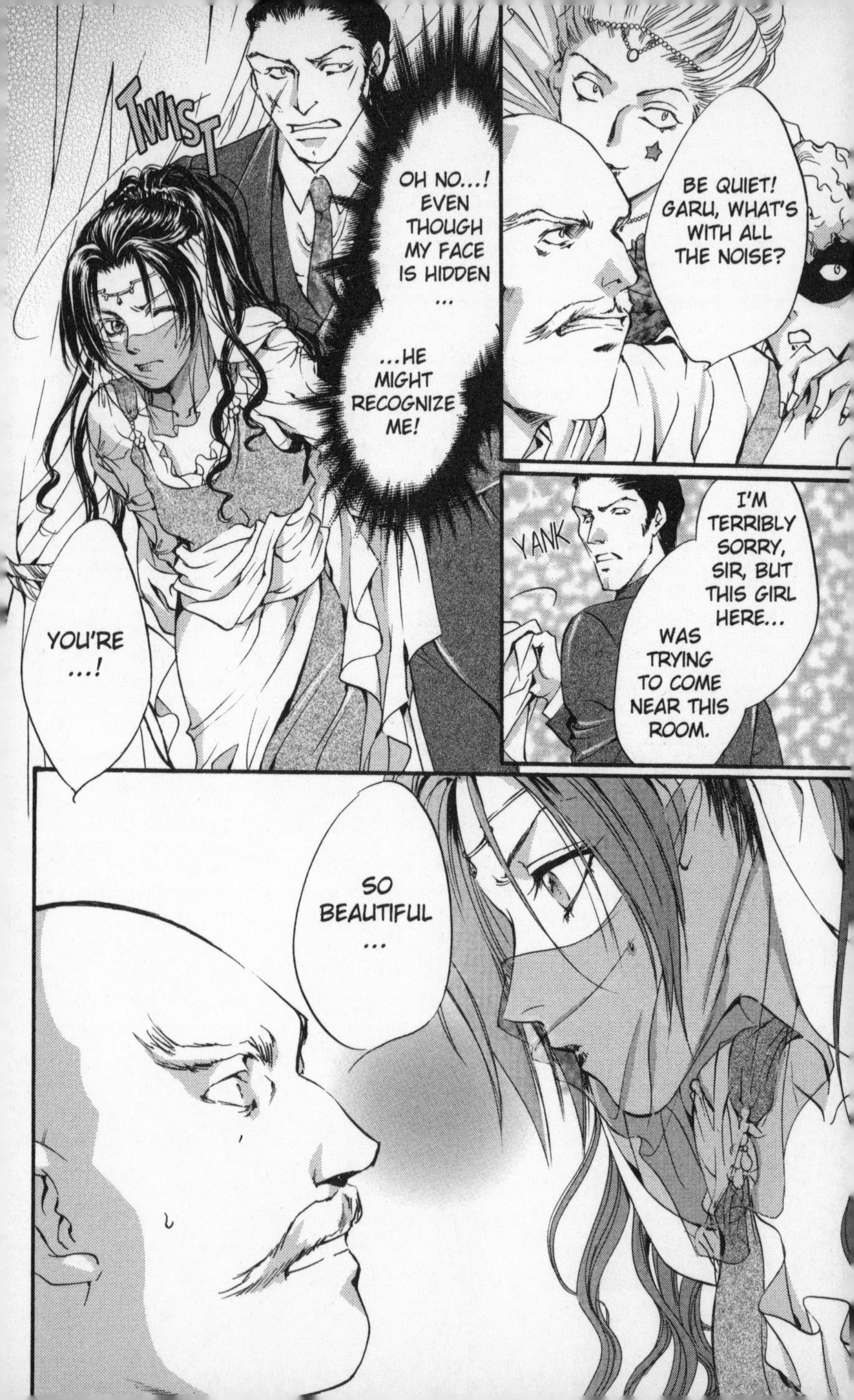
BE QUIET! GARU, WHAT'S WITH ALL THE NOISE?
YANK
I'M TERRIBLY SORRY, SIR, BUT THIS GIRL HERE...
WAS TRYING TO COME NEAR THIS ROOM.
TWIST
OH NO...! EVEN THOUGH MY FACE IS HIDDEN...
...HE MIGHT RECOGNIZE ME!
YOU'RE...!
SO BEAUTIFUL...

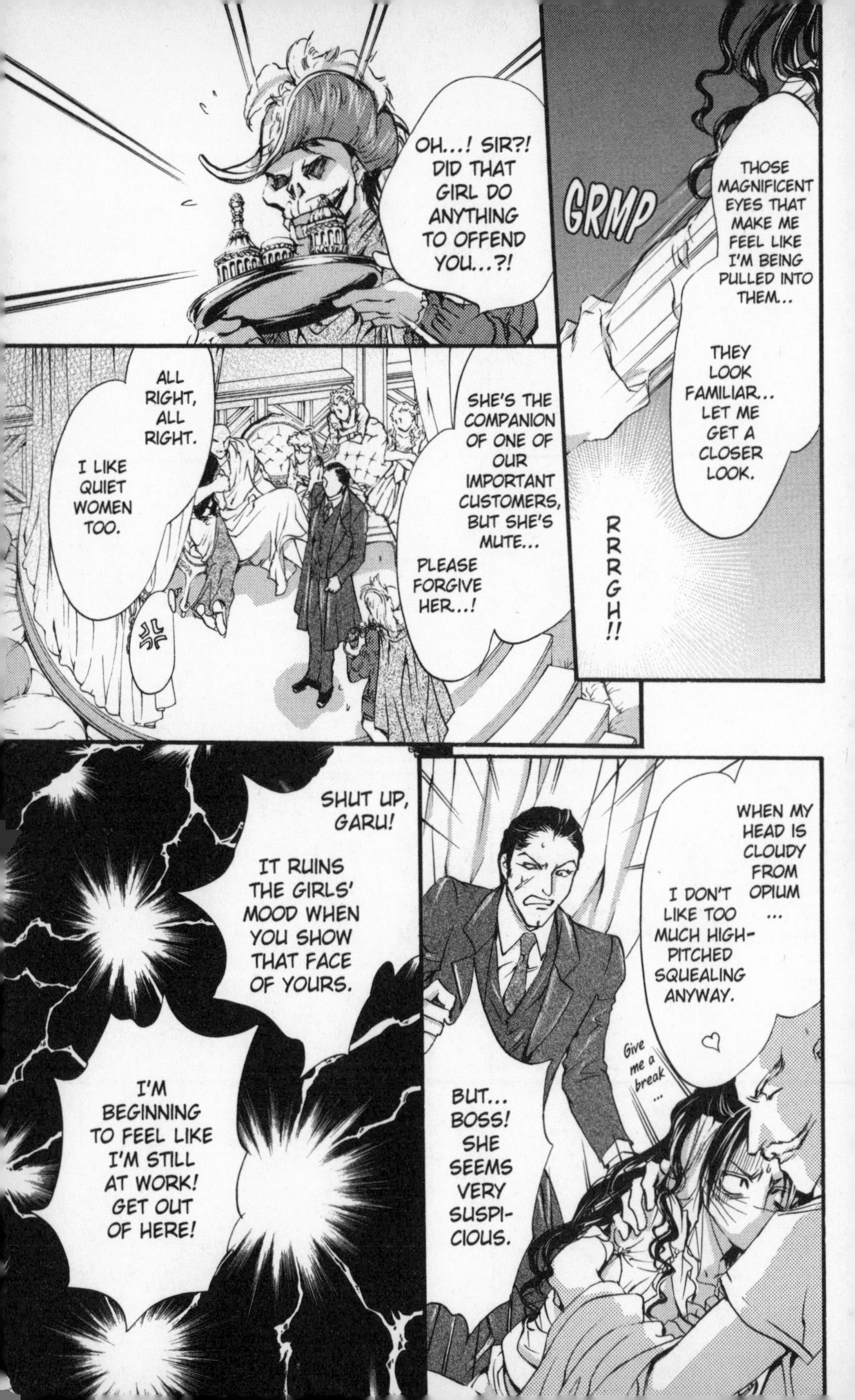
THOSE MAGNIFICENT EYES THAT MAKE ME FEEL LIKE I'M BEING PULLED INTO THEM...
GRMP
THEY LOOK FAMILIAR... LET ME GET A CLOSER LOOK.
RRRGH!!
OH...! SIR?! DID THAT GIRL DO ANYTHING TO OFFEND YOU...?!
SHE'S THE COMPANION OF ONE OF OUR IMPORTANT CUSTOMERS, BUT SHE'S MUTE...
PLEASE FORGIVE HER...!
ALL RIGHT, ALL RIGHT.
I LIKE QUIET WOMEN TOO.
WHEN MY HEAD IS CLOUDY FROM OPIUM...
I DON'T LIKE TOO MUCH HIGH-PITCHED SQUEALING ANYWAY.
♥
Give me a break...
BUT... BOSS! SHE SEEMS VERY SUSPICIOUS.
SHUT UP, GARU!
IT RUINS THE GIRLS' MOOD WHEN YOU SHOW THAT FACE OF YOURS.
I'M BEGINNING TO FEEL LIKE I'M STILL AT WORK! GET OUT OF HERE!

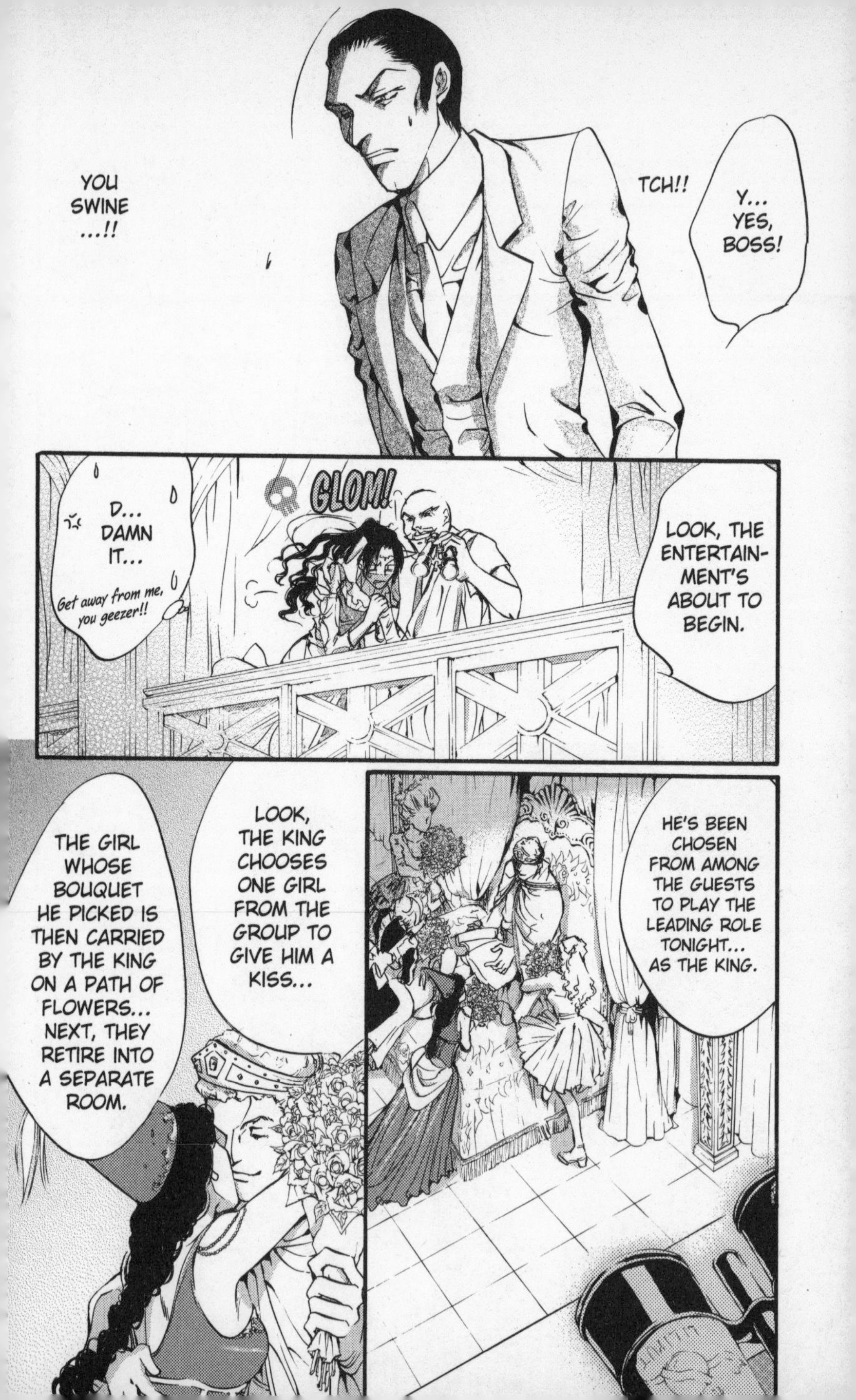
Y... YES, BOSS!
TCH!!
YOU SWINE ...!!
LOOK, THE ENTERTAINMENT'S ABOUT TO BEGIN.
GLOM!
D... DAMN IT...
Get away from me, you geezer!!
HE'S BEEN CHOSEN FROM AMONG THE GUESTS TO PLAY THE LEADING ROLE TONIGHT... AS THE KING.
LOOK, THE KING CHOOSES ONE GIRL FROM THE GROUP TO GIVE HIM A KISS...
THE GIRL WHOSE BOUQUET HE PICKED IS THEN CARRIED BY THE KING ON A PATH OF FLOWERS... NEXT, THEY RETIRE INTO A SEPARATE ROOM.

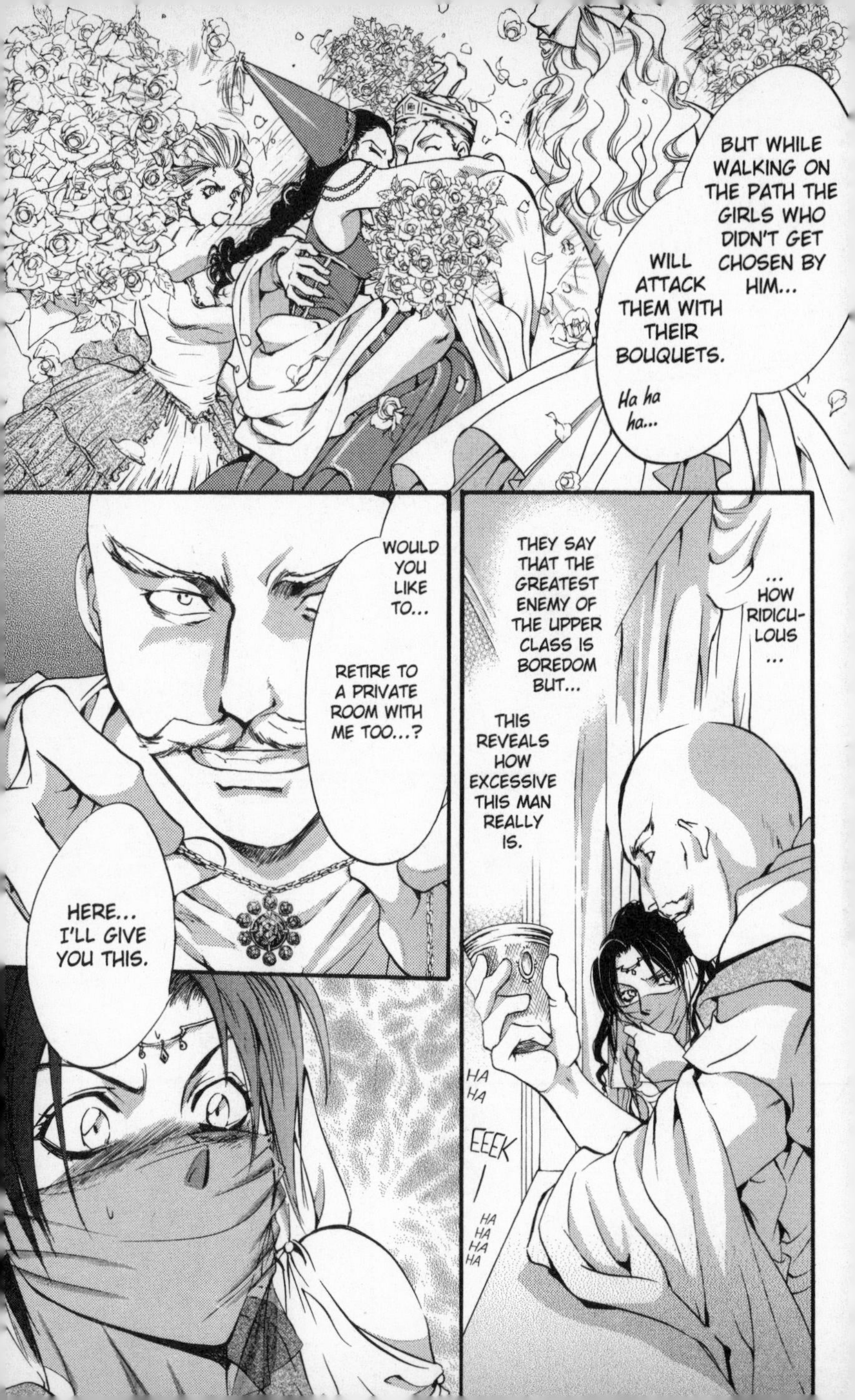
BUT WHILE WALKING ON THE PATH THE GIRLS WHO DIDN'T GET CHOSEN BY HIM...
WILL ATTACK THEM WITH THEIR BOUQUETS.
Ha ha ha...
THEY SAY THAT THE GREATEST ENEMY OF THE UPPER CLASS IS BOREDOM BUT...
...HOW RIDICULOUS...
THIS REVEALS HOW EXCESSIVE THIS MAN REALLY IS.
HA HA
EEEK!
HA HA HA HA
WOULD YOU LIKE TO...
RETIRE TO A PRIVATE ROOM WITH ME TOO...?
HERE... I'LL GIVE YOU THIS.

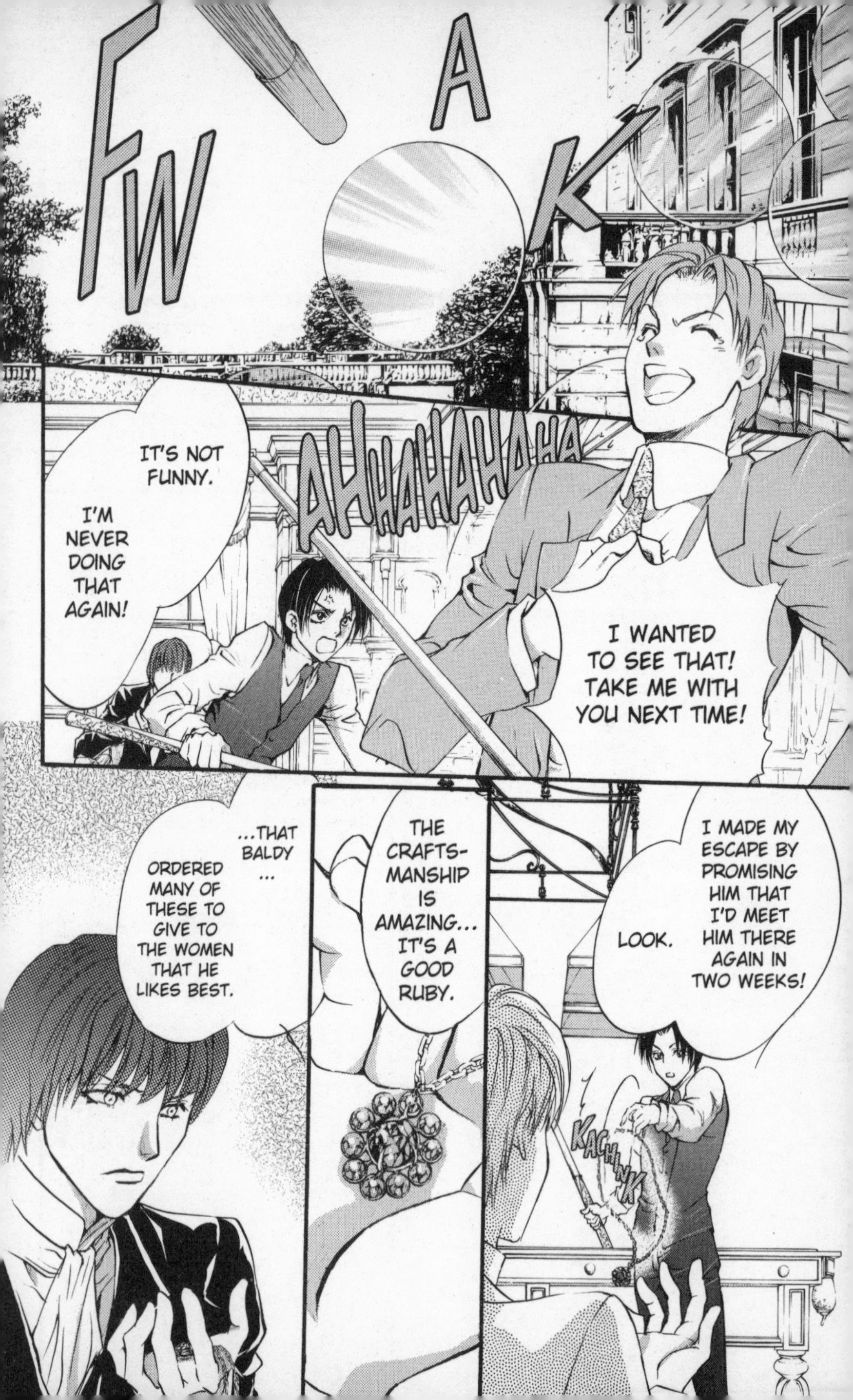
FWAK
AHAHAHAHAHA
I WANTED TO SEE THAT! TAKE ME WITH YOU NEXT TIME!
IT'S NOT FUNNY.
I'M NEVER DOING THAT AGAIN!
I MADE MY ESCAPE BY PROMISING HIM THAT I'D MEET HIM THERE AGAIN IN TWO WEEKS!
LOOK.
KACHINK
THE CRAFTS-MANSHIP IS AMAZING... IT'S A GOOD RUBY.
...THAT BALDY ...
ORDERED MANY OF THESE TO GIVE TO THE WOMEN THAT HE LIKES BEST.

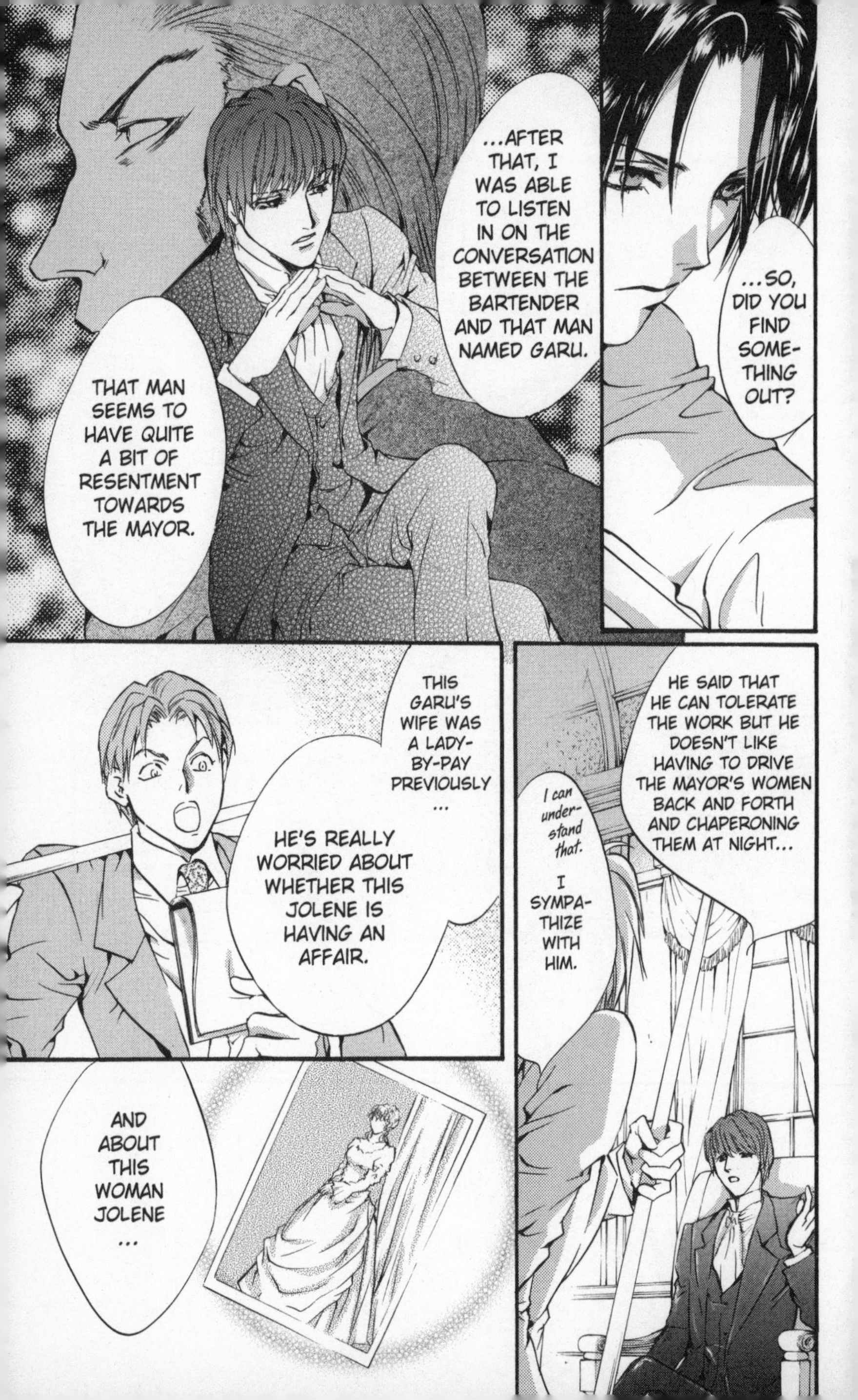
...SO, DID YOU FIND SOME-THING OUT?
...AFTER THAT, I WAS ABLE TO LISTEN IN ON THE CONVERSATION BETWEEN THE BARTENDER AND THAT MAN NAMED GARU.
THAT MAN SEEMS TO HAVE QUITE A BIT OF RESENTMENT TOWARDS THE MAYOR.
HE SAID THAT HE CAN TOLERATE THE WORK BUT HE DOESN'T LIKE HAVING TO DRIVE THE MAYOR'S WOMEN BACK AND FORTH AND CHAPERONING THEM AT NIGHT...
I can under-stand that.
I SYMPA-THIZE WITH HIM.
THIS GARU'S WIFE WAS A LADY-BY-PAY PREVIOUSLY ...
HE'S REALLY WORRIED ABOUT WHETHER THIS JOLENE IS HAVING AN AFFAIR.
AND ABOUT THIS WOMAN JOLENE ...

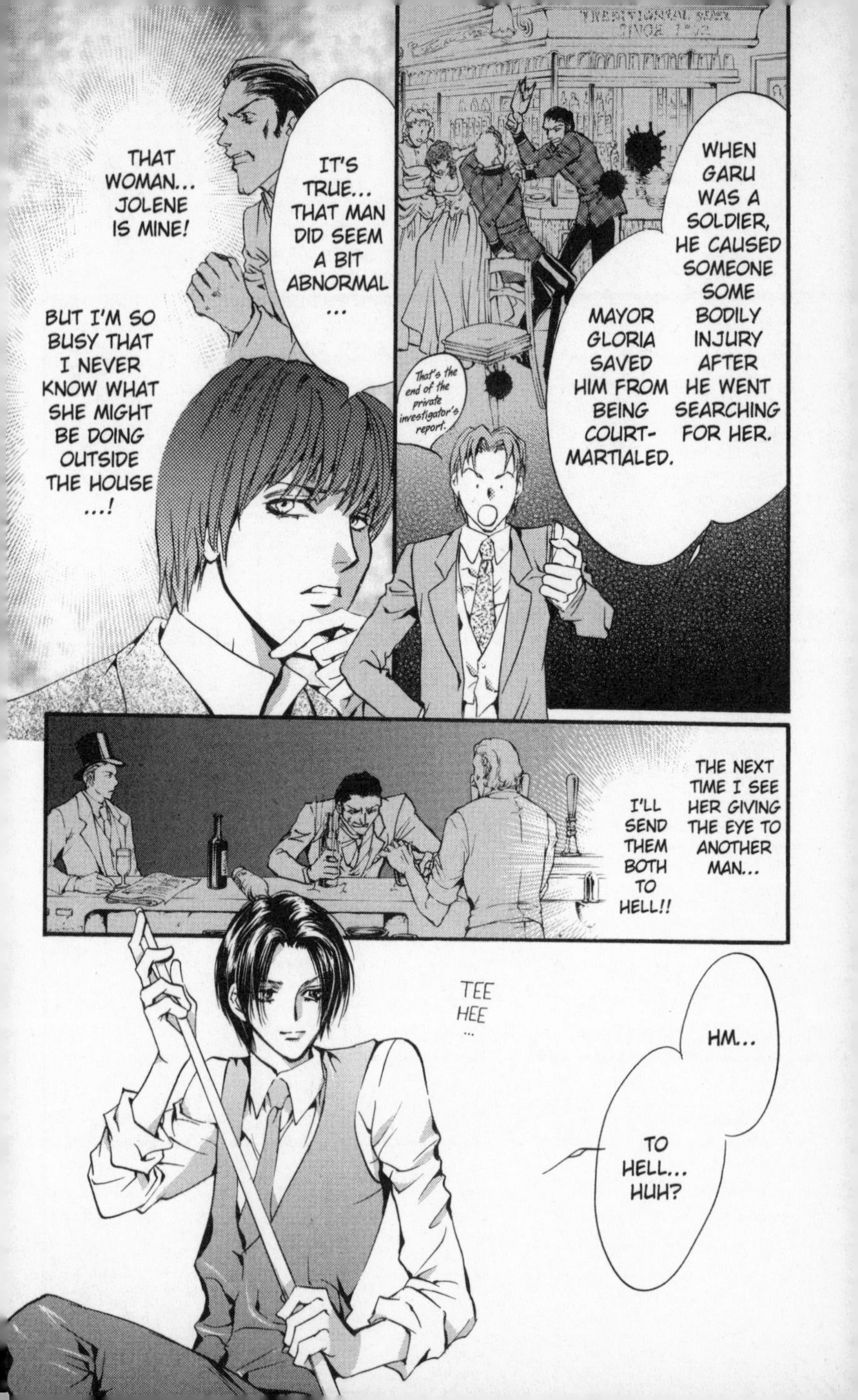
WHEN GARU WAS A SOLDIER, HE CAUSED SOMEONE SOME BODILY INJURY AFTER HE WENT SEARCHING FOR HER.
MAYOR GLORIA SAVED HIM FROM BEING COURT-MARTIALED.
That's the end of the private investigator's report.
IT'S TRUE... THAT MAN DID SEEM A BIT ABNORMAL...
THAT WOMAN... JOLENE IS MINE!
BUT I'M SO BUSY THAT I NEVER KNOW WHAT SHE MIGHT BE DOING OUTSIDE THE HOUSE...!
THE NEXT TIME I SEE HER GIVING THE EYE TO ANOTHER MAN...
I'LL SEND THEM BOTH TO HELL!!
HM...
TO HELL... HUH?
TEE HEE...

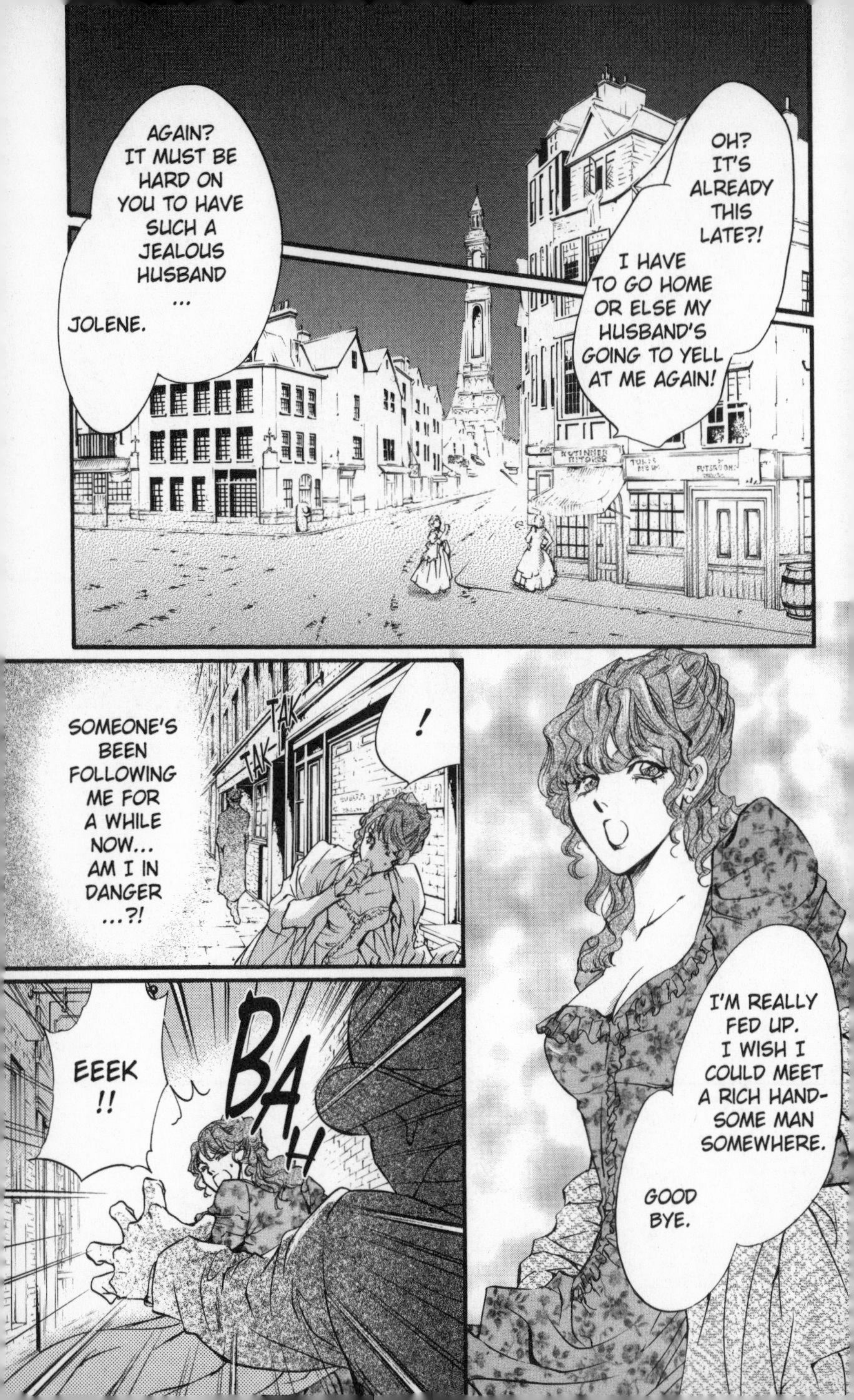
OH? IT'S ALREADY THIS LATE?!
I HAVE TO GO HOME OR ELSE MY HUSBAND'S GOING TO YELL AT ME AGAIN!
AGAIN? IT MUST BE HARD ON YOU TO HAVE SUCH A JEALOUS HUSBAND ... JOLENE.
I'M REALLY FED UP. I WISH I COULD MEET A RICH HAND-SOME MAN SOMEWHERE.
GOOD BYE.
!
TAK-TAK
SOMEONE'S BEEN FOLLOWING ME FOR A WHILE NOW... AM I IN DANGER ...?!
EEEK !!
BAH

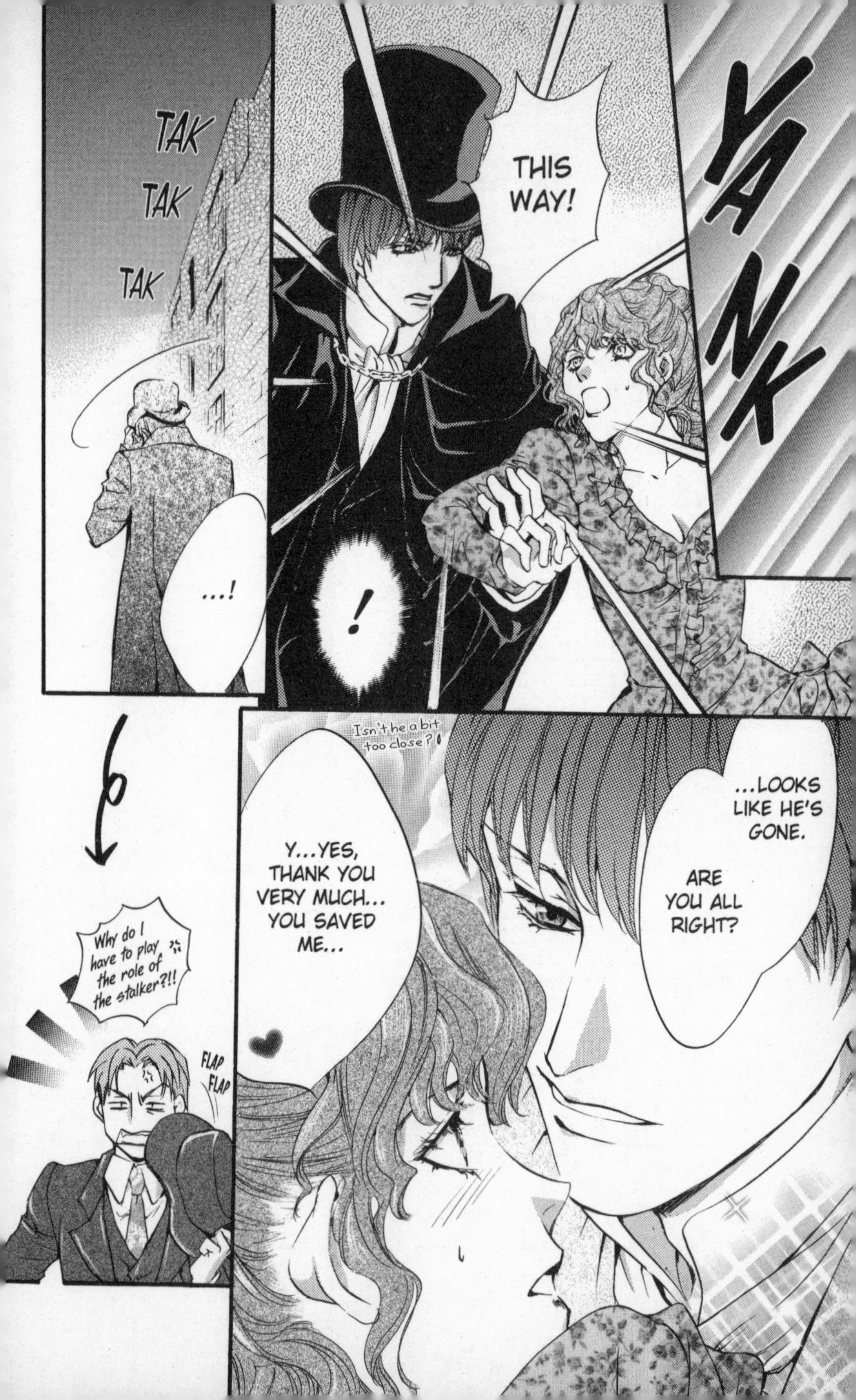
YANK
THIS WAY!
!
TAK
TAK
TAK
...!
...LOOKS LIKE HE'S GONE.
ARE YOU ALL RIGHT?
Y...YES, THANK YOU VERY MUCH... YOU SAVED ME...
Isn't he a bit too close?
Why do I have to play the role of the stalker?!!
FLAP
FLAP

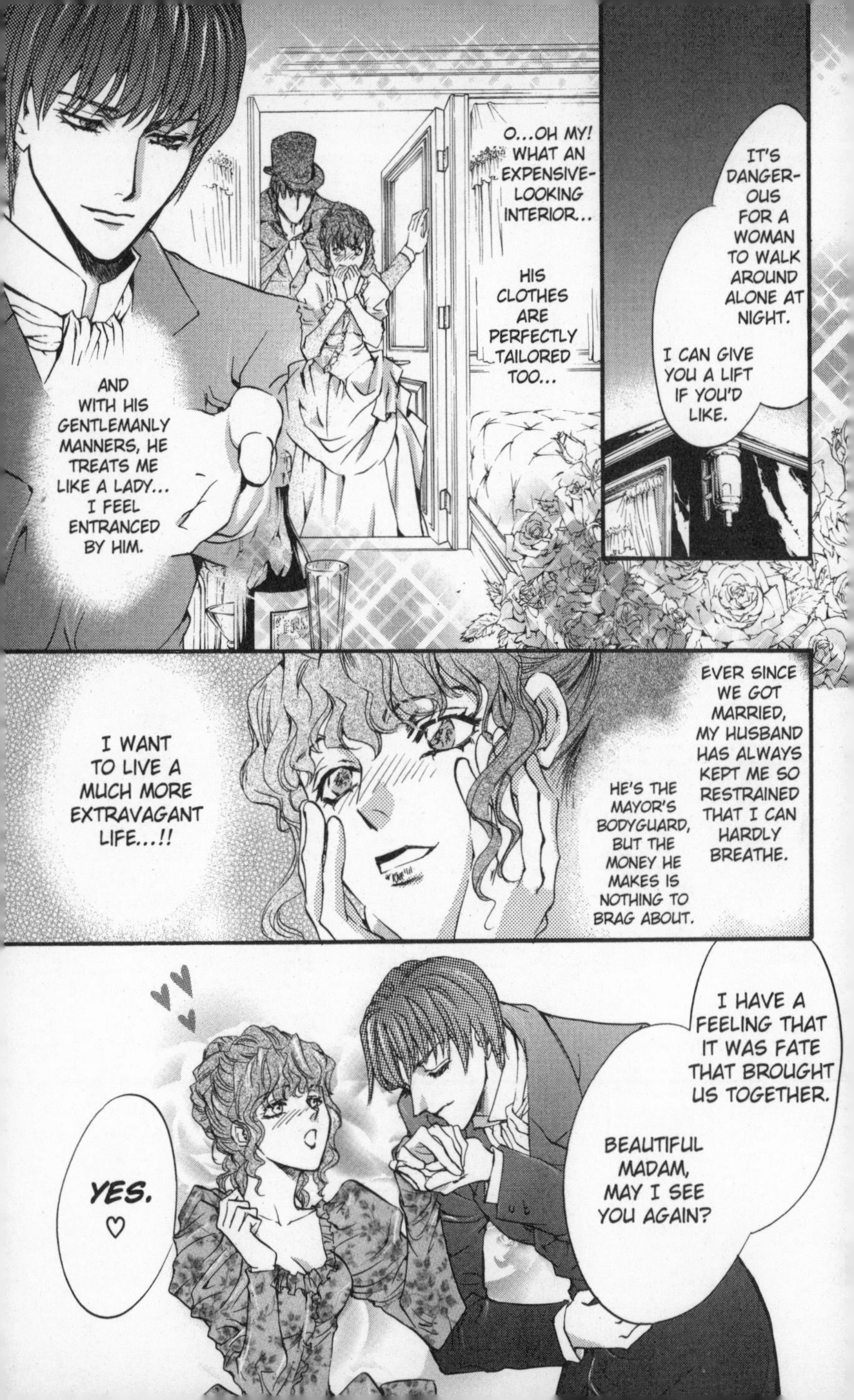
IT'S DANGEROUS FOR A WOMAN TO WALK AROUND ALONE AT NIGHT.
I CAN GIVE YOU A LIFT IF YOU'D LIKE.
O...OH MY! WHAT AN EXPENSIVE-LOOKING INTERIOR...
HIS CLOTHES ARE PERFECTLY TAILORED TOO...
AND WITH HIS GENTLEMANLY MANNERS, HE TREATS ME LIKE A LADY... I FEEL ENTRANCED BY HIM.
EVER SINCE WE GOT MARRIED, MY HUSBAND HAS ALWAYS KEPT ME SO RESTRAINED THAT I CAN HARDLY BREATHE.
HE'S THE MAYOR'S BODYGUARD, BUT THE MONEY HE MAKES IS NOTHING TO BRAG ABOUT.
I WANT TO LIVE A MUCH MORE EXTRAVAGANT LIFE...!!
I HAVE A FEELING THAT IT WAS FATE THAT BROUGHT US TOGETHER.
BEAUTIFUL MADAM, MAY I SEE YOU AGAIN?
YES. ♡

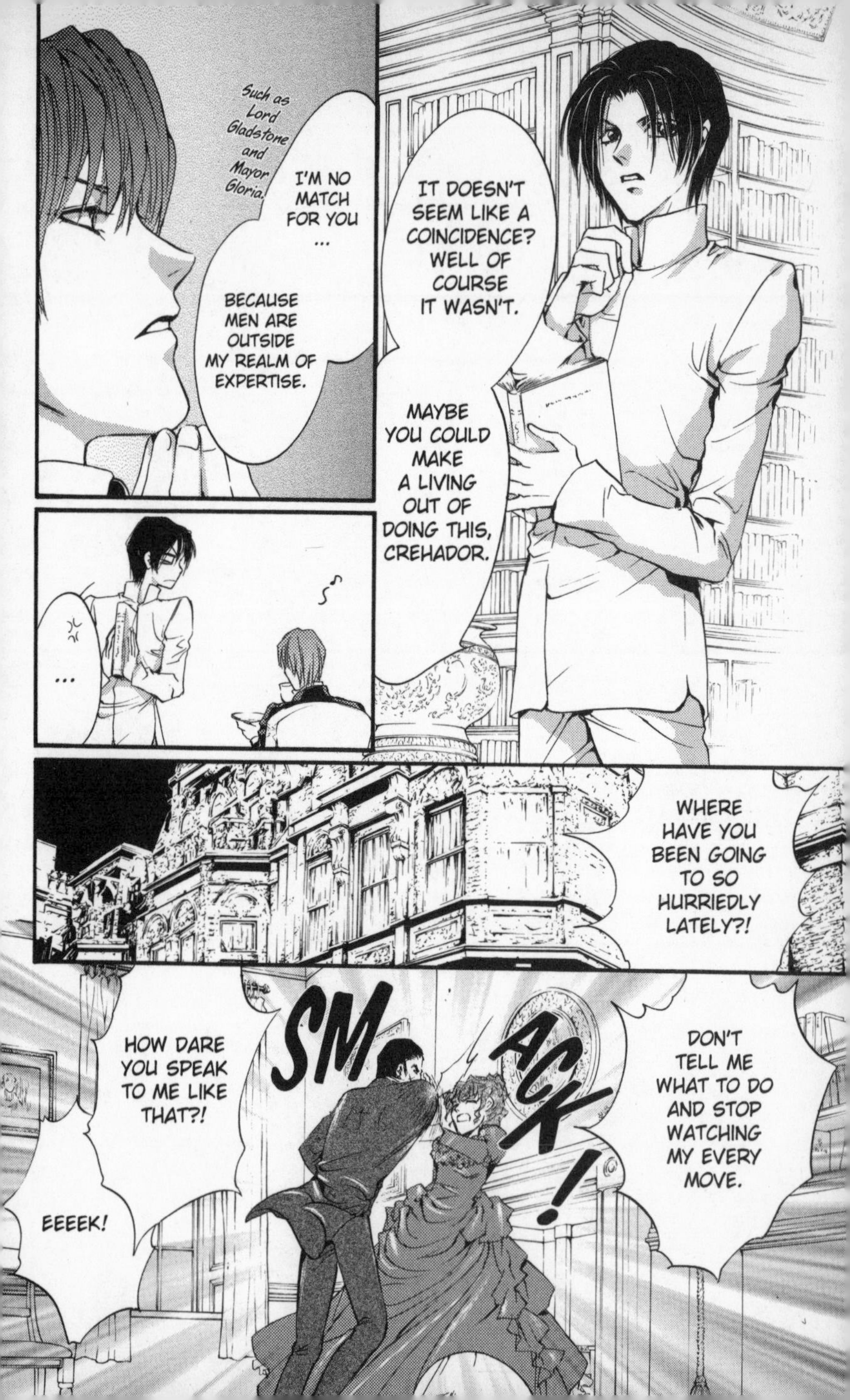
IT DOESN'T SEEM LIKE A COINCIDENCE? WELL OF COURSE IT WASN'T.
MAYBE YOU COULD MAKE A LIVING OUT OF DOING THIS, CREHADOR.
I'M NO MATCH FOR YOU ...
BECAUSE MEN ARE OUTSIDE MY REALM OF EXPERTISE.
Such as Lord Gladstone and Mayor Gloria.
...
WHERE HAVE YOU BEEN GOING TO SO HURRIEDLY LATELY?!
DON'T TELL ME WHAT TO DO AND STOP WATCHING MY EVERY MOVE.
SMACK!
HOW DARE YOU SPEAK TO ME LIKE THAT?!
EEEEK!

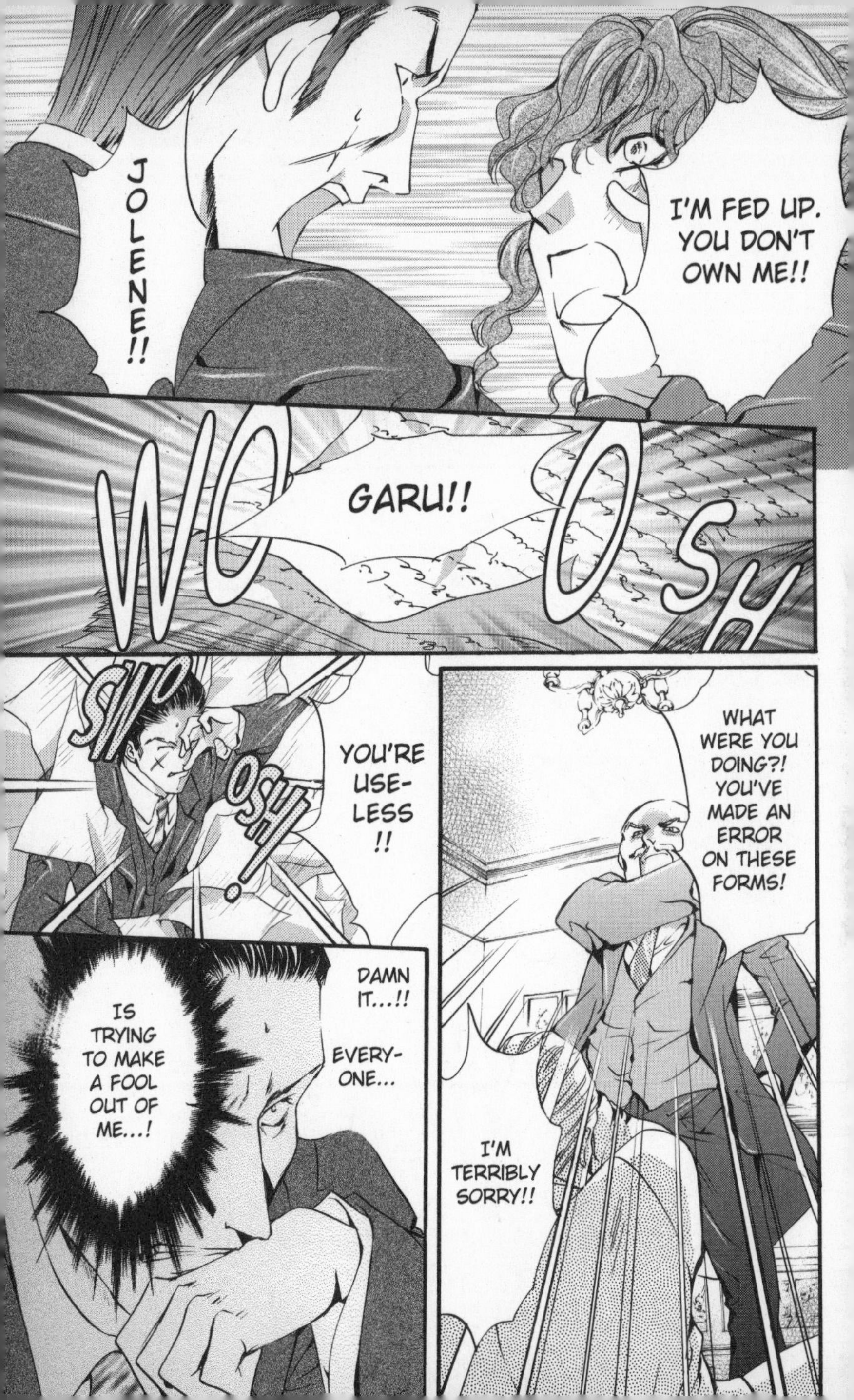
I'M FED UP. YOU DON'T OWN ME!!
JOLENE!!
WOOSH
GARU!!
WHAT WERE YOU DOING?! YOU'VE MADE AN ERROR ON THESE FORMS!
I'M TERRIBLY SORRY!!
YOU'RE USE-LESS!!
SWOOSH!
DAMN IT...!!
EVERY-ONE...
IS TRYING TO MAKE A FOOL OUT OF ME...!

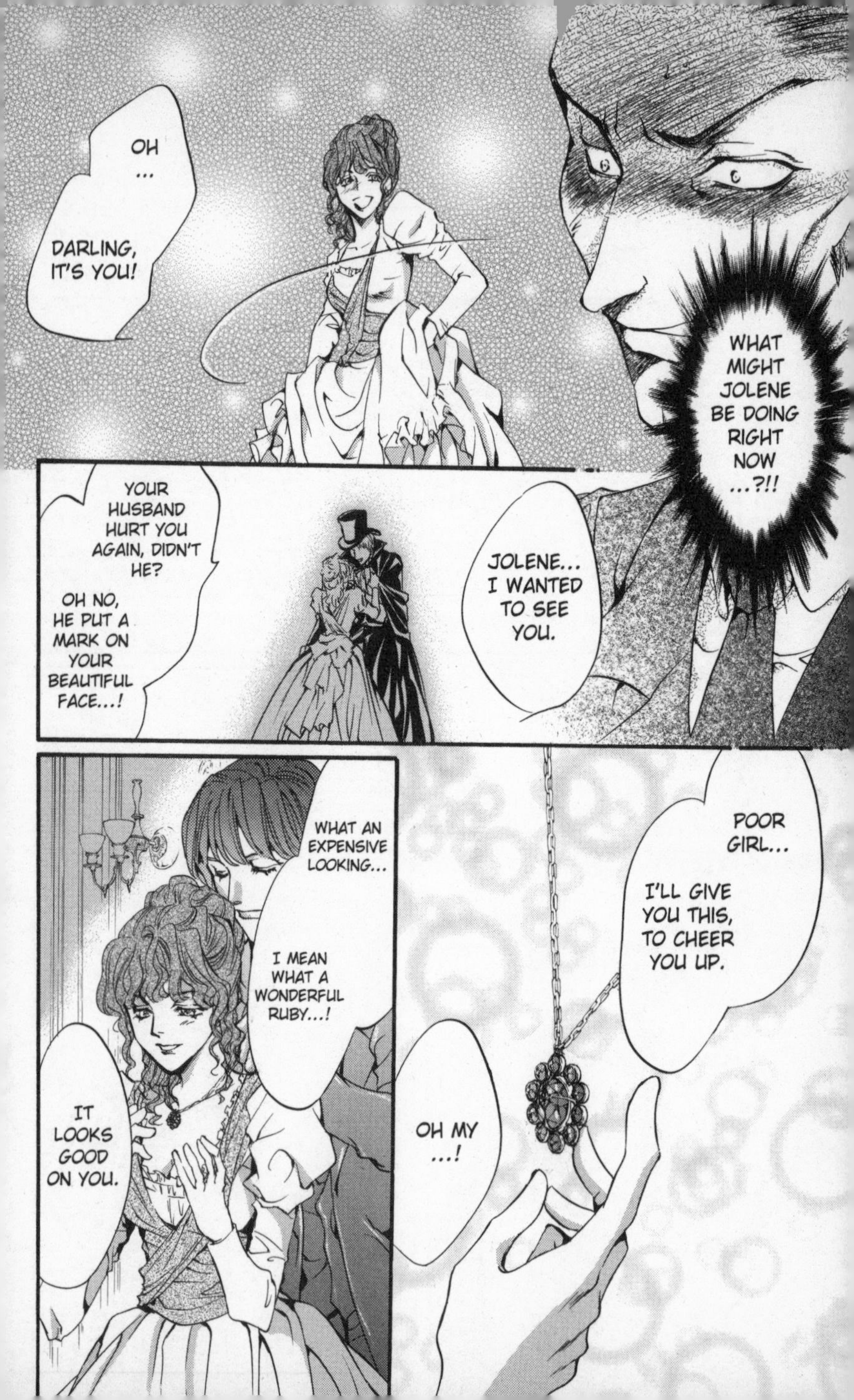
WHAT MIGHT JOLENE BE DOING RIGHT NOW ...?!!
OH ...
DARLING, IT'S YOU!
JOLENE... I WANTED TO SEE YOU.
YOUR HUSBAND HURT YOU AGAIN, DIDN'T HE?
OH NO, HE PUT A MARK ON YOUR BEAUTIFUL FACE...!
POOR GIRL...
I'LL GIVE YOU THIS, TO CHEER YOU UP.
OH MY ...!
WHAT AN EXPENSIVE LOOKING...
I MEAN WHAT A WONDERFUL RUBY...!
IT LOOKS GOOD ON YOU.

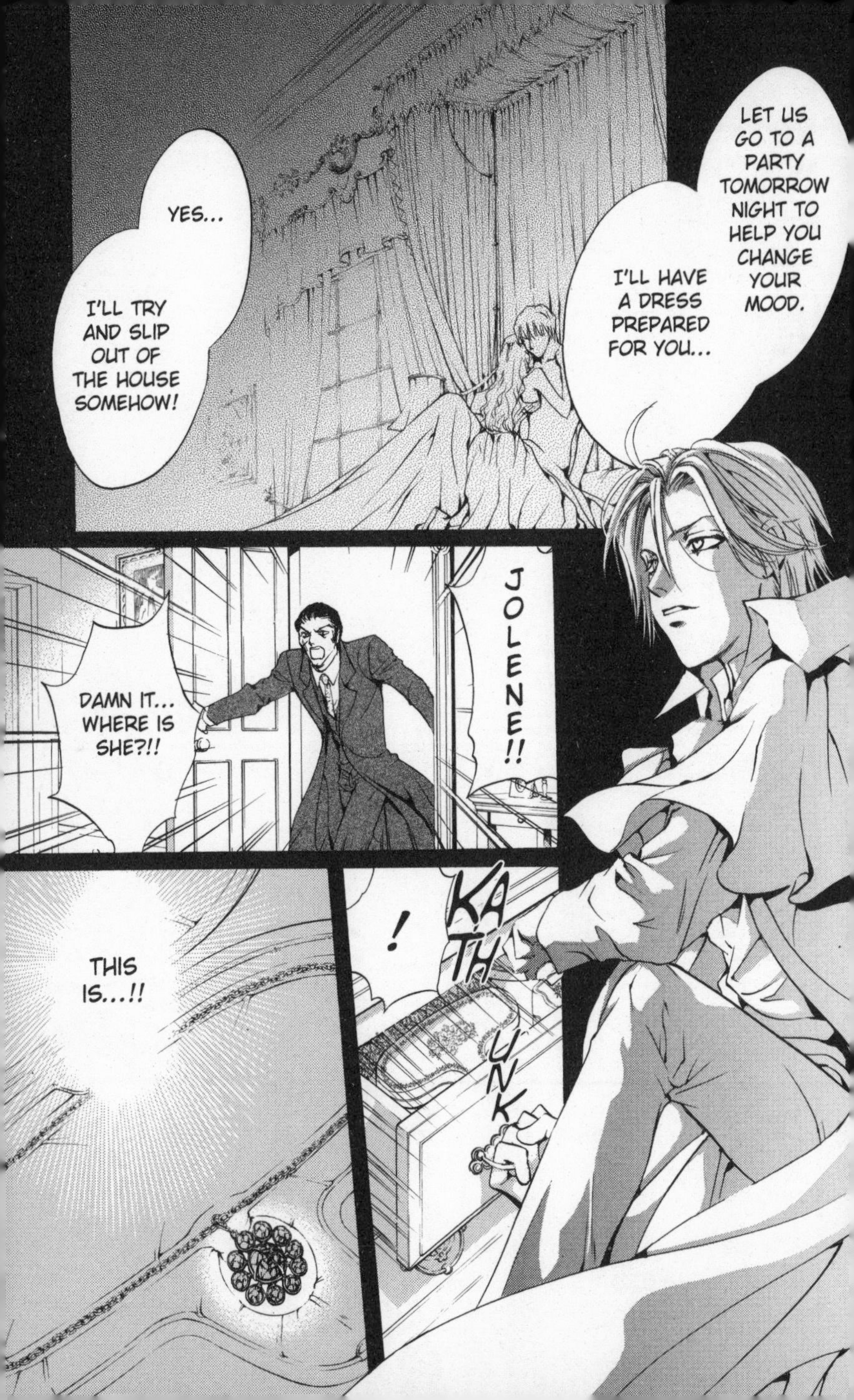
LET US GO TO A PARTY TOMORROW NIGHT TO HELP YOU CHANGE YOUR MOOD.
I'LL HAVE A DRESS PREPARED FOR YOU...
YES...
I'LL TRY AND SLIP OUT OF THE HOUSE SOMEHOW!
JOLENE!!
DAMN IT... WHERE IS SHE?!!
KATHUNK
!
THIS IS...!!

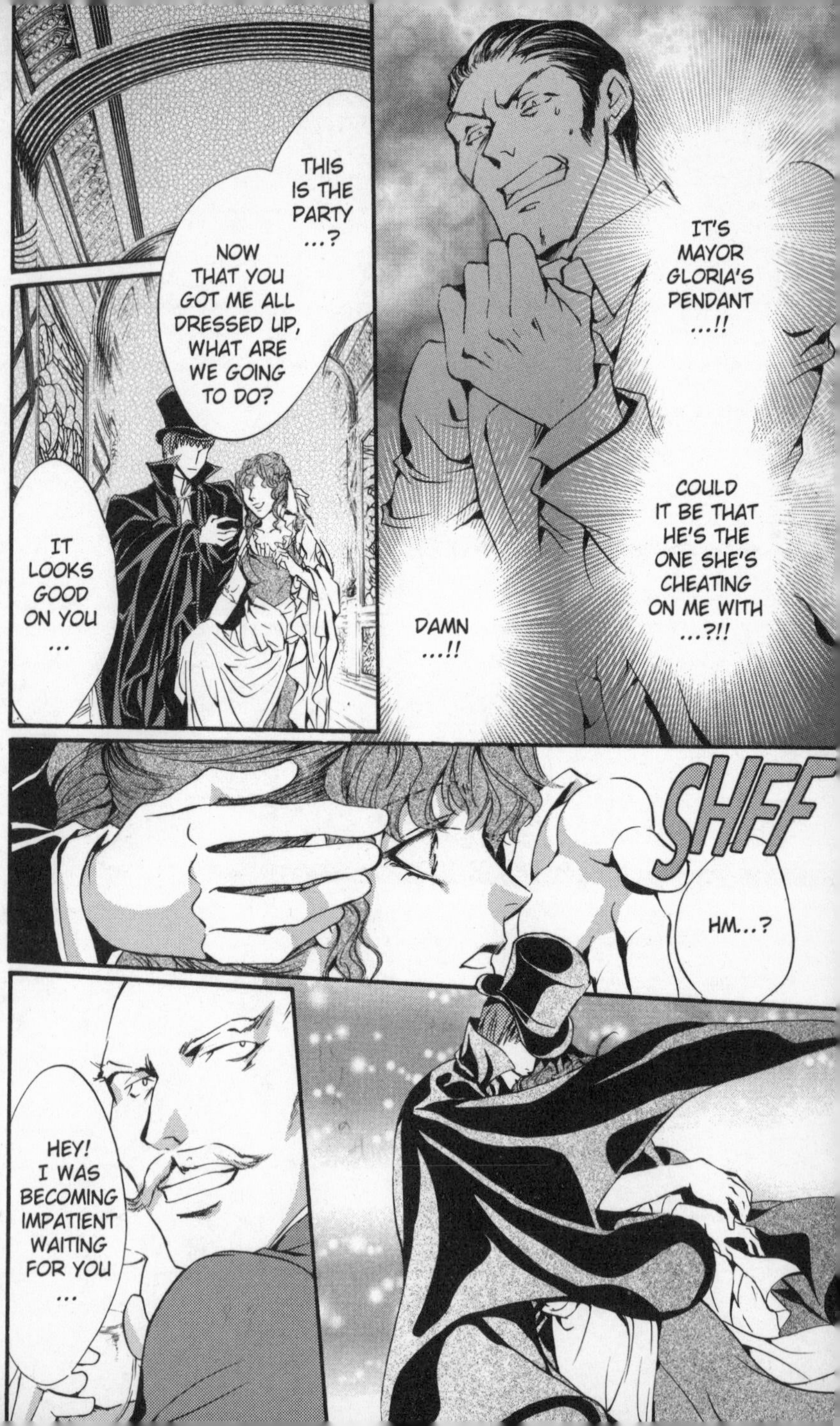
IT'S MAYOR GLORIA'S PENDANT ...!!
COULD IT BE THAT HE'S THE ONE SHE'S CHEATING ON ME WITH ...?!!
DAMN ...!!
THIS IS THE PARTY ...?
NOW THAT YOU GOT ME ALL DRESSED UP, WHAT ARE WE GOING TO DO?
IT LOOKS GOOD ON YOU ...
SHFF
HM...?
HEY! I WAS BECOMING IMPATIENT WAITING FOR YOU ...

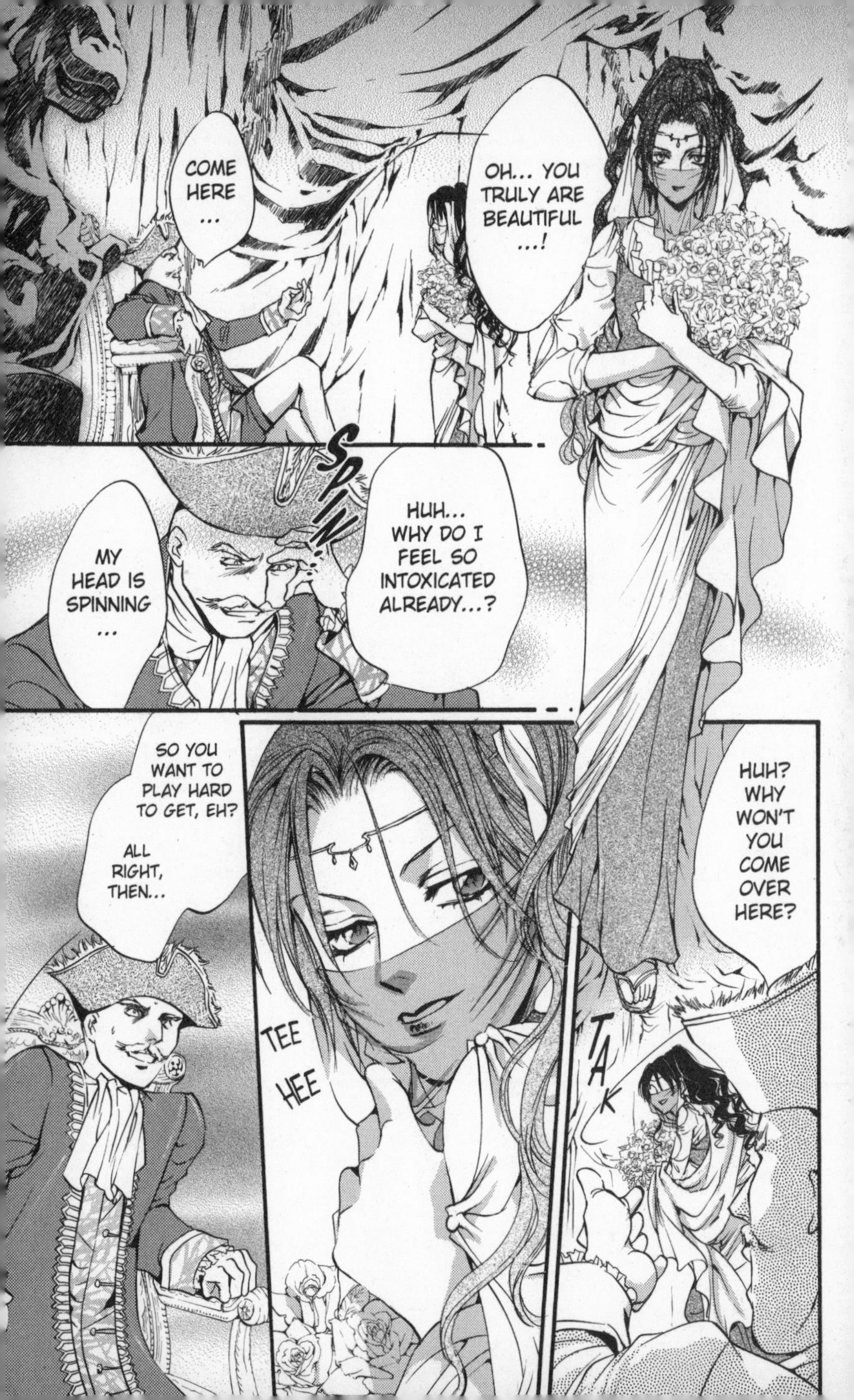
OH... YOU TRULY ARE BEAUTIFUL...!
COME HERE...
SPIN!!
HUH... WHY DO I FEEL SO INTOXICATED ALREADY...?
MY HEAD IS SPINNING...
HUH? WHY WON'T YOU COME OVER HERE?
TAK
TEE HEE
SO YOU WANT TO PLAY HARD TO GET, EH?
ALL RIGHT, THEN...

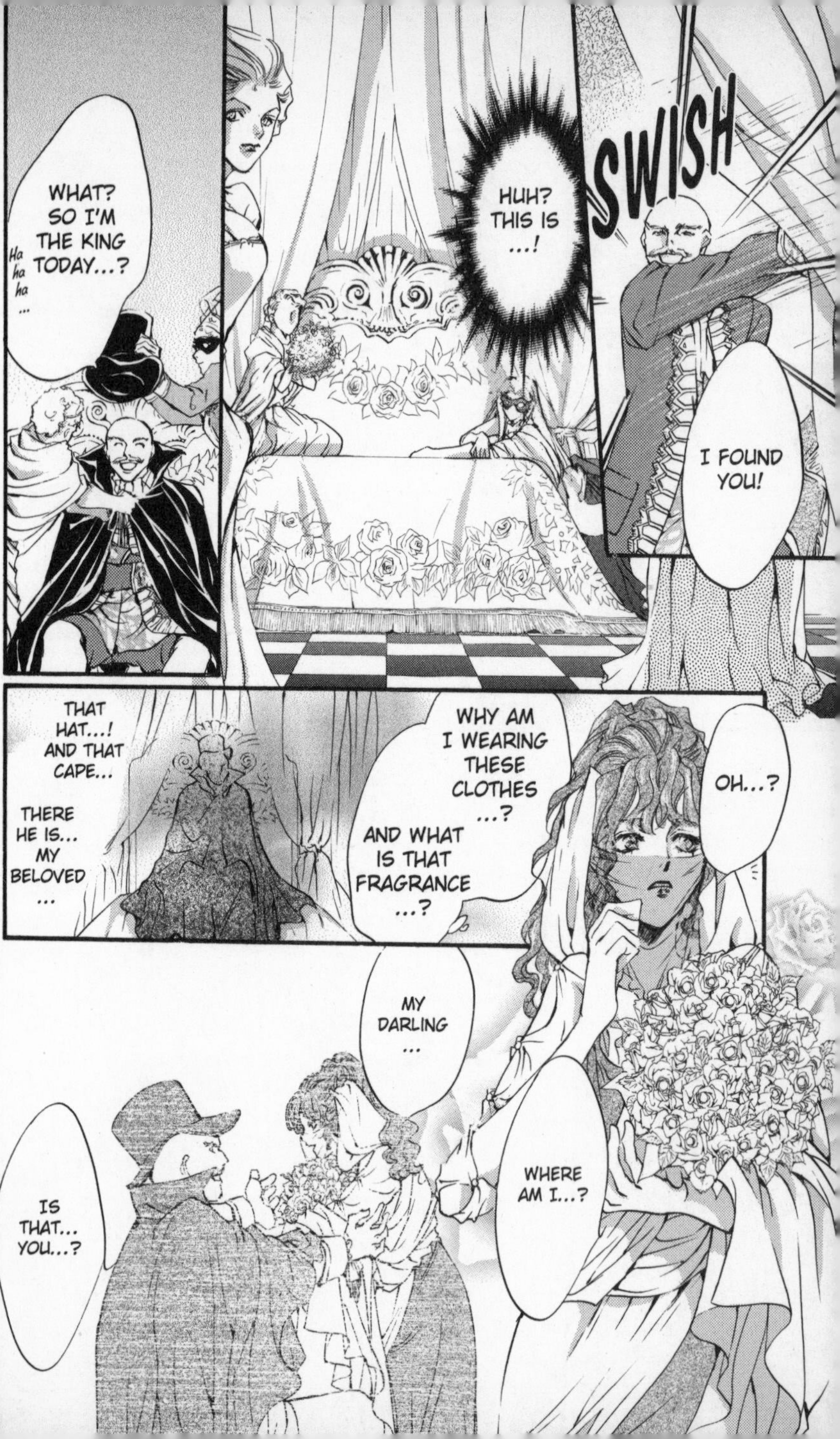
SWISH
I FOUND YOU!
HUH? THIS IS ...!
Ha ha ha ...
WHAT? SO I'M THE KING TODAY...?
OH...?
WHERE AM I...?
WHY AM I WEARING THESE CLOTHES ...?
AND WHAT IS THAT FRAGRANCE ...?
THAT HAT...! AND THAT CAPE...
THERE HE IS... MY BELOVED ...
MY DARLING ...
IS THAT... YOU...?

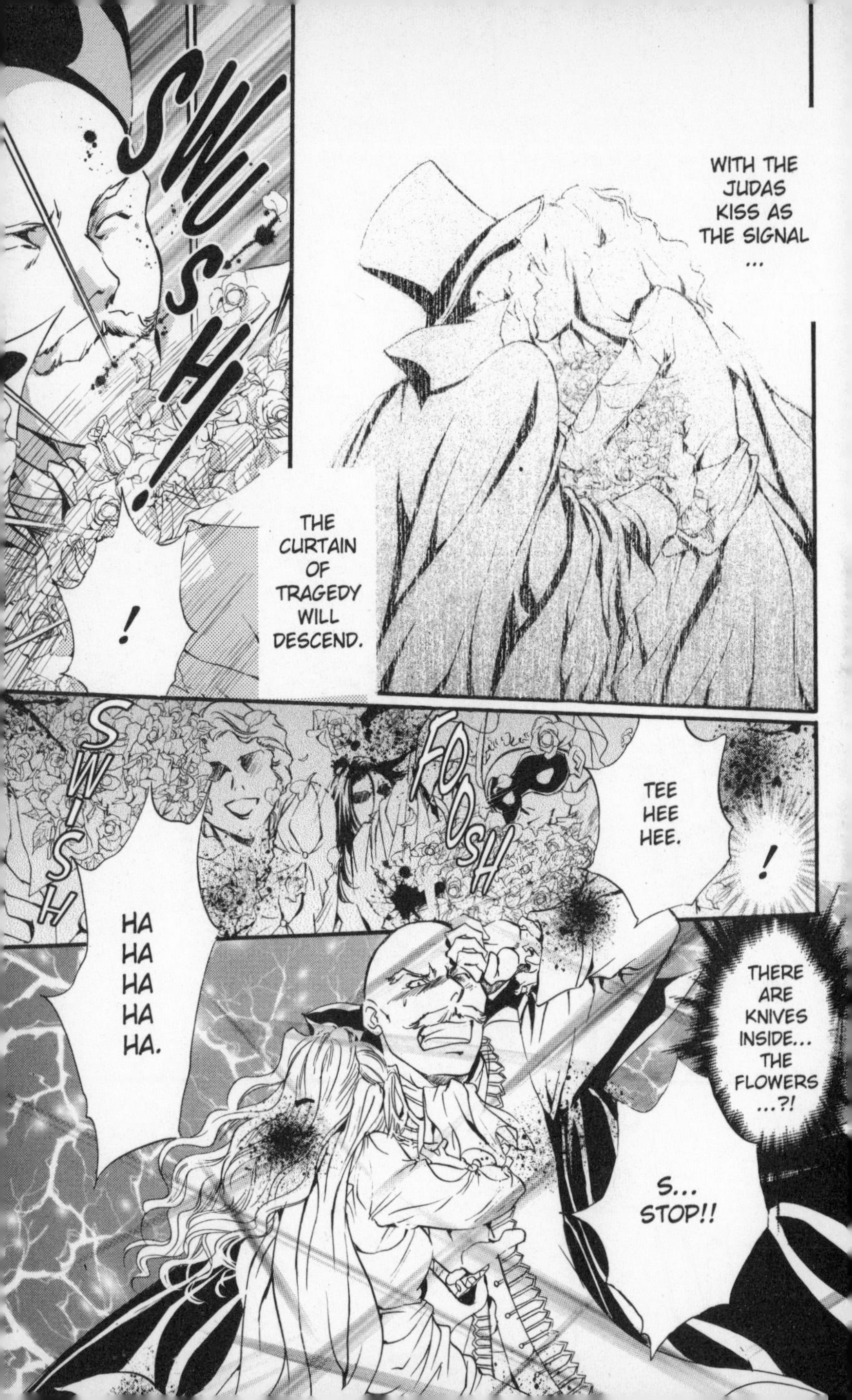
WITH THE JUDAS KISS AS THE SIGNAL ...
THE CURTAIN OF TRAGEDY WILL DESCEND.
SWUSH!
!
!
TEE HEE HEE.
FOOSH
SWISH
THERE ARE KNIVES INSIDE... THE FLOWERS ...?!
S... STOP!!
HA HA HA HA HA.

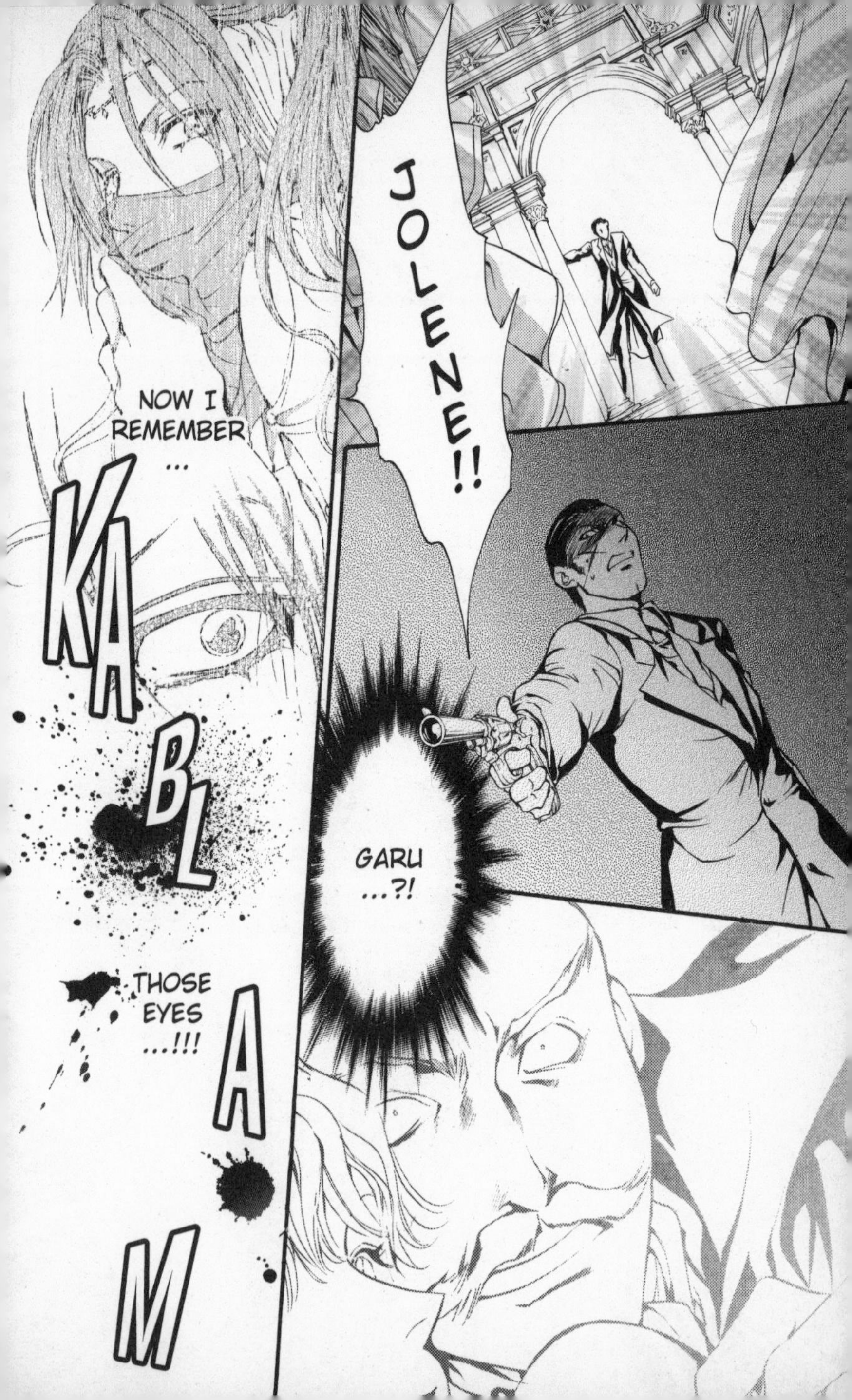
JOLENE!!
GARU ...?!
NOW I REMEMBER ...
KABLAM
THOSE EYES ...!!!

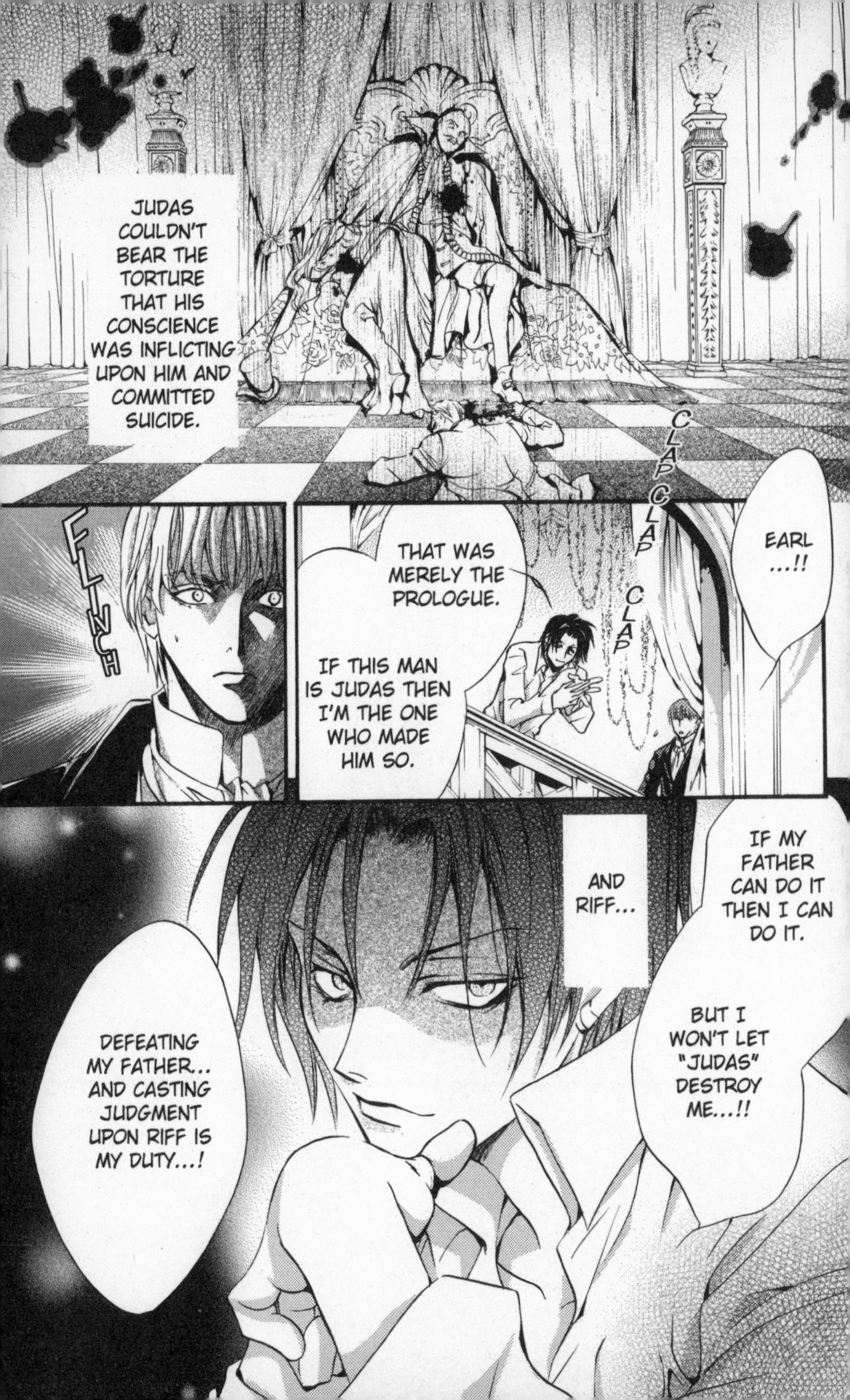
JUDAS COULDN'T BEAR THE TORTURE THAT HIS CONSCIENCE WAS INFLICTING UPON HIM AND COMMITTED SUICIDE.
CLAP CLAP
EARL ...!!
CLAP CLAP
THAT WAS MERELY THE PROLOGUE.
IF THIS MAN IS JUDAS THEN I'M THE ONE WHO MADE HIM SO.
FLINCH
IF MY FATHER CAN DO IT THEN I CAN DO IT.
AND RIFF...
BUT I WON'T LET "JUDAS" DESTROY ME...!!
DEFEATING MY FATHER... AND CASTING JUDGMENT UPON RIFF IS MY DUTY...!

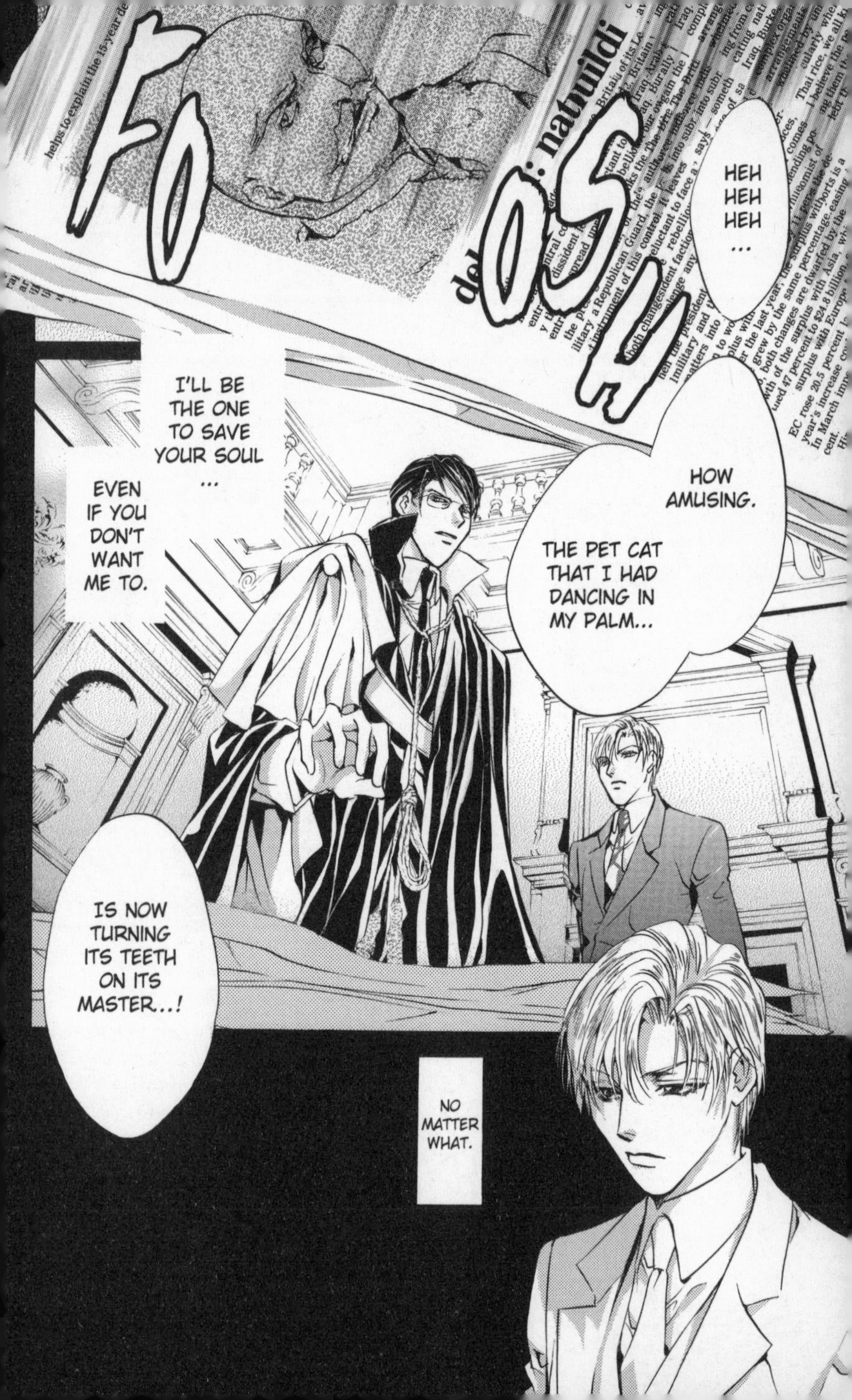
FOOSH
HEH HEH HEH ...
HOW AMUSING.
THE PET CAT THAT I HAD DANCING IN MY PALM...
I'LL BE THE ONE TO SAVE YOUR SOUL ...
EVEN IF YOU DON'T WANT ME TO.
IS NOW TURNING ITS TEETH ON ITS MASTER...!
NO MATTER WHAT.

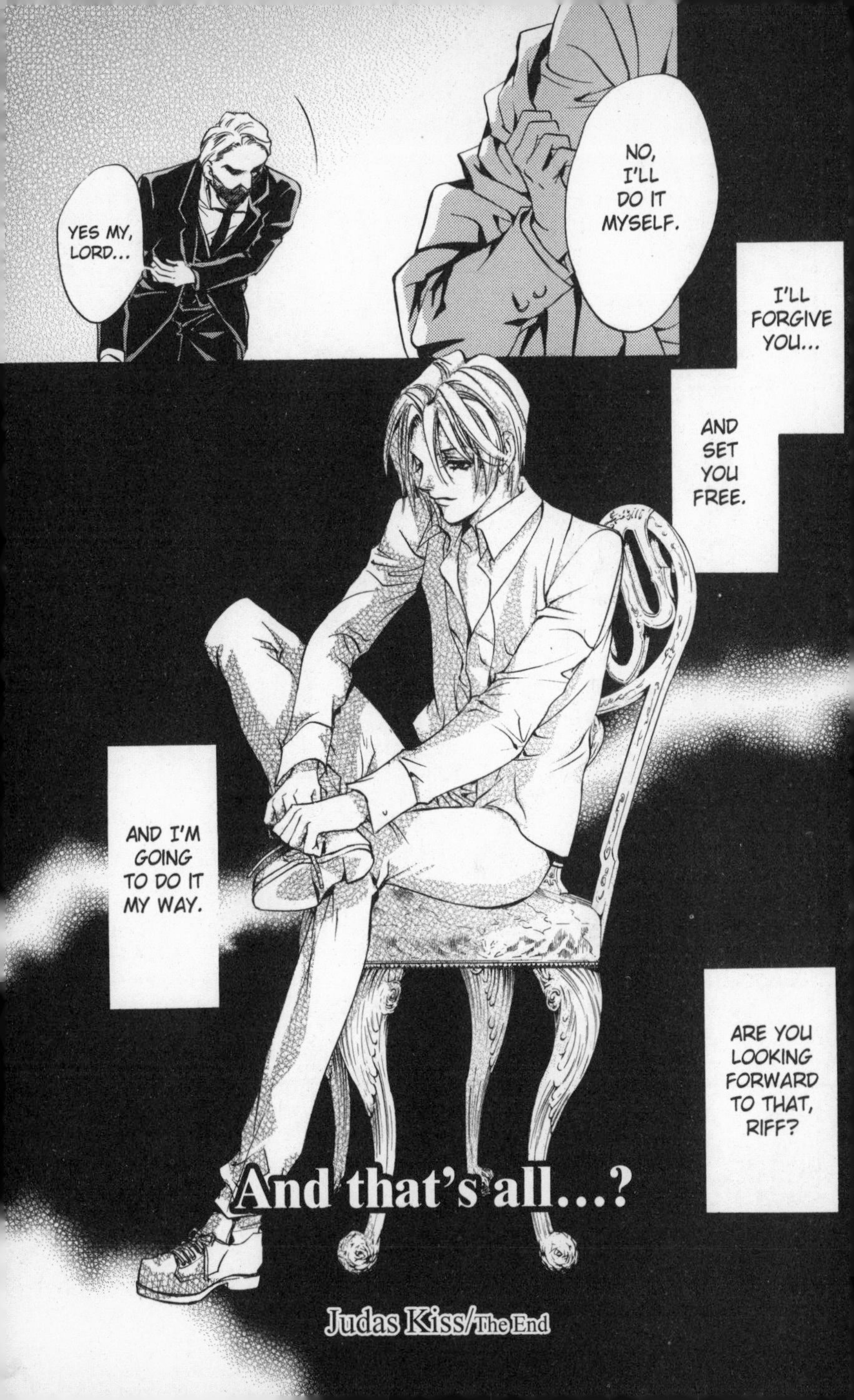
NO, I'LL DO IT MYSELF.
YES MY, LORD...
I'LL FORGIVE YOU...
AND SET YOU FREE.
AND I'M GOING TO DO IT MY WAY.
ARE YOU LOOKING FORWARD TO THAT, RIFF?
And that's all...?
Judas Kiss/The End

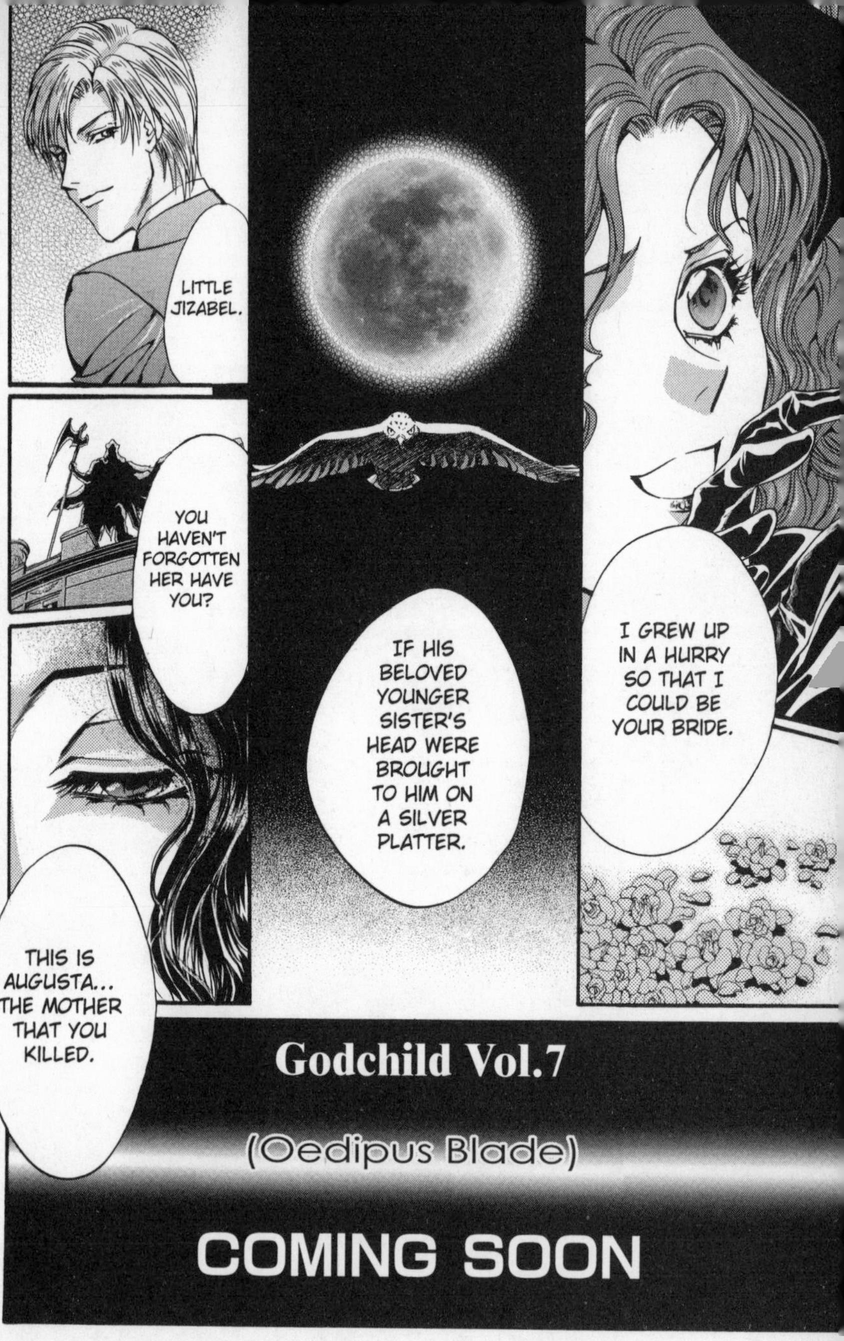

I GREW UP IN A HURRY SO THAT I COULD BE YOUR BRIDE.
IF HIS BELOVED YOUNGER SISTER'S HEAD WERE BROUGHT TO HIM ON A SILVER PLATTER.
LITTLE JIZABEL.
YOU HAVEN'T FORGOTTEN HER HAVE YOU?
THIS IS AUGUSTA... THE MOTHER THAT YOU KILLED.
Godchild Vol.7
(Oedipus Blade)
COMING SOON

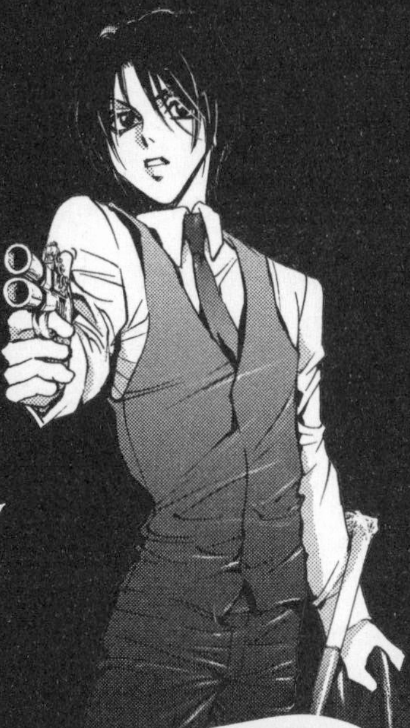

Creator: Kaori Yuki

Date of Birth: December 18

Blood Type: B

Major Works: *Angel Sanctuary* and *The Cain Saga*

Kaori Yuki was born in Tokyo and started drawing at a very early age. Following her debut work *Natsufuku no Erie* (Ellie in Summer Clothes) in the Japanese magazine *Bessatsu Hana to Yume* (1987), she wrote a compelling series of short stories: *Zankoku na Douwatachi* (Cruel Fairy Tales), *Neji* (Screw), and *Sareki Ôkoku* (Gravel Kingdom).

As proven by her best-selling series *Angel Sanctuary* and *The Cain Saga*, her celebrated body of work has etched an indelible mark on the gothic comics genre. She likes mysteries and British films, and is a fan of the movie *Dead Poets Society* and the show *Twin Peaks*.

ILLUMINATING THE DARK SIDE

Our Interview with *Godchild* creator Kaori Yuki

ANGEL SANCTUARY Tenshi Kinryou Ku © Kaori Yuki 1994/HAKUSENSHA, Inc.

Creator Kaori Yuki became a professional manga artist in 1987, with the debut of *Natsufuku no Erie* (*Ellie in Summer Clothes*) in the Japanese magazine *Bessatsu Hana to Yume,* and is perhaps best known for her gothic manga series *Angel Sanctuary* and *The Cain Saga.* Though she dwells on the darker side of life in her manga, she was willing to enlighten us on how she creates suspense and horror in her stories, which *Godchild* characters she most likes to draw, and why she hopes American readers will like her work.

Shojo Beat: Your artwork is beautiful. Do you have formal training in art or drawing?

Kaori Yuki: I went to art school, but because they didn't specifically teach illustration there, I'm mostly self-taught. I just drew a lot and learned on my own.

SB: When you are creating, do you write the story first before you start drawing, or do you just make it up as you go along?

KY: I create the story as I draw, so I make them together. I come up with a rough story and fill in the details by the time it's due.

SB: What inspired you to become a manga artist?

KY: I think it turned out that way because I was moony and have dazedly thought about stories since I was a child. I liked drawing too. I just found myself somehow being a manga creator.

SB: What are some other manga or comic artists whose work you admire, and why?

KY: There are a lot of creators that I like. I admire Ms. Ryoko Yamagishi.* She can describe feelings so clearly, impressively, or horrifically, depending on the situation, and I cried many times when reading her stories. I also admire her realistic illustrations. She's very original too. I think she is a bright person.

SB: Your manga often involves dark themes, such as death, heaven and hell, and murder. What is it about these types of themes that interests you? Is there a genre that you want to explore but haven't?

KY: For some reason, I'm attracted to mysterious things, scary things that are unexplained. I may be the type who gets killed by my curiosity. I want to try drawing a mystery set in the Japanese Meiji and Taisho eras.

SB: How do you go about creating suspense, mystery, and horror in your manga? Are there key story elements necessary for achieving these effects?

KY: I try to fill screens with lots of black tones, exaggerate expressions of characters to add a realistic sensation, or make the stage setting luxurious. What else? Sometimes I try to start stories with ordinary scenes so that scary scenes stand out.

SB: *Godchild* is set in nineteenth century London. Why did you choose this setting for the story, and how did you go about capturing its essence?

KY: I watched and admired movies from that period. The darker, grislier side of the luxurious and elegant upper class charmed me. Women's dresses and accessories were wonderful too.

SB: Of all the characters in *Godchild*, which do you enjoy drawing the most? Why?

KY: In the beginning, I had fun drawing the evil doctor. Throughout the series, Mary Weather was very fun to draw, and I drew her dresses and hairstyles elaborately. It took time, though.

SB: What are your top three favorite gothic, thriller, or true-crime movies of all time? How about books?

KY: Because I don't read novels, I'll just give movies…Hmm. I like movies like *Alien II, Carrie,* and *Phenomena,* although is *Alien II* an action movie? Oh, this is less famous, but I liked a movie called *Paperhouse.* That's not scary, though.

SB: Do you have a message for your American readers?

KY: In Japan, my manga is a little crowded (in terms of drawing) by shojo manga standards, and the story lines tend to be complicated and cruel, so many people don't care for it. I will be glad if American readers can connect with my manga even a little. After all, my youth was filled with MTV and Western movies; they influenced me so much and allowed me to become the story creator I am today. ✳

*Ryoko Yamagishi is best known for her manga *Hiizurutokoro no Tenshi* (or *Emperor of the Rising Sun*), featuring a prince with supernatural powers.

*This interview with Kaori Yuki originally ran in the September 2005 issue of *Shojo Beat* magazine.

GODCHILD, vol. 6
The Shojo Beat Manga Edition

STORY & ART BY KAORI YUKI

Translation/Akira Watanabe
Touch-up Art & Lettering/James Gaubatz
Design/Courtney Utt
Editor/Joel Enos

Managing Editor/Megan Bates
Editorial Director/Elizabeth Kawasaki
VP & Editor in Chief/Yumi Hoashi
Sr. Director of Acquisitions/Rika Inouye
Sr. VP of Marketing/Liza Coppola
Exec. VP of Sales & Marketing/John Easum
Publisher/Hyoe Narita

Published by VIZ Media, LLC
P.O. Box 77010
San Francisco, CA 94107

Shojo Beat Manga Edition
10 9 8 7 6 5 4 3 2 1
First printing, August 2007

store.viz.com

Read Kaori Yuki's entire Earl Cain Series

Series 1: *The Cain Saga*: Forgotten Juliet
Series 2: *The Cain Saga*: The Sound of a Boy Hatching
Series 3: *The Cain Saga*: Kafka
Series 4: *The Cain Saga*: The Seal of the Red Ram, Volumes 1 & 2
Series 5: *Godchild*, Volumes 1-8

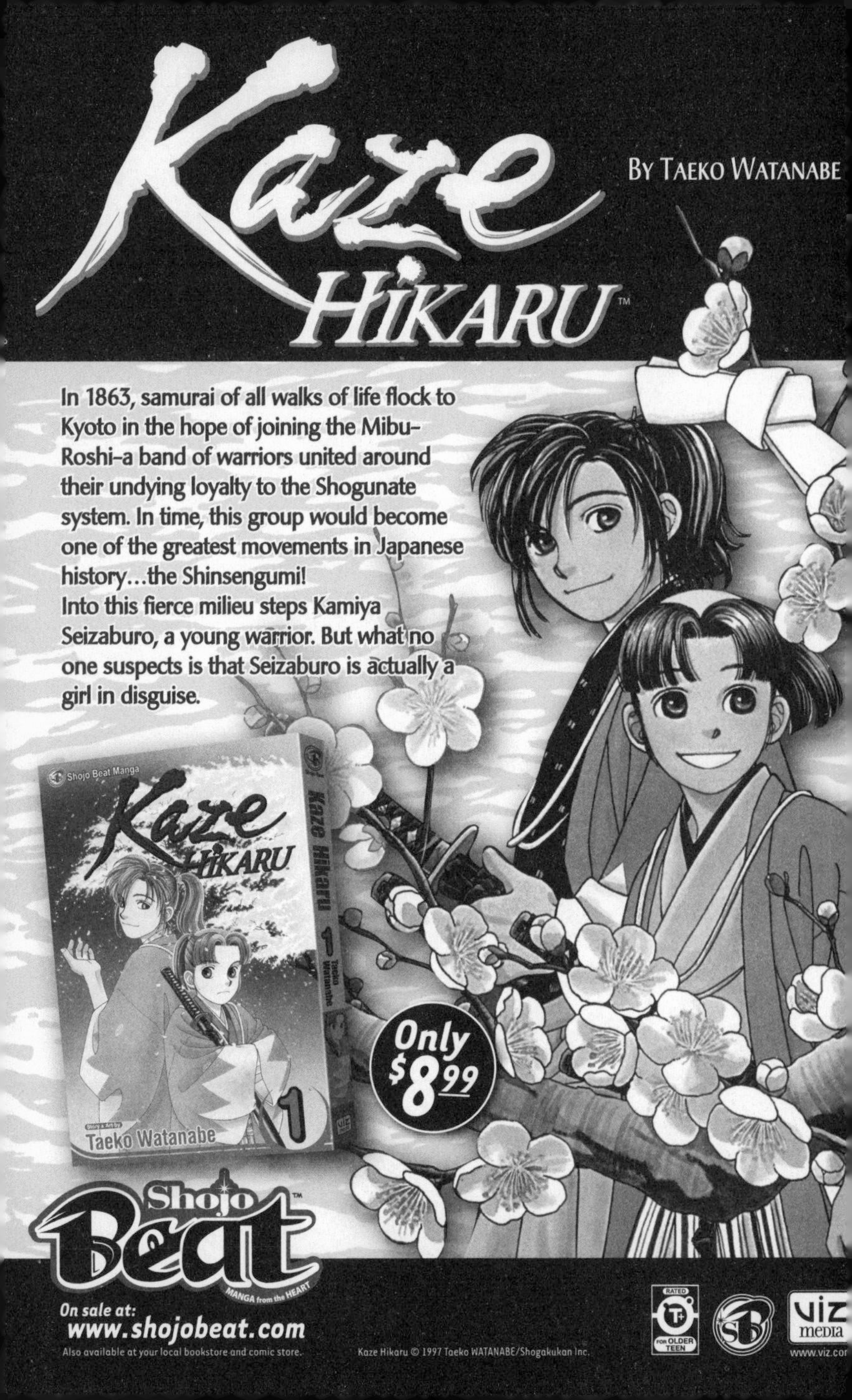
Kaze Hikaru™
By Taeko Watanabe
In 1863, samurai of all walks of life flock to Kyoto in the hope of joining the Mibu-Roshi–a band of warriors united around their undying loyalty to the Shogunate system. In time, this group would become one of the greatest movements in Japanese history…the Shinsengumi!
Into this fierce milieu steps Kamiya Seizaburo, a young warrior. But what no one suspects is that Seizaburo is actually a girl in disguise.
Shojo Beat Manga
Kaze Hikaru
Story & Art by
Taeko Watanabe
1
Only $8.99
Shojo Beat™
MANGA from the HEART
On sale at:
www.shojobeat.com
Also available at your local bookstore and comic store.
Kaze Hikaru © 1997 Taeko WATANABE/Shogakukan Inc.
RATED T+ FOR OLDER TEEN
VIZ media
www.viz.com